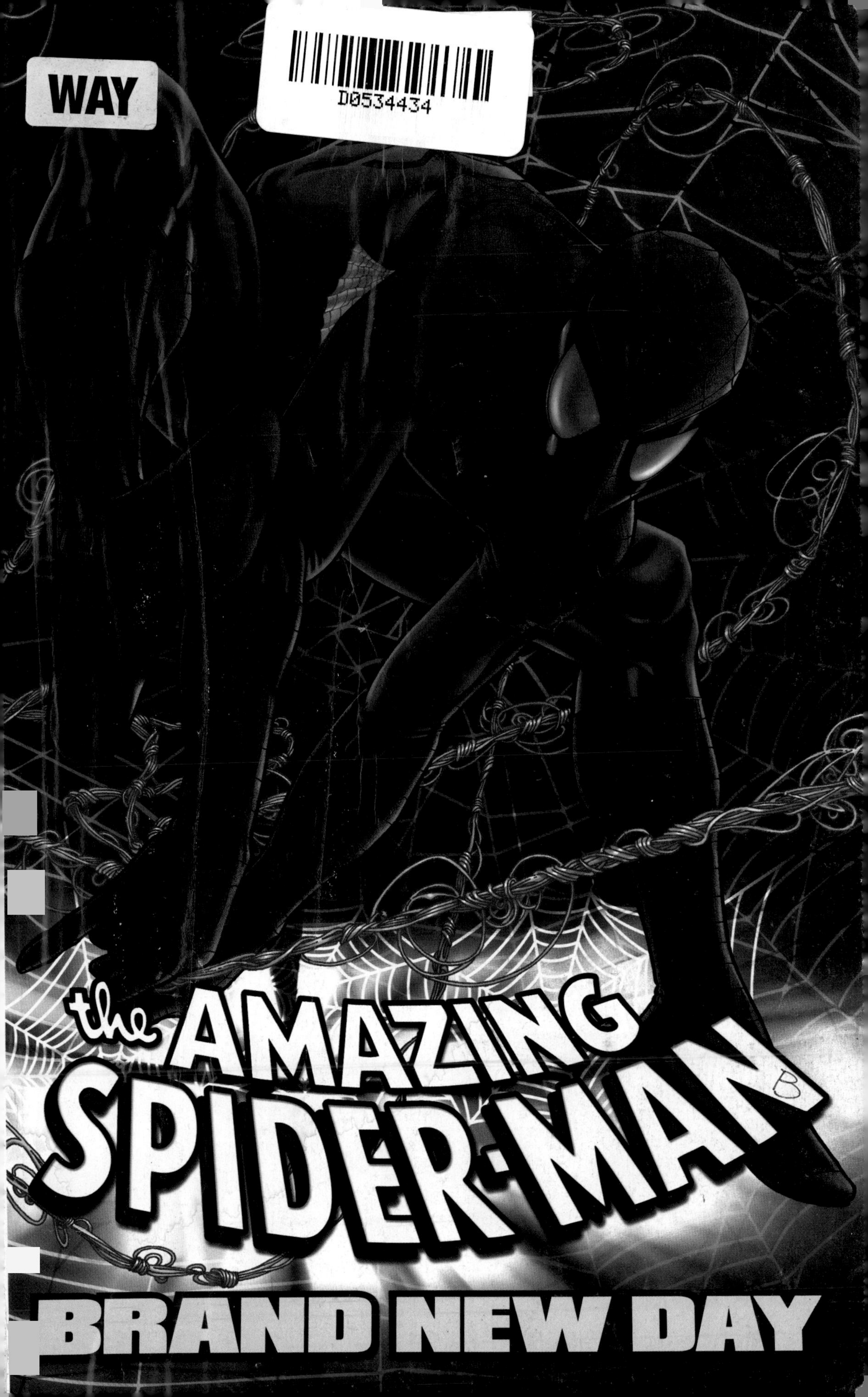
the AMAZING
SPIDER-MAN
BRAND NEW DAY

the AMAZING SPIDER-MAN

BRAND NEW DAY

AMAZING SPIDER-MAN #552-554
Writer: **BOB GALE** • Penciler: **PHIL JIMENEZ**
Inker: **ANDY LANNING** with **DANNY MIKI** & **PHIL JIMENEZ**
Colorist: **JEROMY COX**

AMAZING SPIDER-MAN #555-557
Writer: **ZEB WELLS** • Pencils: **CHRIS BACHALO**
Inker: **TIM TOWNSEND** with **MARK IRWIN, WAYNE FAUCHER,**
JAIME MENDOZA & **AL VEY**
Colorists: **CHRIS BACHALO** & **STUDIO F'S ANTONIO FABELA**

AMAZING SPIDER-MAN #558
Writer: **BOB GALE** • Penciler: **BARRY KITSON**
Inker: **MARK FARMER**
Colorists: **AVALON'S IAN HANNIN** & **MATT MILLA**
Special thanks to **JAMES HODGKINS**

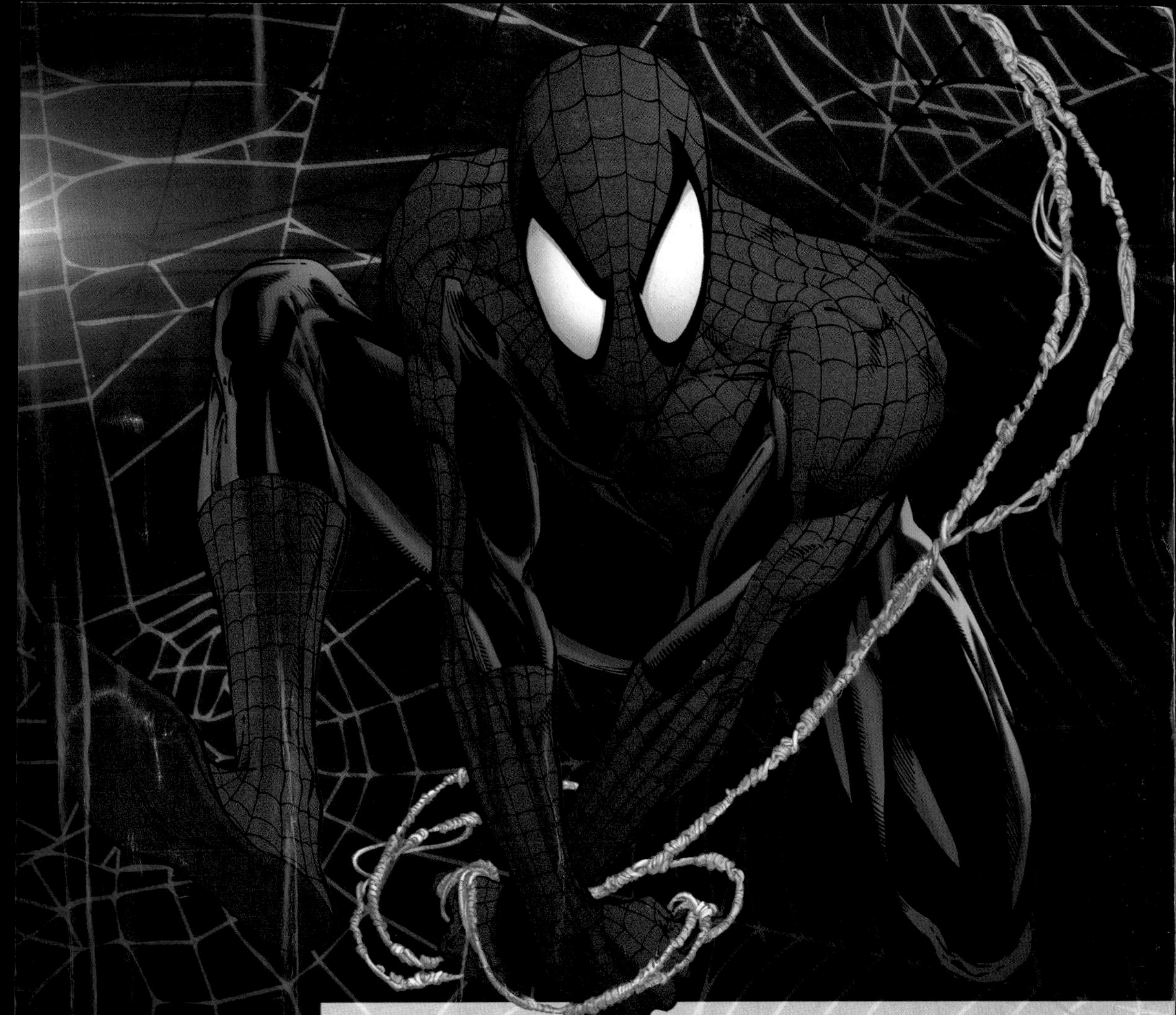

Letters: **VC'S CORY PETIT** with **JOE CARAMAGNA**
Spidey's Braintrust: **BOB GALE**, **MARC GUGGENHEIM**, **DAN SLOTT** & **ZEB WELLS**
Assistant Editor: **TOM BRENNAN**
Editor: **STEPHEN WACKER**
Executive Editor: **TOM BREVOORT**

Collection Editor: **JENNIFER GRÜNWALD**
Assistant Editors: **CORY LEVINE** & **JOHN DENNING**
Editor, Special Projects: **MARK D. BEAZLEY**
Senior Editor, Special Projects: **JEFF YOUNGQUIST**
Senior Vice President of Sales: **DAVID GABRIEL**
Production: **JERRY KALINOWSKI**
Book Designer: **RODOLFO MURAGUCHI**

Editor in Chief: **JOE QUESADA**
Publisher: **DAN BUCKLEY**

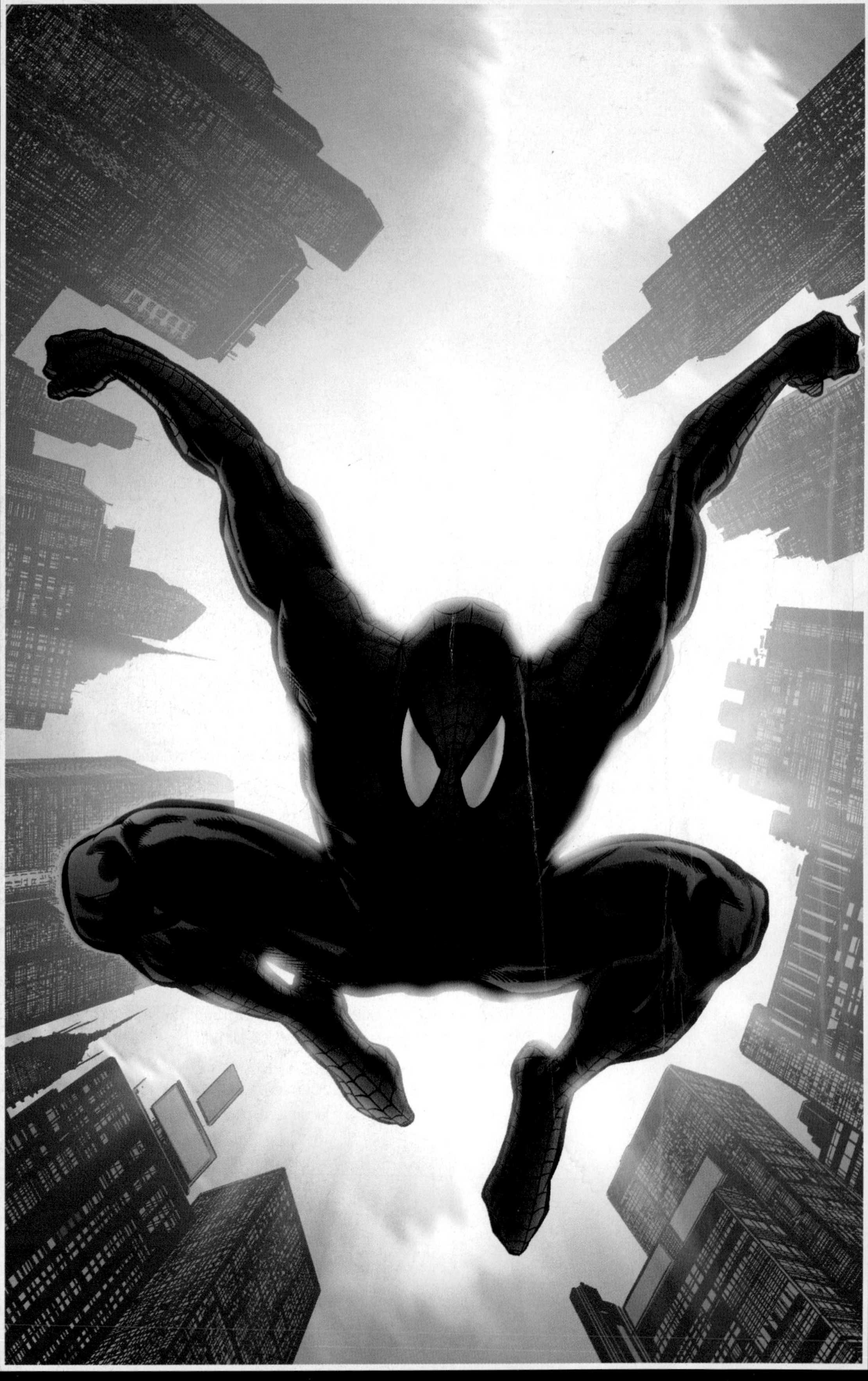

AMAZING SPIDER-MAN #552

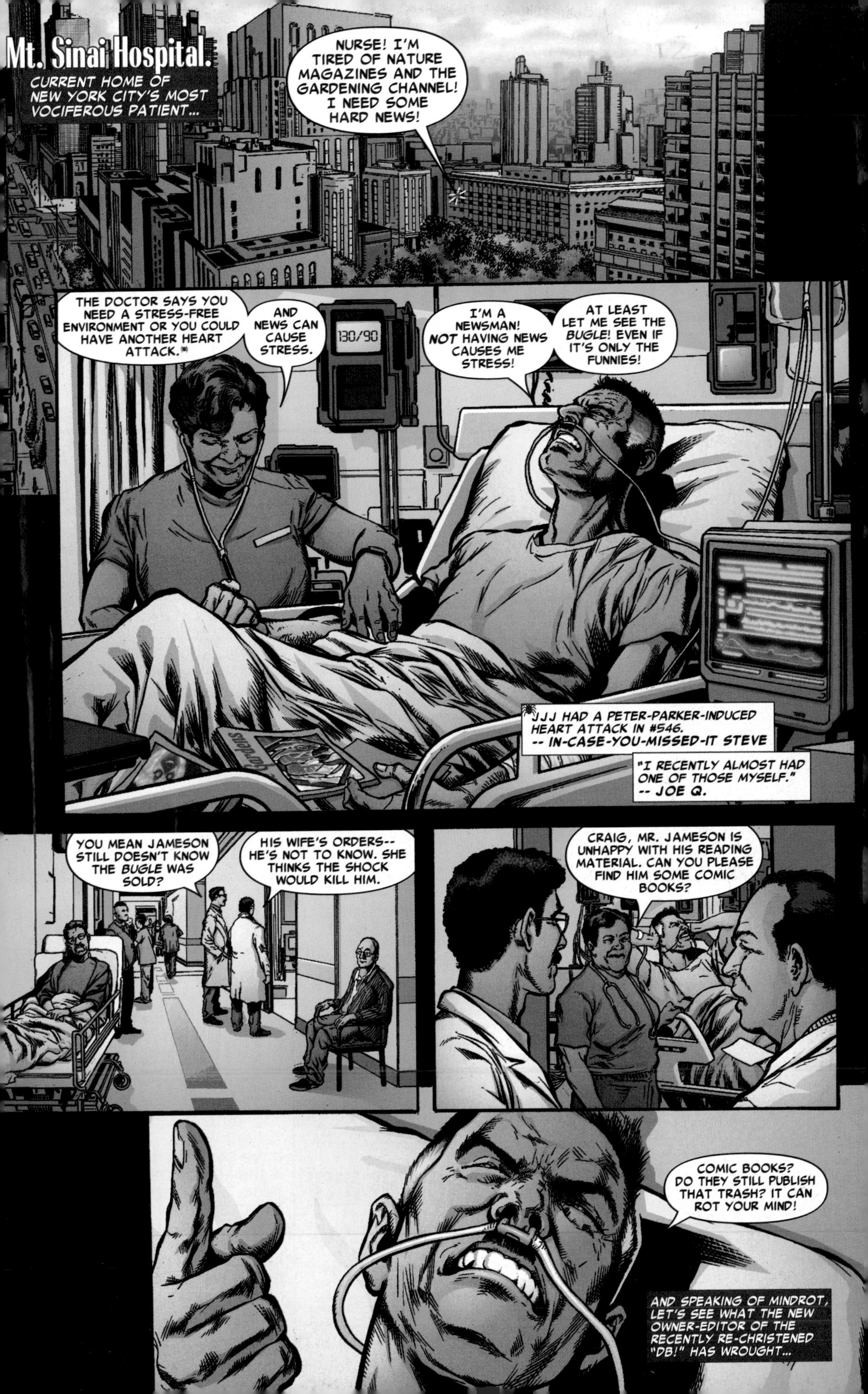
Mt. Sinai Hospital.
CURRENT HOME OF NEW YORK CITY'S MOST VOCIFEROUS PATIENT...
NURSE! I'M TIRED OF NATURE MAGAZINES AND THE GARDENING CHANNEL! I NEED SOME HARD NEWS!
THE DOCTOR SAYS YOU NEED A STRESS-FREE ENVIRONMENT OR YOU COULD HAVE ANOTHER HEART ATTACK.*
AND NEWS CAN CAUSE STRESS.
130/90
I'M A NEWSMAN! NOT HAVING NEWS CAUSES ME STRESS!
AT LEAST LET ME SEE THE BUGLE! EVEN IF IT'S ONLY THE FUNNIES!
Gardens
*JJJ HAD A PETER-PARKER-INDUCED HEART ATTACK IN #546. -- IN-CASE-YOU-MISSED-IT STEVE
"I RECENTLY ALMOST HAD ONE OF THOSE MYSELF." -- JOE Q.
YOU MEAN JAMESON STILL DOESN'T KNOW THE BUGLE WAS SOLD?
HIS WIFE'S ORDERS-- HE'S NOT TO KNOW. SHE THINKS THE SHOCK WOULD KILL HIM.
CRAIG, MR. JAMESON IS UNHAPPY WITH HIS READING MATERIAL. CAN YOU PLEASE FIND HIM SOME COMIC BOOKS?
COMIC BOOKS? DO THEY STILL PUBLISH THAT TRASH? IT CAN ROT YOUR MIND!
AND SPEAKING OF MINDROT, LET'S SEE WHAT THE NEW OWNER-EDITOR OF THE RECENTLY RE-CHRISTENED "DB!" HAS WROUGHT...

THE OFFICIAL NEWSPAPER OF SPIDER-MAN

THE DB

WEIRD WEATHER AHEAD: CHANCE OF SNOW BY THE END OF THE WEEK! TIPS ON HOW TO SURVIVE!

50 CENTS • THUR

SPIDER-MAN: SERIAL KILLER!

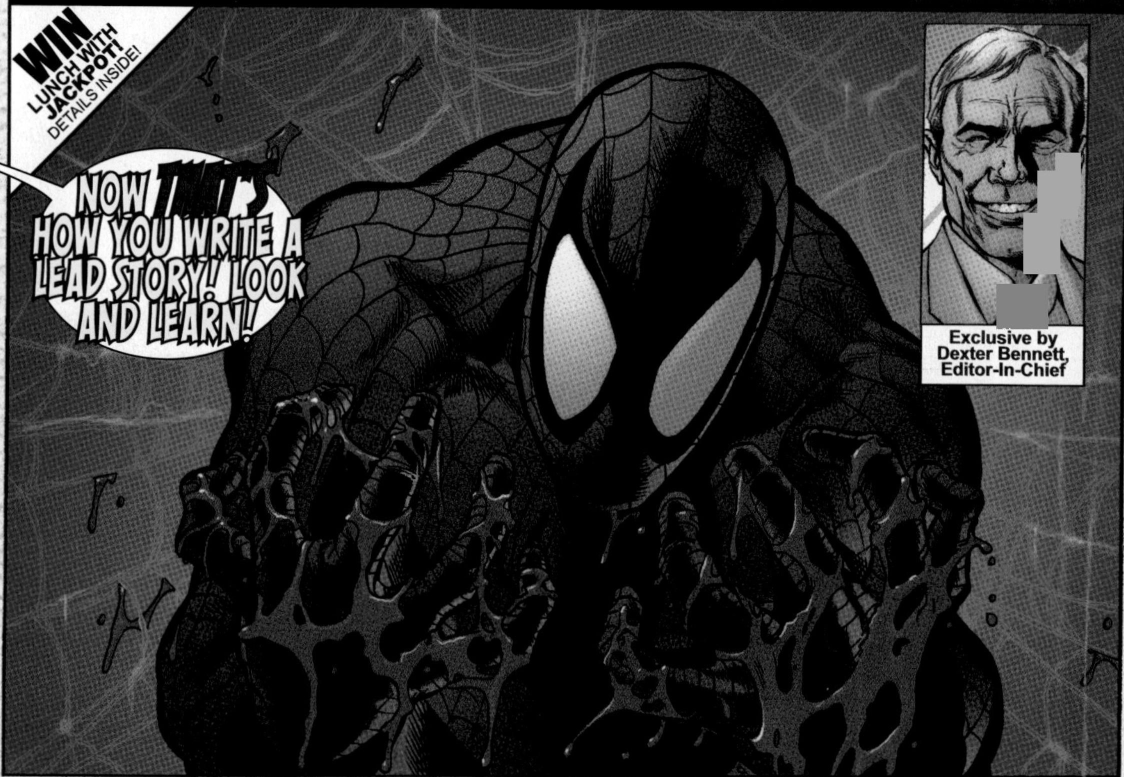

WIN LUNCH WITH JACKPOT! DETAILS INSIDE!
NOW THAT'S HOW YOU WRITE A LEAD STORY! LOOK AND LEARN!

Exclusive by Dexter Bennett, Editor-In-Chief

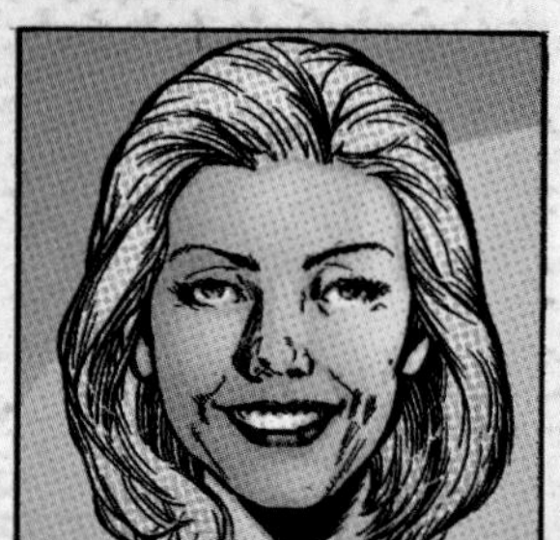

Lisa Parfrey

LISA PARFREY FUNERAL TODAY

Councilwoman Lisa Parfrey, candidate for Mayor, will be buried today in a private ceremony at Forest Hills Cemetery. Parfrey, 52, was found savagely murdered three days ago after being kidnapped from a political debate at the Apollo Theatre by a mysterious super human known as Menace. Menace is the only suspect in the brutal killing. Parfrey's tragic demise shocked the...

CONTINUED ON A-3

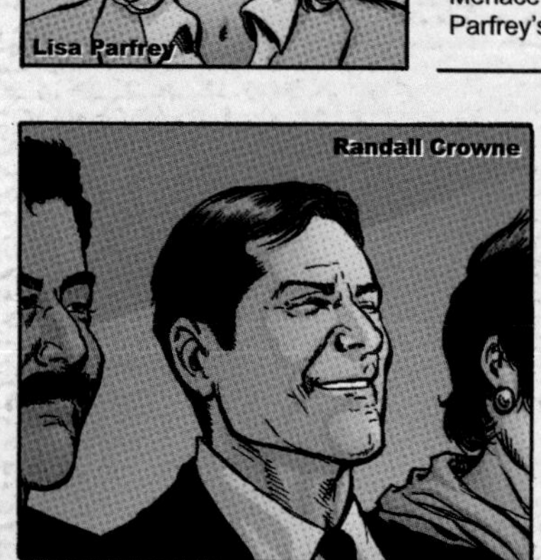

Randall Crowne

WILL CROWNE RUN UNOPPOSED?

With no serious prospect stepping up to take the place of the late Mayoral candidate Lisa Parfrey, it is possible that Randall Crowne may become New York's next mayor by default. If so, it will be the first time in the history of the city that...

CONTINUED ON A-6

POLICE SPIDER-MA TO REC MURDE

EXCLUSIVE TO THE DB!

In off the record conversations with DB Staffers, police have confirmed that Spider-Man is the key suspect in the string of recent murders that has shocked this city. Although Police have been reticent to discuss the specifics of the murders, so-called "Spider Tracers" have definitely been found on each victim, leaving no doubt as to the involvement of Spider-Man. Spider-Man is already wanted for violations of...

CONTINUED ON A-2

JUST BLAME SPIDER-MAN

Bob Gale-writer **Phil Jimenez**-pencils **Andy Lanning**-inks **Jeromy Cox**-colors **VC's Cory Petit**-letters
Thomas Brennan-assistant editor **Stephen Whack Her**-editor **Tom Brevoort**-executive editor
Joe Quesada-editor-in-chief **Dan Buckley**-publisher **Gale, Guggenheim, Slott, Wells**-Spidey Braintrust

Lorem ipsum dolor sit amet, consectetuer adipiscing elit. Morbi vel risus. Aenean sagittis urna eget massa. Donec faucibus odio bibendum sem. Nam ultrices egestas orci. Morbi quis neque ac arcu convallis imperdiet. Nullam euismod. Nullam arcu arcu, elementum a, gravida vitae, condimentum quis, nibh. Suspendisse pretium cursus orci. Cum sociis natoque penatibus et magnis dis parturient montes, nascetur ridiculus mus. Quisque in nibh eget lacus dignissim auctor. Praesent nec turpis accumsan dui ultrices fringilla. Sed ornare. Aliquam leo risus, condimentum eu, euismod sed, sodales et, elit. Cras gravida lorem ac orci. Etiam sed dolor eu lorem vulputate elementum.

Ut quis sem sit amet neque pharetra pretium. Lorem ipsum dolor sit amet, consectetuer adipiscing elit.

quis leo. Vestibulum ante ipsum primis in faucibus orci luctus et ultrices posuere cubilia Curae; Ut pharetra malesuada lorem. Praesent luctus, dui sit amet pretium cursus, nisi purus ornare libero, quis lacinia neque enim nec libero. Aliquam ut dui sit amet orci tincidunt posuere. Nullam mattis urna vitae ante. Vestibulum urna.

Etiam malesuada. Aliquam vulputate dolor nec elit. Etiam feugiat nisl in turpis. Sed in nunc. Donec convallis libero non risus. Maecenas sit amet diam. Suspendisse nonummy facilisis eros. Morbi tempus turpis ac tortor. Proin ultrices sodales urna. Duis semper. Aliquam interdum gravida lectus. Lorem ipsum dolor sit amet, consectetuer adipiscing elit. In elementum tincidunt lorem. Fusce neque. Cum sociis natoque penatibus et magnis dis parturient montes, nascetur ridiculus mus. Vestibulum ante ipsum primis in faucibus orci luctus et

Aliquam sit amet mi nec tellus congue faucibus. Suspendisse ut erat. Nulla pretium scelerisque lorem. Vivamus sit amet mi eu sem elementum aliquet. Duis quis lorem et nibh dignissim sodales. Mauris urna. Phasellus ullamcorper dui at urna. Donec turpis arcu, lacinia vel, dapibus volutpat, ullamcorper quis, turpis. Curabitur enim orci, egestas convallis, adipiscing sit amet, dignissim sit amet, tortor. Sed eu arcu quis tellus iaculis aliquet. Integer vel quam. Suspendisse potenti. Curabitur et lacus. Fusce dapibus mauris quis mauris.

Nam lacus risus, dictum vel, euismod vel, commodo sed, justo. Sed condimentum nulla eget erat. Vestibulum pharetra mollis turpis. Maecenas diam quam, vulputate eu, porta at, porta eu, ante. Praesent adipiscing, mauris eu viverra commodo, neque tellus sagittis magna, id viverra tellus nibh in risus. Integer tellus nisi, ornare nec,

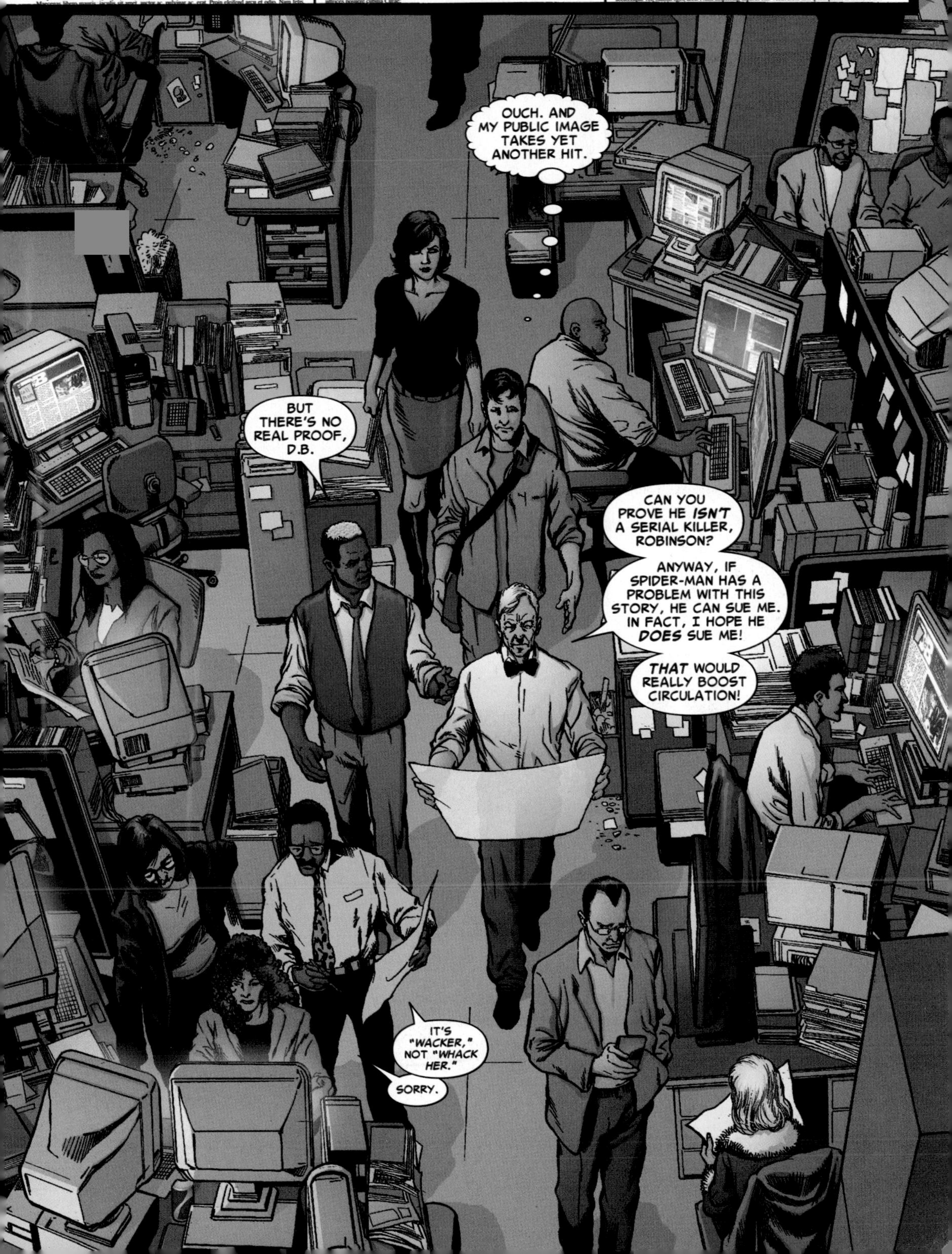
OUCH. AND MY PUBLIC IMAGE TAKES YET ANOTHER HIT.
BUT THERE'S NO REAL PROOF, D.B.
CAN YOU PROVE HE *ISN'T* A SERIAL KILLER, ROBINSON?
ANYWAY, IF SPIDER-MAN HAS A PROBLEM WITH THIS STORY, HE CAN SUE ME. IN FACT, I HOPE HE *DOES* SUE ME!
THAT WOULD REALLY BOOST CIRCULATION!
IT'S "WACKER," NOT "WHACK HER."
SORRY.

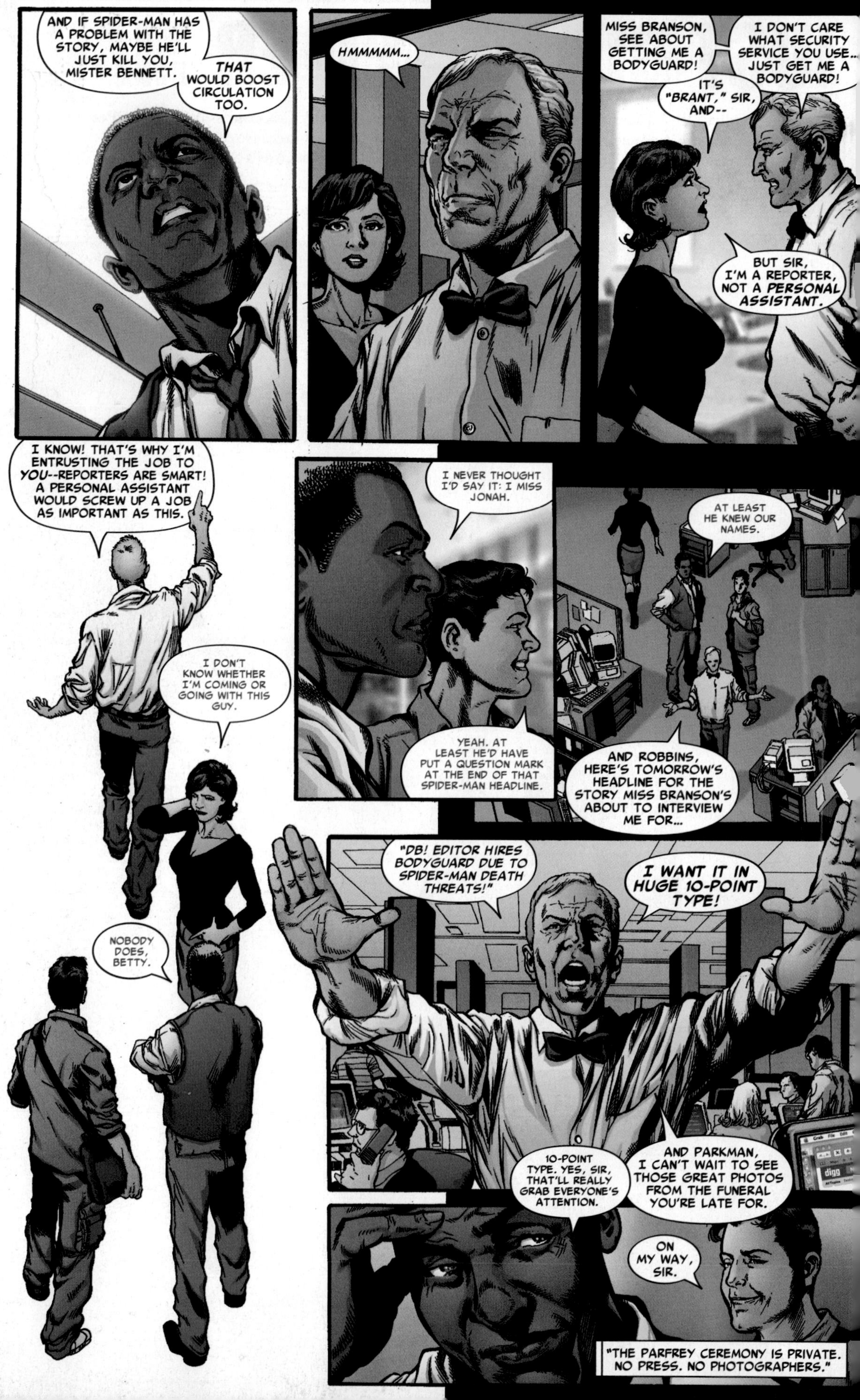
AND IF SPIDER-MAN HAS A PROBLEM WITH THE STORY, MAYBE HE'LL JUST KILL YOU, MISTER BENNETT.
THAT WOULD BOOST CIRCULATION TOO.
HMMMMM...
MISS BRANSON, SEE ABOUT GETTING ME A BODYGUARD!
IT'S "BRANT," SIR, AND--
I DON'T CARE WHAT SECURITY SERVICE YOU USE... JUST GET ME A BODYGUARD!
BUT SIR, I'M A REPORTER, NOT A PERSONAL ASSISTANT.
I KNOW! THAT'S WHY I'M ENTRUSTING THE JOB TO YOU--REPORTERS ARE SMART! A PERSONAL ASSISTANT WOULD SCREW UP A JOB AS IMPORTANT AS THIS.
I DON'T KNOW WHETHER I'M COMING OR GOING WITH THIS GUY.
NOBODY DOES, BETTY.
I NEVER THOUGHT I'D SAY IT: I MISS JONAH.
YEAH. AT LEAST HE'D HAVE PUT A QUESTION MARK AT THE END OF THAT SPIDER-MAN HEADLINE.
AT LEAST HE KNEW OUR NAMES.
AND ROBBINS, HERE'S TOMORROW'S HEADLINE FOR THE STORY MISS BRANSON'S ABOUT TO INTERVIEW ME FOR...
"DB! EDITOR HIRES BODYGUARD DUE TO SPIDER-MAN DEATH THREATS!"
I WANT IT IN HUGE 10-POINT TYPE!
10-POINT TYPE. YES, SIR, THAT'LL REALLY GRAB EVERYONE'S ATTENTION.
AND PARKMAN, I CAN'T WAIT TO SEE THOSE GREAT PHOTOS FROM THE FUNERAL YOU'RE LATE FOR.
ON MY WAY, SIR.
"THE PARFREY CEREMONY IS PRIVATE. NO PRESS. NO PHOTOGRAPHERS."

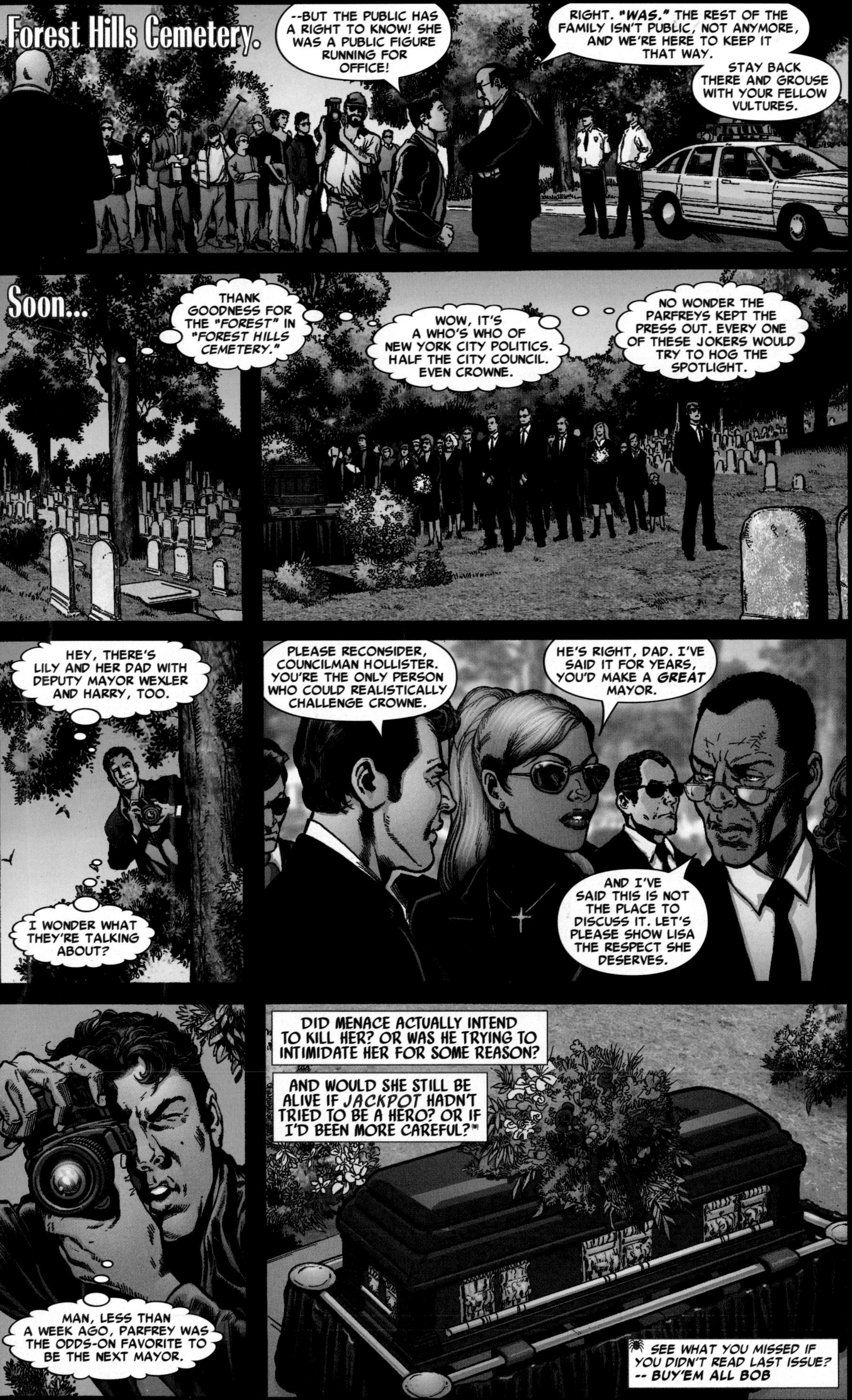
Forest Hills Cemetery.
--BUT THE PUBLIC HAS A RIGHT TO KNOW! SHE WAS A PUBLIC FIGURE RUNNING FOR OFFICE!
RIGHT. "WAS." THE REST OF THE FAMILY ISN'T PUBLIC, NOT ANYMORE, AND WE'RE HERE TO KEEP IT THAT WAY.
STAY BACK THERE AND GROUSE WITH YOUR FELLOW VULTURES.
Soon...
THANK GOODNESS FOR THE "FOREST" IN "FOREST HILLS CEMETERY."
WOW, IT'S A WHO'S WHO OF NEW YORK CITY POLITICS. HALF THE CITY COUNCIL. EVEN CROWNE.
NO WONDER THE PARFREYS KEPT THE PRESS OUT. EVERY ONE OF THESE JOKERS WOULD TRY TO HOG THE SPOTLIGHT.
HEY, THERE'S LILY AND HER DAD WITH DEPUTY MAYOR WEXLER AND HARRY, TOO.
I WONDER WHAT THEY'RE TALKING ABOUT?
PLEASE RECONSIDER, COUNCILMAN HOLLISTER. YOU'RE THE ONLY PERSON WHO COULD REALISTICALLY CHALLENGE CROWNE.
HE'S RIGHT, DAD. I'VE SAID IT FOR YEARS, YOU'D MAKE A GREAT MAYOR.
AND I'VE SAID THIS IS NOT THE PLACE TO DISCUSS IT. LET'S PLEASE SHOW LISA THE RESPECT SHE DESERVES.
MAN, LESS THAN A WEEK AGO, PARFREY WAS THE ODDS-ON FAVORITE TO BE THE NEXT MAYOR.
DID MENACE ACTUALLY INTEND TO KILL HER? OR WAS HE TRYING TO INTIMIDATE HER FOR SOME REASON?
AND WOULD SHE STILL BE ALIVE IF JACKPOT HADN'T TRIED TO BE A HERO? OR IF I'D BEEN MORE CAREFUL?*
*SEE WHAT YOU MISSED IF YOU DIDN'T READ LAST ISSUE? -- BUY'EM ALL BOB

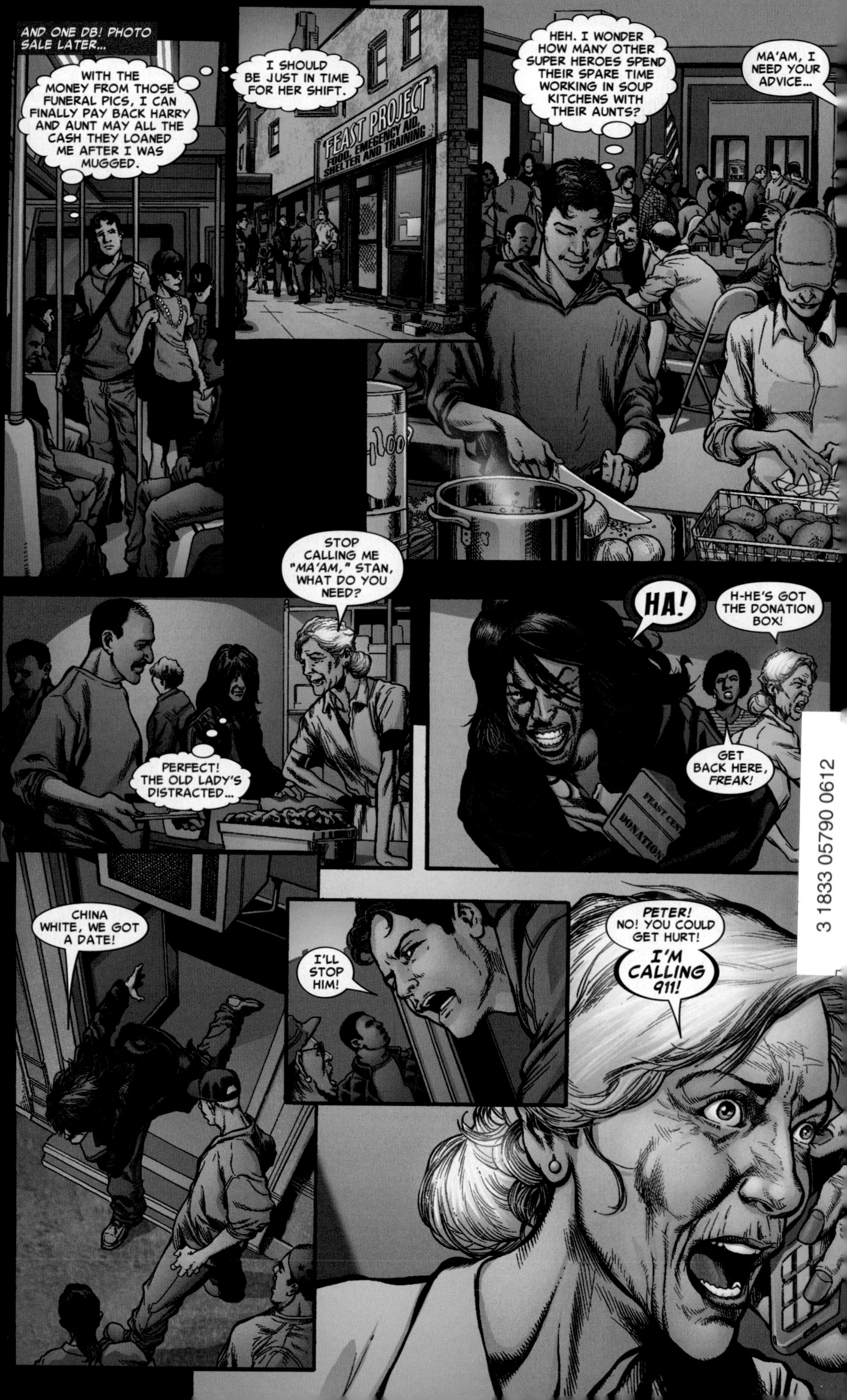
AND ONE DB! PHOTO SALE LATER...
WITH THE MONEY FROM THOSE FUNERAL PICS, I CAN FINALLY PAY BACK HARRY AND AUNT MAY ALL THE CASH THEY LOANED ME AFTER I WAS MUGGED.
I SHOULD BE JUST IN TIME FOR HER SHIFT.
FEAST PROJECT
FOOD, EMERGENCY AID, SHELTER AND TRAINING
HEH. I WONDER HOW MANY OTHER SUPER HEROES SPEND THEIR SPARE TIME WORKING IN SOUP KITCHENS WITH THEIR AUNTS?
MA'AM, I NEED YOUR ADVICE...
STOP CALLING ME "MA'AM," STAN, WHAT DO YOU NEED?
PERFECT! THE OLD LADY'S DISTRACTED...
HA!
H-HE'S GOT THE DONATION BOX!
GET BACK HERE, *FREAK!*
DONATION
CHINA WHITE, WE GOT A DATE!
I'LL STOP HIM!
PETER! NO! YOU COULD GET HURT!
I'M CALLING 911!

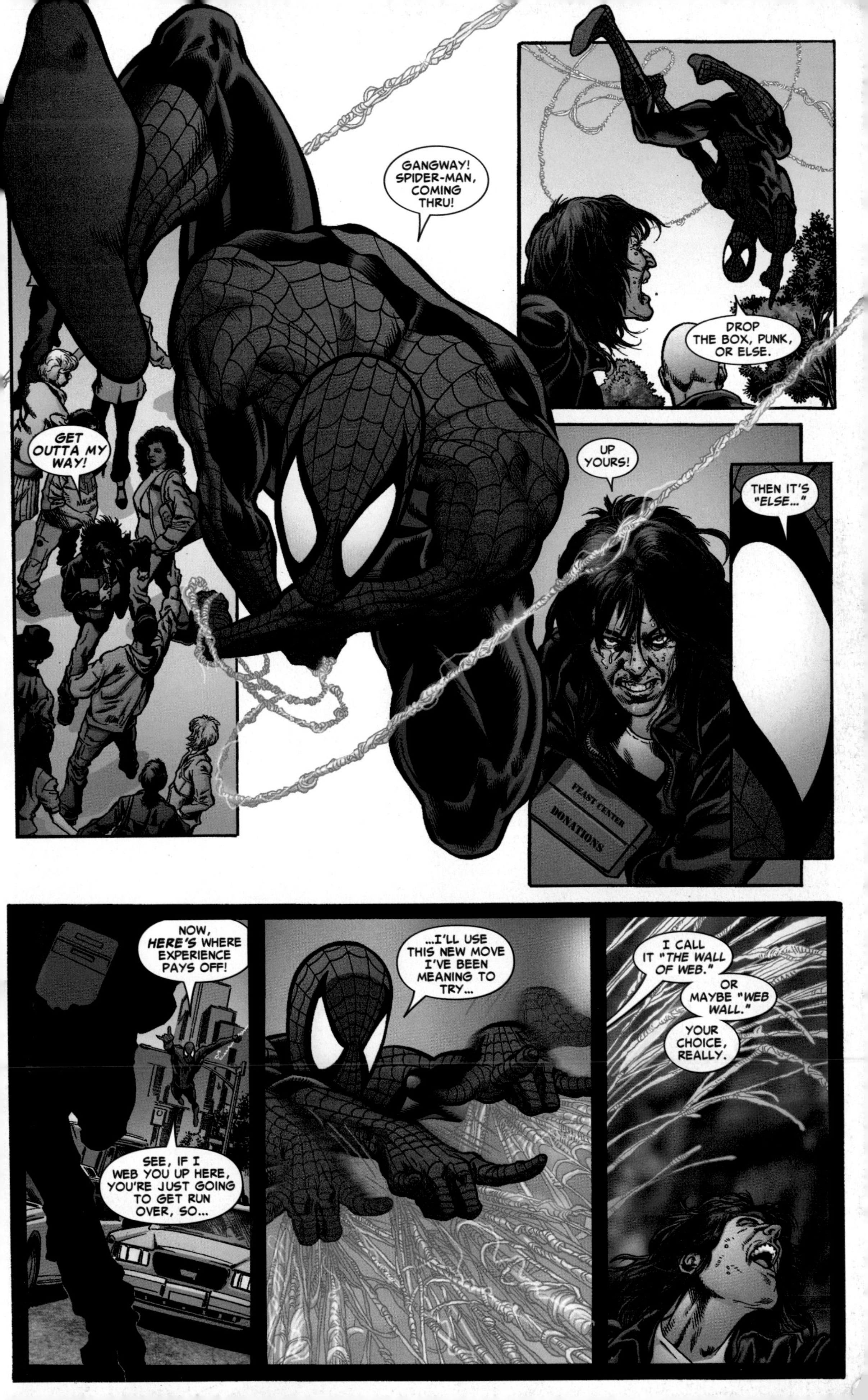
GANGWAY! SPIDER-MAN, COMING THRU!
DROP THE BOX, PUNK, OR ELSE.
GET OUTTA MY WAY!
UP YOURS!
THEN IT'S "ELSE..."
FEAST CENTER
DONATIONS
NOW, HERE'S WHERE EXPERIENCE PAYS OFF!
SEE, IF I WEB YOU UP HERE, YOU'RE JUST GOING TO GET RUN OVER, SO...
...I'LL USE THIS NEW MOVE I'VE BEEN MEANING TO TRY...
I CALL IT "THE WALL OF WEB."
OR MAYBE "WEB WALL."
YOUR CHOICE, REALLY.

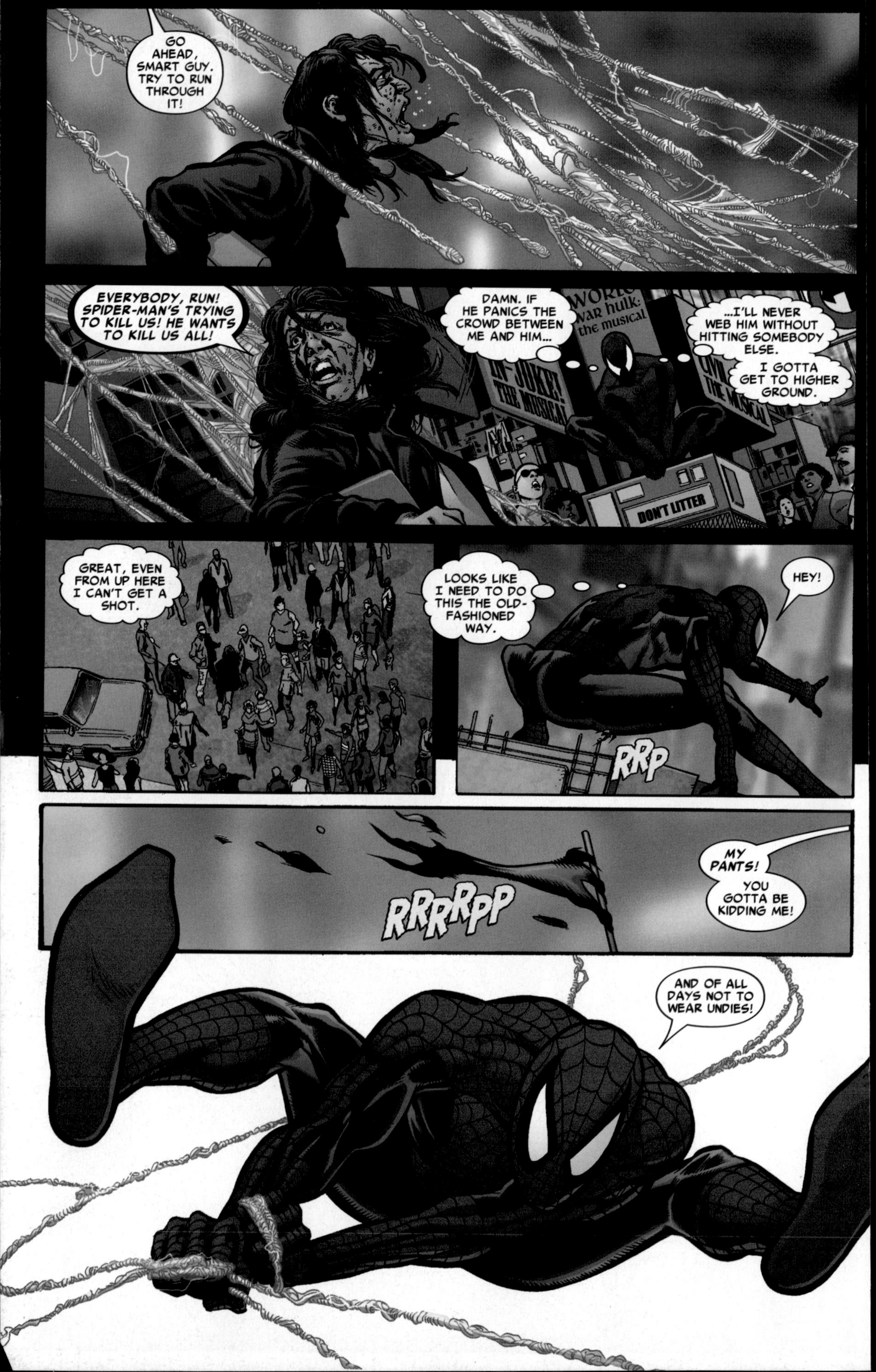

GO AHEAD, SMART GUY. TRY TO RUN THROUGH IT!
EVERYBODY, RUN! SPIDER-MAN'S TRYING TO KILL US! HE WANTS TO KILL US ALL!
DAMN. IF HE PANICS THE CROWD BETWEEN ME AND HIM...
...I'LL NEVER WEB HIM WITHOUT HITTING SOMEBODY ELSE.
I GOTTA GET TO HIGHER GROUND.
WORLD WAR HULK: the musical
IN-JOKE! THE MUSICAL
DON'T LITTER
GREAT, EVEN FROM UP HERE I CAN'T GET A SHOT.
LOOKS LIKE I NEED TO DO THIS THE OLD-FASHIONED WAY.
HEY!
RRP
RRRRPP
MY PANTS!
YOU GOTTA BE KIDDING ME!
AND OF ALL DAYS NOT TO WEAR UNDIES!

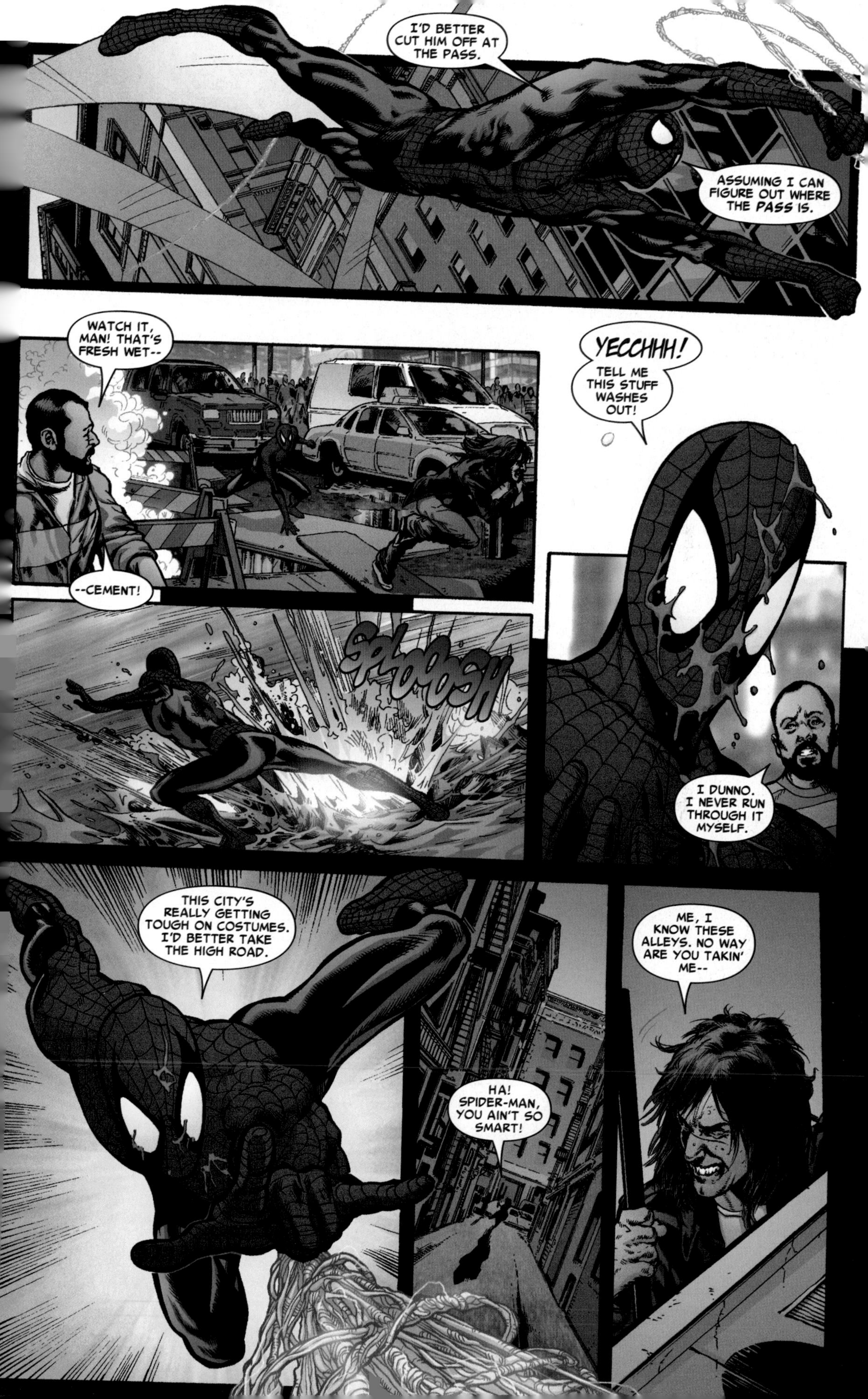
I'D BETTER CUT HIM OFF AT THE PASS.
ASSUMING I CAN FIGURE OUT WHERE THE PASS IS.
WATCH IT, MAN! THAT'S FRESH WET--
--CEMENT!
SPLOOOSH
YECCHHH!
TELL ME THIS STUFF WASHES OUT!
I DUNNO. I NEVER RUN THROUGH IT MYSELF.
THIS CITY'S REALLY GETTING TOUGH ON COSTUMES. I'D BETTER TAKE THE HIGH ROAD.
ME, I KNOW THESE ALLEYS. NO WAY ARE YOU TAKIN' ME--
HA! SPIDER-MAN, YOU AIN'T SO SMART!

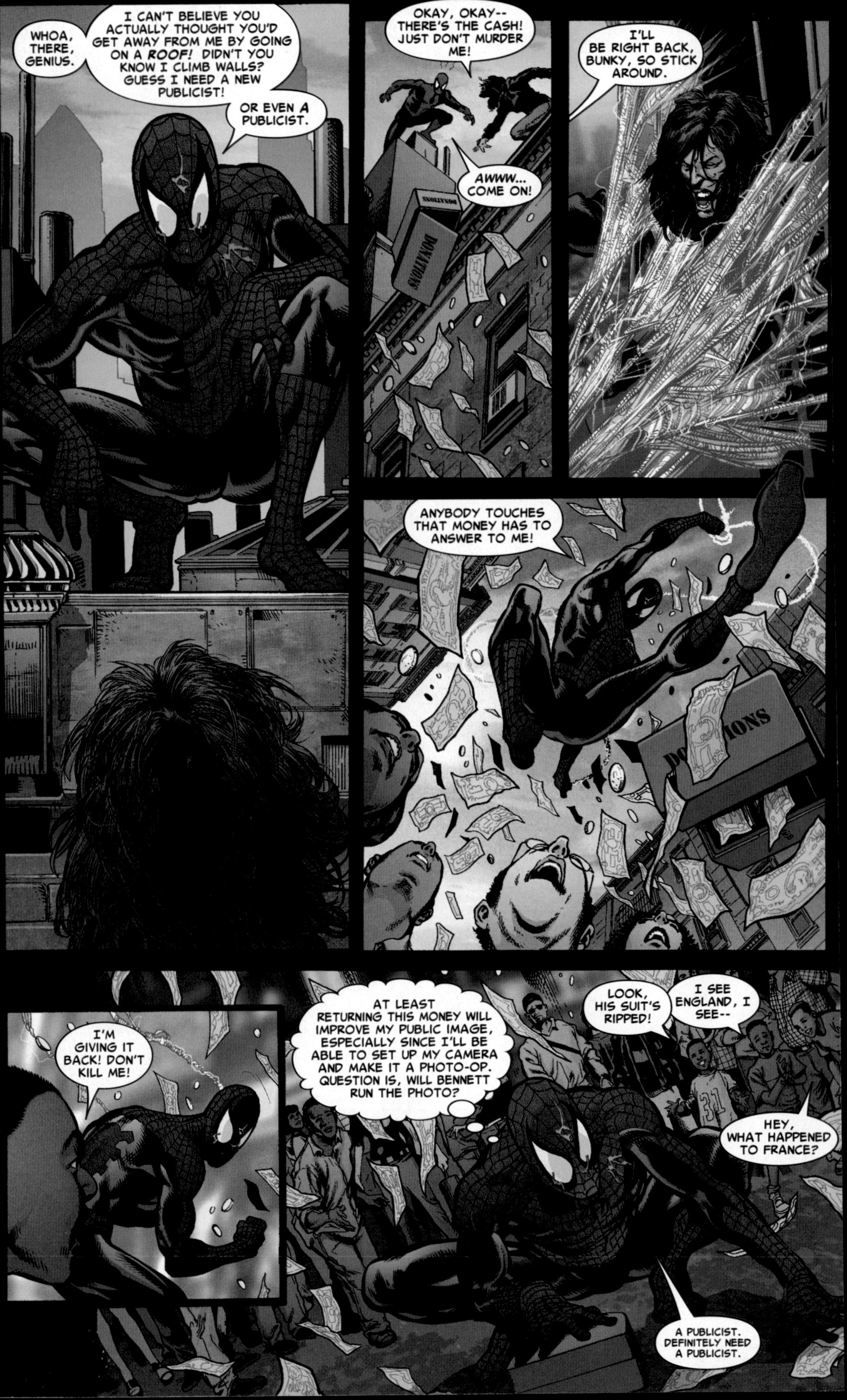
WHOA, THERE, GENIUS.
I CAN'T BELIEVE YOU ACTUALLY THOUGHT YOU'D GET AWAY FROM ME BY GOING ON A ROOF! DIDN'T YOU KNOW I CLIMB WALLS? GUESS I NEED A NEW PUBLICIST!
OR EVEN A PUBLICIST.
OKAY, OKAY-- THERE'S THE CASH! JUST DON'T MURDER ME!
AWWW... COME ON!
DONATIONS
I'LL BE RIGHT BACK, BUNKY, SO STICK AROUND.
ANYBODY TOUCHES THAT MONEY HAS TO ANSWER TO ME!
I'M GIVING IT BACK! DON'T KILL ME!
AT LEAST RETURNING THIS MONEY WILL IMPROVE MY PUBLIC IMAGE, ESPECIALLY SINCE I'LL BE ABLE TO SET UP MY CAMERA AND MAKE IT A PHOTO-OP. QUESTION IS, WILL BENNETT RUN THE PHOTO?
LOOK, HIS SUIT'S RIPPED!
I SEE ENGLAND, I SEE--
HEY, WHAT HAPPENED TO FRANCE?
A PUBLICIST. DEFINITELY NEED A PUBLICIST.

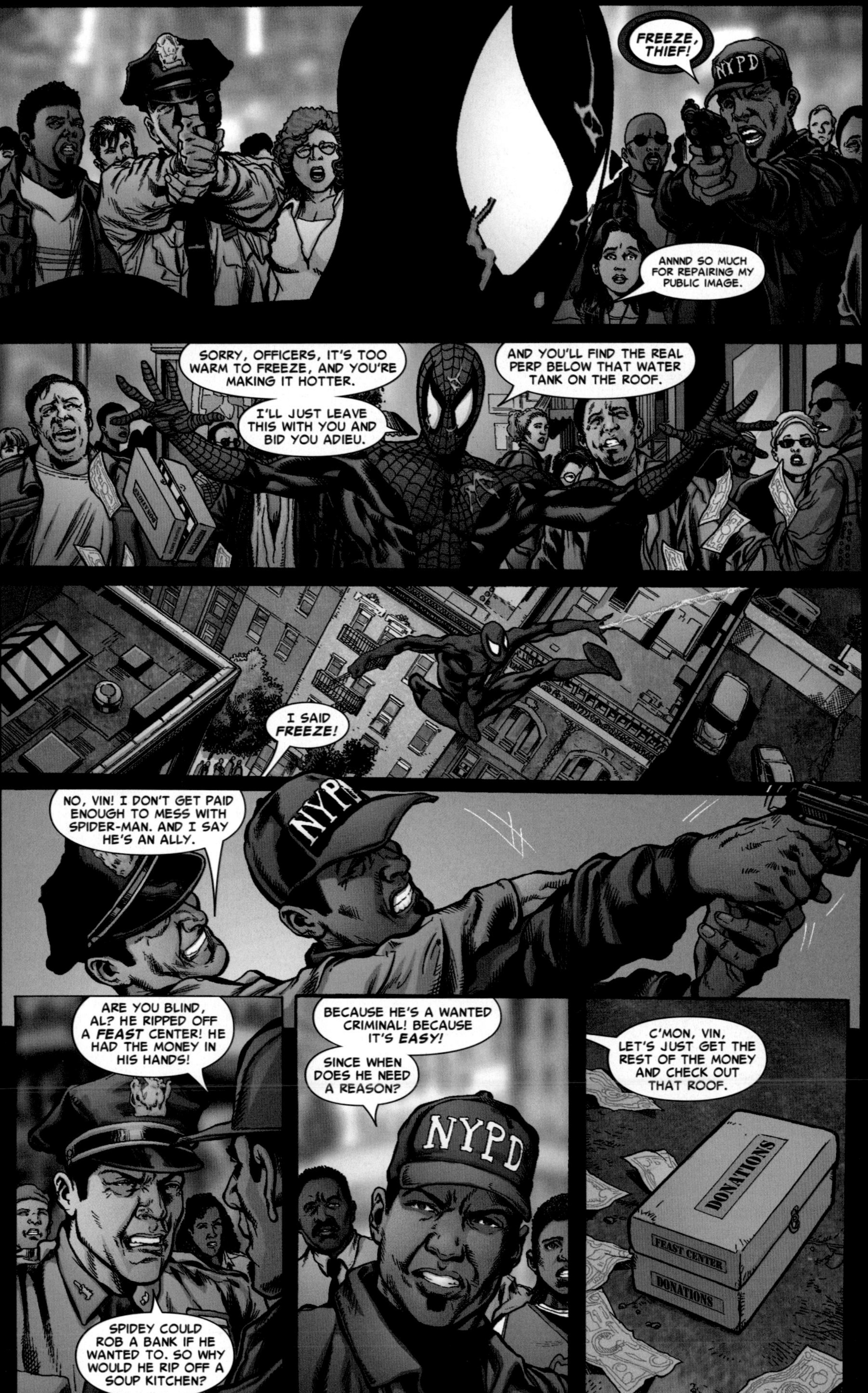
FREEZE, THIEF!
ANNND SO MUCH FOR REPAIRING MY PUBLIC IMAGE.
SORRY, OFFICERS, IT'S TOO WARM TO FREEZE, AND YOU'RE MAKING IT HOTTER.
I'LL JUST LEAVE THIS WITH YOU AND BID YOU ADIEU.
AND YOU'LL FIND THE REAL PERP BELOW THAT WATER TANK ON THE ROOF.
I SAID FREEZE!
NO, VIN! I DON'T GET PAID ENOUGH TO MESS WITH SPIDER-MAN. AND I SAY HE'S AN ALLY.
NYPD
ARE YOU BLIND, AL? HE RIPPED OFF A FEAST CENTER! HE HAD THE MONEY IN HIS HANDS!
SPIDEY COULD ROB A BANK IF HE WANTED TO. SO WHY WOULD HE RIP OFF A SOUP KITCHEN?
BECAUSE HE'S A WANTED CRIMINAL! BECAUSE IT'S EASY!
SINCE WHEN DOES HE NEED A REASON?
NYPD
C'MON, VIN, LET'S JUST GET THE REST OF THE MONEY AND CHECK OUT THAT ROOF.
DONATIONS
FEAST CENTER
DONATIONS

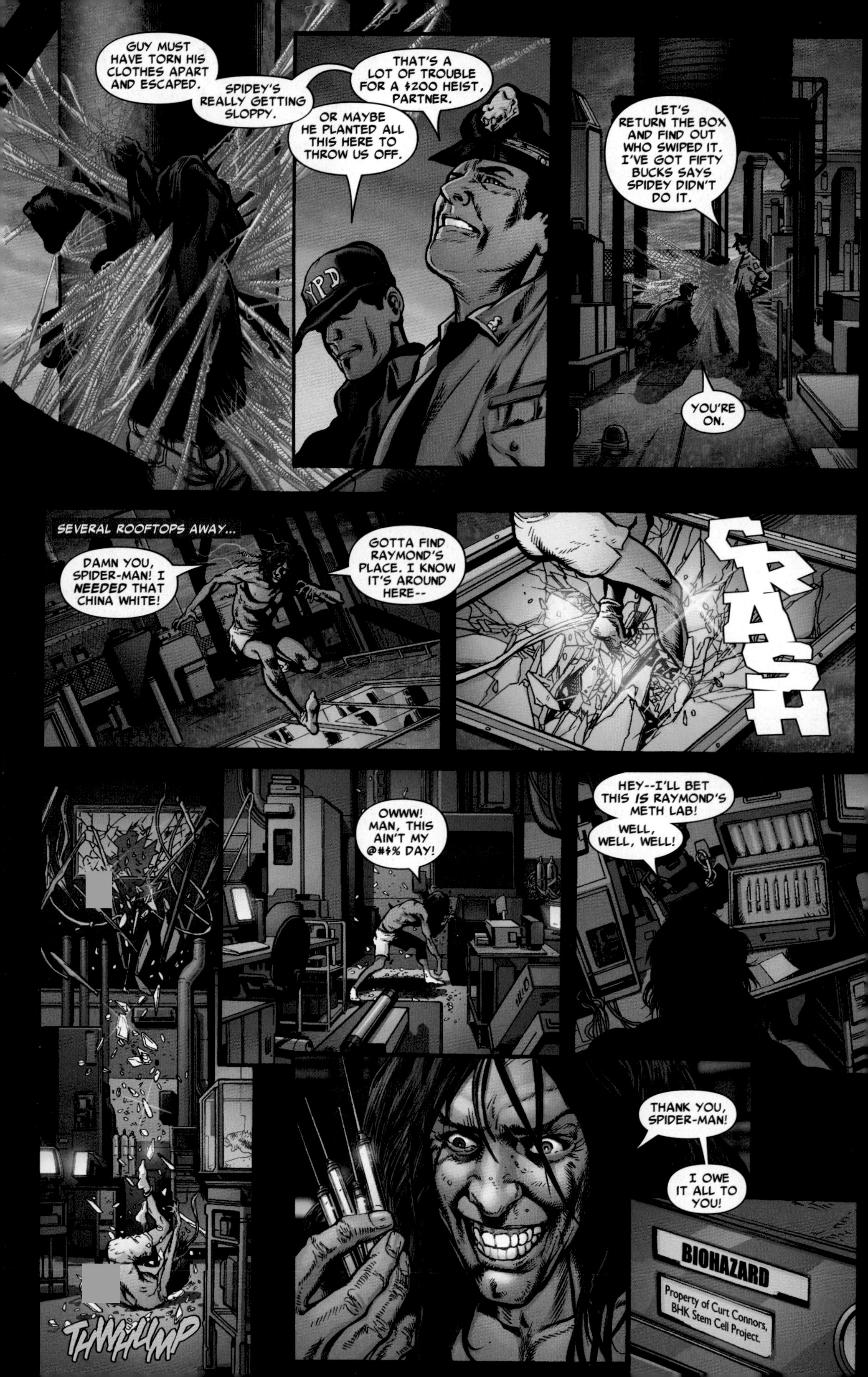
GUY MUST HAVE TORN HIS CLOTHES APART AND ESCAPED.
SPIDEY'S REALLY GETTING SLOPPY.
THAT'S A LOT OF TROUBLE FOR A $200 HEIST, PARTNER.
OR MAYBE HE PLANTED ALL THIS HERE TO THROW US OFF.
YPD
LET'S RETURN THE BOX AND FIND OUT WHO SWIPED IT. I'VE GOT FIFTY BUCKS SAYS SPIDEY DIDN'T DO IT.
YOU'RE ON.
SEVERAL ROOFTOPS AWAY...
DAMN YOU, SPIDER-MAN! I NEEDED THAT CHINA WHITE!
GOTTA FIND RAYMOND'S PLACE. I KNOW IT'S AROUND HERE--
CRASH
THWHUMP
OWWW! MAN, THIS AIN'T MY @#$% DAY!
HEY--I'LL BET THIS IS RAYMOND'S METH LAB!
WELL, WELL, WELL!
THANK YOU, SPIDER-MAN!
I OWE IT ALL TO YOU!
BIOHAZARD
Property of Curt Connors, BHK Stem Cell Project.

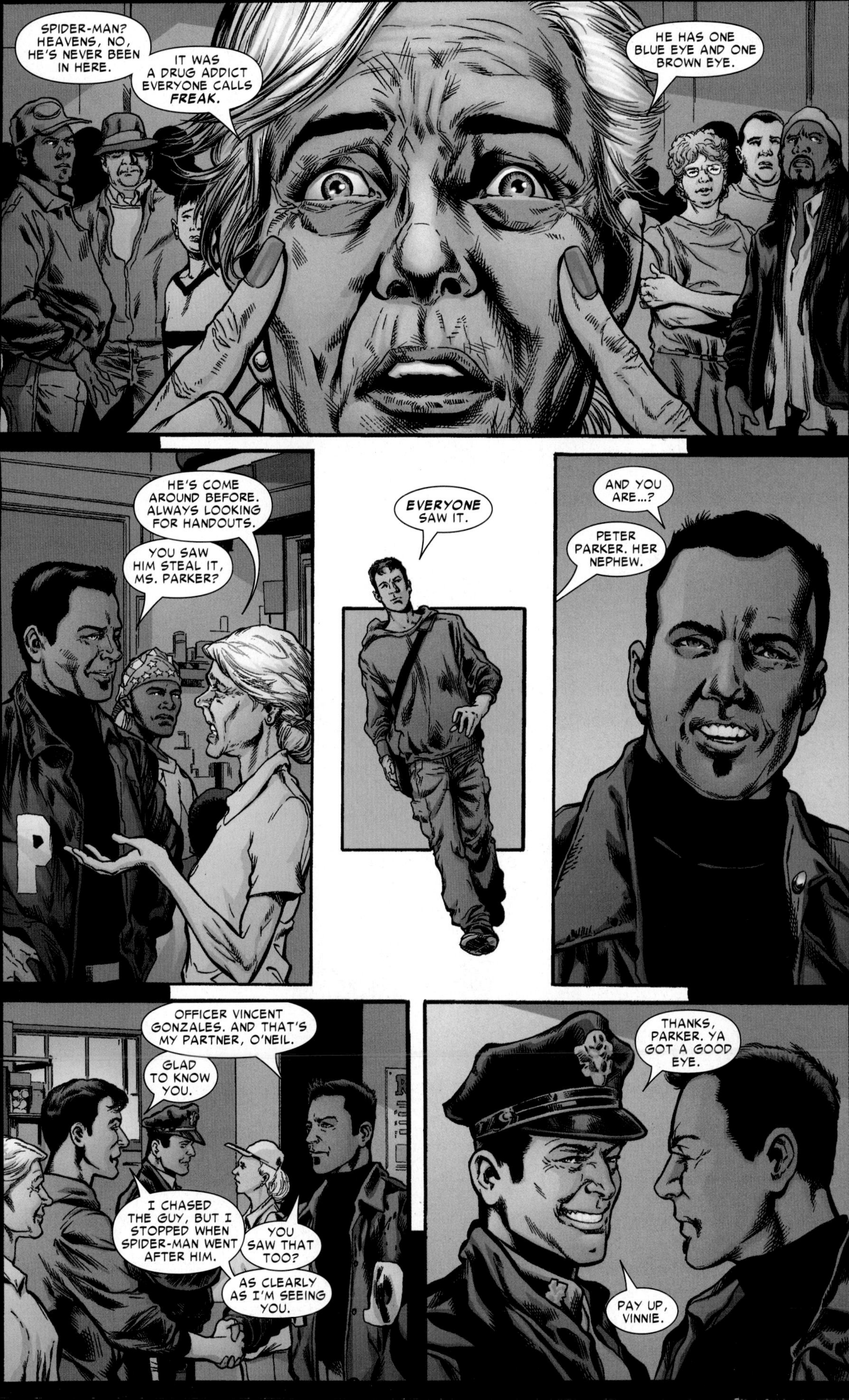
SPIDER-MAN? HEAVENS, NO, HE'S NEVER BEEN IN HERE.
IT WAS A DRUG ADDICT EVERYONE CALLS *FREAK.*
HE HAS ONE BLUE EYE AND ONE BROWN EYE.
HE'S COME AROUND BEFORE. ALWAYS LOOKING FOR HANDOUTS.
YOU SAW HIM STEAL IT, MS. PARKER?
EVERYONE SAW IT.
AND YOU ARE...?
PETER PARKER. HER NEPHEW.
OFFICER VINCENT GONZALES. AND THAT'S MY PARTNER, O'NEIL.
GLAD TO KNOW YOU.
I CHASED THE GUY, BUT I STOPPED WHEN SPIDER-MAN WENT AFTER HIM.
YOU SAW THAT TOO?
AS CLEARLY AS I'M SEEING YOU.
THANKS, PARKER. YA GOT A GOOD EYE.
PAY UP, VINNIE.

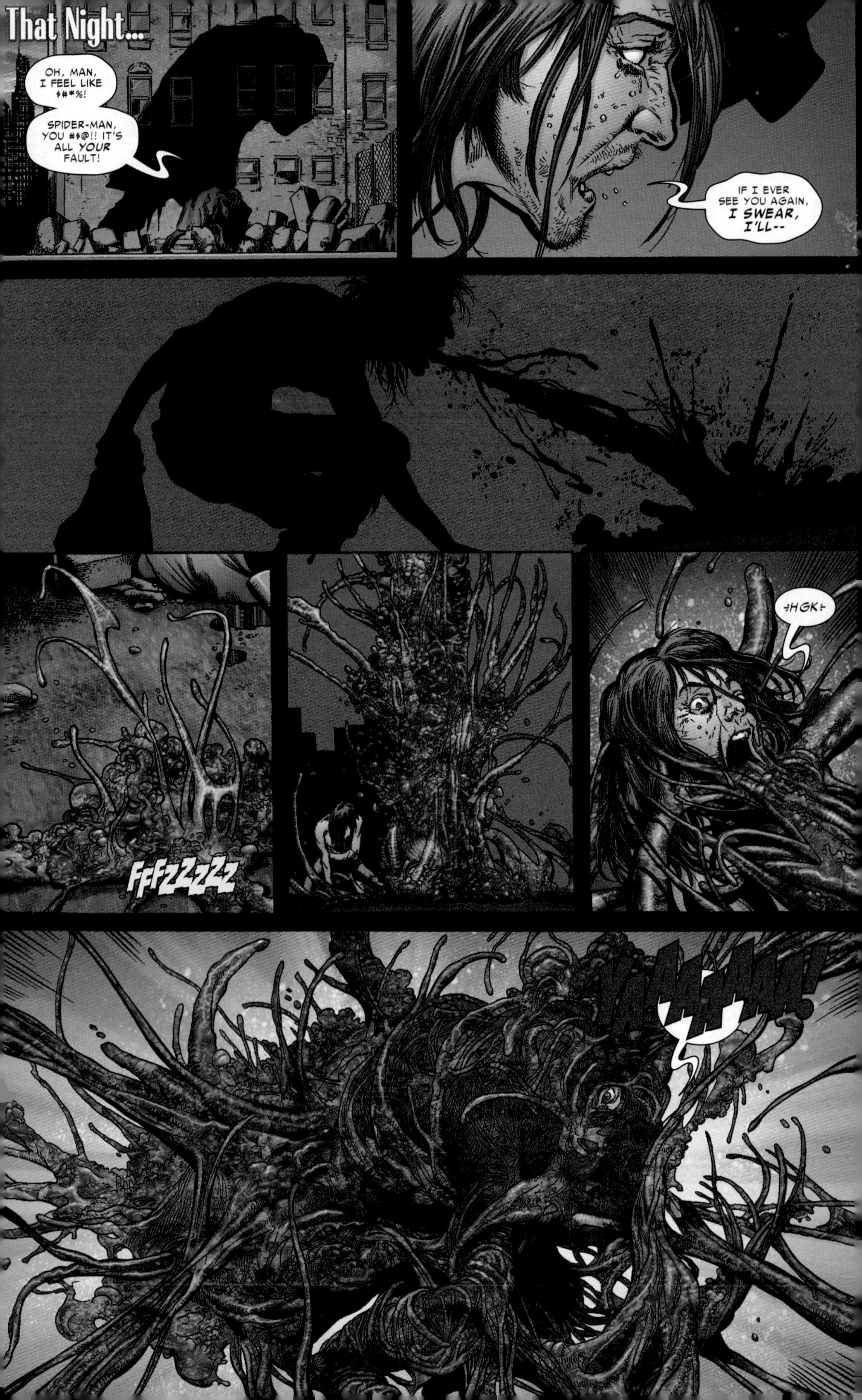
That Night...
OH, MAN, I FEEL LIKE $#*%!
SPIDER-MAN, YOU #$@!! IT'S ALL YOUR FAULT!
IF I EVER SEE YOU AGAIN, I SWEAR, I'LL--
FFFZZZZZ
HGK

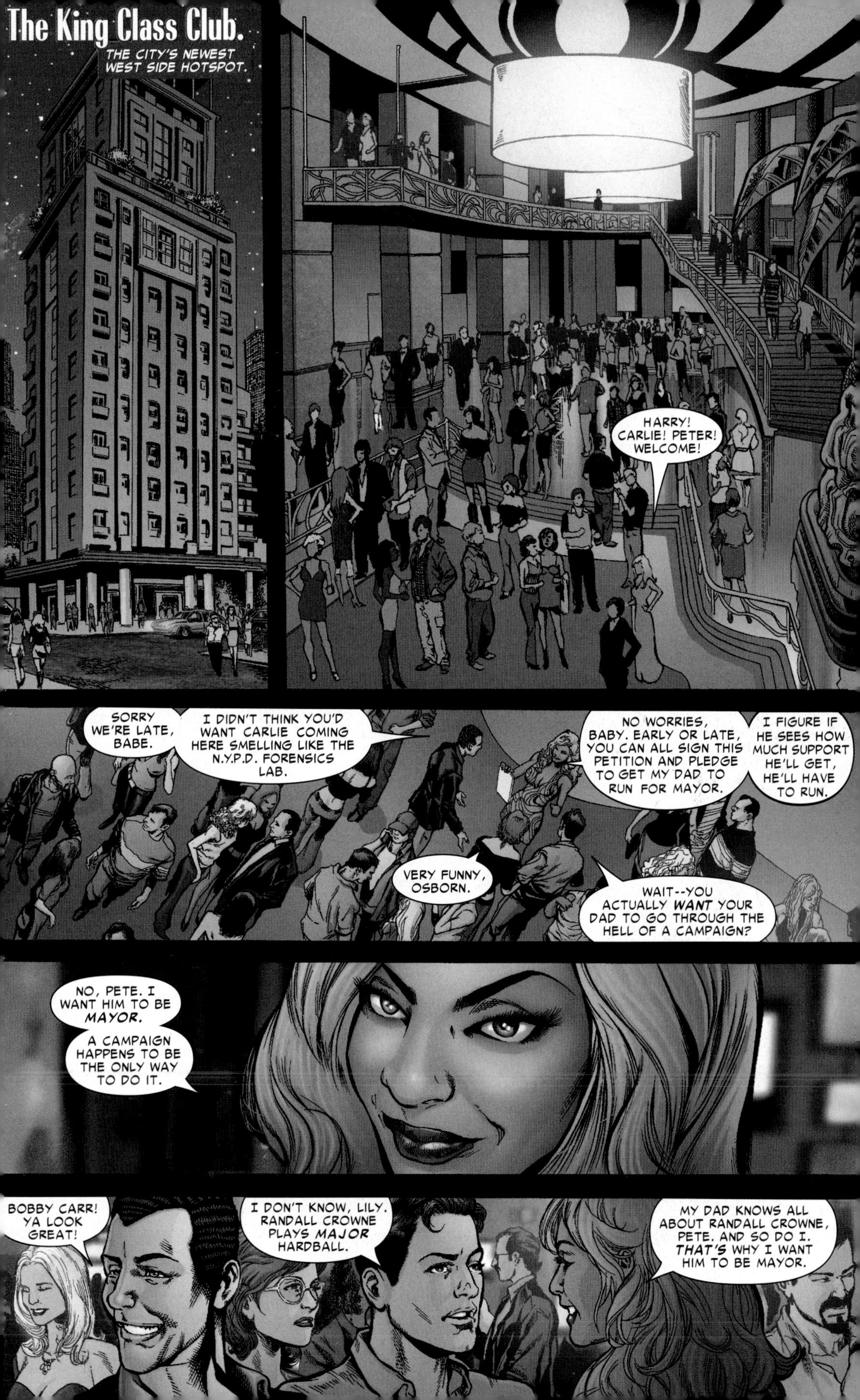
The King Class Club.
THE CITY'S NEWEST WEST SIDE HOTSPOT.
HARRY! CARLIE! PETER! WELCOME!
SORRY WE'RE LATE, BABE.
I DIDN'T THINK YOU'D WANT CARLIE COMING HERE SMELLING LIKE THE N.Y.P.D. FORENSICS LAB.
NO WORRIES, BABY. EARLY OR LATE, YOU CAN ALL SIGN THIS PETITION AND PLEDGE TO GET MY DAD TO RUN FOR MAYOR.
I FIGURE IF HE SEES HOW MUCH SUPPORT HE'LL GET, HE'LL HAVE TO RUN.
VERY FUNNY, OSBORN.
WAIT--YOU ACTUALLY *WANT* YOUR DAD TO GO THROUGH THE HELL OF A CAMPAIGN?
NO, PETE. I WANT HIM TO BE *MAYOR.*
A CAMPAIGN HAPPENS TO BE THE ONLY WAY TO DO IT.
BOBBY CARR! YA LOOK GREAT!
I DON'T KNOW, LILY. RANDALL CROWNE PLAYS *MAJOR* HARDBALL.
MY DAD KNOWS ALL ABOUT RANDALL CROWNE, PETE. AND SO DO I. *THAT'S* WHY I WANT HIM TO BE MAYOR.

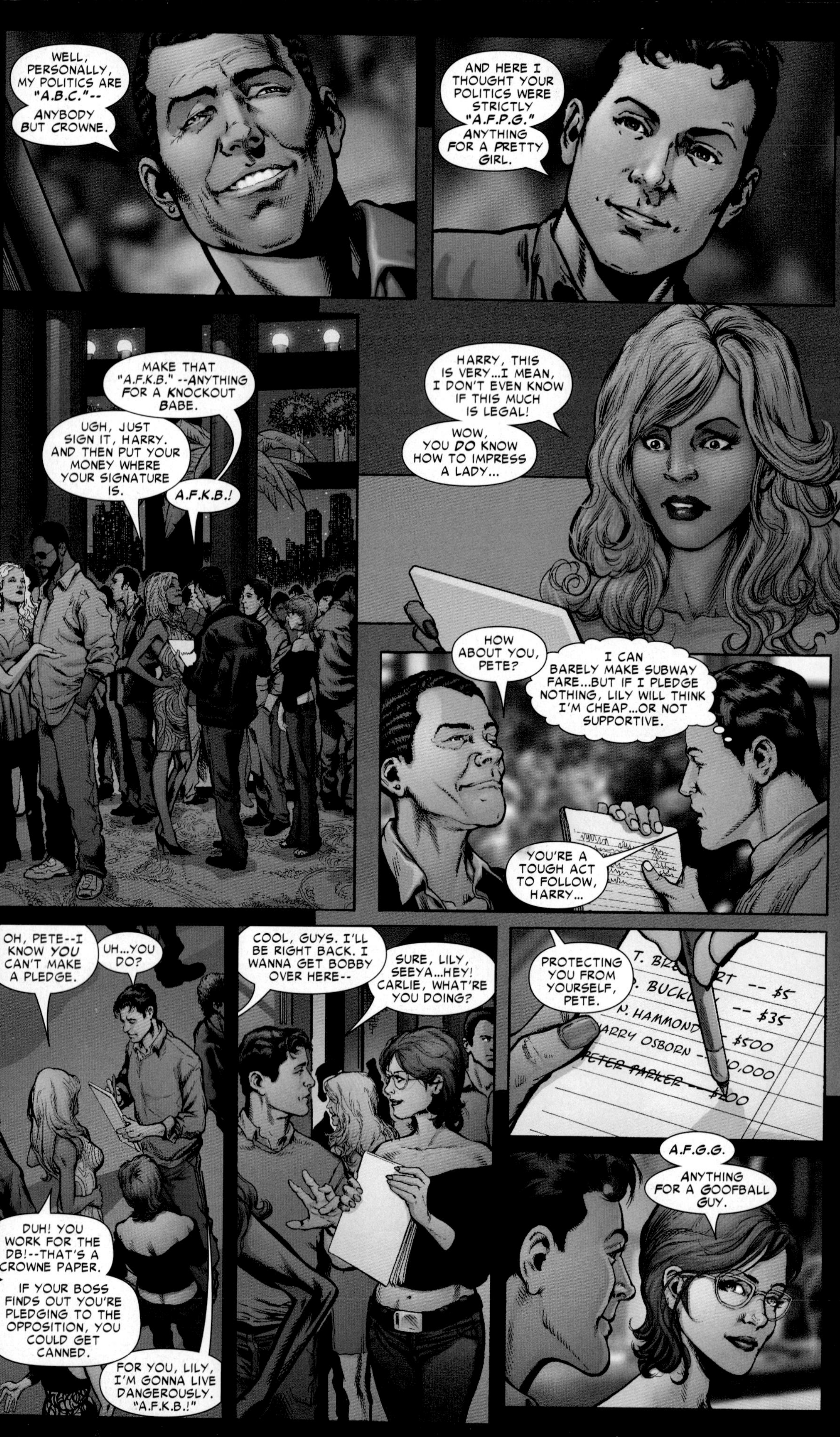
WELL, PERSONALLY, MY POLITICS ARE "A.B.C."--
ANYBODY BUT CROWNE.
AND HERE I THOUGHT YOUR POLITICS WERE STRICTLY "A.F.P.G." ANYTHING FOR A PRETTY GIRL.
MAKE THAT "A.F.K.B." --ANYTHING FOR A KNOCKOUT BABE.
UGH, JUST SIGN IT, HARRY. AND THEN PUT YOUR MONEY WHERE YOUR SIGNATURE IS.
A.F.K.B.!
HARRY, THIS IS VERY...I MEAN, I DON'T EVEN KNOW IF THIS MUCH IS LEGAL!
WOW, YOU DO KNOW HOW TO IMPRESS A LADY...
HOW ABOUT YOU, PETE?
I CAN BARELY MAKE SUBWAY FARE...BUT IF I PLEDGE NOTHING, LILY WILL THINK I'M CHEAP...OR NOT SUPPORTIVE.
YOU'RE A TOUGH ACT TO FOLLOW, HARRY...
OH, PETE--I KNOW YOU CAN'T MAKE A PLEDGE.
UH...YOU DO?
DUH! YOU WORK FOR THE DB!--THAT'S A CROWNE PAPER.
IF YOUR BOSS FINDS OUT YOU'RE PLEDGING TO THE OPPOSITION, YOU COULD GET CANNED.
FOR YOU, LILY, I'M GONNA LIVE DANGEROUSLY. "A.F.K.B.!"
COOL, GUYS. I'LL BE RIGHT BACK. I WANNA GET BOBBY OVER HERE--
SURE, LILY, SEEYA...HEY! CARLIE, WHAT'RE YOU DOING?
PROTECTING YOU FROM YOURSELF, PETE.
N. HAMMOND
HARRY OSBORN
PETER PARKER
$5
$35
$500
$100
A.F.G.G.
ANYTHING FOR A GOOFBALL GUY.

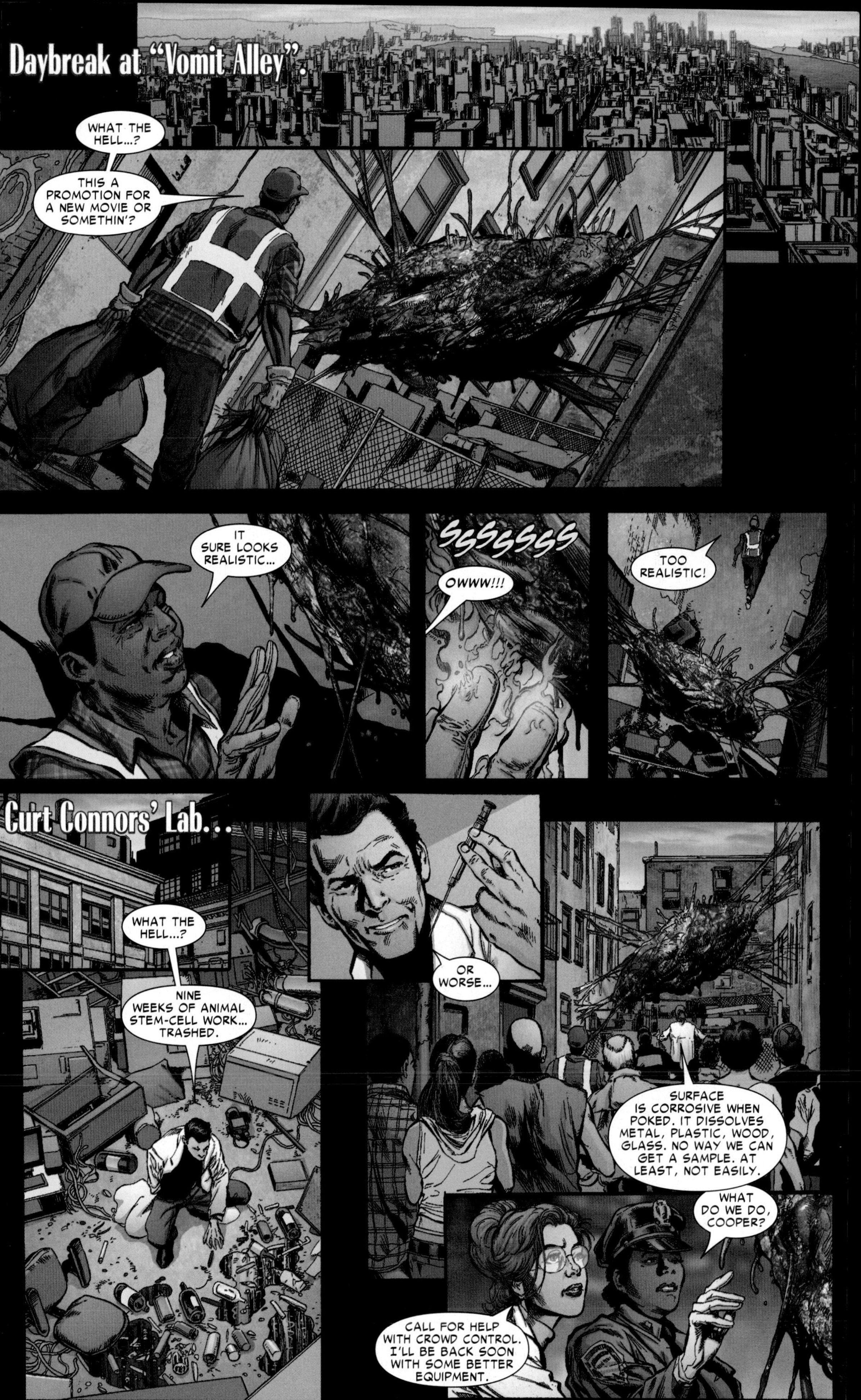
Daybreak at "Vomit Alley".
WHAT THE HELL...?
THIS A PROMOTION FOR A NEW MOVIE OR SOMETHIN'?
IT SURE LOOKS REALISTIC...
SSSSSSS
OWWW!!!
TOO REALISTIC!
Curt Connors' Lab...
WHAT THE HELL...?
NINE WEEKS OF ANIMAL STEM-CELL WORK... TRASHED.
OR WORSE...
SURFACE IS CORROSIVE WHEN POKED. IT DISSOLVES METAL, PLASTIC, WOOD, GLASS. NO WAY WE CAN GET A SAMPLE. AT LEAST, NOT EASILY.
WHAT DO WE DO, COOPER?
CALL FOR HELP WITH CROWD CONTROL. I'LL BE BACK SOON WITH SOME BETTER EQUIPMENT.

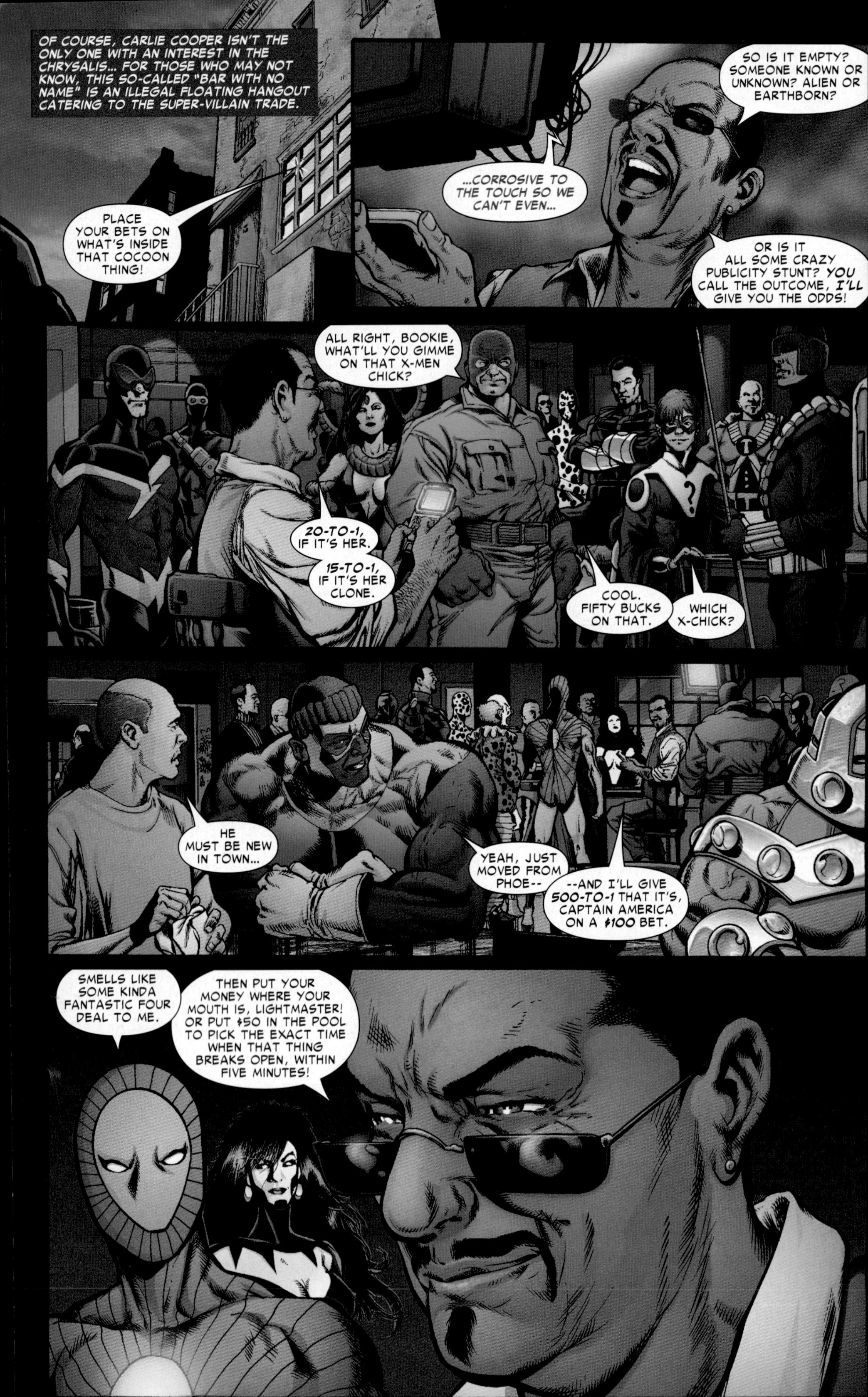
OF COURSE, CARLIE COOPER ISN'T THE ONLY ONE WITH AN INTEREST IN THE CHRYSALIS... FOR THOSE WHO MAY NOT KNOW, THIS SO-CALLED "BAR WITH NO NAME" IS AN ILLEGAL FLOATING HANGOUT CATERING TO THE SUPER-VILLAIN TRADE.
PLACE YOUR BETS ON WHAT'S INSIDE THAT COCOON THING!
...CORROSIVE TO THE TOUCH SO WE CAN'T EVEN...
SO IS IT EMPTY? SOMEONE KNOWN OR UNKNOWN? ALIEN OR EARTHBORN?
OR IS IT ALL SOME CRAZY PUBLICITY STUNT? YOU CALL THE OUTCOME, I'LL GIVE YOU THE ODDS!
ALL RIGHT, BOOKIE, WHAT'LL YOU GIMME ON THAT X-MEN CHICK?
20-TO-1, IF IT'S HER.
15-TO-1, IF IT'S HER CLONE.
COOL. FIFTY BUCKS ON THAT.
WHICH X-CHICK?
HE MUST BE NEW IN TOWN...
YEAH, JUST MOVED FROM PHOE--
--AND I'LL GIVE 500-TO-1 THAT IT'S, CAPTAIN AMERICA ON A $100 BET.
SMELLS LIKE SOME KINDA FANTASTIC FOUR DEAL TO ME.
THEN PUT YOUR MONEY WHERE YOUR MOUTH IS, LIGHTMASTER! OR PUT $50 IN THE POOL TO PICK THE EXACT TIME WHEN THAT THING BREAKS OPEN, WITHIN FIVE MINUTES!

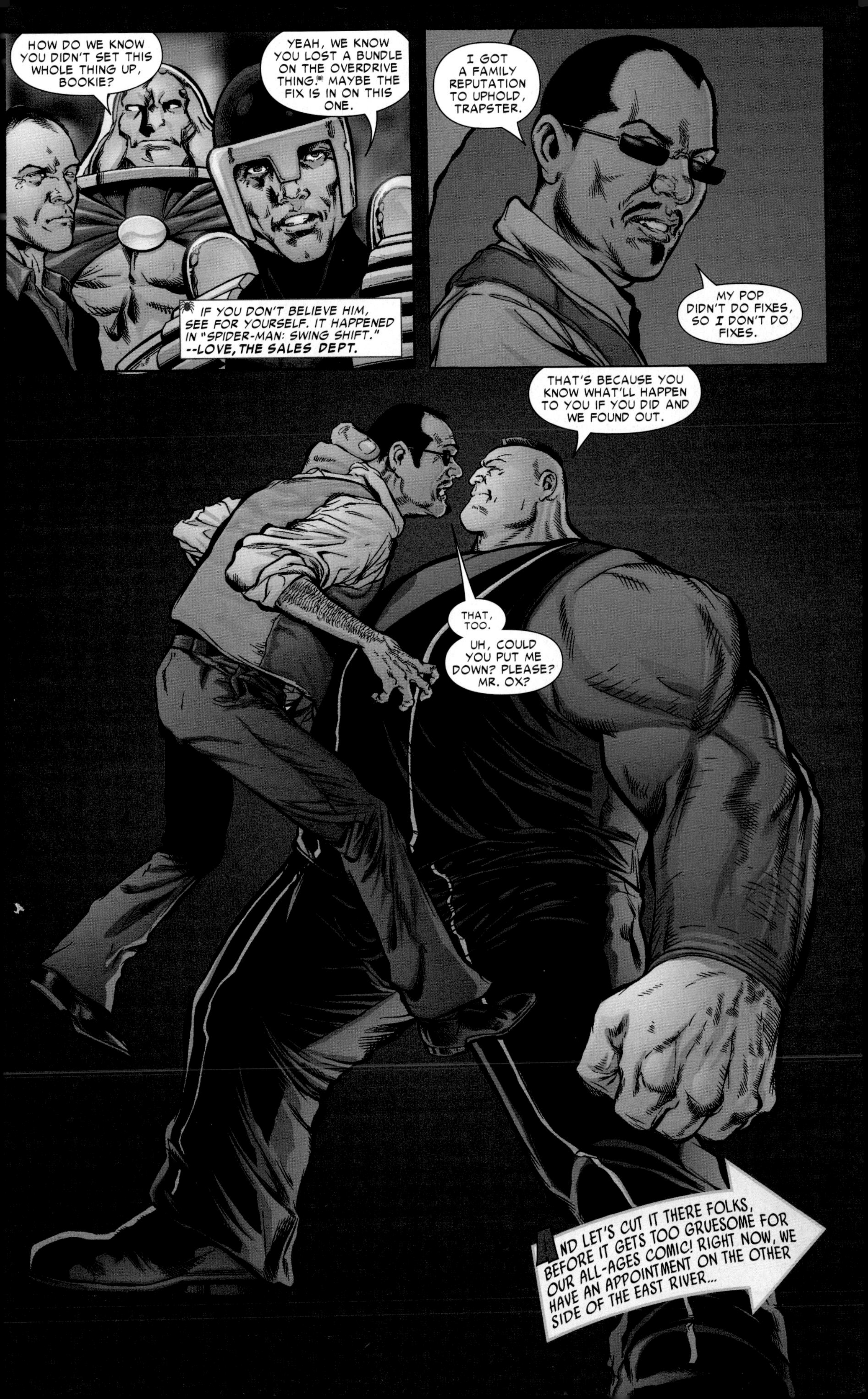
HOW DO WE KNOW YOU DIDN'T SET THIS WHOLE THING UP, BOOKIE?
YEAH, WE KNOW YOU LOST A BUNDLE ON THE OVERDRIVE THING.* MAYBE THE FIX IS IN ON THIS ONE.
*IF YOU DON'T BELIEVE HIM, SEE FOR YOURSELF. IT HAPPENED IN "SPIDER-MAN: SWING SHIFT." --LOVE, THE SALES DEPT.
I GOT A FAMILY REPUTATION TO UPHOLD, TRAPSTER.
MY POP DIDN'T DO FIXES, SO I DON'T DO FIXES.
THAT'S BECAUSE YOU KNOW WHAT'LL HAPPEN TO YOU IF YOU DID AND WE FOUND OUT.
THAT, TOO.
UH, COULD YOU PUT ME DOWN? PLEASE? MR. OX?
AND LET'S CUT IT THERE FOLKS, BEFORE IT GETS TOO GRUESOME FOR OUR ALL-AGES COMIC! RIGHT NOW, WE HAVE AN APPOINTMENT ON THE OTHER SIDE OF THE EAST RIVER...

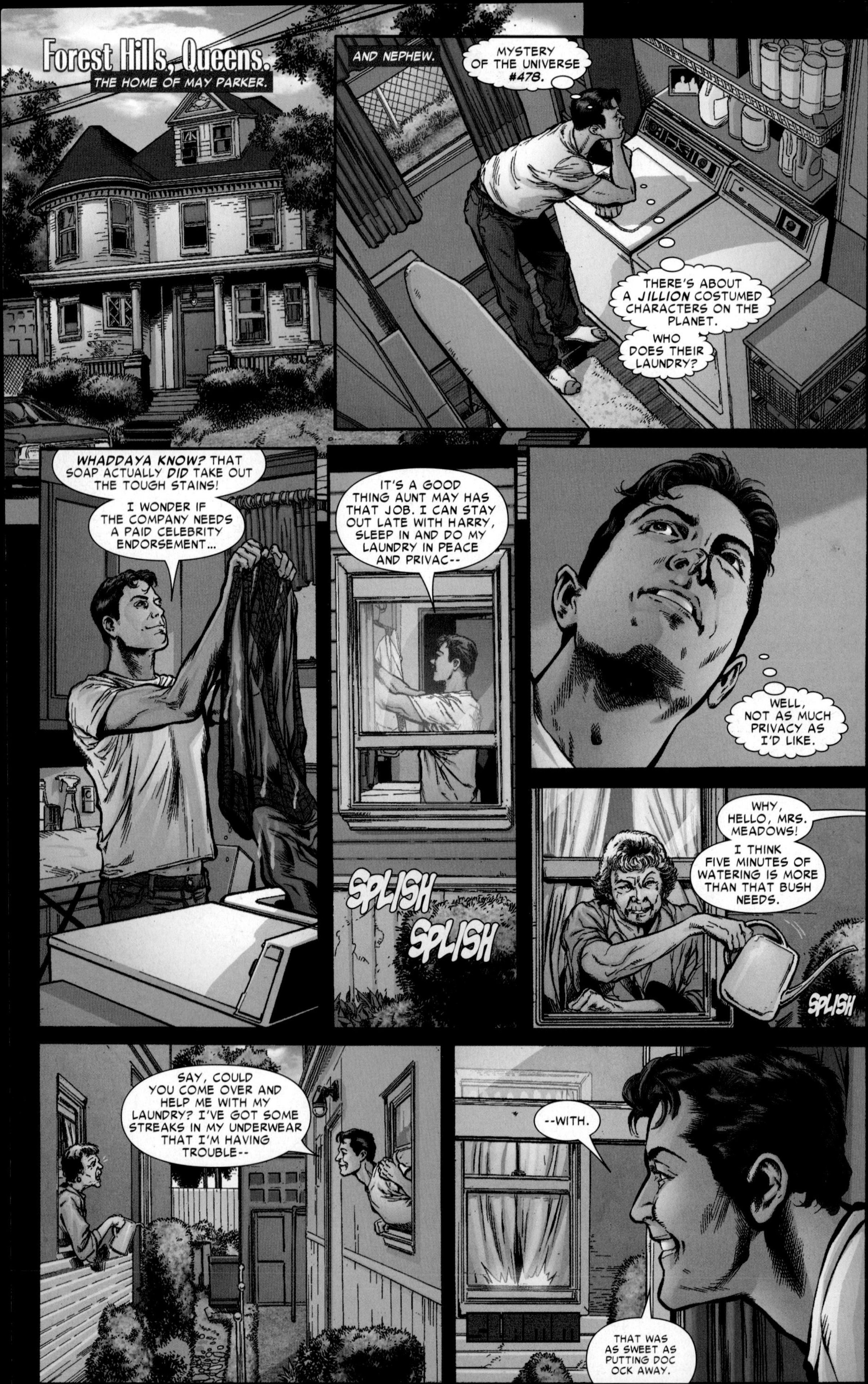
Forest Hills, Queens.
THE HOME OF MAY PARKER.
AND NEPHEW.
MYSTERY OF THE UNIVERSE #478.
THERE'S ABOUT A JILLION COSTUMED CHARACTERS ON THE PLANET.
WHO DOES THEIR LAUNDRY?
WHADDAYA KNOW? THAT SOAP ACTUALLY DID TAKE OUT THE TOUGH STAINS!
I WONDER IF THE COMPANY NEEDS A PAID CELEBRITY ENDORSEMENT...
IT'S A GOOD THING AUNT MAY HAS THAT JOB. I CAN STAY OUT LATE WITH HARRY, SLEEP IN AND DO MY LAUNDRY IN PEACE AND PRIVAC--
SPLISH
SPLISH
WELL, NOT AS MUCH PRIVACY AS I'D LIKE.
WHY, HELLO, MRS. MEADOWS!
I THINK FIVE MINUTES OF WATERING IS MORE THAN THAT BUSH NEEDS.
SPLISH
SAY, COULD YOU COME OVER AND HELP ME WITH MY LAUNDRY? I'VE GOT SOME STREAKS IN MY UNDERWEAR THAT I'M HAVING TROUBLE--
--WITH.
THAT WAS AS SWEET AS PUTTING DOC OCK AWAY.

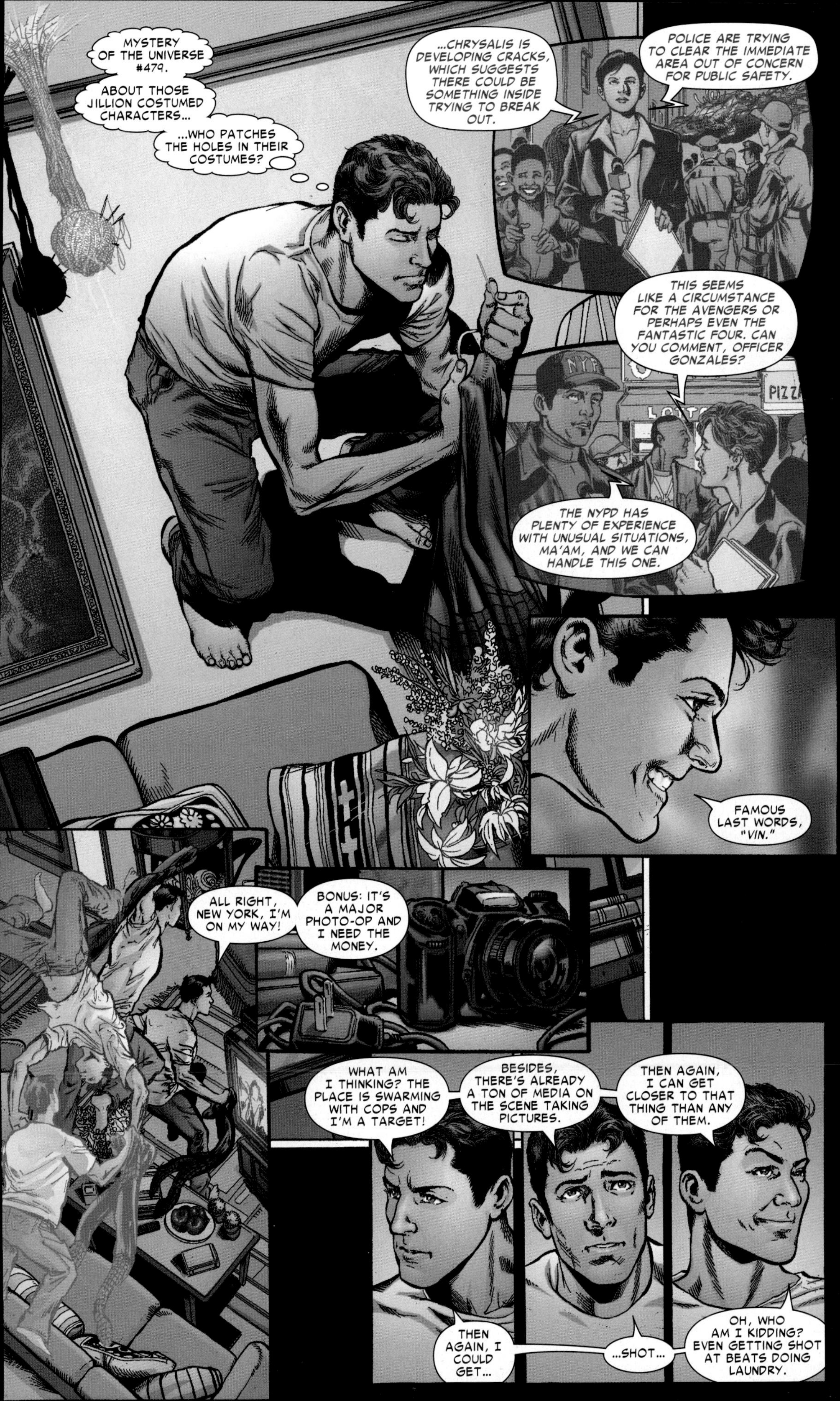
MYSTERY OF THE UNIVERSE #479.
ABOUT THOSE JILLION COSTUMED CHARACTERS...
...WHO PATCHES THE HOLES IN THEIR COSTUMES?
...CHRYSALIS IS DEVELOPING CRACKS, WHICH SUGGESTS THERE COULD BE SOMETHING INSIDE TRYING TO BREAK OUT.
POLICE ARE TRYING TO CLEAR THE IMMEDIATE AREA OUT OF CONCERN FOR PUBLIC SAFETY.
THIS SEEMS LIKE A CIRCUMSTANCE FOR THE AVENGERS OR PERHAPS EVEN THE FANTASTIC FOUR. CAN YOU COMMENT, OFFICER GONZALES?
NYPD
PIZZA
THE NYPD HAS PLENTY OF EXPERIENCE WITH UNUSUAL SITUATIONS, MA'AM, AND WE CAN HANDLE THIS ONE.
FAMOUS LAST WORDS, "VIN."
ALL RIGHT, NEW YORK, I'M ON MY WAY!
BONUS: IT'S A MAJOR PHOTO-OP AND I NEED THE MONEY.
WHAT AM I THINKING? THE PLACE IS SWARMING WITH COPS AND I'M A TARGET!
BESIDES, THERE'S ALREADY A TON OF MEDIA ON THE SCENE TAKING PICTURES.
THEN AGAIN, I CAN GET CLOSER TO THAT THING THAN ANY OF THEM.
THEN AGAIN, I COULD GET...
...SHOT...
OH, WHO AM I KIDDING? EVEN GETTING SHOT AT BEATS DOING LAUNDRY.

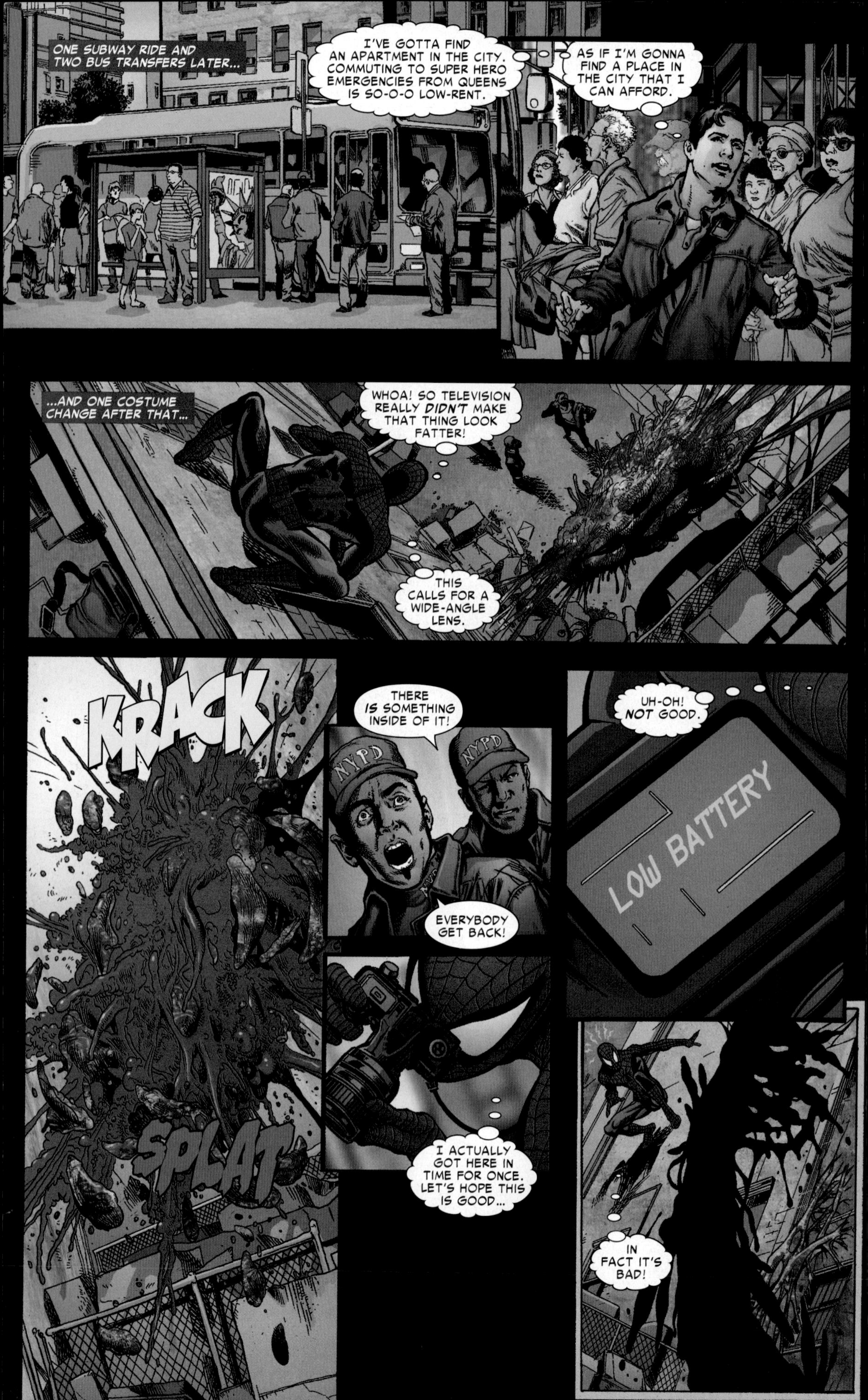
ONE SUBWAY RIDE AND TWO BUS TRANSFERS LATER...
I'VE GOTTA FIND AN APARTMENT IN THE CITY. COMMUTING TO SUPER HERO EMERGENCIES FROM QUEENS IS SO-O-O LOW-RENT.
AS IF I'M GONNA FIND A PLACE IN THE CITY THAT I CAN AFFORD.
...AND ONE COSTUME CHANGE AFTER THAT...
WHOA! SO TELEVISION REALLY DIDN'T MAKE THAT THING LOOK FATTER!
THIS CALLS FOR A WIDE-ANGLE LENS.
KRACK
SPLAT
THERE IS SOMETHING INSIDE OF IT!
EVERYBODY GET BACK!
I ACTUALLY GOT HERE IN TIME FOR ONCE. LET'S HOPE THIS IS GOOD...
UH-OH! NOT GOOD.
LOW BATTERY
IN FACT IT'S BAD!

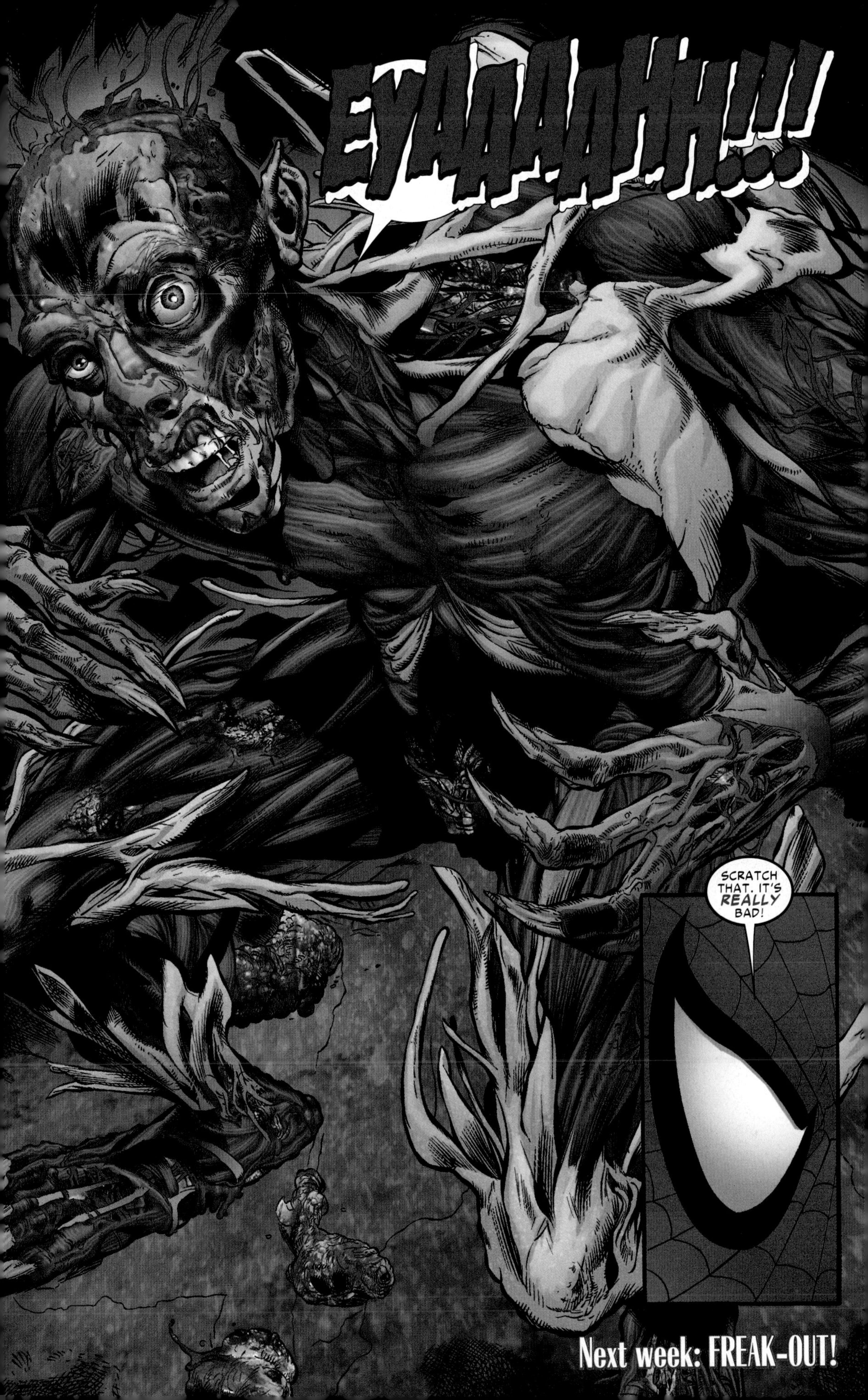
EYAAAAHH!!!
SCRATCH THAT. IT'S REALLY BAD!
Next week: FREAK-OUT!

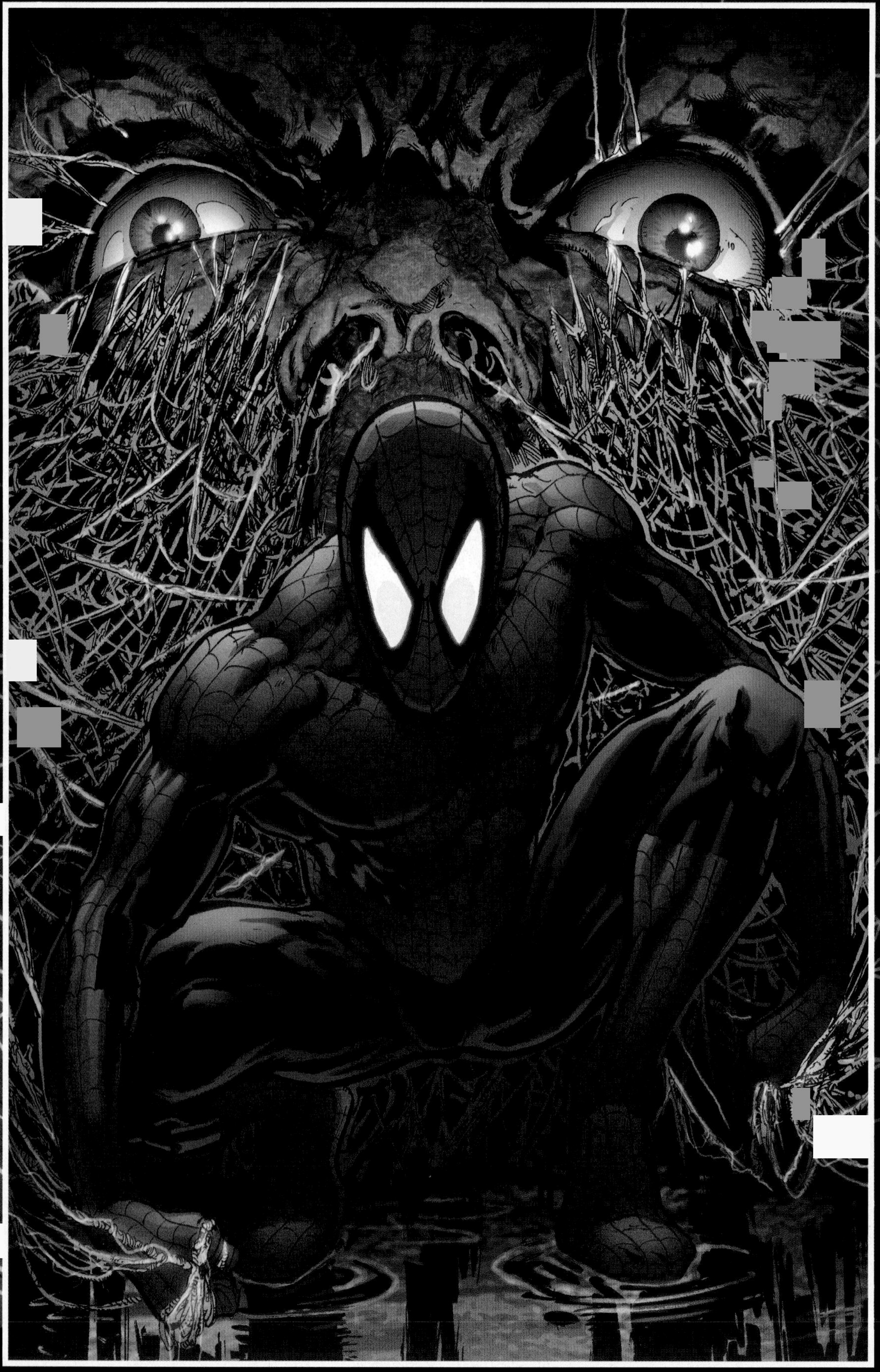

AMAZING SPIDER-MAN #553

WHILE ATTENDING A DEMONSTRATION IN RADIOLOGY, HIGH SCHOOL STUDENT **PETER PARKER** WAS BITTEN BY A SPIDER WHICH HAD ACCIDENTALLY BEEN EXPOSED TO **RADIOACTIVE RAYS.** THROUGH A MIRACLE OF SCIENCE, PETER SOON FOUND THAT HE HAD **GAINED** THE SPIDER'S POWERS...AND HAD, IN EFFECT, BECOME A HUMAN SPIDER! FROM THAT DAY ON HE WAS...

THE AMAZING SPIDER-MAN™
FREAK-OUT!

BOB GALE WRITER | **PHIL JIMENEZ** PENCILS | **ANDY LANNING** INKS

JEROMY COX COLORS | **VC'S JOE CARAMAGNA** LETTERS | **TOM BRENNAN** ASSISTANT EDITOR | **STEPHEN WACKER** FREAK | **TOM BREVOORT** EXECUTIVE EDITOR | **JOE QUESADA** EDITOR IN CHIEF | **DAN BUCKLEY** PUBLISHER

GALE, GUGGENHEIM, SLOTT & WELLS SPIDEY'S BRAINTRUST

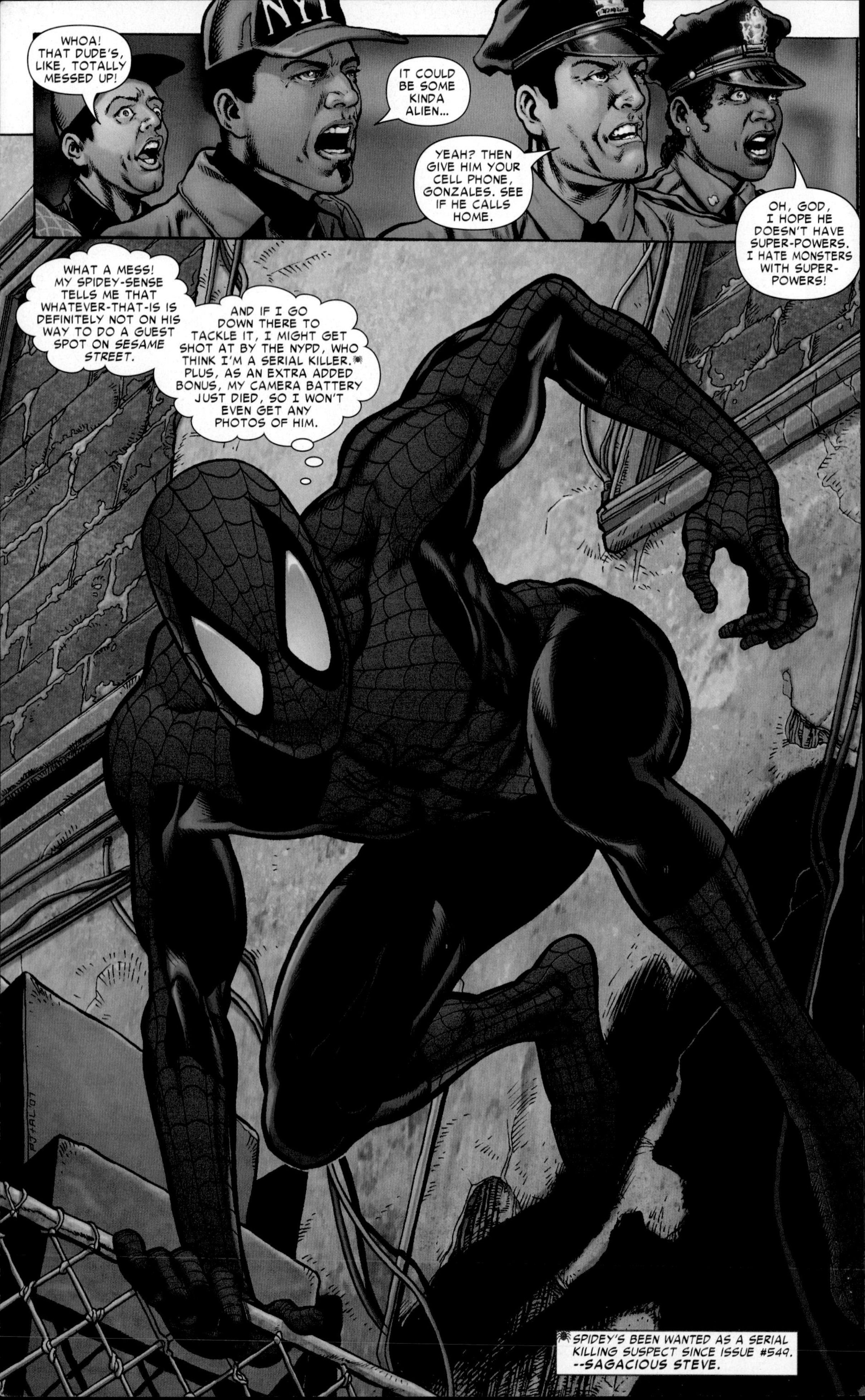
WHOA! THAT DUDE'S, LIKE, TOTALLY MESSED UP!
IT COULD BE SOME KINDA ALIEN...
YEAH? THEN GIVE HIM YOUR CELL PHONE, GONZALES. SEE IF HE CALLS HOME.
OH, GOD, I HOPE HE DOESN'T HAVE SUPER-POWERS. I HATE MONSTERS WITH SUPER-POWERS!
WHAT A MESS! MY SPIDEY-SENSE TELLS ME THAT WHATEVER-THAT-IS IS DEFINITELY NOT ON HIS WAY TO DO A GUEST SPOT ON *SESAME STREET.*
AND IF I GO DOWN THERE TO TACKLE IT, I MIGHT GET SHOT AT BY THE NYPD, WHO THINK I'M A SERIAL KILLER. PLUS, AS AN EXTRA ADDED BONUS, MY CAMERA BATTERY JUST DIED, SO I WON'T EVEN GET ANY PHOTOS OF HIM.
SPIDEY'S BEEN WANTED AS A SERIAL KILLING SUSPECT SINCE ISSUE #549. --SAGACIOUS STEVE.

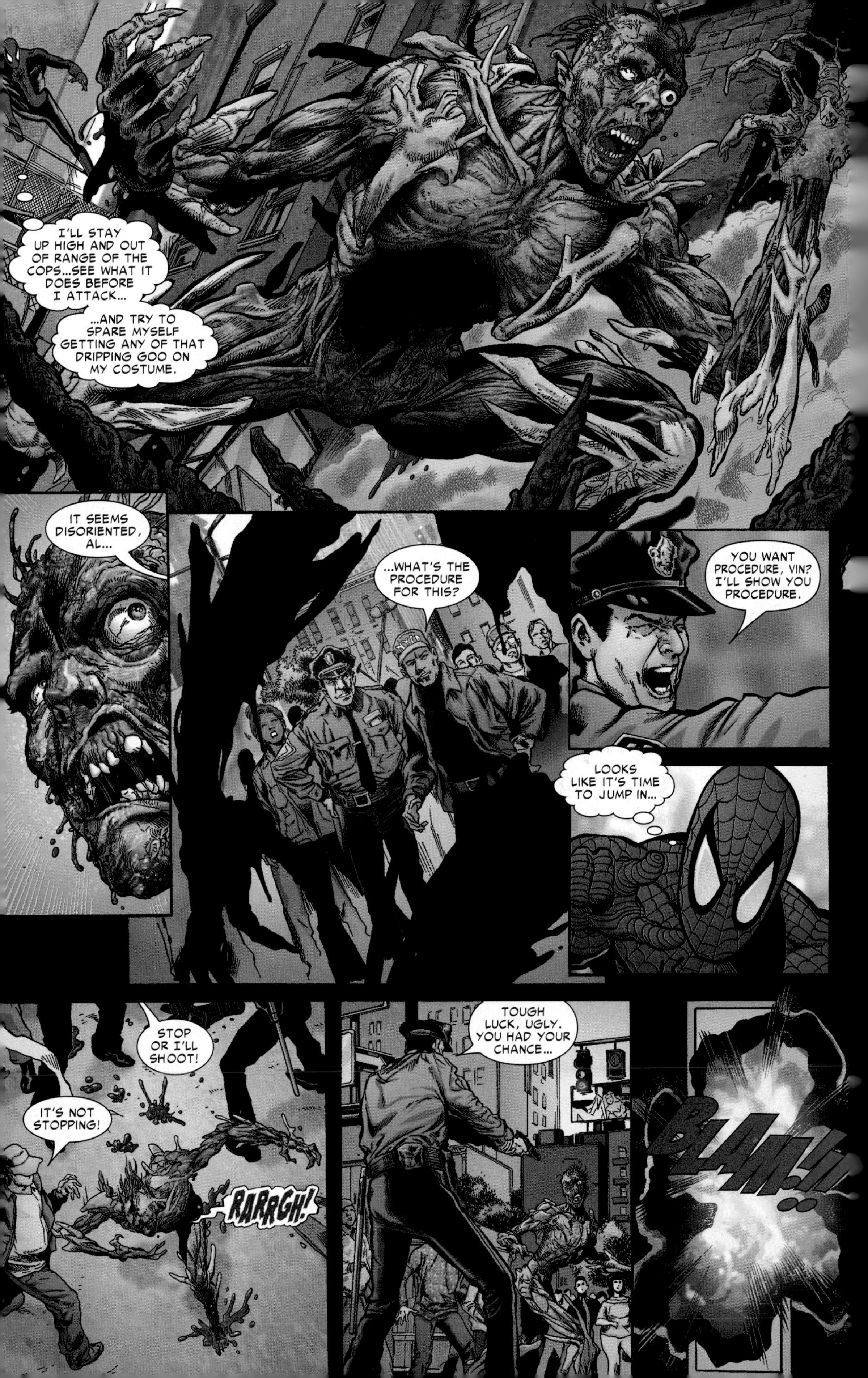

I'LL STAY UP HIGH AND OUT OF RANGE OF THE COPS...SEE WHAT IT DOES BEFORE I ATTACK...
...AND TRY TO SPARE MYSELF GETTING ANY OF THAT DRIPPING GOO ON MY COSTUME.
IT SEEMS DISORIENTED, AL...
...WHAT'S THE PROCEDURE FOR THIS?
YOU WANT PROCEDURE, VIN? I'LL SHOW YOU PROCEDURE.
LOOKS LIKE IT'S TIME TO JUMP IN...
STOP OR I'LL SHOOT!
IT'S NOT STOPPING!
RARRGH!
TOUGH LUCK, UGLY. YOU HAD YOUR CHANCE...
BLAM!!!

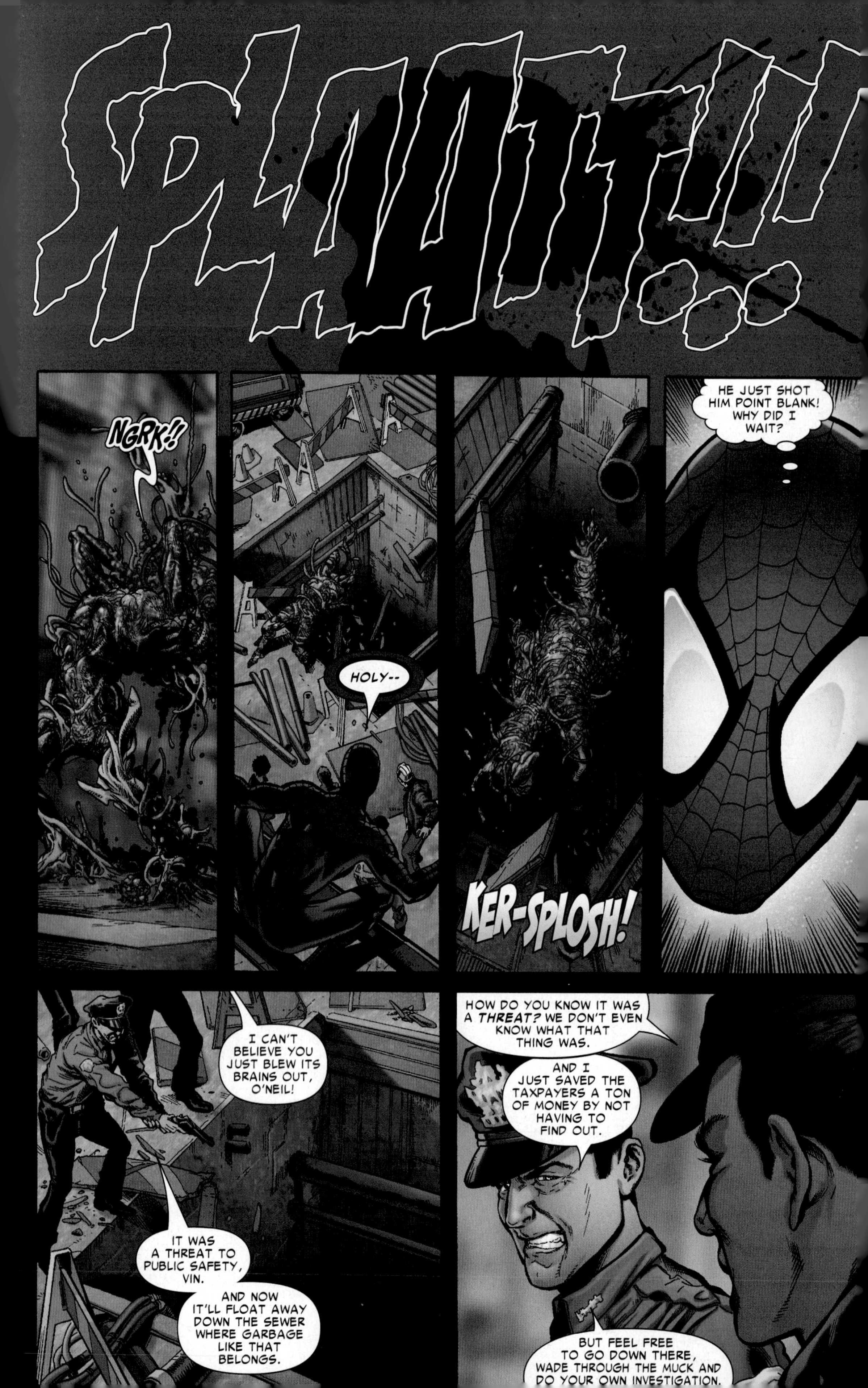
SPLOOOT!!!
NGRK!!
HOLY--
KER-SPLOSH!
HE JUST SHOT HIM POINT BLANK! WHY DID I WAIT?
I CAN'T BELIEVE YOU JUST BLEW ITS BRAINS OUT, O'NEIL!
IT WAS A THREAT TO PUBLIC SAFETY, VIN.
AND NOW IT'LL FLOAT AWAY DOWN THE SEWER WHERE GARBAGE LIKE THAT BELONGS.
HOW DO YOU KNOW IT WAS A *THREAT?* WE DON'T EVEN KNOW WHAT THAT THING WAS.
AND I JUST SAVED THE TAXPAYERS A TON OF MONEY BY NOT HAVING TO FIND OUT.
BUT FEEL FREE TO GO DOWN THERE, WADE THROUGH THE MUCK AND DO YOUR OWN INVESTIGATION.

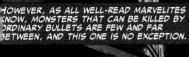

HOWEVER, AS ALL WELL-READ MARVELITES KNOW, MONSTERS THAT CAN BE KILLED BY ORDINARY BULLETS ARE FEW AND FAR BETWEEN, AND THIS ONE IS NO EXCEPTION.

AS FREAK FLOATS DOWNSTREAM, HIS BLOOD, INFECTED WITH DR. CONNORS' EXPERIMENTAL ANIMAL STEM CELLS, FORMS ANOTHER CHRYSALIS AROUND HIM. SO WE CAN BE SURE WE HAVEN'T SEEN THE LAST OF HIM...

"WHEN YOU'VE BEEN A COP AS LONG AS I HAVE, YOU CAN TELL THE DIFFERENCE BETWEEN THE GOOD GUYS AND THE BAD GUYS, VIN."

TAKE SPIDER-MAN F'RINSTANCE.

GOOD GUY. AND A GOOD GUY FOR US, TOO. REMEMBER, VIN, IF YOU MAKE A MISTAKE OR DESTROY SOME PROPERTY, YOU CAN ALWAYS BLAME IT ON SPIDER-MAN.

JUST MY LUCK. ONE COP THINKS I'M *NOT* A SERIAL KILLER...

...AND HE'S A TRIGGER-HAPPY COWBOY WHO THINKS OF ME AS THE DOG WHO ATE HIS HOMEWORK.

WHATEVER THAT THING WAS, IT DIDN'T DESERVE TO GET TAKEN DOWN LIKE THAT. I GUESS I FROZE UP BECAUSE I'M SO FREAKED OUT ABOUT GETTING SHOT AT MYSELF.

THIS DAY IS ALREADY OFF TO A LOUSY START. HOPEFULLY, IT CAN'T GET ANY WORSE.

OH YES IT CAN, SPIDER-MAN. JUST BE PATIENT!

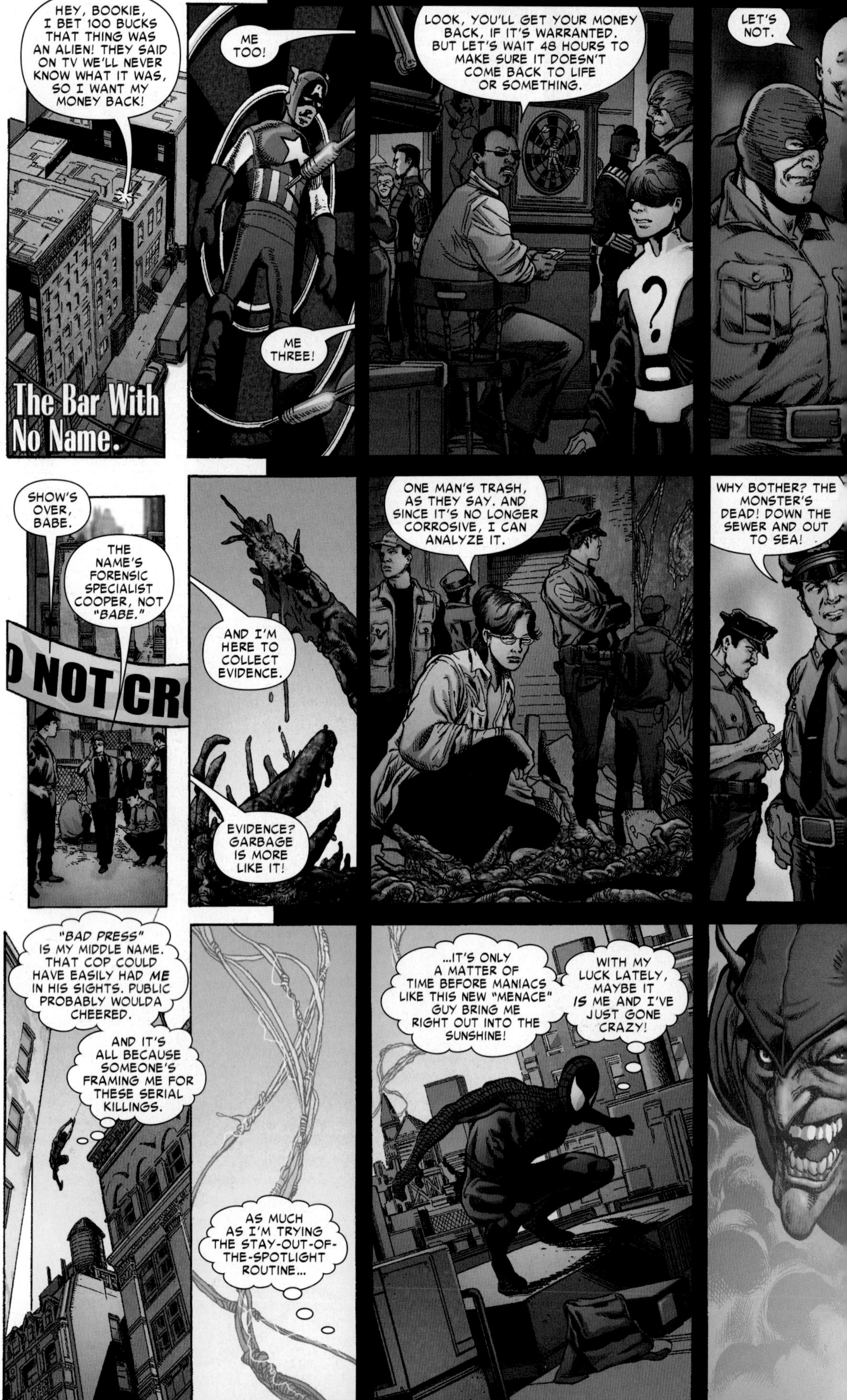
HEY, BOOKIE, I BET 100 BUCKS THAT THING WAS AN ALIEN! THEY SAID ON TV WE'LL NEVER KNOW WHAT IT WAS, SO I WANT MY MONEY BACK!
The Bar With No Name.
ME TOO!
ME THREE!
LOOK, YOU'LL GET YOUR MONEY BACK, IF IT'S WARRANTED. BUT LET'S WAIT 48 HOURS TO MAKE SURE IT DOESN'T COME BACK TO LIFE OR SOMETHING.
LET'S NOT.
SHOW'S OVER, BABE.
THE NAME'S FORENSIC SPECIALIST COOPER, NOT "BABE."
O NOT CRO
AND I'M HERE TO COLLECT EVIDENCE.
EVIDENCE? GARBAGE IS MORE LIKE IT!
ONE MAN'S TRASH, AS THEY SAY. AND SINCE IT'S NO LONGER CORROSIVE, I CAN ANALYZE IT.
WHY BOTHER? THE MONSTER'S DEAD! DOWN THE SEWER AND OUT TO SEA!
"BAD PRESS" IS MY MIDDLE NAME. THAT COP COULD HAVE EASILY HAD ME IN HIS SIGHTS. PUBLIC PROBABLY WOULDA CHEERED.
AND IT'S ALL BECAUSE SOMEONE'S FRAMING ME FOR THESE SERIAL KILLINGS.
AS MUCH AS I'M TRYING THE STAY-OUT-OF-THE-SPOTLIGHT ROUTINE...
...IT'S ONLY A MATTER OF TIME BEFORE MANIACS LIKE THIS NEW "MENACE" GUY BRING ME RIGHT OUT INTO THE SUNSHINE!
WITH MY LUCK LATELY, MAYBE IT IS ME AND I'VE JUST GONE CRAZY!

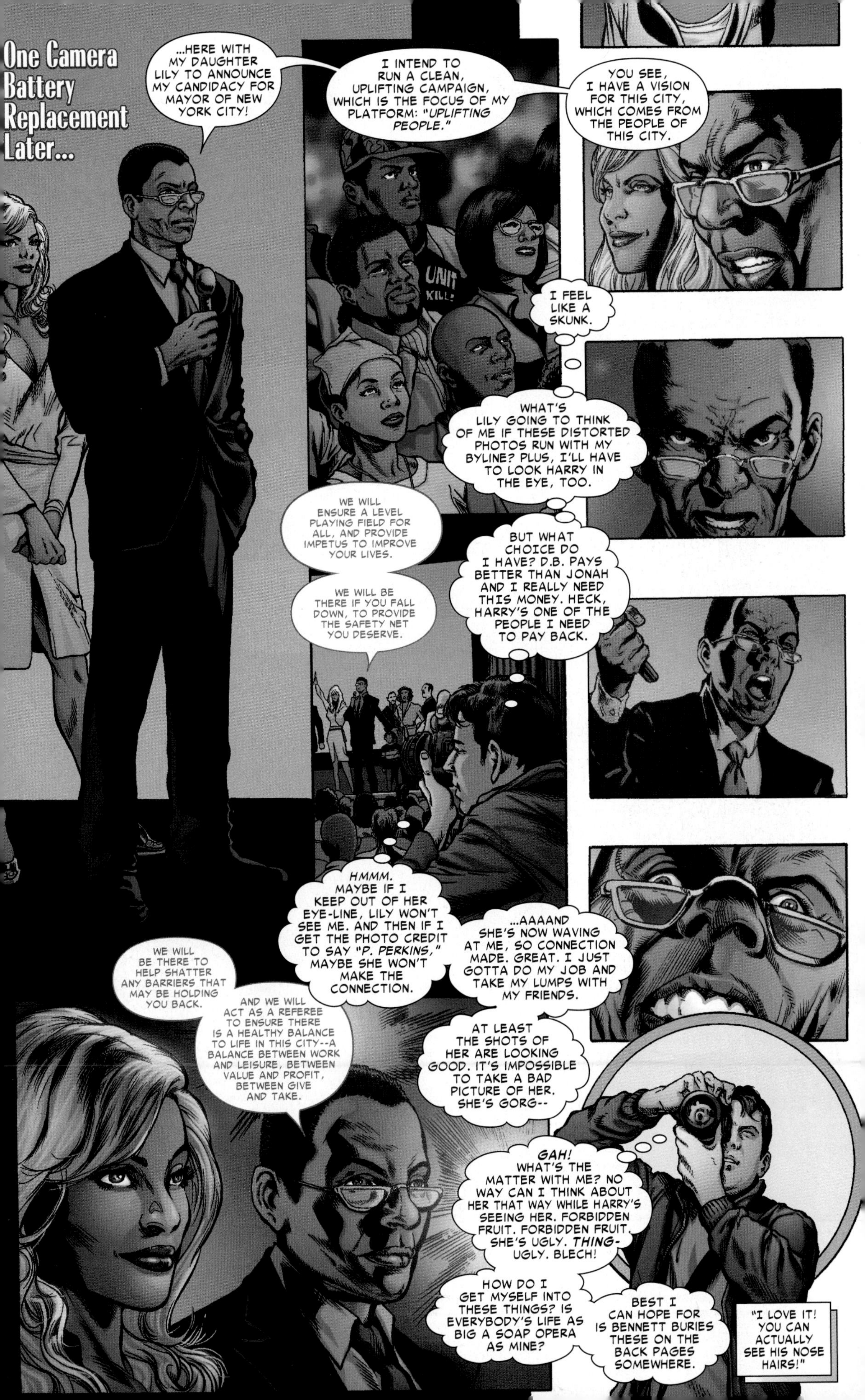
One Camera Battery Replacement Later...
...HERE WITH MY DAUGHTER LILY TO ANNOUNCE MY CANDIDACY FOR MAYOR OF NEW YORK CITY!
I INTEND TO RUN A CLEAN, UPLIFTING CAMPAIGN, WHICH IS THE FOCUS OF MY PLATFORM: "UPLIFTING PEOPLE."
YOU SEE, I HAVE A VISION FOR THIS CITY, WHICH COMES FROM THE PEOPLE OF THIS CITY.
I FEEL LIKE A SKUNK.
WHAT'S LILY GOING TO THINK OF ME IF THESE DISTORTED PHOTOS RUN WITH MY BYLINE? PLUS, I'LL HAVE TO LOOK HARRY IN THE EYE, TOO.
WE WILL ENSURE A LEVEL PLAYING FIELD FOR ALL, AND PROVIDE IMPETUS TO IMPROVE YOUR LIVES.
WE WILL BE THERE IF YOU FALL DOWN, TO PROVIDE THE SAFETY NET YOU DESERVE.
BUT WHAT CHOICE DO I HAVE? D.B. PAYS BETTER THAN JONAH AND I REALLY NEED THIS MONEY. HECK, HARRY'S ONE OF THE PEOPLE I NEED TO PAY BACK.
HMMM. MAYBE IF I KEEP OUT OF HER EYE-LINE, LILY WON'T SEE ME. AND THEN IF I GET THE PHOTO CREDIT TO SAY "P. PERKINS," MAYBE SHE WON'T MAKE THE CONNECTION.
...AAAAND SHE'S NOW WAVING AT ME, SO CONNECTION MADE. GREAT. I JUST GOTTA DO MY JOB AND TAKE MY LUMPS WITH MY FRIENDS.
WE WILL BE THERE TO HELP SHATTER ANY BARRIERS THAT MAY BE HOLDING YOU BACK.
AND WE WILL ACT AS A REFEREE TO ENSURE THERE IS A HEALTHY BALANCE TO LIFE IN THIS CITY--A BALANCE BETWEEN WORK AND LEISURE, BETWEEN VALUE AND PROFIT, BETWEEN GIVE AND TAKE.
AT LEAST THE SHOTS OF HER ARE LOOKING GOOD. IT'S IMPOSSIBLE TO TAKE A BAD PICTURE OF HER. SHE'S GORG--
GAH! WHAT'S THE MATTER WITH ME? NO WAY CAN I THINK ABOUT HER THAT WAY WHILE HARRY'S SEEING HER. FORBIDDEN FRUIT. FORBIDDEN FRUIT. SHE'S UGLY. THING-UGLY. BLECH!
HOW DO I GET MYSELF INTO THESE THINGS? IS EVERYBODY'S LIFE AS BIG A SOAP OPERA AS MINE?
BEST I CAN HOPE FOR IS BENNETT BURIES THESE ON THE BACK PAGES SOMEWHERE.
"I LOVE IT! YOU CAN ACTUALLY SEE HIS NOSE HAIRS!"

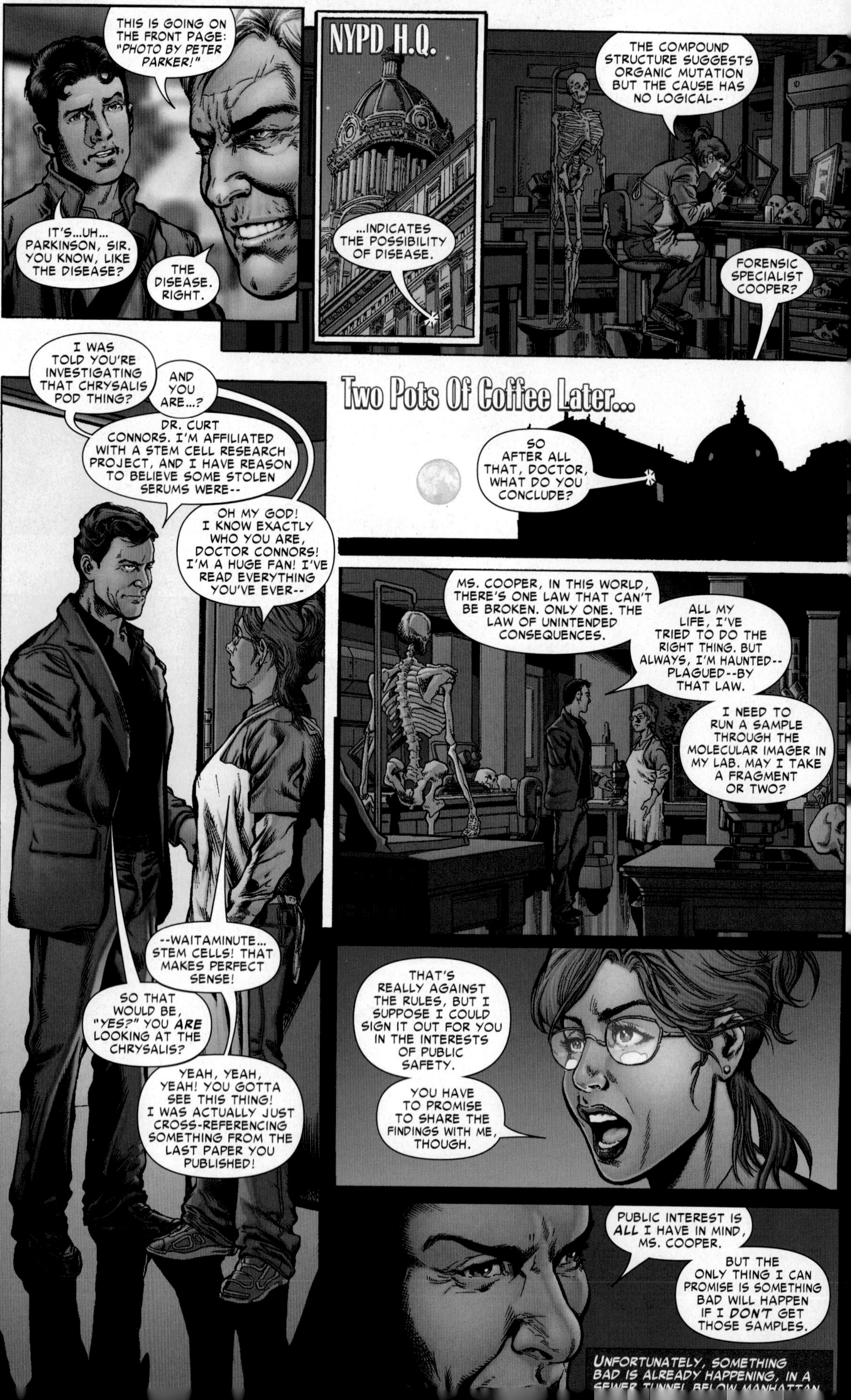
THIS IS GOING ON THE FRONT PAGE: "PHOTO BY PETER PARKER!"
IT'S...UH... PARKINSON, SIR. YOU KNOW, LIKE THE DISEASE?
THE DISEASE. RIGHT.
NYPD H.Q.
...INDICATES THE POSSIBILITY OF DISEASE.
THE COMPOUND STRUCTURE SUGGESTS ORGANIC MUTATION BUT THE CAUSE HAS NO LOGICAL--
FORENSIC SPECIALIST COOPER?
I WAS TOLD YOU'RE INVESTIGATING THAT CHRYSALIS POD THING?
AND YOU ARE...?
DR. CURT CONNORS. I'M AFFILIATED WITH A STEM CELL RESEARCH PROJECT, AND I HAVE REASON TO BELIEVE SOME STOLEN SERUMS WERE--
OH MY GOD! I KNOW EXACTLY WHO YOU ARE, DOCTOR CONNORS! I'M A HUGE FAN! I'VE READ EVERYTHING YOU'VE EVER--
--WAITAMINUTE... STEM CELLS! THAT MAKES PERFECT SENSE!
SO THAT WOULD BE, "YES?" YOU ARE LOOKING AT THE CHRYSALIS?
YEAH, YEAH, YEAH! YOU GOTTA SEE THIS THING! I WAS ACTUALLY JUST CROSS-REFERENCING SOMETHING FROM THE LAST PAPER YOU PUBLISHED!
Two Pots Of Coffee Later...
SO AFTER ALL THAT, DOCTOR, WHAT DO YOU CONCLUDE?
MS. COOPER, IN THIS WORLD, THERE'S ONE LAW THAT CAN'T BE BROKEN. ONLY ONE. THE LAW OF UNINTENDED CONSEQUENCES.
ALL MY LIFE, I'VE TRIED TO DO THE RIGHT THING. BUT ALWAYS, I'M HAUNTED--PLAGUED--BY THAT LAW.
I NEED TO RUN A SAMPLE THROUGH THE MOLECULAR IMAGER IN MY LAB. MAY I TAKE A FRAGMENT OR TWO?
THAT'S REALLY AGAINST THE RULES, BUT I SUPPOSE I COULD SIGN IT OUT FOR YOU IN THE INTERESTS OF PUBLIC SAFETY.
YOU HAVE TO PROMISE TO SHARE THE FINDINGS WITH ME, THOUGH.
PUBLIC INTEREST IS ALL I HAVE IN MIND, MS. COOPER.
BUT THE ONLY THING I CAN PROMISE IS SOMETHING BAD WILL HAPPEN IF I DON'T GET THOSE SAMPLES.
UNFORTUNATELY, SOMETHING BAD IS ALREADY HAPPENING, IN A

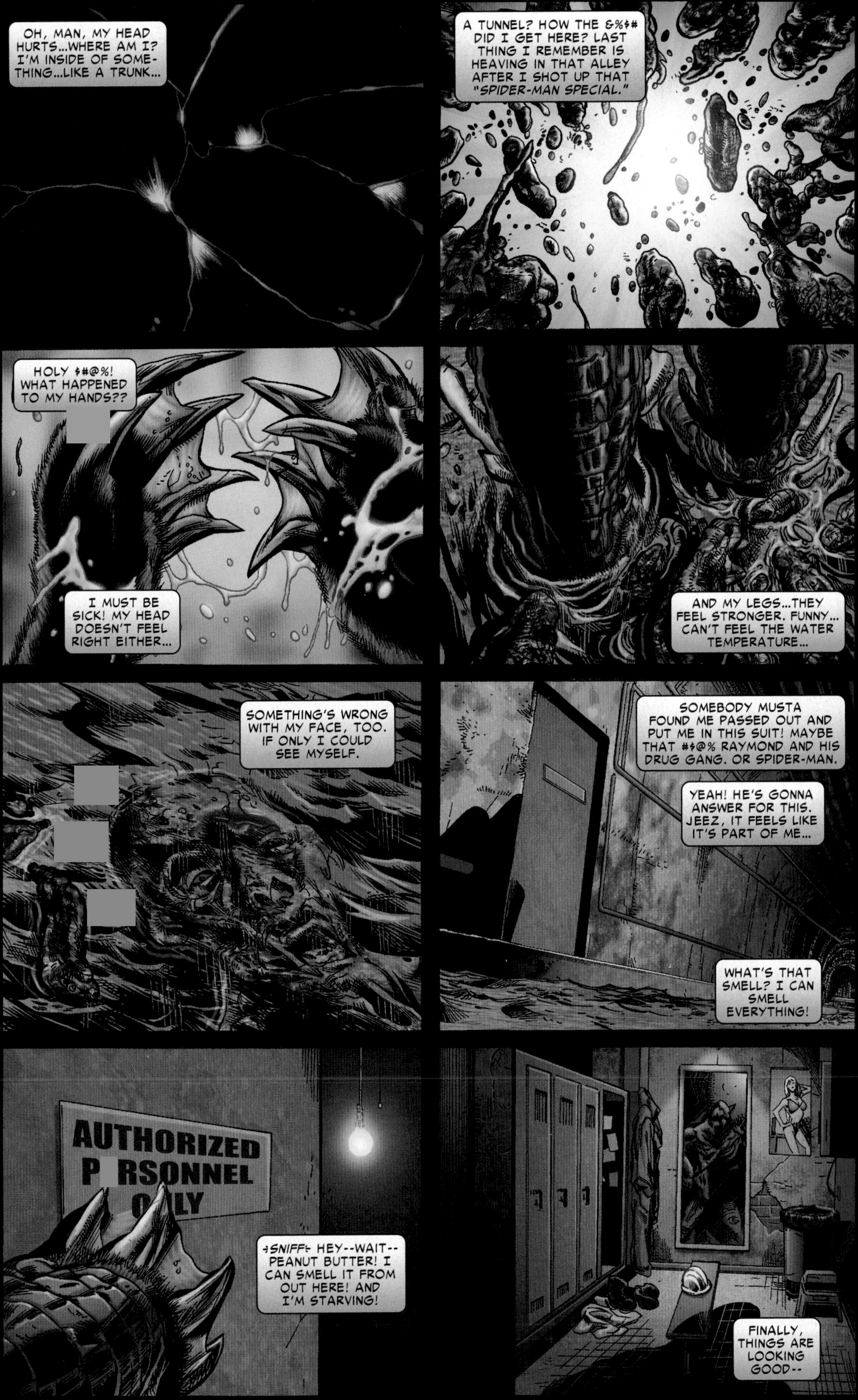
OH, MAN, MY HEAD HURTS...WHERE AM I? I'M INSIDE OF SOMETHING...LIKE A TRUNK...
A TUNNEL? HOW THE &%$# DID I GET HERE? LAST THING I REMEMBER IS HEAVING IN THAT ALLEY AFTER I SHOT UP THAT "SPIDER-MAN SPECIAL."
HOLY $#@%! WHAT HAPPENED TO MY HANDS??
I MUST BE SICK! MY HEAD DOESN'T FEEL RIGHT EITHER...
AND MY LEGS...THEY FEEL STRONGER. FUNNY... CAN'T FEEL THE WATER TEMPERATURE...
SOMETHING'S WRONG WITH MY FACE, TOO. IF ONLY I COULD SEE MYSELF.
SOMEBODY MUSTA FOUND ME PASSED OUT AND PUT ME IN THIS SUIT! MAYBE THAT #$@% RAYMOND AND HIS DRUG GANG. OR SPIDER-MAN.
YEAH! HE'S GONNA ANSWER FOR THIS. JEEZ, IT FEELS LIKE IT'S PART OF ME...
WHAT'S THAT SMELL? I CAN SMELL EVERYTHING!
AUTHORIZED
P RSONNEL
SNIFF HEY--WAIT--PEANUT BUTTER! I CAN SMELL IT FROM OUT HERE! AND I'M STARVING!
FINALLY, THINGS ARE LOOKING GOOD--

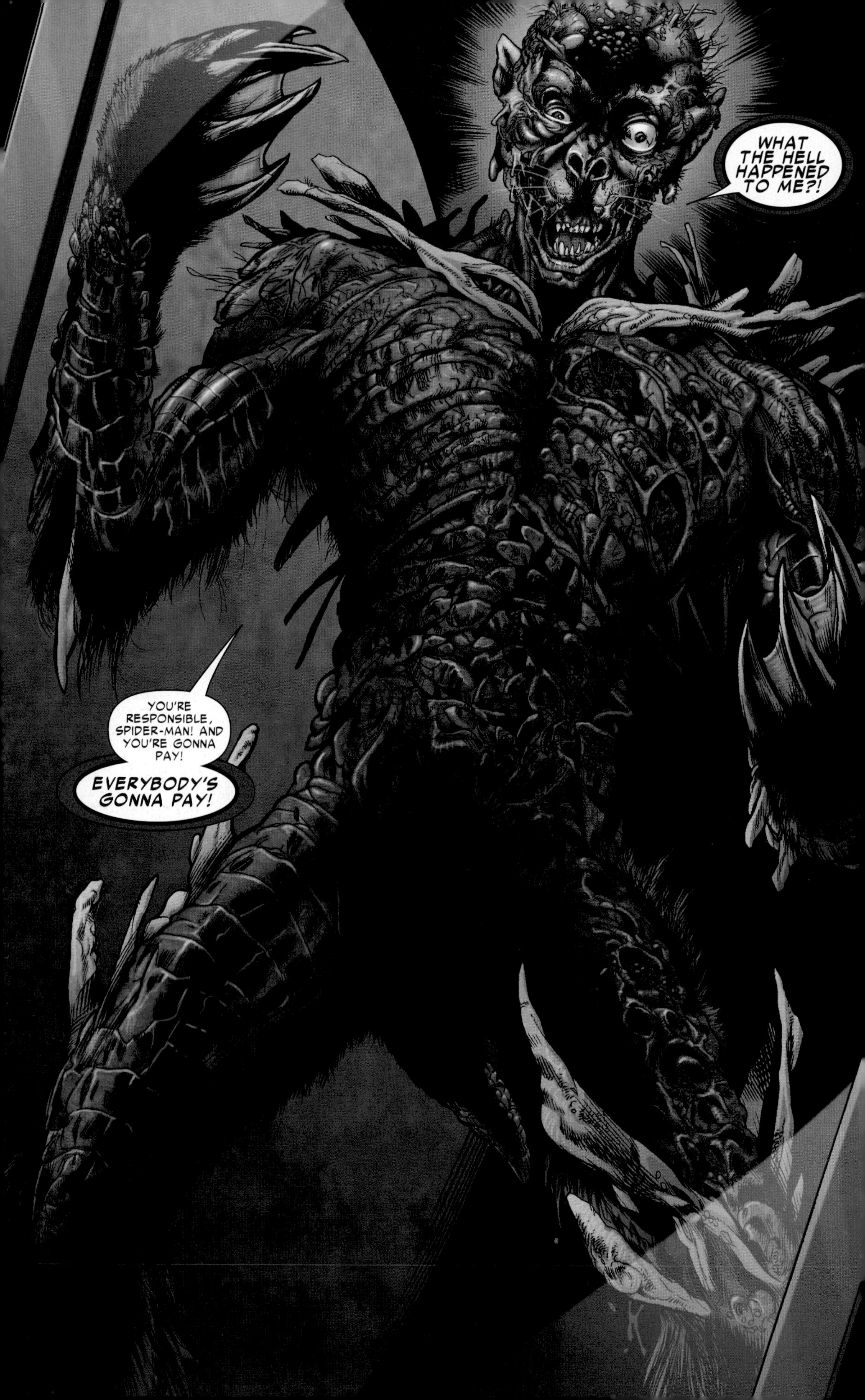
WHAT THE HELL HAPPENED TO ME?!
YOU'RE RESPONSIBLE, SPIDER-MAN! AND YOU'RE GONNA PAY!
EVERYBODY'S GONNA PAY!

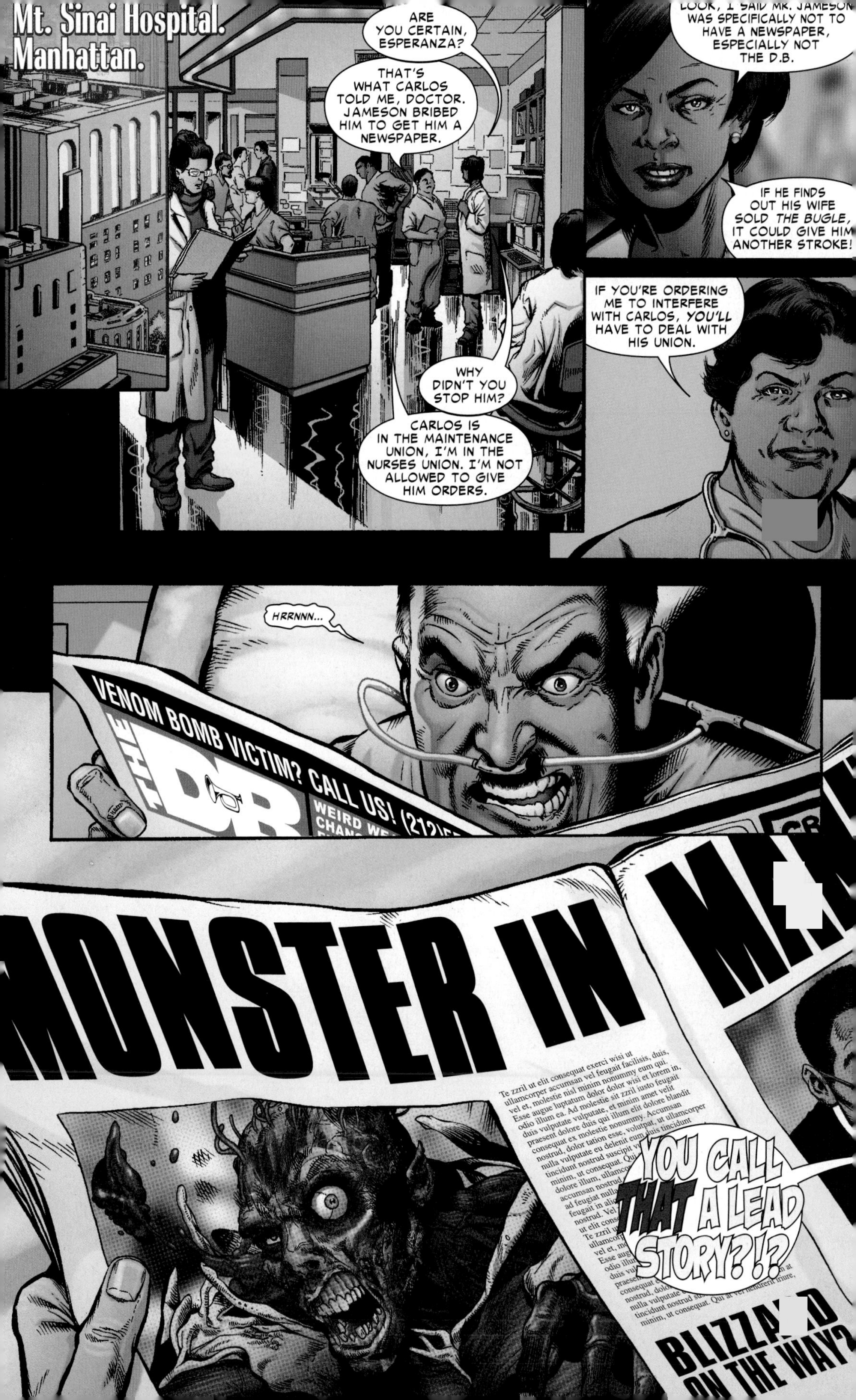

Mt. Sinai Hospital. Manhattan.
ARE YOU CERTAIN, ESPERANZA?
THAT'S WHAT CARLOS TOLD ME, DOCTOR. JAMESON BRIBED HIM TO GET HIM A NEWSPAPER.
WHY DIDN'T YOU STOP HIM?
CARLOS IS IN THE MAINTENANCE UNION, I'M IN THE NURSES UNION. I'M NOT ALLOWED TO GIVE HIM ORDERS.
LOOK, I SAID MR. JAMESON WAS SPECIFICALLY NOT TO HAVE A NEWSPAPER, ESPECIALLY NOT THE D.B.
IF HE FINDS OUT HIS WIFE SOLD *THE BUGLE*, IT COULD GIVE HIM ANOTHER STROKE!
IF YOU'RE ORDERING ME TO INTERFERE WITH CARLOS, *YOU'LL* HAVE TO DEAL WITH HIS UNION.
HRRNNN...
THE DB
VENOM BOMB VICTIM? CALL US! (212)
MONSTER IN
YOU CALL *THAT* A LEAD STORY?!?
ON THE WAY?

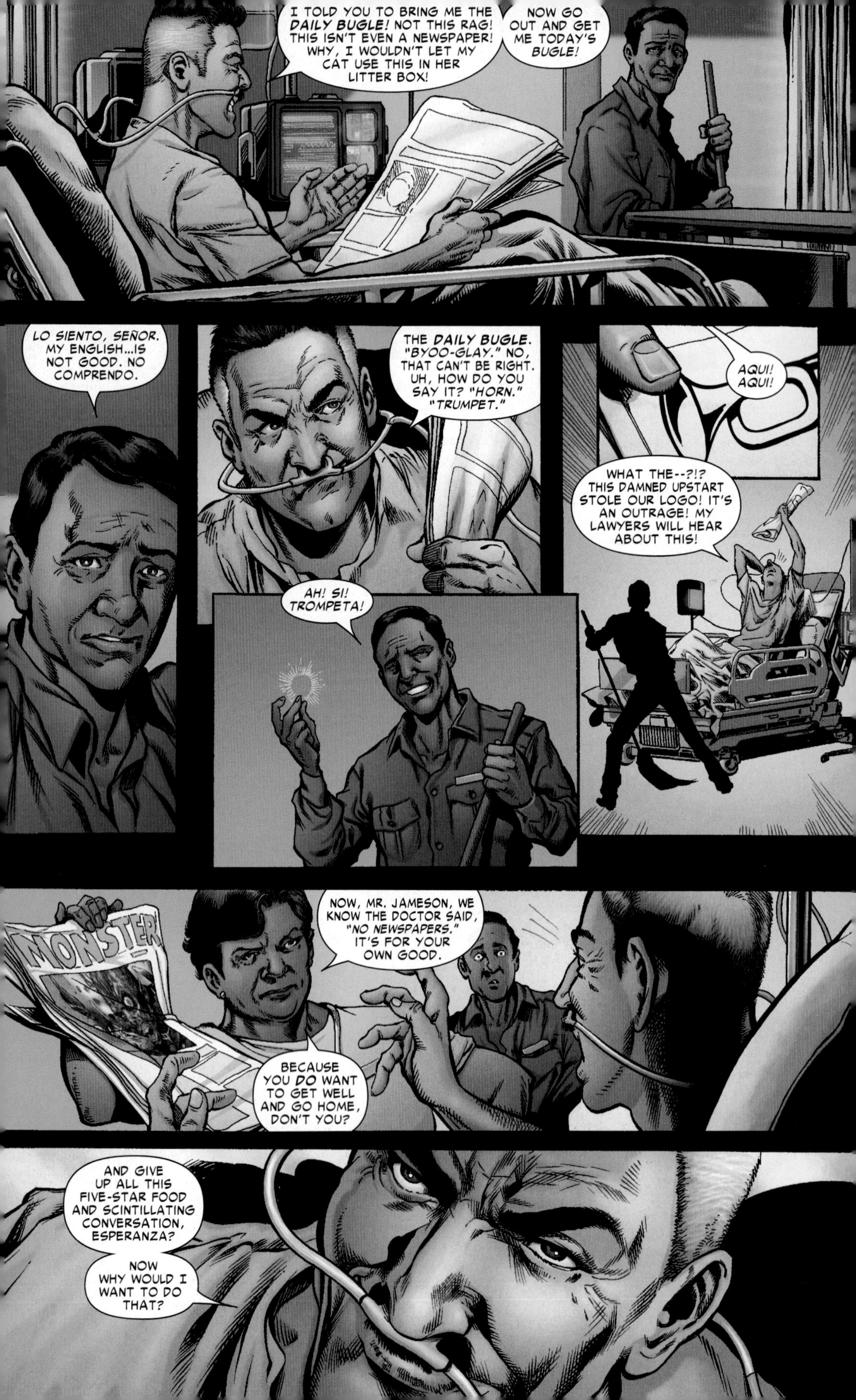
I TOLD YOU TO BRING ME THE DAILY BUGLE! NOT THIS RAG! THIS ISN'T EVEN A NEWSPAPER! WHY, I WOULDN'T LET MY CAT USE THIS IN HER LITTER BOX!
NOW GO OUT AND GET ME TODAY'S BUGLE!
LO SIENTO, SEÑOR. MY ENGLISH...IS NOT GOOD. NO COMPRENDO.
THE DAILY BUGLE. "BYOO-GLAY." NO, THAT CAN'T BE RIGHT. UH, HOW DO YOU SAY IT? "HORN." "TRUMPET."
AH! SI! TROMPETA!
AQUI! AQUI!
WHAT THE--?!? THIS DAMNED UPSTART STOLE OUR LOGO! IT'S AN OUTRAGE! MY LAWYERS WILL HEAR ABOUT THIS!
MONSTER
NOW, MR. JAMESON, WE KNOW THE DOCTOR SAID, "NO NEWSPAPERS." IT'S FOR YOUR OWN GOOD.
BECAUSE YOU DO WANT TO GET WELL AND GO HOME, DON'T YOU?
AND GIVE UP ALL THIS FIVE-STAR FOOD AND SCINTILLATING CONVERSATION, ESPERANZA?
NOW WHY WOULD I WANT TO DO THAT?

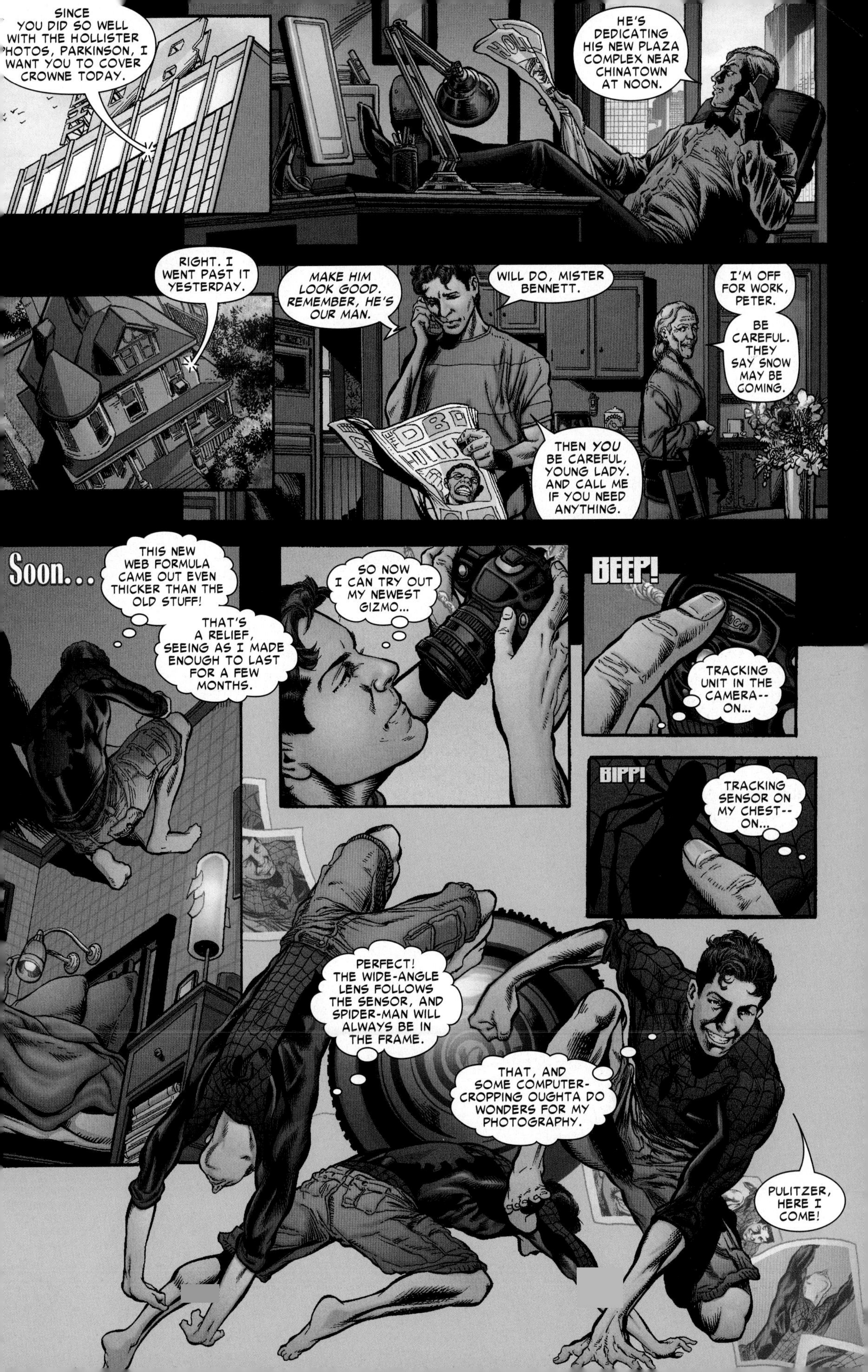
SINCE YOU DID SO WELL WITH THE HOLLISTER PHOTOS, PARKINSON, I WANT YOU TO COVER CROWNE TODAY.
HE'S DEDICATING HIS NEW PLAZA COMPLEX NEAR CHINATOWN AT NOON.
RIGHT. I WENT PAST IT YESTERDAY.
MAKE HIM LOOK GOOD. REMEMBER, HE'S OUR MAN.
WILL DO, MISTER BENNETT.
I'M OFF FOR WORK, PETER.
BE CAREFUL. THEY SAY SNOW MAY BE COMING.
THEN YOU BE CAREFUL, YOUNG LADY. AND CALL ME IF YOU NEED ANYTHING.
Soon...
THIS NEW WEB FORMULA CAME OUT EVEN THICKER THAN THE OLD STUFF!
THAT'S A RELIEF, SEEING AS I MADE ENOUGH TO LAST FOR A FEW MONTHS.
SO NOW I CAN TRY OUT MY NEWEST GIZMO...
BEEP!
TRACKING UNIT IN THE CAMERA-- ON...
BIPP!
TRACKING SENSOR ON MY CHEST-- ON...
PERFECT! THE WIDE-ANGLE LENS FOLLOWS THE SENSOR, AND SPIDER-MAN WILL ALWAYS BE IN THE FRAME.
THAT, AND SOME COMPUTER-CROPPING OUGHTA DO WONDERS FOR MY PHOTOGRAPHY.
PULITZER, HERE I COME!

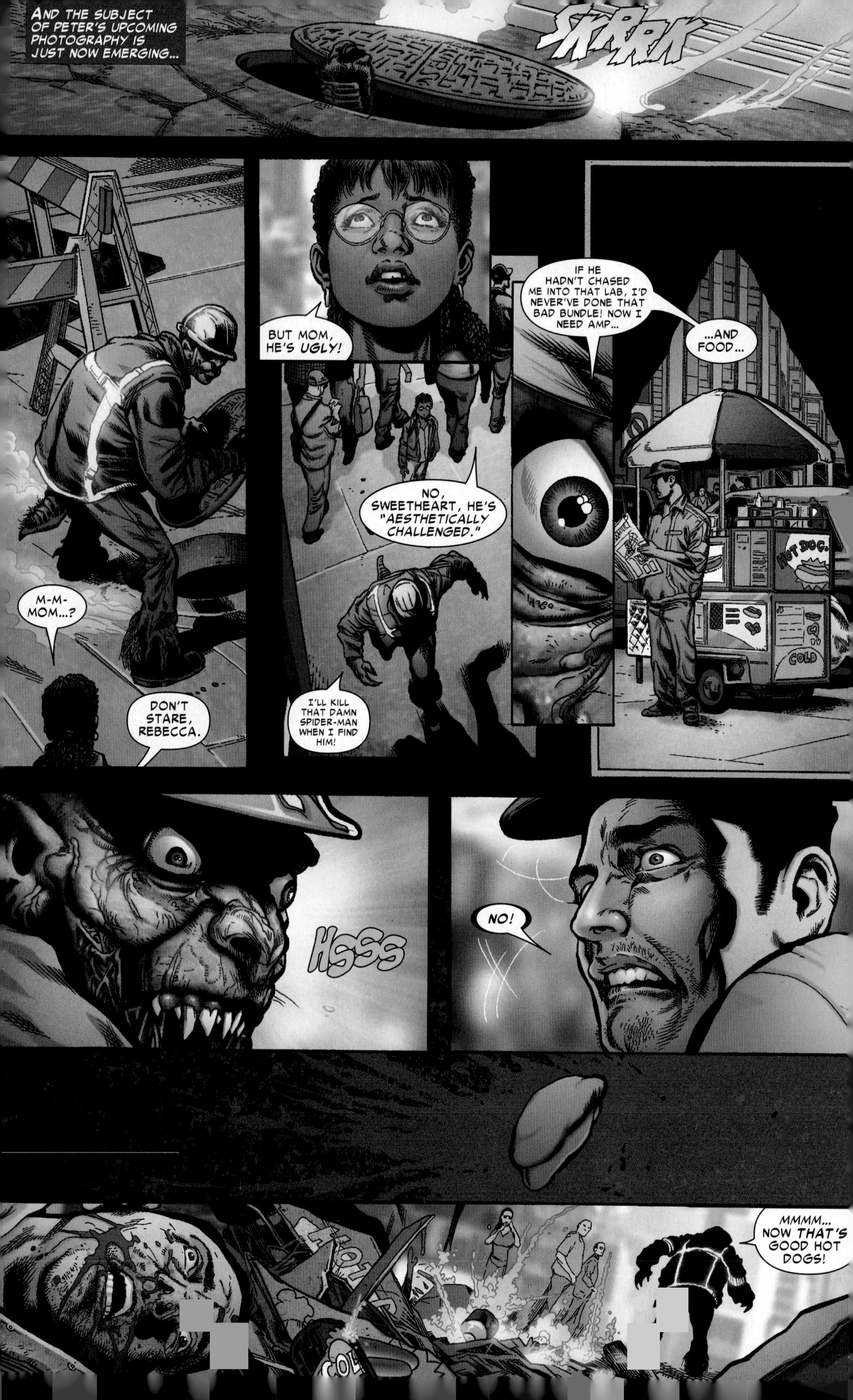
AND THE SUBJECT OF PETER'S UPCOMING PHOTOGRAPHY IS JUST NOW EMERGING...
SKRRK
M-M-MOM...?
DON'T STARE, REBECCA.
BUT MOM, HE'S UGLY!
NO, SWEETHEART, HE'S "AESTHETICALLY CHALLENGED."
I'LL KILL THAT DAMN SPIDER-MAN WHEN I FIND HIM!
IF HE HADN'T CHASED ME INTO THAT LAB, I'D NEVER'VE DONE THAT BAD BUNDLE! NOW I NEED AMP...
...AND FOOD...
HOT DOG
COLD
HSSS
NO!
MMMM... NOW THAT'S GOOD HOT DOGS!

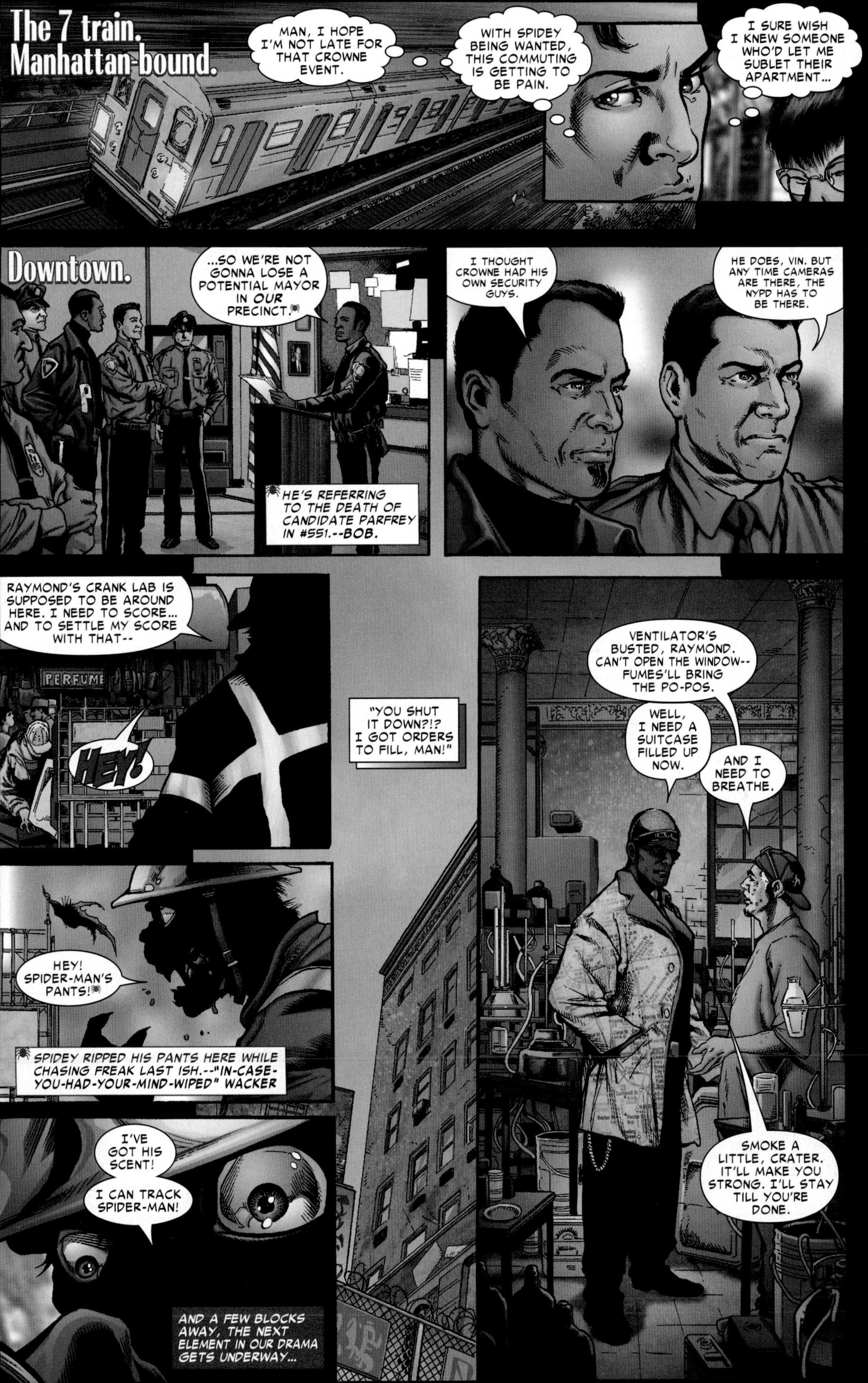
The 7 train. Manhattan-bound.
MAN, I HOPE I'M NOT LATE FOR THAT CROWNE EVENT.
WITH SPIDEY BEING WANTED, THIS COMMUTING IS GETTING TO BE PAIN.
I SURE WISH I KNEW SOMEONE WHO'D LET ME SUBLET THEIR APARTMENT...
Downtown.
...SO WE'RE NOT GONNA LOSE A POTENTIAL MAYOR IN OUR PRECINCT.
HE'S REFERRING TO THE DEATH OF CANDIDATE PARFREY IN #551.--BOB.
I THOUGHT CROWNE HAD HIS OWN SECURITY GUYS.
HE DOES, VIN. BUT ANY TIME CAMERAS ARE THERE, THE NYPD HAS TO BE THERE.
RAYMOND'S CRANK LAB IS SUPPOSED TO BE AROUND HERE. I NEED TO SCORE... AND TO SETTLE MY SCORE WITH THAT--
PERFUME
HEY!
HEY! SPIDER-MAN'S PANTS!
SPIDEY RIPPED HIS PANTS HERE WHILE CHASING FREAK LAST ISH.--"IN-CASE-YOU-HAD-YOUR-MIND-WIPED" WACKER
I'VE GOT HIS SCENT!
I CAN TRACK SPIDER-MAN!
AND A FEW BLOCKS AWAY, THE NEXT ELEMENT IN OUR DRAMA GETS UNDERWAY...
"YOU SHUT IT DOWN?!? I GOT ORDERS TO FILL, MAN!"
VENTILATOR'S BUSTED, RAYMOND. CAN'T OPEN THE WINDOW-- FUMES'LL BRING THE PO-POS.
WELL, I NEED A SUITCASE FILLED UP NOW.
AND I NEED TO BREATHE.
SMOKE A LITTLE, CRATER. IT'LL MAKE YOU STRONG. I'LL STAY TILL YOU'RE DONE.

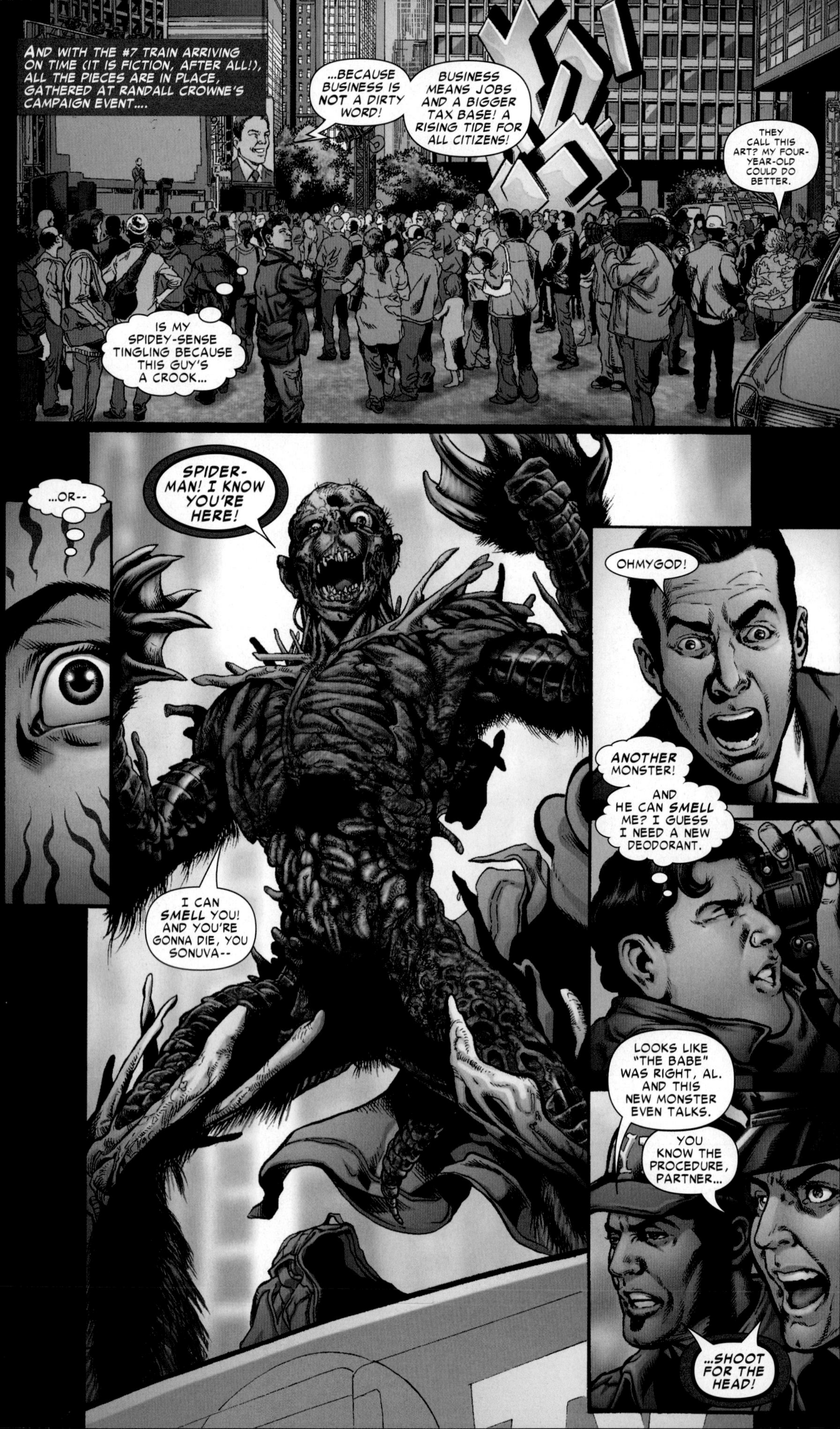

AND WITH THE #7 TRAIN ARRIVING ON TIME (IT IS FICTION, AFTER ALL!), ALL THE PIECES ARE IN PLACE, GATHERED AT RANDALL CROWNE'S CAMPAIGN EVENT....
...BECAUSE BUSINESS IS NOT A DIRTY WORD!
BUSINESS MEANS JOBS AND A BIGGER TAX BASE! A RISING TIDE FOR ALL CITIZENS!
THEY CALL THIS ART? MY FOUR-YEAR-OLD COULD DO BETTER.
IS MY SPIDEY-SENSE TINGLING BECAUSE THIS GUY'S A CROOK...
...OR--
SPIDER-MAN! I KNOW YOU'RE HERE!
OHMYGOD!
ANOTHER MONSTER!
I CAN SMELL YOU! AND YOU'RE GONNA DIE, YOU SONUVA--
AND HE CAN SMELL ME? I GUESS I NEED A NEW DEODORANT.
LOOKS LIKE "THE BABE" WAS RIGHT, AL. AND THIS NEW MONSTER EVEN TALKS.
YOU KNOW THE PROCEDURE, PARTNER...
...SHOOT FOR THE HEAD!

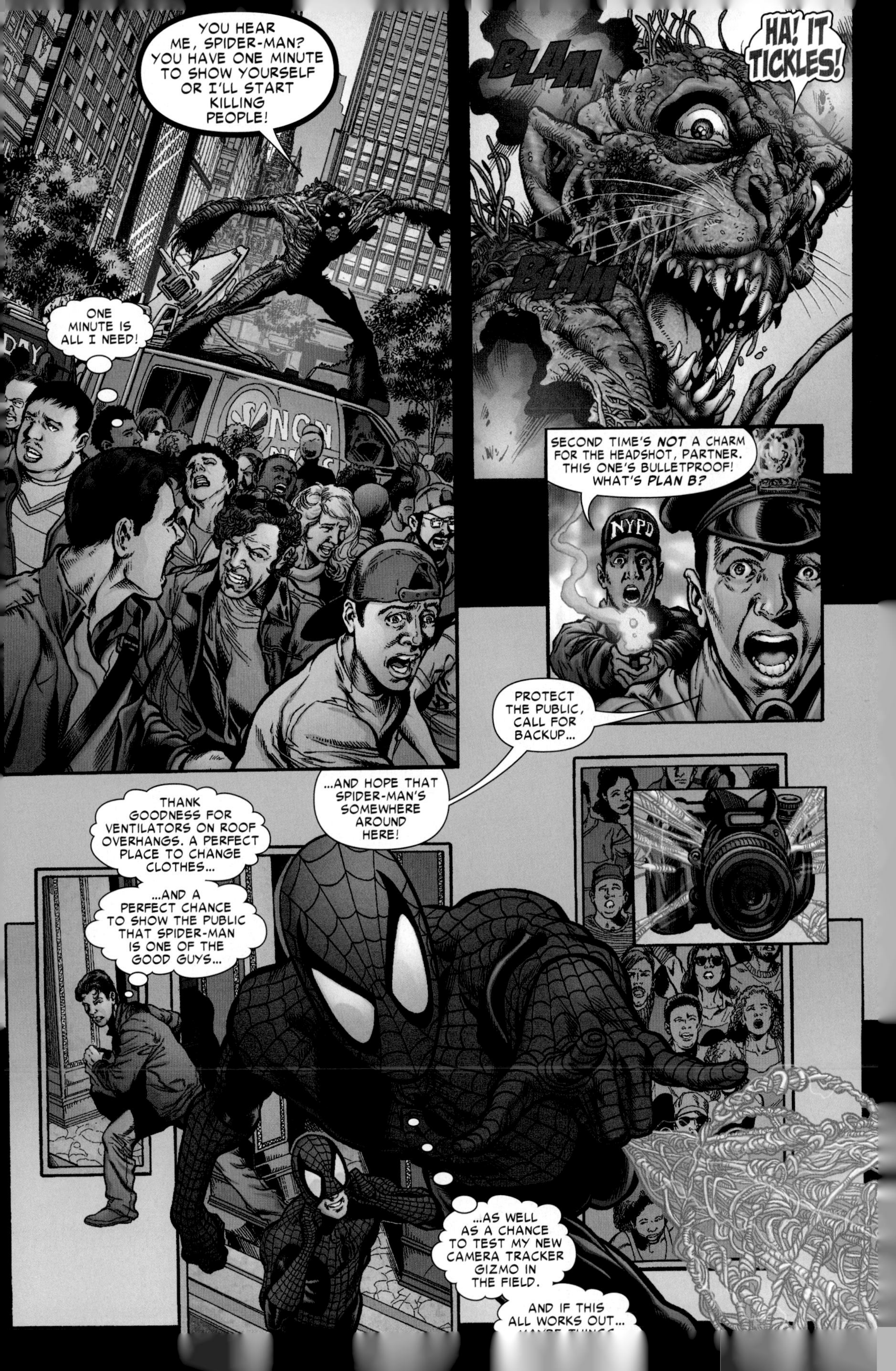
YOU HEAR ME, SPIDER-MAN? YOU HAVE ONE MINUTE TO SHOW YOURSELF OR I'LL START KILLING PEOPLE!
ONE MINUTE IS ALL I NEED!
BLAM
HA! IT TICKLES!
BLAM
SECOND TIME'S *NOT* A CHARM FOR THE HEADSHOT, PARTNER. THIS ONE'S BULLETPROOF! WHAT'S *PLAN B?*
NYPD
PROTECT THE PUBLIC, CALL FOR BACKUP...
...AND HOPE THAT SPIDER-MAN'S SOMEWHERE AROUND HERE!
THANK GOODNESS FOR VENTILATORS ON ROOF OVERHANGS. A PERFECT PLACE TO CHANGE CLOTHES...
...AND A PERFECT CHANCE TO SHOW THE PUBLIC THAT SPIDER-MAN IS ONE OF THE GOOD GUYS...
...AS WELL AS A CHANCE TO TEST MY NEW CAMERA TRACKER GIZMO IN THE FIELD.
AND IF THIS ALL WORKS OUT...

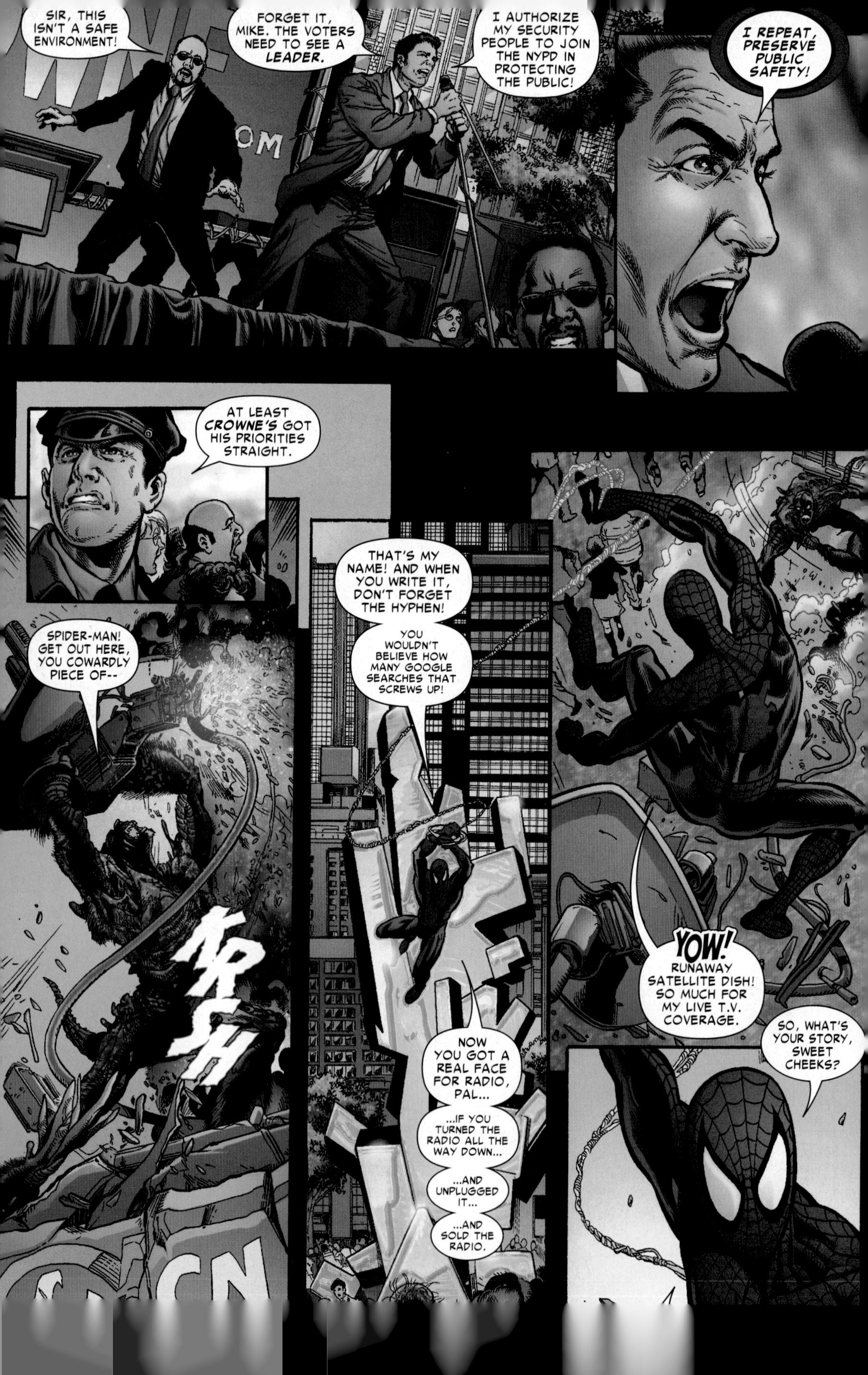
SIR, THIS ISN'T A SAFE ENVIRONMENT!
FORGET IT, MIKE. THE VOTERS NEED TO SEE A LEADER.
I AUTHORIZE MY SECURITY PEOPLE TO JOIN THE NYPD IN PROTECTING THE PUBLIC!
I REPEAT, PRESERVE PUBLIC SAFETY!
AT LEAST CROWNE'S GOT HIS PRIORITIES STRAIGHT.
SPIDER-MAN! GET OUT HERE, YOU COWARDLY PIECE OF--
KRSH
THAT'S MY NAME! AND WHEN YOU WRITE IT, DON'T FORGET THE HYPHEN!
YOU WOULDN'T BELIEVE HOW MANY GOOGLE SEARCHES THAT SCREWS UP!
NOW YOU GOT A REAL FACE FOR RADIO, PAL...
...IF YOU TURNED THE RADIO ALL THE WAY DOWN...
...AND UNPLUGGED IT...
...AND SOLD THE RADIO.
YOW! RUNAWAY SATELLITE DISH! SO MUCH FOR MY LIVE T.V. COVERAGE.
SO, WHAT'S YOUR STORY, SWEET CHEEKS?

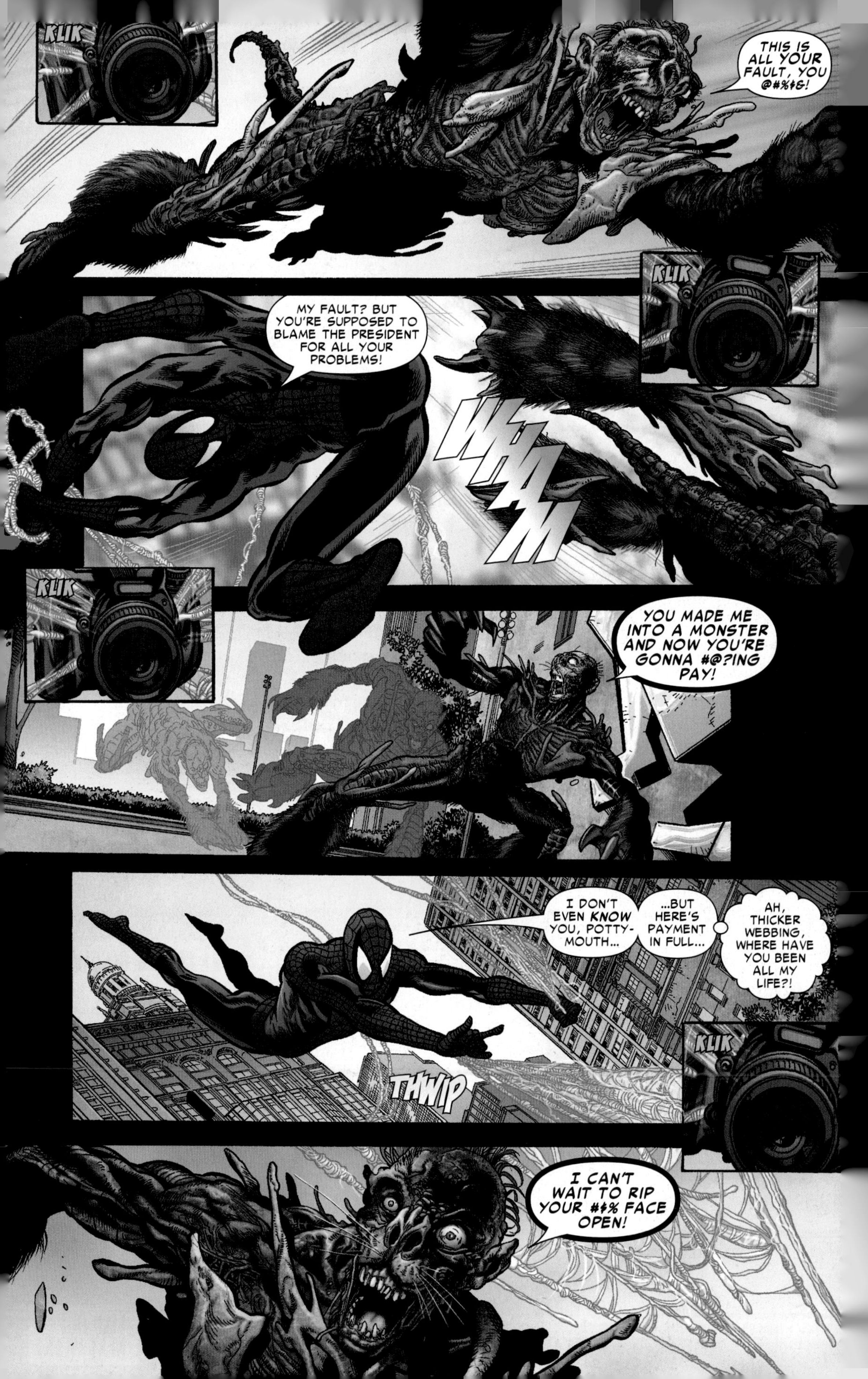
KLIK
THIS IS ALL YOUR FAULT, YOU @#%$&!
KLIK
MY FAULT? BUT YOU'RE SUPPOSED TO BLAME THE PRESIDENT FOR ALL YOUR PROBLEMS!
WHAM
KLIK
YOU MADE ME INTO A MONSTER AND NOW YOU'RE GONNA #@?ING PAY!
I DON'T EVEN KNOW YOU, POTTY-MOUTH...
...BUT HERE'S PAYMENT IN FULL...
AH, THICKER WEBBING, WHERE HAVE YOU BEEN ALL MY LIFE?!
THWIP
KLIK
I CAN'T WAIT TO RIP YOUR #$% FACE OPEN!

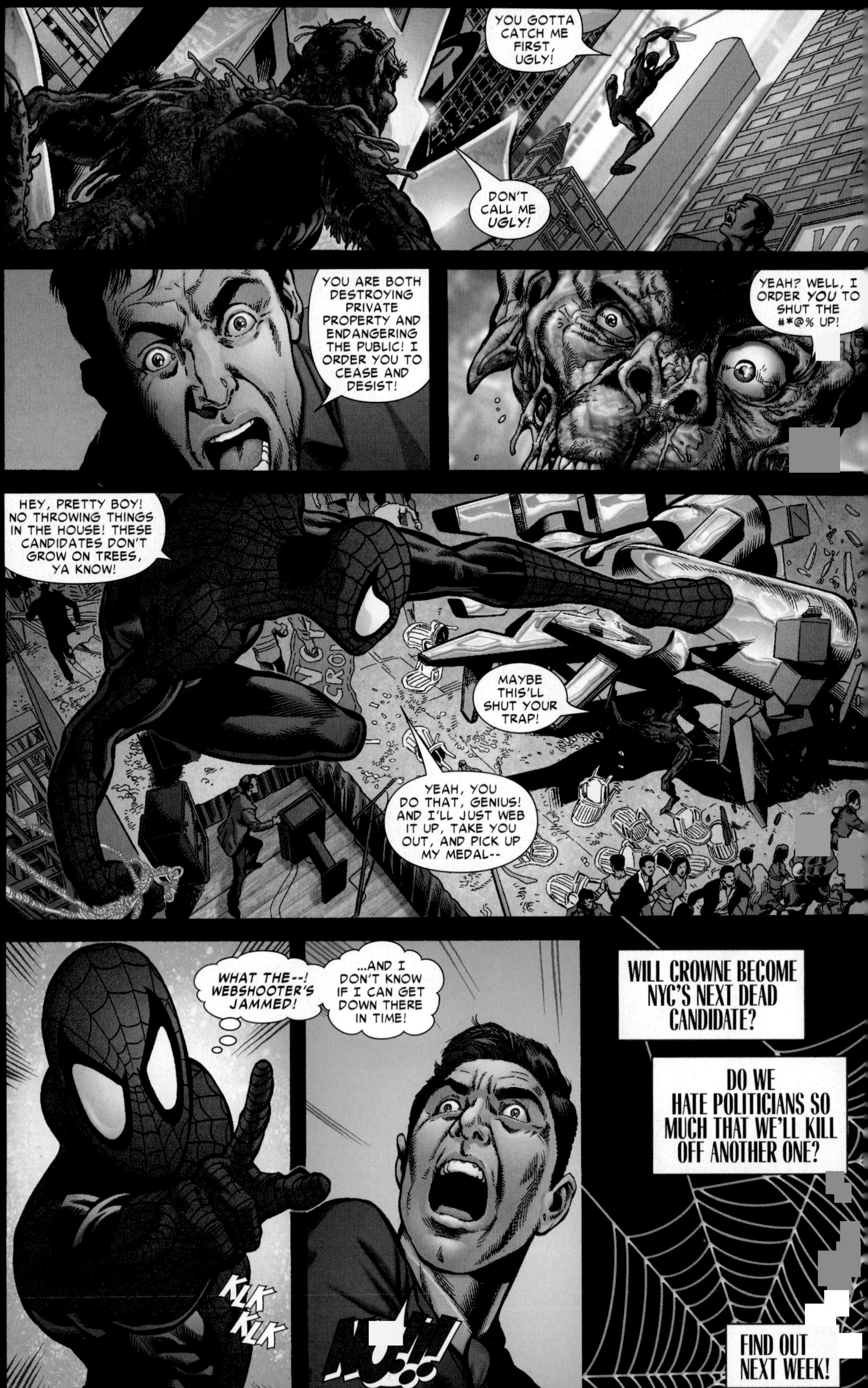

YOU GOTTA CATCH ME FIRST, UGLY!
DON'T CALL ME UGLY!
YOU ARE BOTH DESTROYING PRIVATE PROPERTY AND ENDANGERING THE PUBLIC! I ORDER YOU TO CEASE AND DESIST!
YEAH? WELL, I ORDER YOU TO SHUT THE #*@% UP!
HEY, PRETTY BOY! NO THROWING THINGS IN THE HOUSE! THESE CANDIDATES DON'T GROW ON TREES, YA KNOW!
MAYBE THIS'LL SHUT YOUR TRAP!
YEAH, YOU DO THAT, GENIUS! AND I'LL JUST WEB IT UP, TAKE YOU OUT, AND PICK UP MY MEDAL--
WHAT THE--! WEBSHOOTER'S JAMMED!
...AND I DON'T KNOW IF I CAN GET DOWN THERE IN TIME!
KLK KLK
WILL CROWNE BECOME NYC'S NEXT DEAD CANDIDATE?
DO WE HATE POLITICIANS SO MUCH THAT WE'LL KILL OFF ANOTHER ONE?
FIND OUT NEXT WEEK!

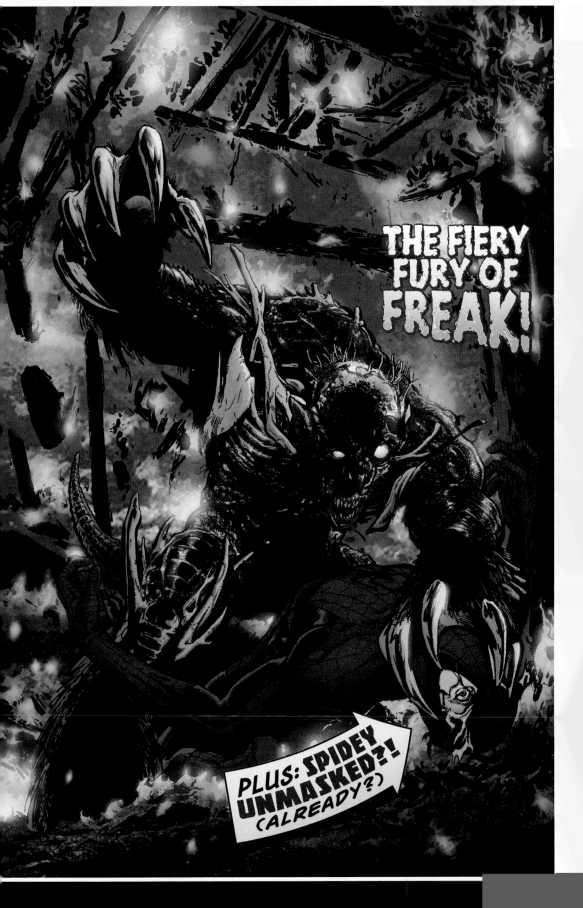

THE FIERY
FURY OF
FREAK!

PLUS: SPIDEY
UNMASKED?!
(ALREADY?)

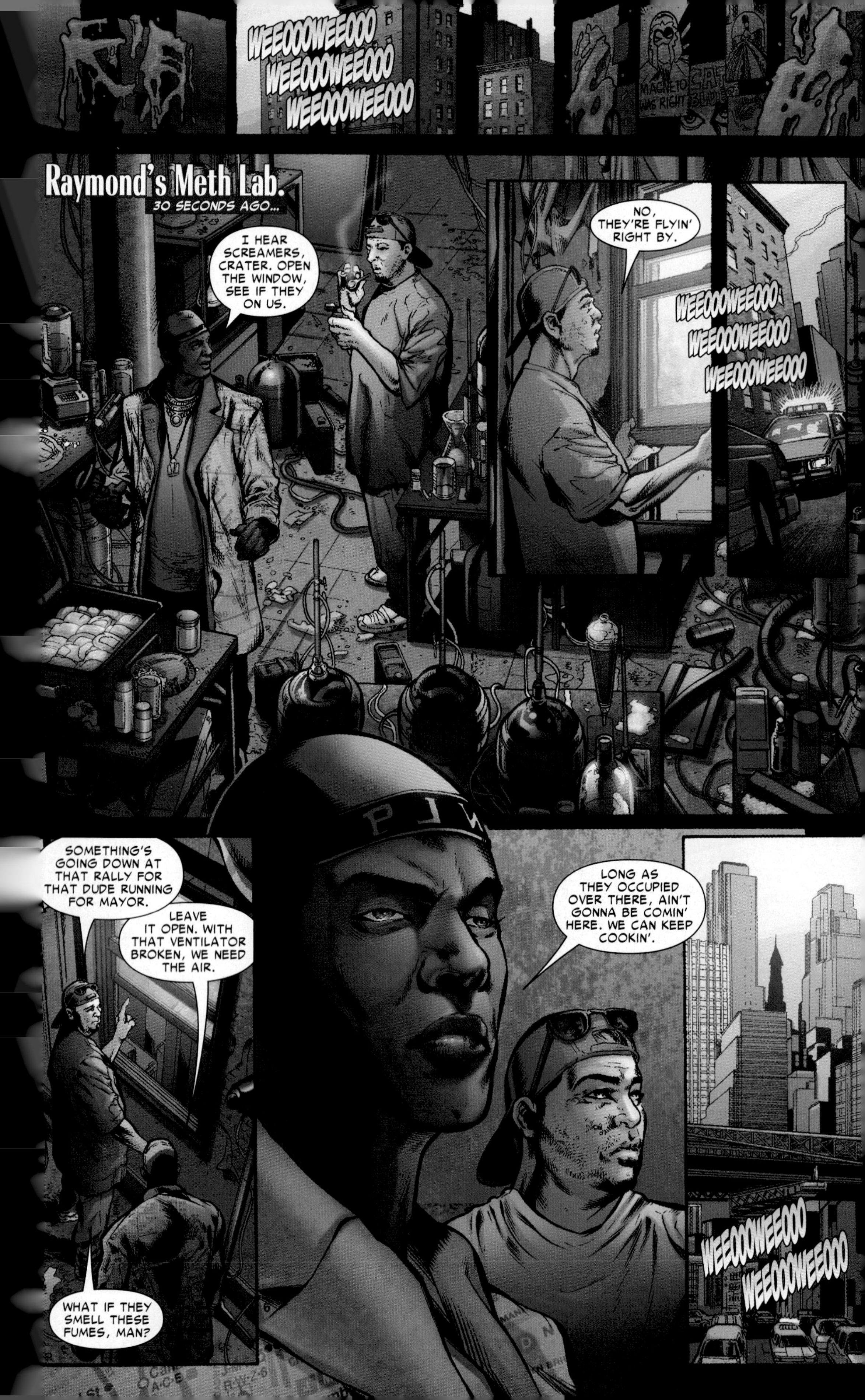

WEEOOOWEEOOO
WEEOOOWEEOOO
WEEOOOWEEOOO
MAGNETO WAS RIGHT
Raymond's Meth Lab.
30 SECONDS AGO...
I HEAR SCREAMERS, CRATER. OPEN THE WINDOW, SEE IF THEY ON US.
NO, THEY'RE FLYIN' RIGHT BY.
WEEOOOWEEOOO
WEEOOOWEEOOO
WEEOOOWEEOOO
SOMETHING'S GOING DOWN AT THAT RALLY FOR THAT DUDE RUNNING FOR MAYOR.
LEAVE IT OPEN. WITH THAT VENTILATOR BROKEN, WE NEED THE AIR.
WHAT IF THEY SMELL THESE FUMES, MAN?
LONG AS THEY OCCUPIED OVER THERE, AIN'T GONNA BE COMIN' HERE. WE CAN KEEP COOKIN'.
WEEOOOWEEOOO
WEEOOOWEEOOO

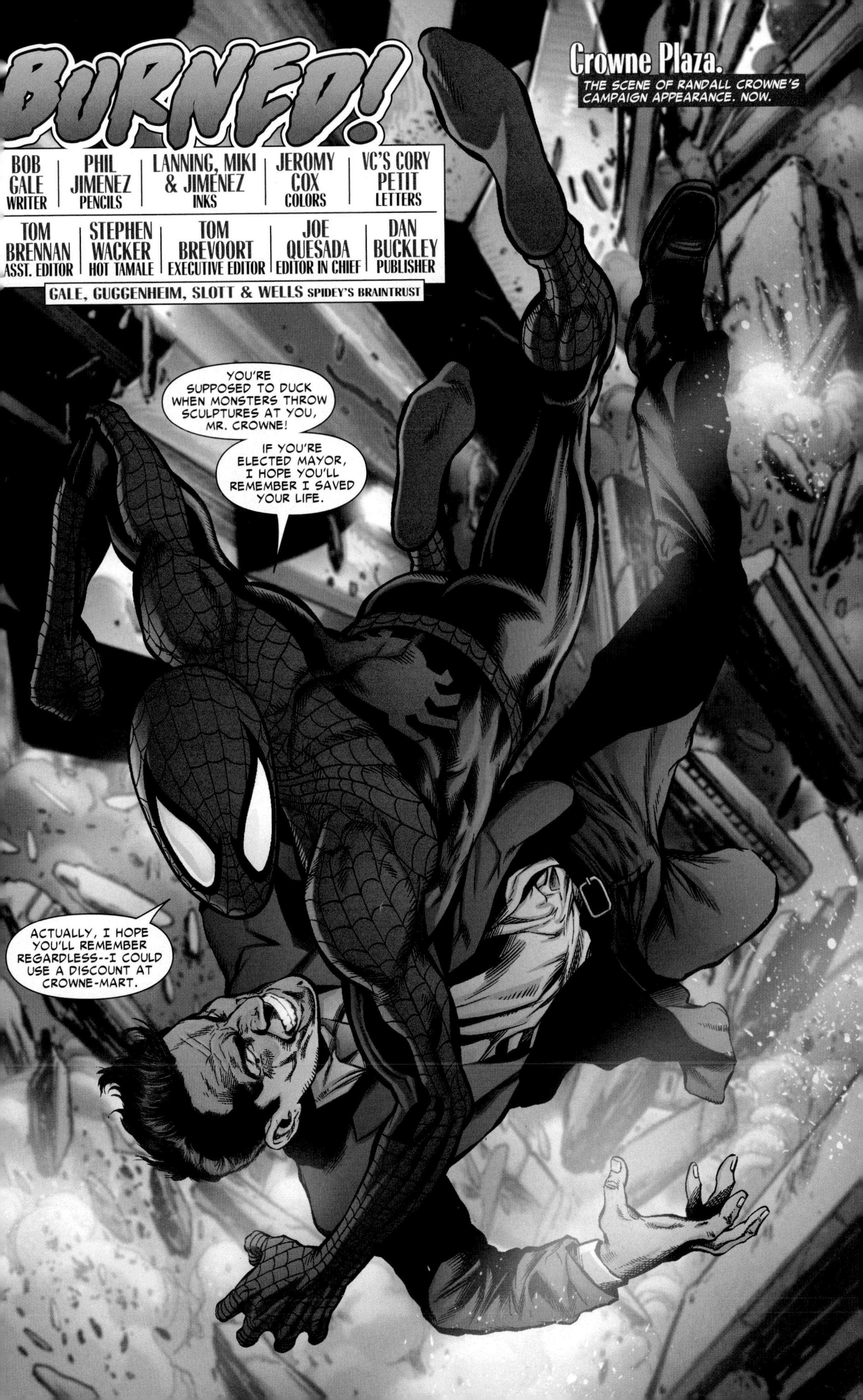
BURNED!
BOB GALE WRITER
PHIL JIMENEZ PENCILS
LANNING, MIKI & JIMENEZ INKS
JEROMY COX COLORS
VC'S CORY PETIT LETTERS
TOM BRENNAN ASST. EDITOR
STEPHEN WACKER HOT TAMALE
TOM BREVOORT EXECUTIVE EDITOR
JOE QUESADA EDITOR IN CHIEF
DAN BUCKLEY PUBLISHER
GALE, GUGGENHEIM, SLOTT & WELLS SPIDEY'S BRAINTRUST
Crowne Plaza.
THE SCENE OF RANDALL CROWNE'S CAMPAIGN APPEARANCE. NOW.
YOU'RE SUPPOSED TO DUCK WHEN MONSTERS THROW SCULPTURES AT YOU, MR. CROWNE!
IF YOU'RE ELECTED MAYOR, I HOPE YOU'LL REMEMBER I SAVED YOUR LIFE.
ACTUALLY, I HOPE YOU'LL REMEMBER REGARDLESS--I COULD USE A DISCOUNT AT CROWNE-MART.

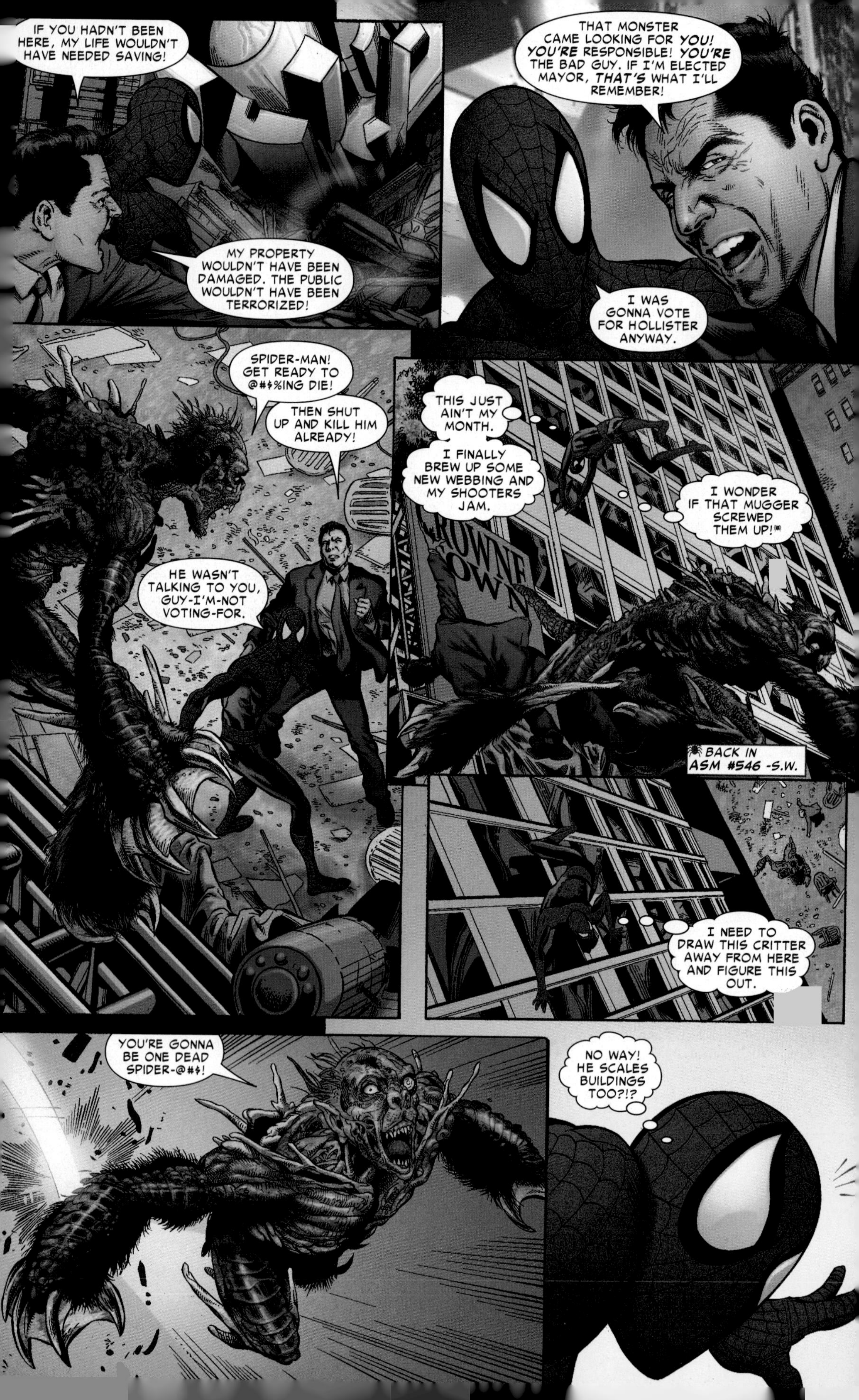

IF YOU HADN'T BEEN HERE, MY LIFE WOULDN'T HAVE NEEDED SAVING!
MY PROPERTY WOULDN'T HAVE BEEN DAMAGED. THE PUBLIC WOULDN'T HAVE BEEN TERRORIZED!
THAT MONSTER CAME LOOKING FOR YOU! YOU'RE RESPONSIBLE! YOU'RE THE BAD GUY. IF I'M ELECTED MAYOR, THAT'S WHAT I'LL REMEMBER!
I WAS GONNA VOTE FOR HOLLISTER ANYWAY.
SPIDER-MAN! GET READY TO @#$%ING DIE!
THEN SHUT UP AND KILL HIM ALREADY!
HE WASN'T TALKING TO YOU, GUY-I'M-NOT VOTING-FOR.
THIS JUST AIN'T MY MONTH.
I FINALLY BREW UP SOME NEW WEBBING AND MY SHOOTERS JAM.
I WONDER IF THAT MUGGER SCREWED THEM UP!*
*BACK IN ASM #546 -S.W.
I NEED TO DRAW THIS CRITTER AWAY FROM HERE AND FIGURE THIS OUT.
YOU'RE GONNA BE ONE DEAD SPIDER-@#$!
NO WAY! HE SCALES BUILDINGS TOO?!?

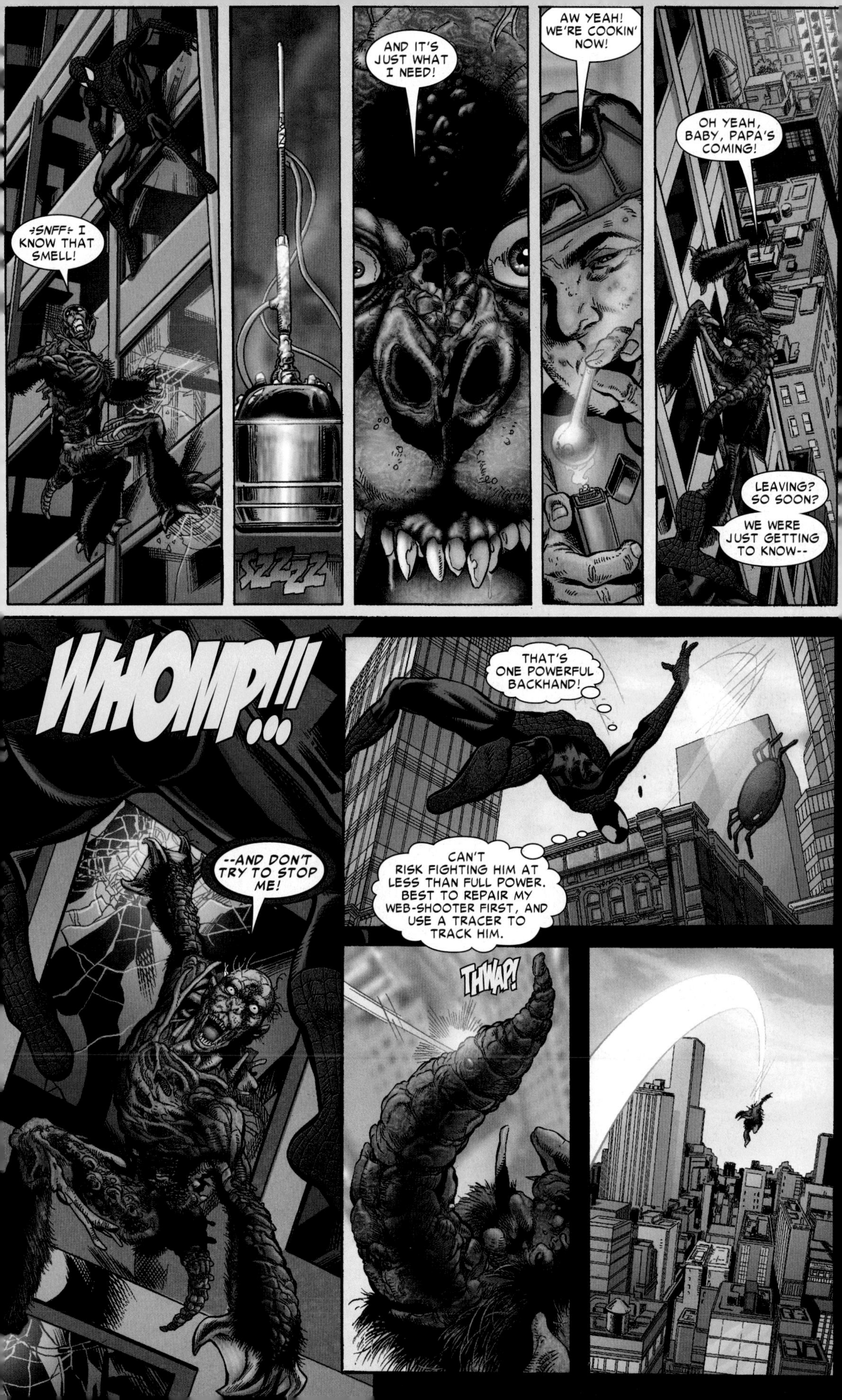

-SNFF- I KNOW THAT SMELL!
SZZZZ
AND IT'S JUST WHAT I NEED!
AW YEAH! WE'RE COOKIN' NOW!
OH YEAH, BABY, PAPA'S COMING!
LEAVING? SO SOON?
WE WERE JUST GETTING TO KNOW--
WHOMP!!!...
--AND DON'T TRY TO STOP ME!
THAT'S ONE POWERFUL BACKHAND!
CAN'T RISK FIGHTING HIM AT LESS THAN FULL POWER. BEST TO REPAIR MY WEB-SHOOTER FIRST, AND USE A TRACER TO TRACK HIM.
THWAP!

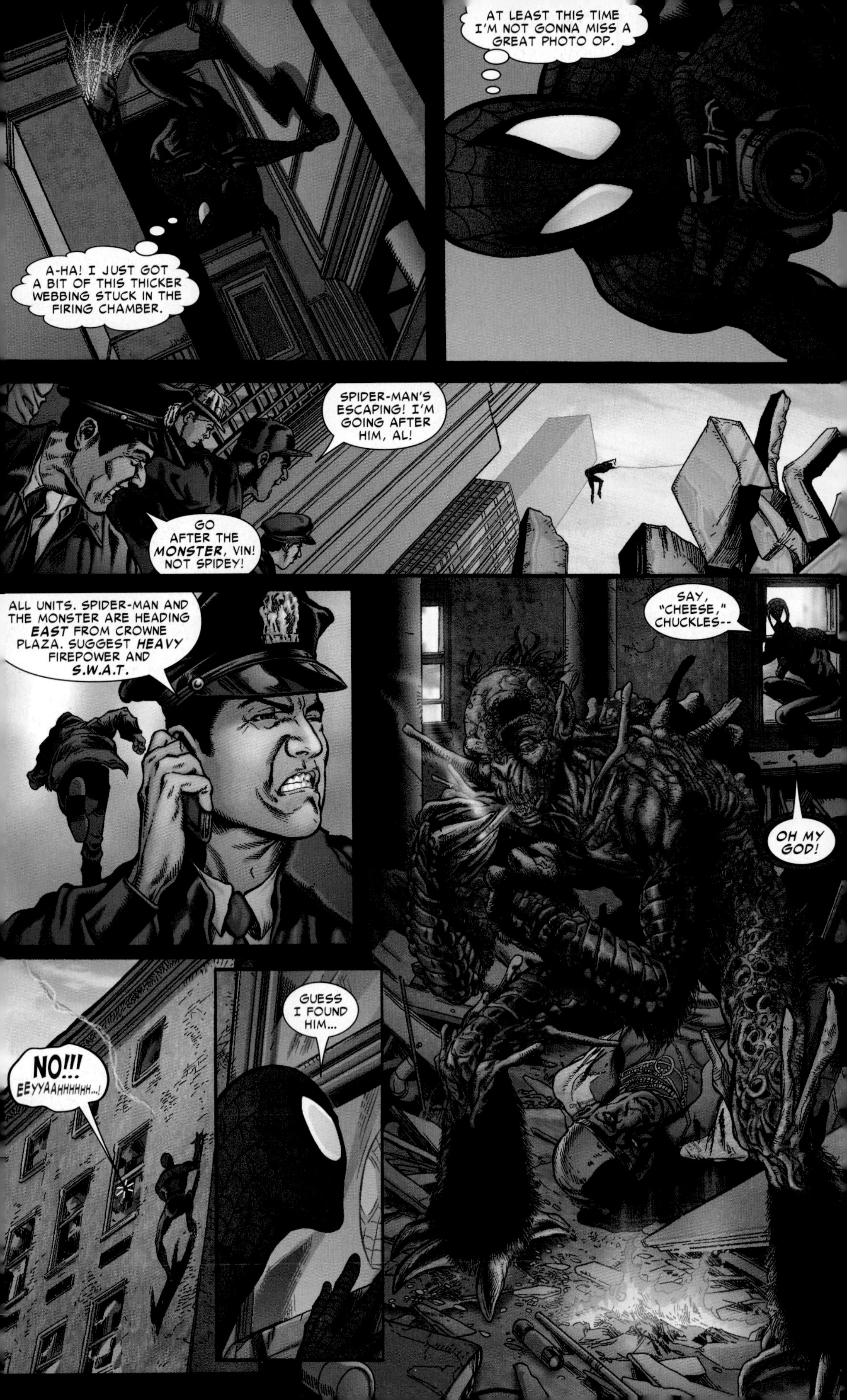
A-HA! I JUST GOT A BIT OF THIS THICKER WEBBING STUCK IN THE FIRING CHAMBER.
AT LEAST THIS TIME I'M NOT GONNA MISS A GREAT PHOTO OP.
SPIDER-MAN'S ESCAPING! I'M GOING AFTER HIM, AL!
GO AFTER THE MONSTER, VIN! NOT SPIDEY!
ALL UNITS. SPIDER-MAN AND THE MONSTER ARE HEADING EAST FROM CROWNE PLAZA. SUGGEST HEAVY FIREPOWER AND S.W.A.T.
SAY, "CHEESE," CHUCKLES--
OH MY GOD!
NO!!! EEYYAAHHHHHH...!
GUESS I FOUND HIM...

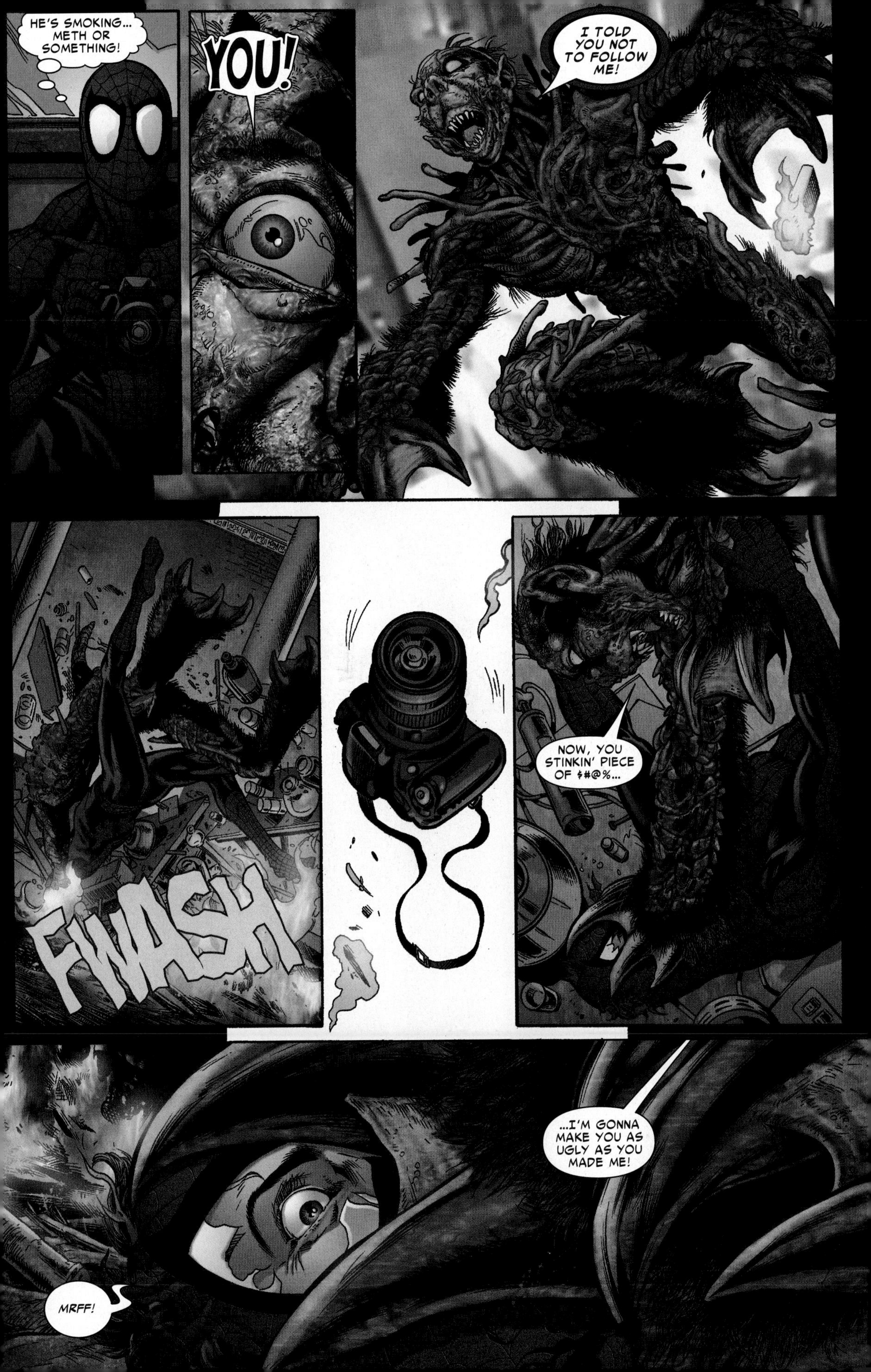
HE'S SMOKING... METH OR SOMETHING!
YOU!
I TOLD YOU NOT TO FOLLOW ME!
FWASH
NOW, YOU STINKIN' PIECE OF $#@%...
...I'M GONNA MAKE YOU AS UGLY AS YOU MADE ME!
MRFF!

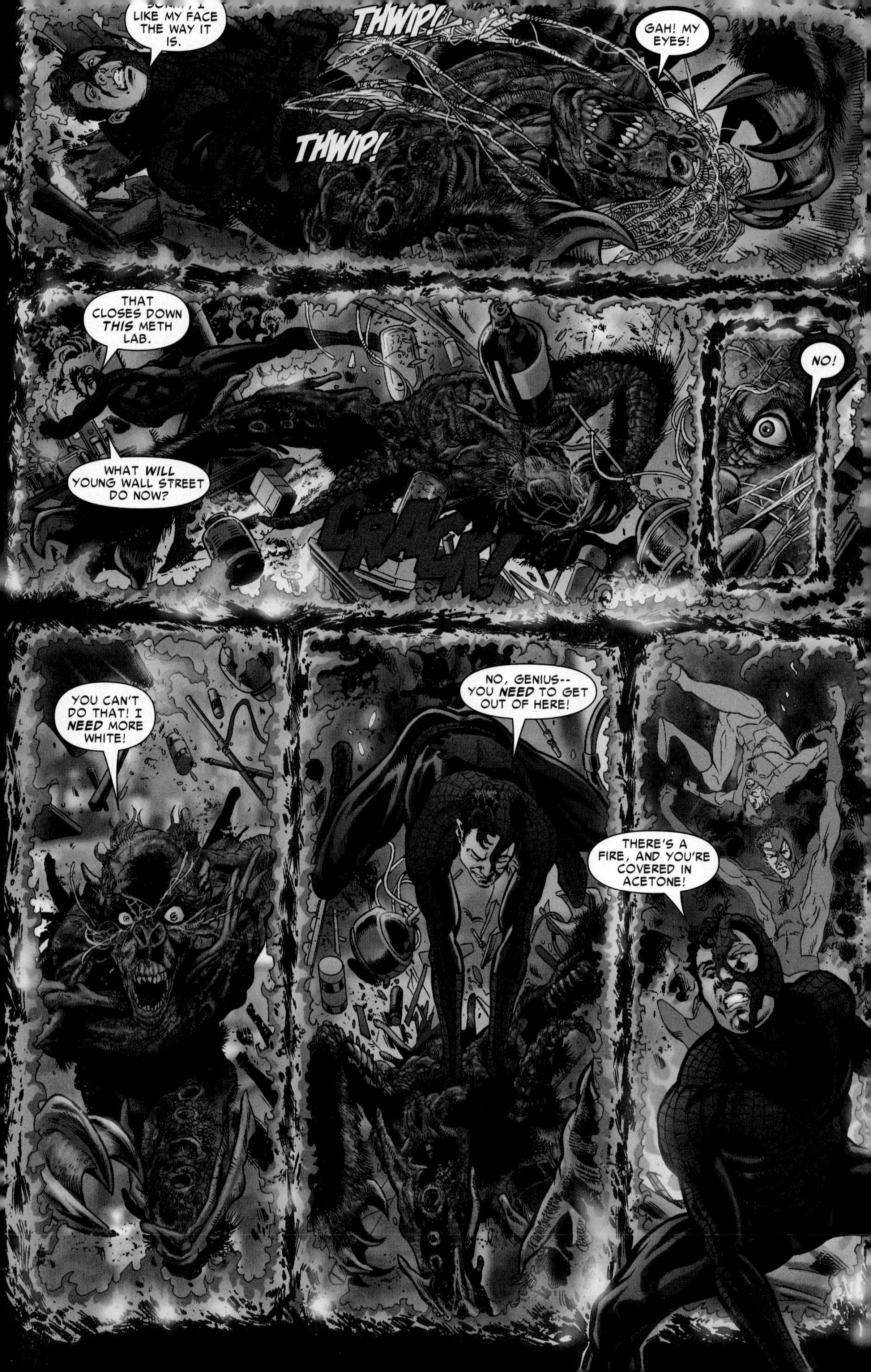

LIKE MY FACE THE WAY IT IS.
THWIP!
GAH! MY EYES!
THWIP!
THAT CLOSES DOWN THIS METH LAB.
WHAT WILL YOUNG WALL STREET DO NOW?
CRACK!
NO!
YOU CAN'T DO THAT! I NEED MORE WHITE!
NO, GENIUS-- YOU NEED TO GET OUT OF HERE!
THERE'S A FIRE, AND YOU'RE COVERED IN ACETONE!

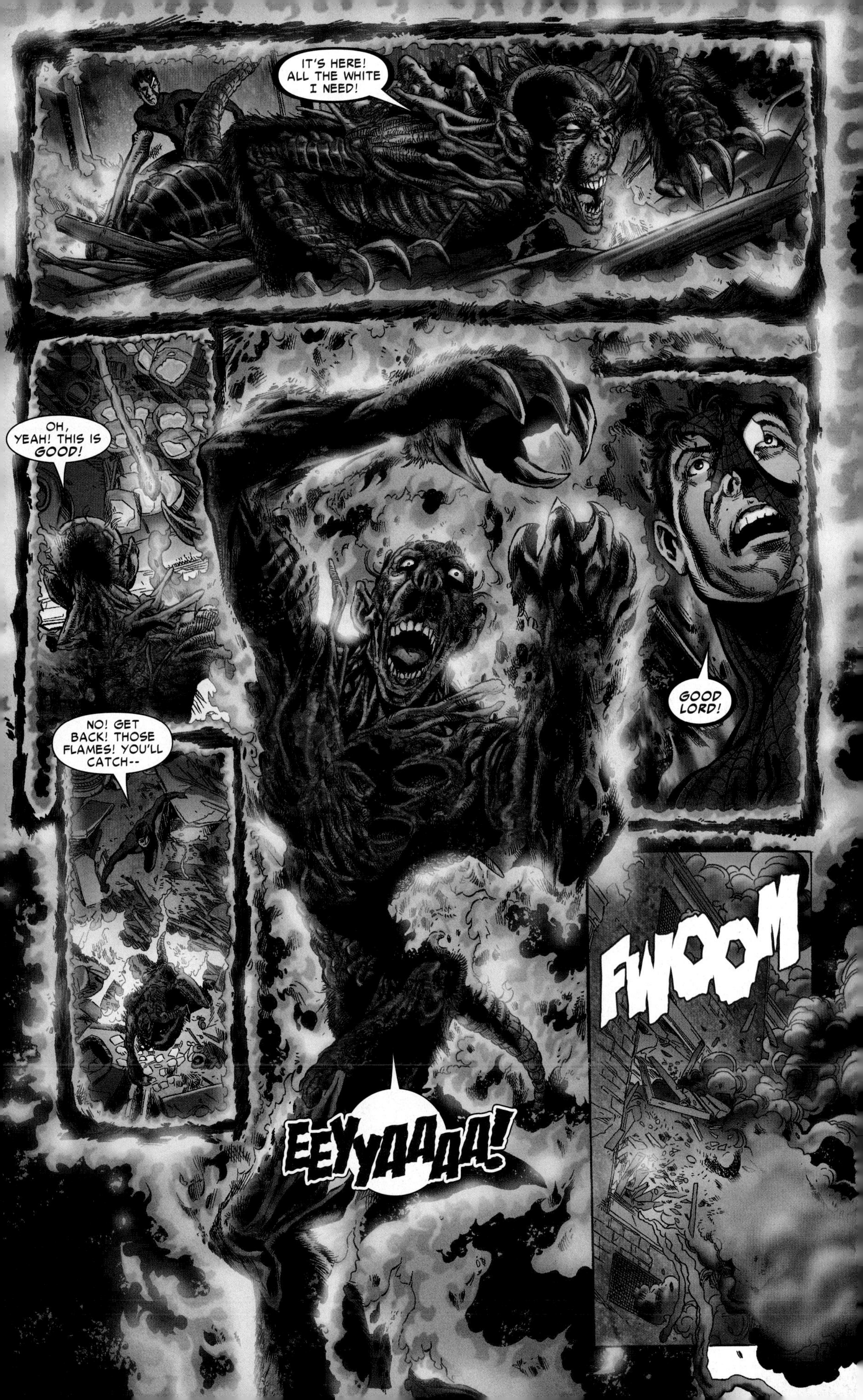
IT'S HERE! ALL THE WHITE I NEED!
OH, YEAH! THIS IS GOOD!
GOOD LORD!
NO! GET BACK! THOSE FLAMES! YOU'LL CATCH--
EEYYAAAA!
FWOOM

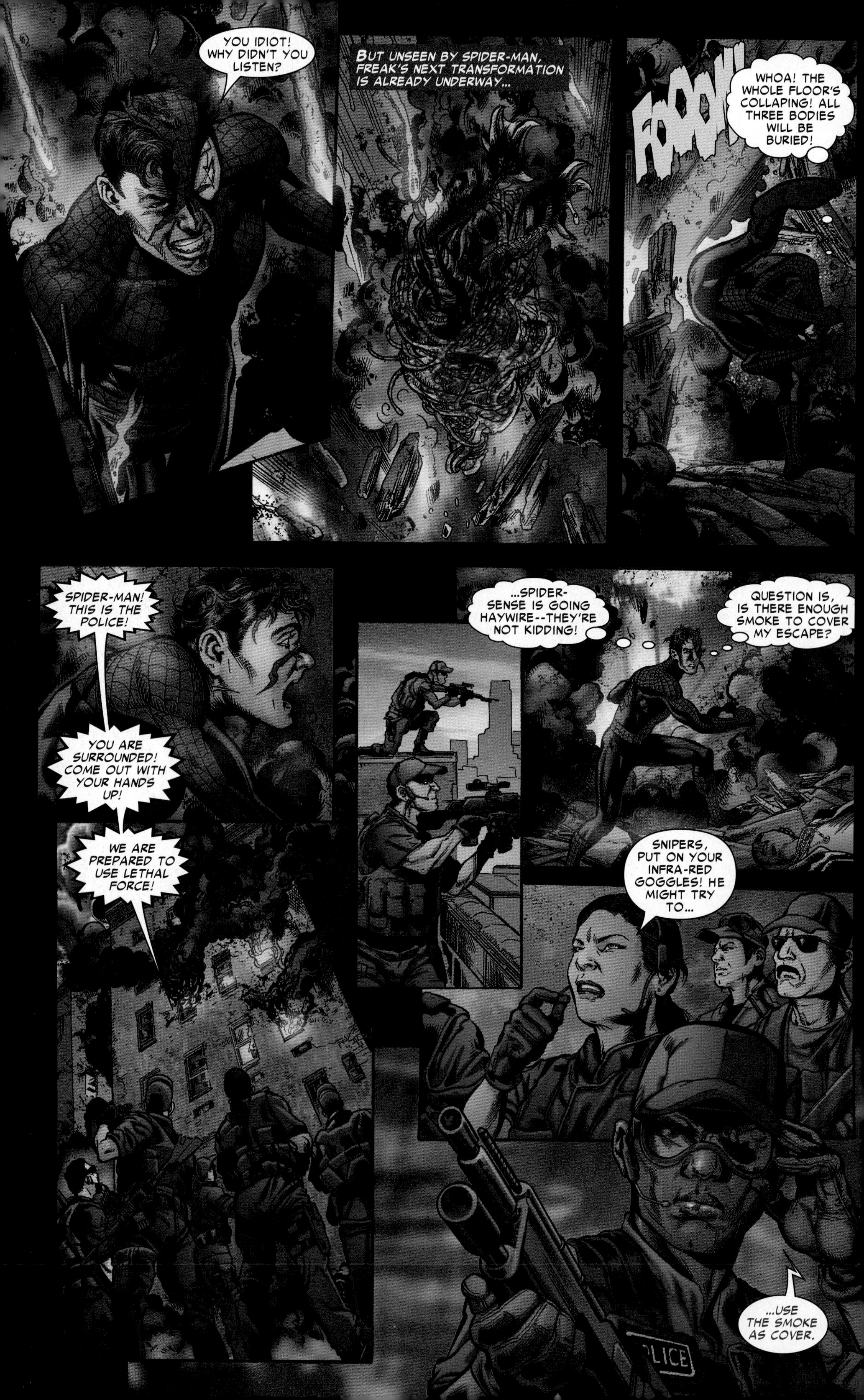
YOU IDIOT! WHY DIDN'T YOU LISTEN?
BUT UNSEEN BY SPIDER-MAN, FREAK'S NEXT TRANSFORMATION IS ALREADY UNDERWAY...
FOOOM!
WHOA! THE WHOLE FLOOR'S COLLAPING! ALL THREE BODIES WILL BE BURIED!
SPIDER-MAN! THIS IS THE POLICE!
YOU ARE SURROUNDED! COME OUT WITH YOUR HANDS UP!
WE ARE PREPARED TO USE LETHAL FORCE!
...SPIDER-SENSE IS GOING HAYWIRE--THEY'RE NOT KIDDING!
QUESTION IS, IS THERE ENOUGH SMOKE TO COVER MY ESCAPE?
SNIPERS, PUT ON YOUR INFRA-RED GOGGLES! HE MIGHT TRY TO...
...USE THE SMOKE AS COVER.
POLICE

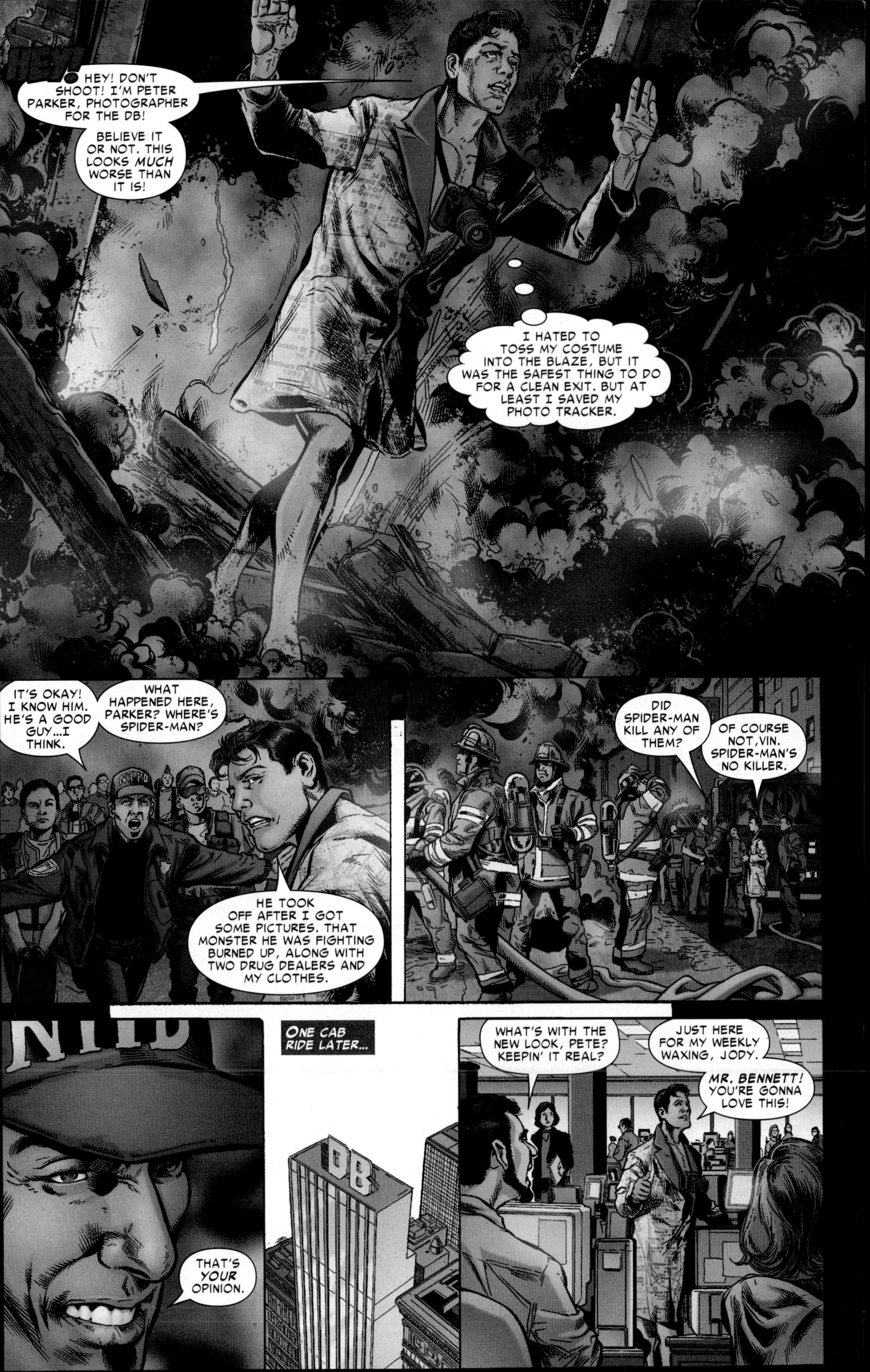
HEY!
HEY! DON'T SHOOT! I'M PETER PARKER, PHOTOGRAPHER FOR THE DB!
BELIEVE IT OR NOT. THIS LOOKS MUCH WORSE THAN IT IS!
I HATED TO TOSS MY COSTUME INTO THE BLAZE, BUT IT WAS THE SAFEST THING TO DO FOR A CLEAN EXIT. BUT AT LEAST I SAVED MY PHOTO TRACKER.
IT'S OKAY! I KNOW HIM. HE'S A GOOD GUY...I THINK.
WHAT HAPPENED HERE, PARKER? WHERE'S SPIDER-MAN?
HE TOOK OFF AFTER I GOT SOME PICTURES. THAT MONSTER HE WAS FIGHTING BURNED UP, ALONG WITH TWO DRUG DEALERS AND MY CLOTHES.
DID SPIDER-MAN KILL ANY OF THEM?
OF COURSE NOT, VIN. SPIDER-MAN'S NO KILLER.
THAT'S YOUR OPINION.
ONE CAB RIDE LATER...
DB
WHAT'S WITH THE NEW LOOK, PETE? KEEPIN' IT REAL?
JUST HERE FOR MY WEEKLY WAXING, JODY.
MR. BENNETT! YOU'RE GONNA LOVE THIS!

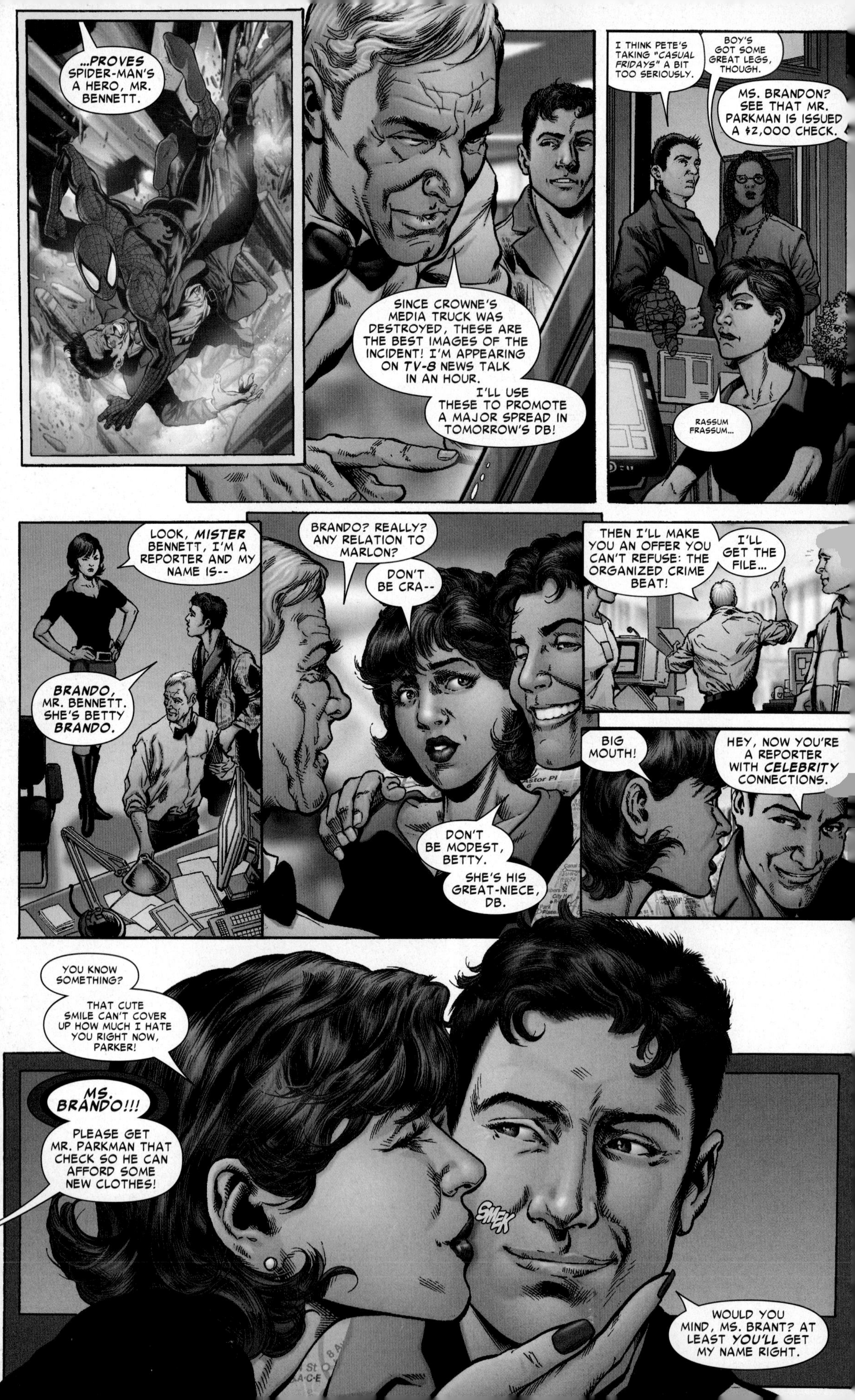
...PROVES SPIDER-MAN'S A HERO, MR. BENNETT.
SINCE CROWNE'S MEDIA TRUCK WAS DESTROYED, THESE ARE THE BEST IMAGES OF THE INCIDENT! I'M APPEARING ON TV-8 NEWS TALK IN AN HOUR.
I'LL USE THESE TO PROMOTE A MAJOR SPREAD IN TOMORROW'S DB!
I THINK PETE'S TAKING "CASUAL FRIDAYS" A BIT TOO SERIOUSLY.
BOY'S GOT SOME GREAT LEGS, THOUGH.
MS. BRANDON? SEE THAT MR. PARKMAN IS ISSUED A $2,000 CHECK.
RASSUM FRASSUM...
LOOK, MISTER BENNETT, I'M A REPORTER AND MY NAME IS--
BRANDO, MR. BENNETT. SHE'S BETTY BRANDO.
BRANDO? REALLY? ANY RELATION TO MARLON?
DON'T BE CRA--
DON'T BE MODEST, BETTY.
SHE'S HIS GREAT-NIECE, DB.
THEN I'LL MAKE YOU AN OFFER YOU CAN'T REFUSE: THE ORGANIZED CRIME BEAT!
I'LL GET THE FILE...
BIG MOUTH!
HEY, NOW YOU'RE A REPORTER WITH CELEBRITY CONNECTIONS.
YOU KNOW SOMETHING?
THAT CUTE SMILE CAN'T COVER UP HOW MUCH I HATE YOU RIGHT NOW, PARKER!
MS. BRANDO!!!
PLEASE GET MR. PARKMAN THAT CHECK SO HE CAN AFFORD SOME NEW CLOTHES!
SMEK
WOULD YOU MIND, MS. BRANT? AT LEAST YOU'LL GET MY NAME RIGHT.

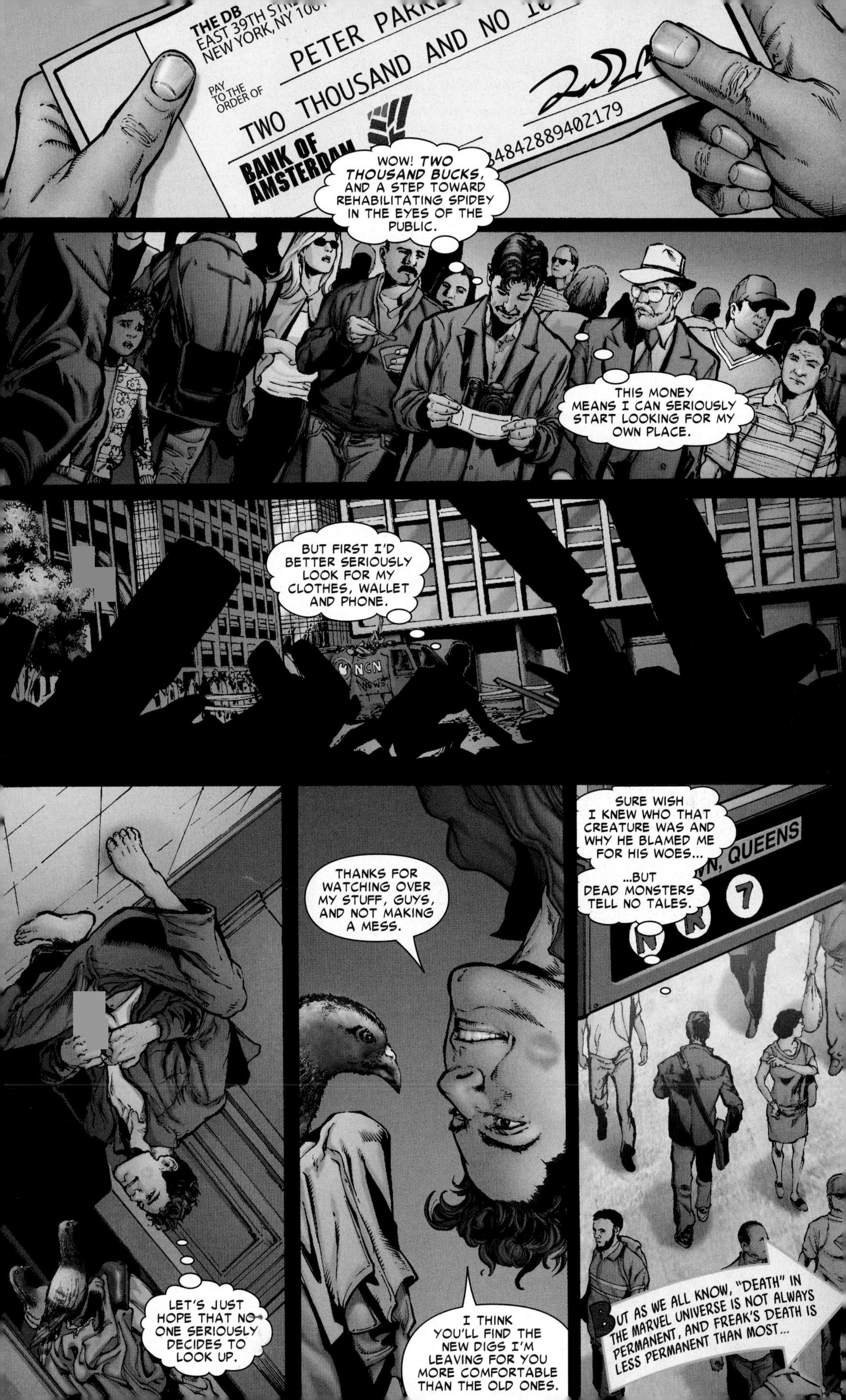
THE DB
EAST 39TH ST
NEW YORK, NY 100
PAY TO THE ORDER OF
PETER PARK
TWO THOUSAND AND NO
BANK OF AMSTERDAM
WOW! TWO THOUSAND BUCKS, AND A STEP TOWARD REHABILITATING SPIDEY IN THE EYES OF THE PUBLIC.
THIS MONEY MEANS I CAN SERIOUSLY START LOOKING FOR MY OWN PLACE.
BUT FIRST I'D BETTER SERIOUSLY LOOK FOR MY CLOTHES, WALLET AND PHONE.
LET'S JUST HOPE THAT NO ONE SERIOUSLY DECIDES TO LOOK UP.
THANKS FOR WATCHING OVER MY STUFF, GUYS, AND NOT MAKING A MESS.
I THINK YOU'LL FIND THE NEW DIGS I'M LEAVING FOR YOU MORE COMFORTABLE THAN THE OLD ONES.
SURE WISH I KNEW WHO THAT CREATURE WAS AND WHY HE BLAMED ME FOR HIS WOES...
...BUT DEAD MONSTERS TELL NO TALES.
BUT AS WE ALL KNOW, "DEATH" IN THE MARVEL UNIVERSE IS NOT ALWAYS PERMANENT, AND FREAK'S DEATH IS LESS PERMANENT THAN MOST...

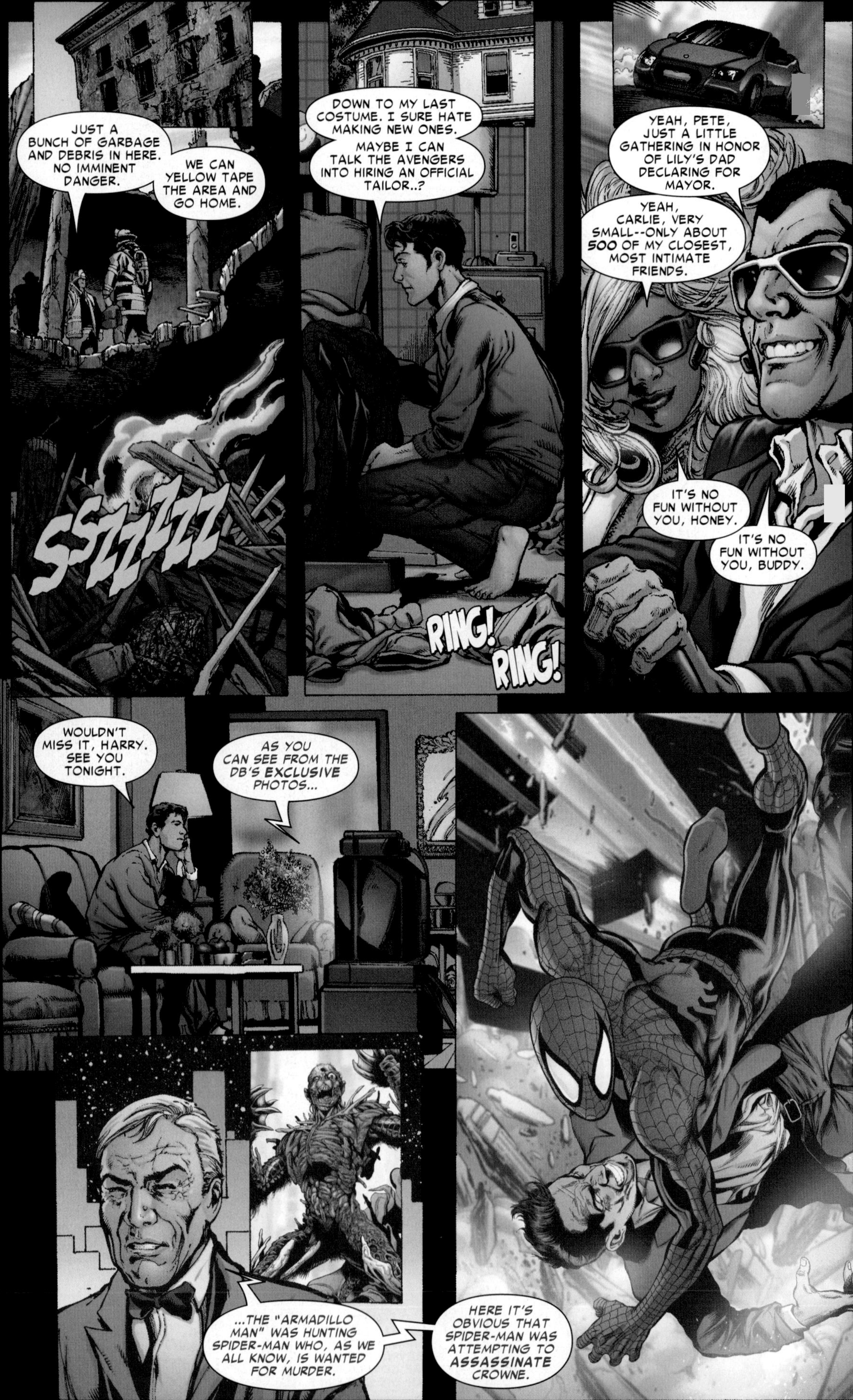
JUST A BUNCH OF GARBAGE AND DEBRIS IN HERE. NO IMMINENT DANGER.
WE CAN YELLOW TAPE THE AREA AND GO HOME.
SSZZZZZ
DOWN TO MY LAST COSTUME. I SURE HATE MAKING NEW ONES.
MAYBE I CAN TALK THE AVENGERS INTO HIRING AN OFFICIAL TAILOR..?
RING!
RING!
YEAH, PETE, JUST A LITTLE GATHERING IN HONOR OF LILY'S DAD DECLARING FOR MAYOR.
YEAH, CARLIE, VERY SMALL--ONLY ABOUT 500 OF MY CLOSEST, MOST INTIMATE FRIENDS.
IT'S NO FUN WITHOUT YOU, HONEY.
IT'S NO FUN WITHOUT YOU, BUDDY.
WOULDN'T MISS IT, HARRY. SEE YOU TONIGHT.
AS YOU CAN SEE FROM THE DB'S EXCLUSIVE PHOTOS...
...THE "ARMADILLO MAN" WAS HUNTING SPIDER-MAN WHO, AS WE ALL KNOW, IS WANTED FOR MURDER.
HERE IT'S OBVIOUS THAT SPIDER-MAN WAS ATTEMPTING TO ASSASSINATE CROWNE.

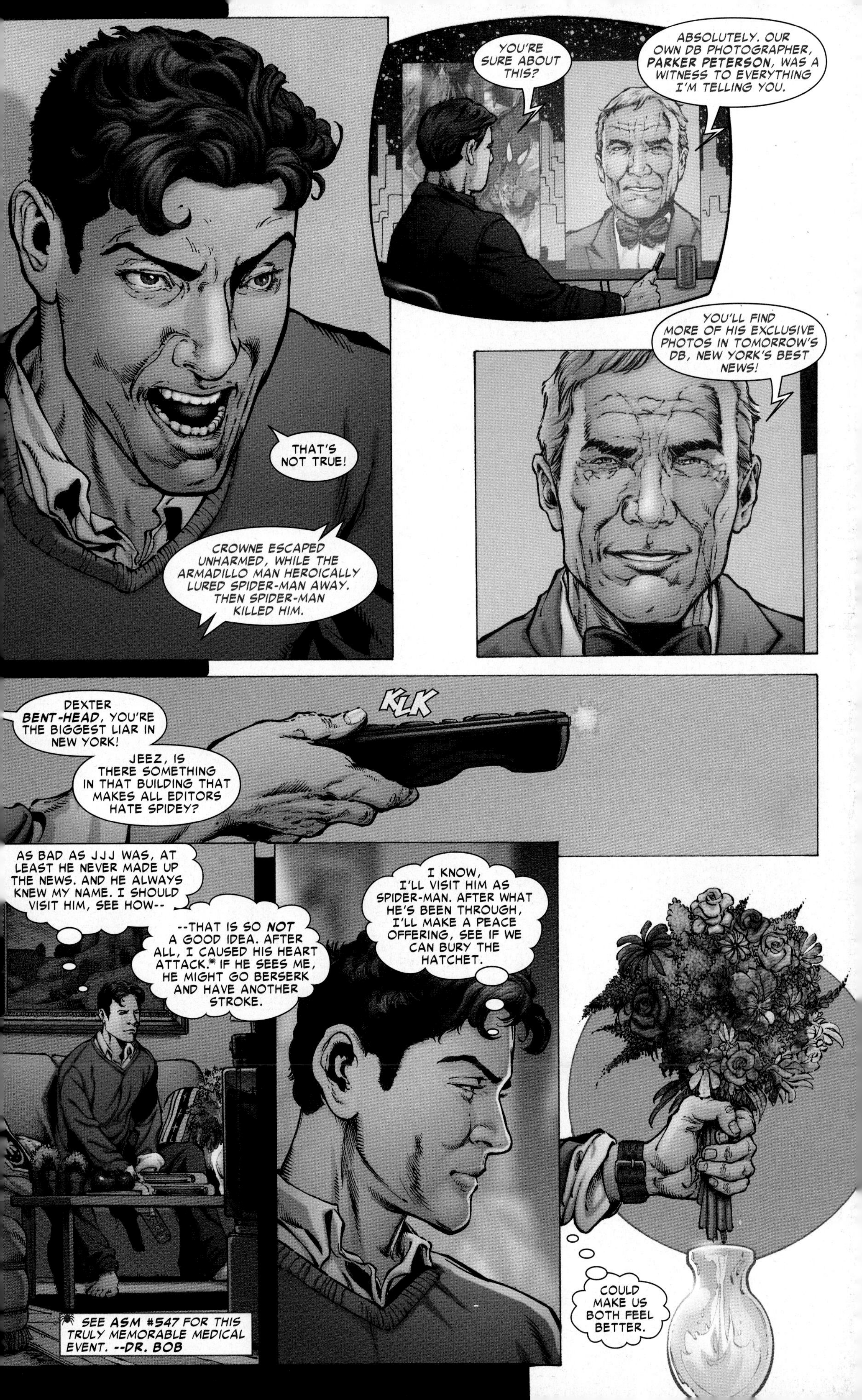
YOU'RE SURE ABOUT THIS?
ABSOLUTELY. OUR OWN DB PHOTOGRAPHER, PARKER PETERSON, WAS A WITNESS TO EVERYTHING I'M TELLING YOU.
THAT'S NOT TRUE!
CROWNE ESCAPED UNHARMED, WHILE THE ARMADILLO MAN HEROICALLY LURED SPIDER-MAN AWAY. THEN SPIDER-MAN KILLED HIM.
YOU'LL FIND MORE OF HIS EXCLUSIVE PHOTOS IN TOMORROW'S DB, NEW YORK'S BEST NEWS!
KLK
DEXTER BENT-HEAD, YOU'RE THE BIGGEST LIAR IN NEW YORK!
JEEZ, IS THERE SOMETHING IN THAT BUILDING THAT MAKES ALL EDITORS HATE SPIDEY?
AS BAD AS JJJ WAS, AT LEAST HE NEVER MADE UP THE NEWS. AND HE ALWAYS KNEW MY NAME. I SHOULD VISIT HIM, SEE HOW--
--THAT IS SO NOT A GOOD IDEA. AFTER ALL, I CAUSED HIS HEART ATTACK.* IF HE SEES ME, HE MIGHT GO BERSERK AND HAVE ANOTHER STROKE.
* SEE ASM #547 FOR THIS TRULY MEMORABLE MEDICAL EVENT. --DR. BOB
I KNOW, I'LL VISIT HIM AS SPIDER-MAN. AFTER WHAT HE'S BEEN THROUGH, I'LL MAKE A PEACE OFFERING, SEE IF WE CAN BURY THE HATCHET.
COULD MAKE US BOTH FEEL BETTER.

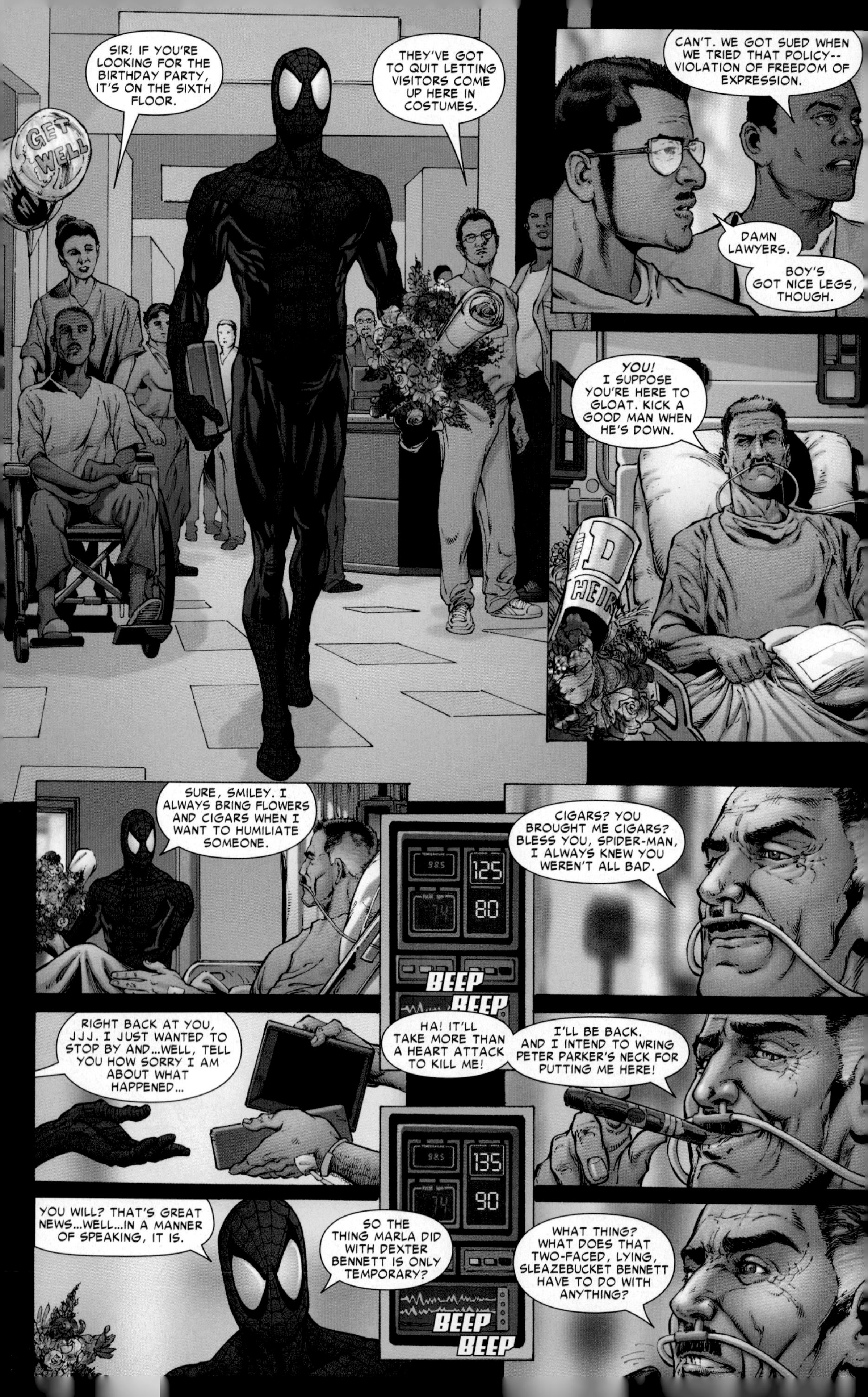
GET WELL
SIR! IF YOU'RE LOOKING FOR THE BIRTHDAY PARTY, IT'S ON THE SIXTH FLOOR.
THEY'VE GOT TO QUIT LETTING VISITORS COME UP HERE IN COSTUMES.
CAN'T. WE GOT SUED WHEN WE TRIED THAT POLICY--VIOLATION OF FREEDOM OF EXPRESSION.
DAMN LAWYERS.
BOY'S GOT NICE LEGS, THOUGH.
YOU! I SUPPOSE YOU'RE HERE TO GLOAT. KICK A GOOD MAN WHEN HE'S DOWN.
SURE, SMILEY. I ALWAYS BRING FLOWERS AND CIGARS WHEN I WANT TO HUMILIATE SOMEONE.
CIGARS? YOU BROUGHT ME CIGARS? BLESS YOU, SPIDER-MAN, I ALWAYS KNEW YOU WEREN'T ALL BAD.
125
80
BEEP BEEP
RIGHT BACK AT YOU, JJJ. I JUST WANTED TO STOP BY AND...WELL, TELL YOU HOW SORRY I AM ABOUT WHAT HAPPENED...
HA! IT'LL TAKE MORE THAN A HEART ATTACK TO KILL ME!
I'LL BE BACK. AND I INTEND TO WRING PETER PARKER'S NECK FOR PUTTING ME HERE!
135
90
YOU WILL? THAT'S GREAT NEWS...WELL...IN A MANNER OF SPEAKING, IT IS.
SO THE THING MARLA DID WITH DEXTER BENNETT IS ONLY TEMPORARY?
WHAT THING? WHAT DOES THAT TWO-FACED, LYING, SLEAZEBUCKET BENNETT HAVE TO DO WITH ANYTHING?
BEEP BEEP

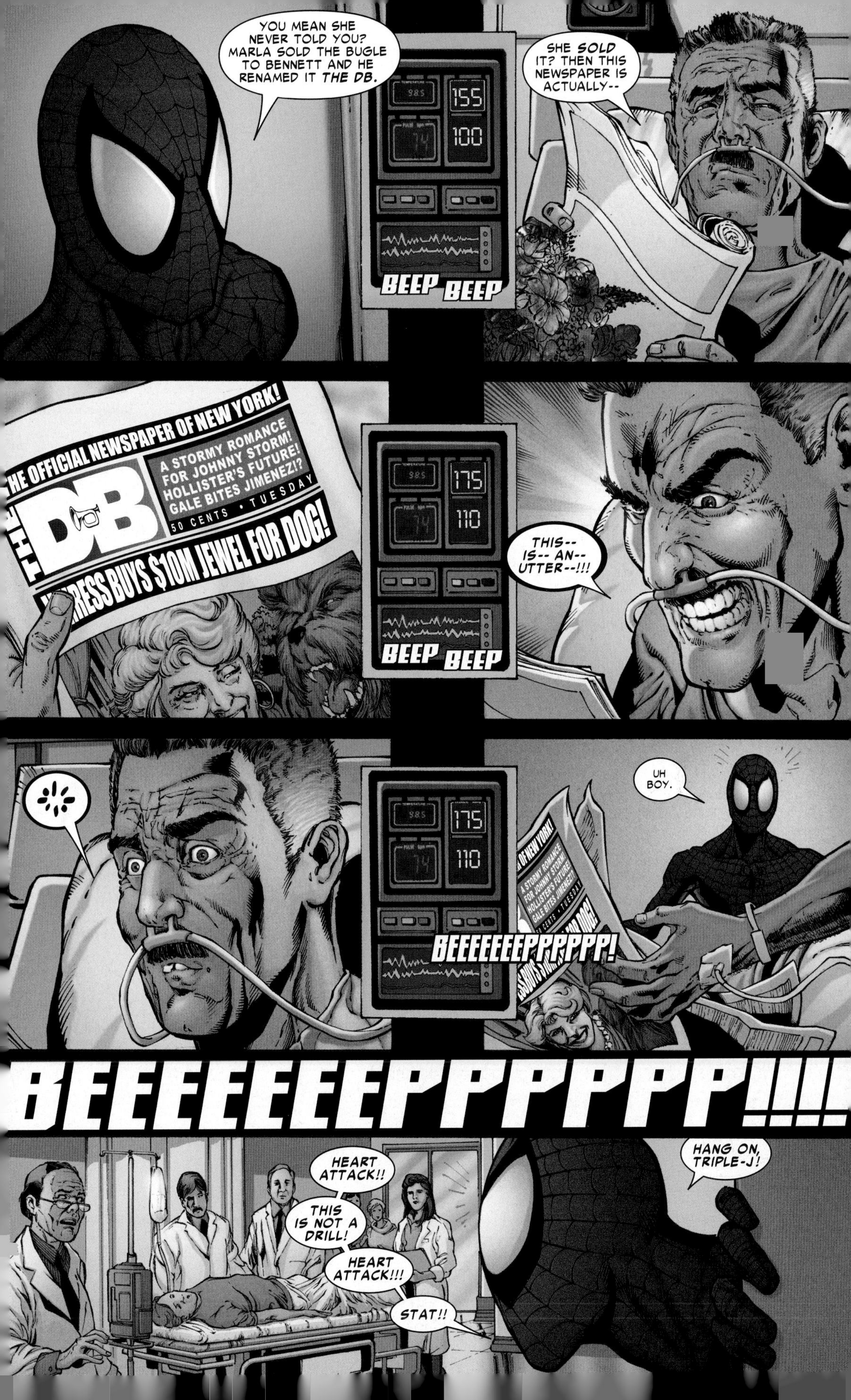

YOU MEAN SHE NEVER TOLD YOU? MARLA SOLD THE BUGLE TO BENNETT AND HE RENAMED IT THE DB.
SHE SOLD IT? THEN THIS NEWSPAPER IS ACTUALLY--
BEEP BEEP
THE OFFICIAL NEWSPAPER OF NEW YORK!
THE DB
A STORMY ROMANCE FOR JOHNNY STORM! HOLLISTER'S FUTURE! GALE BITES JIMENEZ!?
50 CENTS • TUESDAY
ESS BUYS $10M JEWEL FOR DOG!
THIS-- IS-- AN-- UTTER--!!!
BEEP BEEP
UH BOY.
BEEEEEEEPPPPPP!
BEEEEEEEEPPPPPPPP!!!!
HEART ATTACK!!
THIS IS NOT A DRILL!
HEART ATTACK!!!
STAT!!
HANG ON, TRIPLE-J!

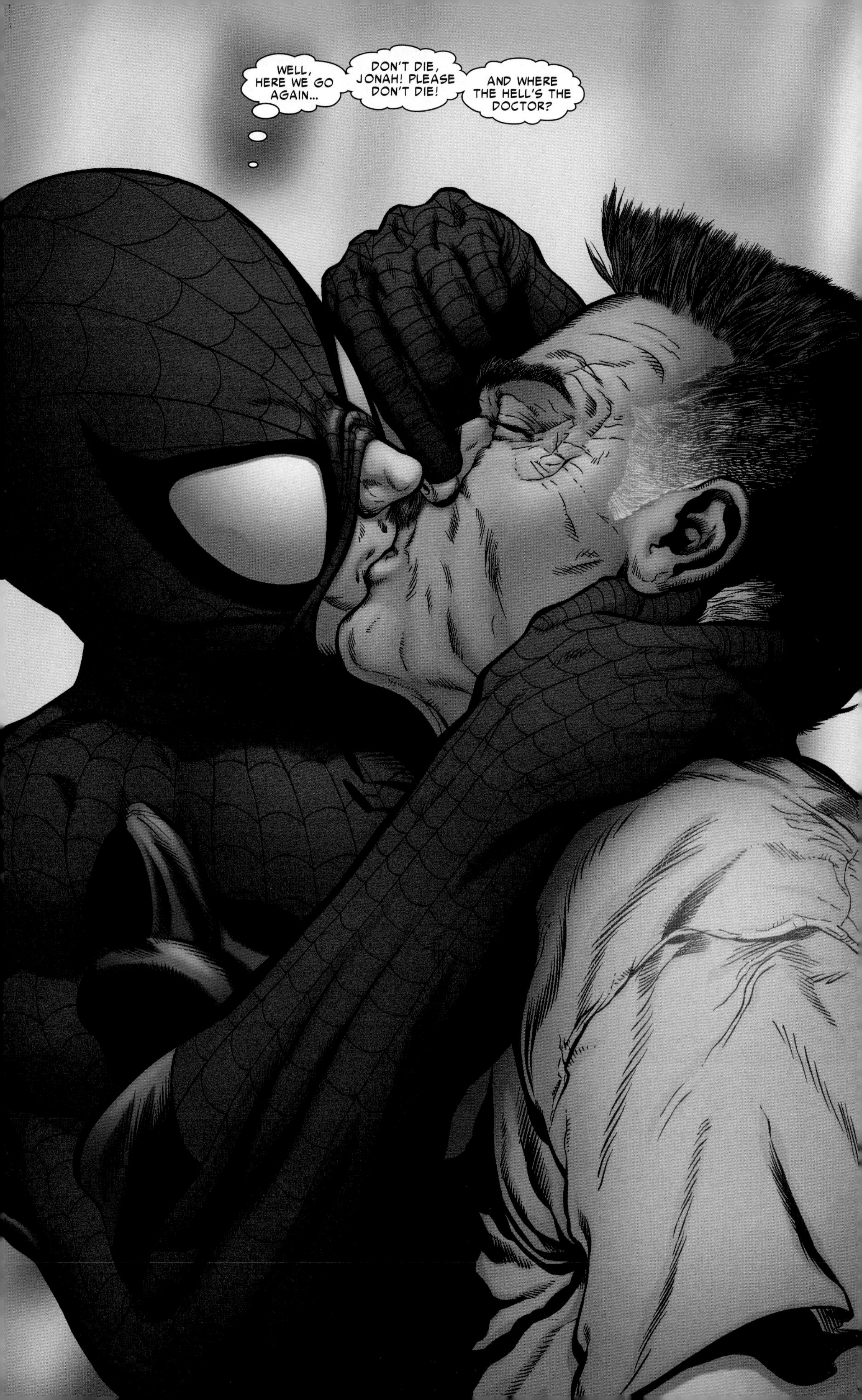
WELL, HERE WE GO AGAIN...
DON'T DIE, JONAH! PLEASE DON'T DIE!
AND WHERE THE HELL'S THE DOCTOR?

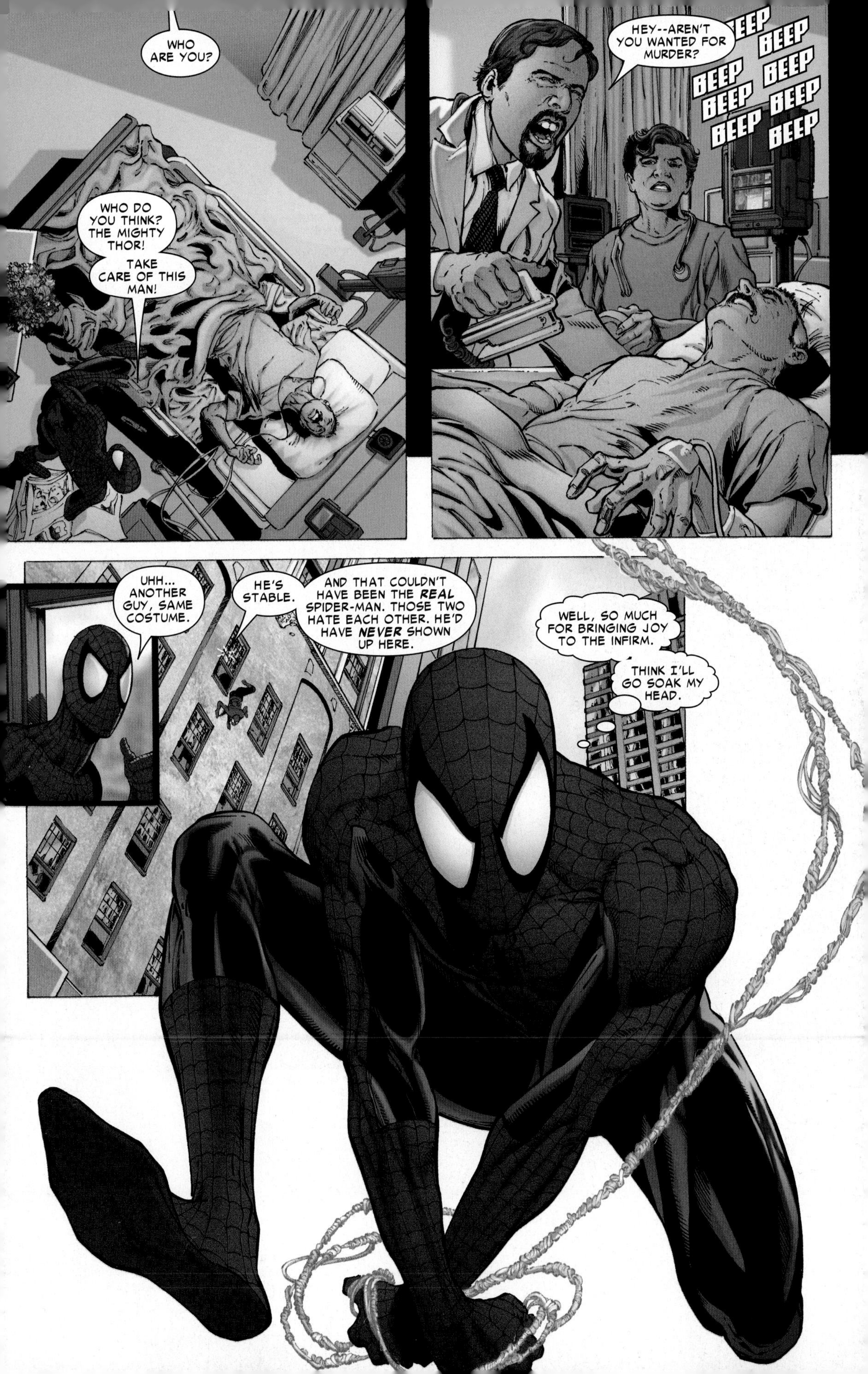

WHO ARE YOU?
WHO DO YOU THINK? THE MIGHTY THOR!
TAKE CARE OF THIS MAN!
HEY--AREN'T YOU WANTED FOR MURDER?
BEEP BEEP BEEP BEEP BEEP BEEP BEEP BEEP BEEP
UHH... ANOTHER GUY, SAME COSTUME.
HE'S STABLE.
AND THAT COULDN'T HAVE BEEN THE *REAL* SPIDER-MAN. THOSE TWO HATE EACH OTHER. HE'D HAVE *NEVER* SHOWN UP HERE.
WELL, SO MUCH FOR BRINGING JOY TO THE INFIRM.
THINK I'LL GO SOAK MY HEAD.

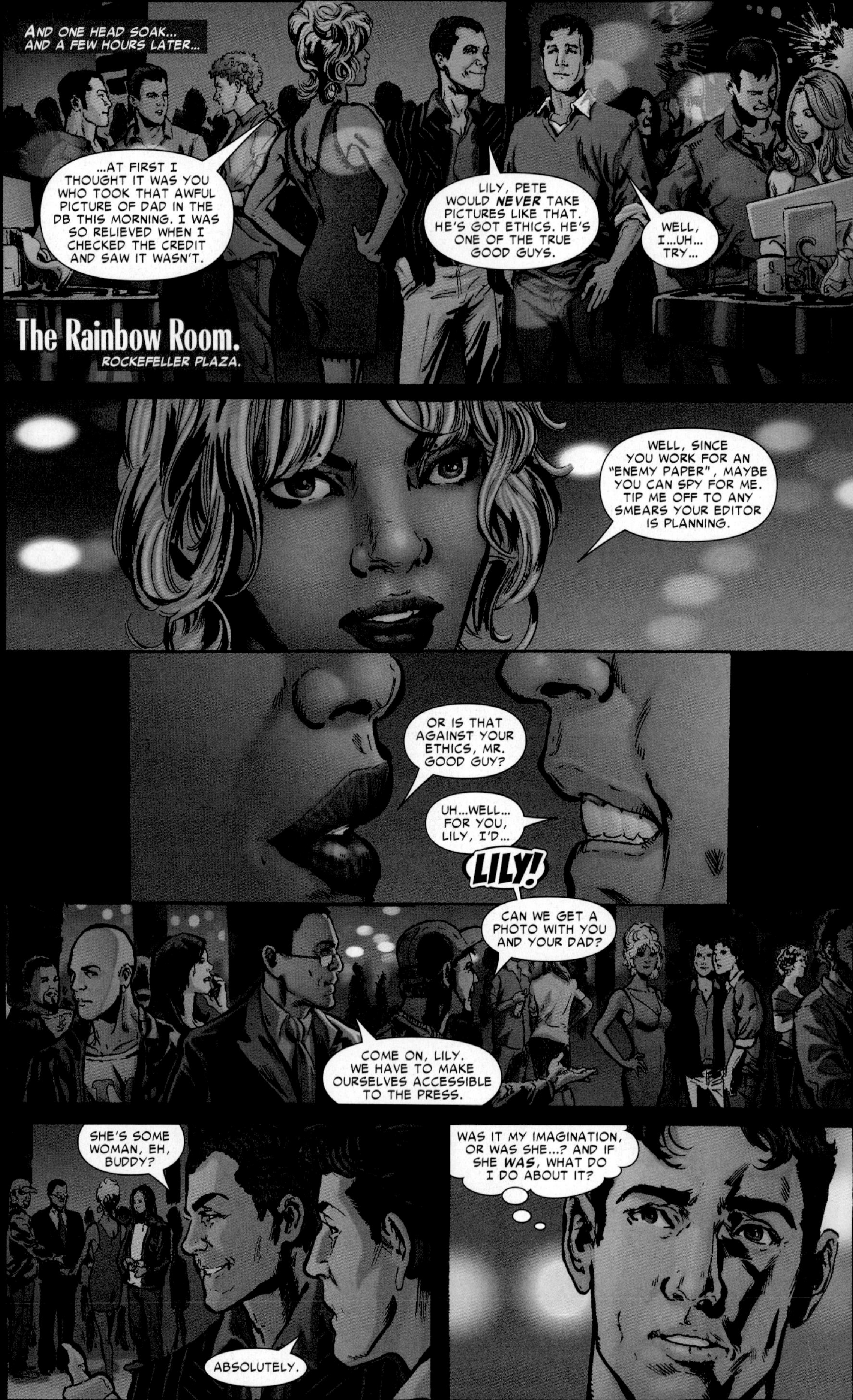
AND ONE HEAD SOAK... AND A FEW HOURS LATER...
...AT FIRST I THOUGHT IT WAS YOU WHO TOOK THAT AWFUL PICTURE OF DAD IN THE DB THIS MORNING. I WAS SO RELIEVED WHEN I CHECKED THE CREDIT AND SAW IT WASN'T.
LILY, PETE WOULD NEVER TAKE PICTURES LIKE THAT. HE'S GOT ETHICS. HE'S ONE OF THE TRUE GOOD GUYS.
WELL, I...UH... TRY...
The Rainbow Room.
ROCKEFELLER PLAZA.
WELL, SINCE YOU WORK FOR AN "ENEMY PAPER", MAYBE YOU CAN SPY FOR ME. TIP ME OFF TO ANY SMEARS YOUR EDITOR IS PLANNING.
OR IS THAT AGAINST YOUR ETHICS, MR. GOOD GUY?
UH...WELL... FOR YOU, LILY, I'D...
LILY!
CAN WE GET A PHOTO WITH YOU AND YOUR DAD?
COME ON, LILY. WE HAVE TO MAKE OURSELVES ACCESSIBLE TO THE PRESS.
SHE'S SOME WOMAN, EH, BUDDY?
ABSOLUTELY.
WAS IT MY IMAGINATION, OR WAS SHE...? AND IF SHE WAS, WHAT DO I DO ABOUT IT?

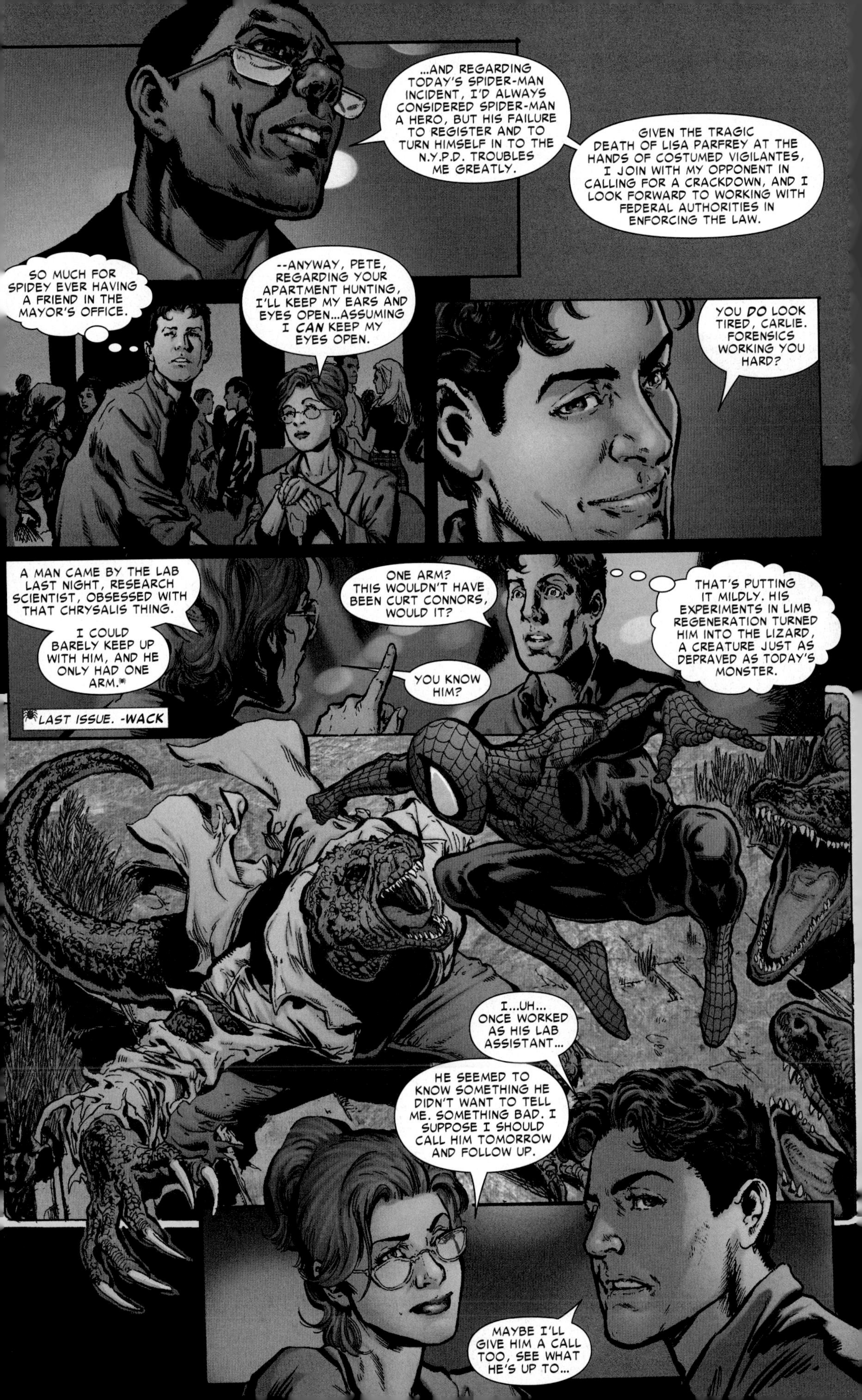
...AND REGARDING TODAY'S SPIDER-MAN INCIDENT, I'D ALWAYS CONSIDERED SPIDER-MAN A HERO, BUT HIS FAILURE TO REGISTER AND TO TURN HIMSELF IN TO THE N.Y.P.D. TROUBLES ME GREATLY.
GIVEN THE TRAGIC DEATH OF LISA PARFREY AT THE HANDS OF COSTUMED VIGILANTES, I JOIN WITH MY OPPONENT IN CALLING FOR A CRACKDOWN, AND I LOOK FORWARD TO WORKING WITH FEDERAL AUTHORITIES IN ENFORCING THE LAW.
SO MUCH FOR SPIDEY EVER HAVING A FRIEND IN THE MAYOR'S OFFICE.
--ANYWAY, PETE, REGARDING YOUR APARTMENT HUNTING, I'LL KEEP MY EARS AND EYES OPEN...ASSUMING I CAN KEEP MY EYES OPEN.
YOU DO LOOK TIRED, CARLIE. FORENSICS WORKING YOU HARD?
A MAN CAME BY THE LAB LAST NIGHT, RESEARCH SCIENTIST, OBSESSED WITH THAT CHRYSALIS THING.
I COULD BARELY KEEP UP WITH HIM, AND HE ONLY HAD ONE ARM.
LAST ISSUE. -WACK
ONE ARM? THIS WOULDN'T HAVE BEEN CURT CONNORS, WOULD IT?
YOU KNOW HIM?
THAT'S PUTTING IT MILDLY. HIS EXPERIMENTS IN LIMB REGENERATION TURNED HIM INTO THE LIZARD, A CREATURE JUST AS DEPRAVED AS TODAY'S MONSTER.
I...UH... ONCE WORKED AS HIS LAB ASSISTANT...
HE SEEMED TO KNOW SOMETHING HE DIDN'T WANT TO TELL ME. SOMETHING BAD. I SUPPOSE I SHOULD CALL HIM TOMORROW AND FOLLOW UP.
MAYBE I'LL GIVE HIM A CALL TOO, SEE WHAT HE'S UP TO...

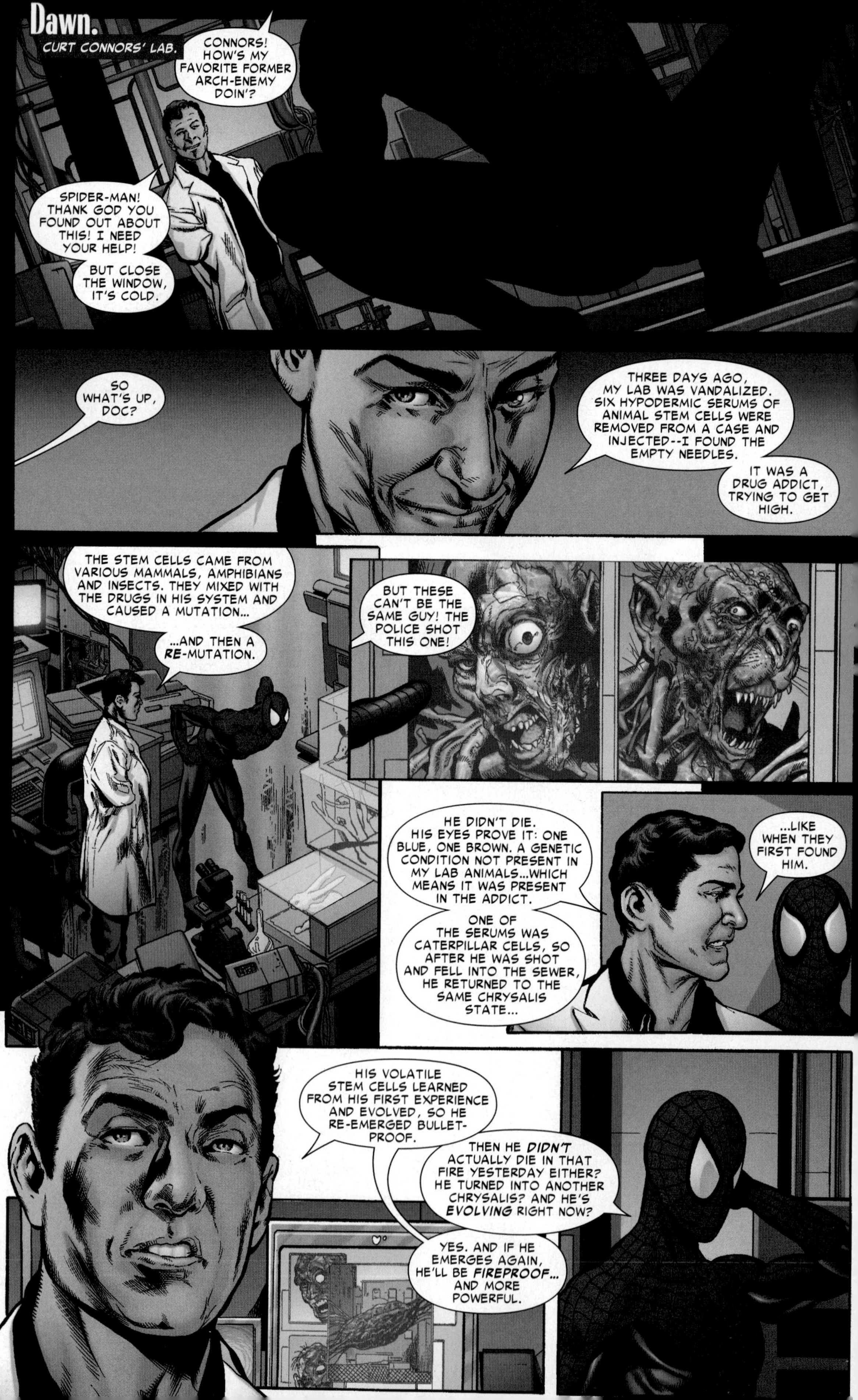
Dawn.
CURT CONNORS' LAB.
CONNORS! HOW'S MY FAVORITE FORMER ARCH-ENEMY DOIN'?
SPIDER-MAN! THANK GOD YOU FOUND OUT ABOUT THIS! I NEED YOUR HELP!
BUT CLOSE THE WINDOW, IT'S COLD.
SO WHAT'S UP, DOC?
THREE DAYS AGO, MY LAB WAS VANDALIZED. SIX HYPODERMIC SERUMS OF ANIMAL STEM CELLS WERE REMOVED FROM A CASE AND INJECTED--I FOUND THE EMPTY NEEDLES.
IT WAS A DRUG ADDICT, TRYING TO GET HIGH.
THE STEM CELLS CAME FROM VARIOUS MAMMALS, AMPHIBIANS AND INSECTS. THEY MIXED WITH THE DRUGS IN HIS SYSTEM AND CAUSED A MUTATION...
...AND THEN A RE-MUTATION.
BUT THESE CAN'T BE THE SAME GUY! THE POLICE SHOT THIS ONE!
HE DIDN'T DIE. HIS EYES PROVE IT: ONE BLUE, ONE BROWN. A GENETIC CONDITION NOT PRESENT IN MY LAB ANIMALS...WHICH MEANS IT WAS PRESENT IN THE ADDICT.
ONE OF THE SERUMS WAS CATERPILLAR CELLS, SO AFTER HE WAS SHOT AND FELL INTO THE SEWER, HE RETURNED TO THE SAME CHRYSALIS STATE...
...LIKE WHEN THEY FIRST FOUND HIM.
HIS VOLATILE STEM CELLS LEARNED FROM HIS FIRST EXPERIENCE AND EVOLVED, SO HE RE-EMERGED BULLET-PROOF.
THEN HE DIDN'T ACTUALLY DIE IN THAT FIRE YESTERDAY EITHER? HE TURNED INTO ANOTHER CHRYSALIS? AND HE'S EVOLVING RIGHT NOW?
YES. AND IF HE EMERGES AGAIN, HE'LL BE FIREPROOF... AND MORE POWERFUL.

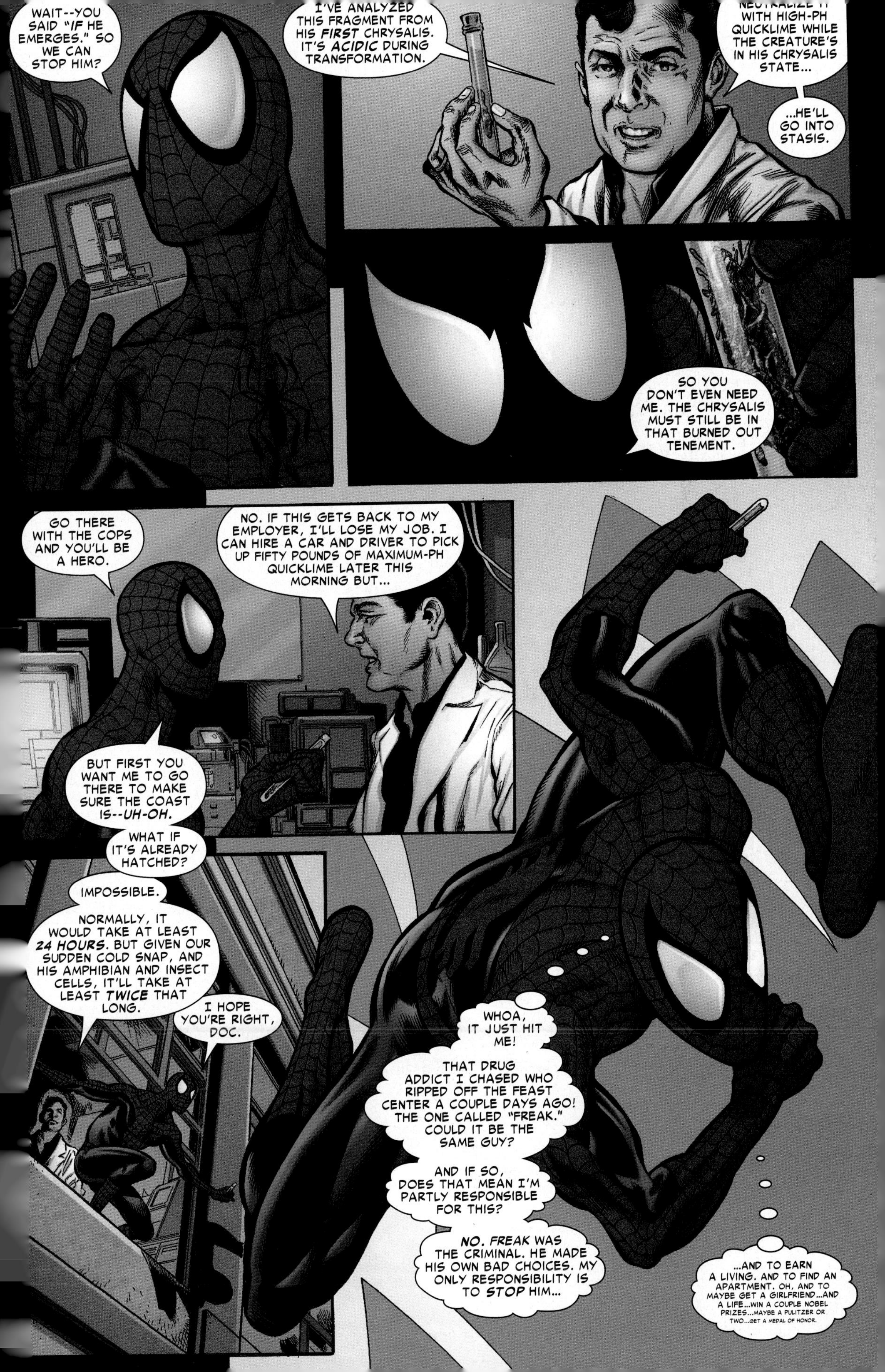
WAIT--YOU SAID "*IF* HE EMERGES." SO WE CAN STOP HIM?
I'VE ANALYZED THIS FRAGMENT FROM HIS *FIRST* CHRYSALIS. IT'S *ACIDIC* DURING TRANSFORMATION.
NEUTRALIZE IT WITH HIGH-PH QUICKLIME WHILE THE CREATURE'S IN HIS CHRYSALIS STATE...
...HE'LL GO INTO STASIS.
SO YOU DON'T EVEN NEED ME. THE CHRYSALIS MUST STILL BE IN THAT BURNED OUT TENEMENT.
GO THERE WITH THE COPS AND YOU'LL BE A HERO.
NO. IF THIS GETS BACK TO MY EMPLOYER, I'LL LOSE MY JOB. I CAN HIRE A CAR AND DRIVER TO PICK UP FIFTY POUNDS OF MAXIMUM-PH QUICKLIME LATER THIS MORNING BUT...
BUT FIRST YOU WANT ME TO GO THERE TO MAKE SURE THE COAST IS--*UH-OH.*
WHAT IF IT'S ALREADY HATCHED?
IMPOSSIBLE.
NORMALLY, IT WOULD TAKE AT LEAST **24 HOURS**. BUT GIVEN OUR SUDDEN COLD SNAP, AND HIS AMPHIBIAN AND INSECT CELLS, IT'LL TAKE AT LEAST *TWICE* THAT LONG.
I HOPE YOU'RE RIGHT, DOC.
WHOA, IT JUST HIT ME!
THAT DRUG ADDICT I CHASED WHO RIPPED OFF THE FEAST CENTER A COUPLE DAYS AGO! THE ONE CALLED "FREAK." COULD IT BE THE SAME GUY?
AND IF SO, DOES THAT MEAN I'M PARTLY RESPONSIBLE FOR THIS?
NO. FREAK WAS THE CRIMINAL. HE MADE HIS OWN BAD CHOICES. MY ONLY RESPONSIBILITY IS TO *STOP* HIM...
...AND TO EARN A LIVING. AND TO FIND AN APARTMENT. OH, AND TO MAYBE GET A GIRLFRIEND...AND A LIFE...WIN A COUPLE NOBEL PRIZES...MAYBE A PULITZER OR TWO...GET A MEDAL OF HONOR.

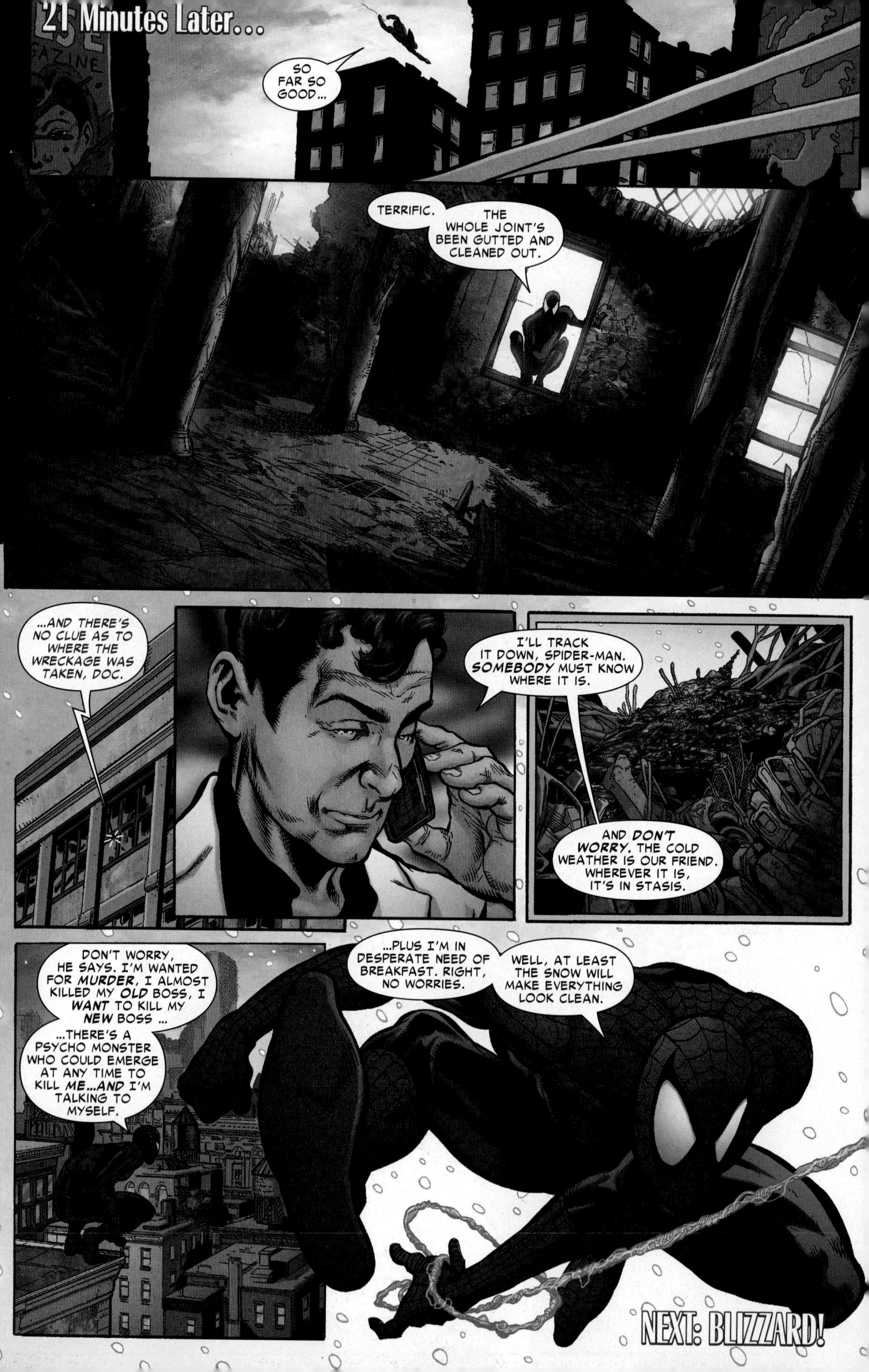
21 Minutes Later...
SO FAR SO GOOD...
TERRIFIC.
THE WHOLE JOINT'S BEEN GUTTED AND CLEANED OUT.
...AND THERE'S NO CLUE AS TO WHERE THE WRECKAGE WAS TAKEN, DOC.
I'LL TRACK IT DOWN, SPIDER-MAN. SOMEBODY MUST KNOW WHERE IT IS.
AND DON'T WORRY. THE COLD WEATHER IS OUR FRIEND. WHEREVER IT IS, IT'S IN STASIS.
DON'T WORRY, HE SAYS. I'M WANTED FOR MURDER, I ALMOST KILLED MY OLD BOSS, I WANT TO KILL MY NEW BOSS ...
...THERE'S A PSYCHO MONSTER WHO COULD EMERGE AT ANY TIME TO KILL ME...AND I'M TALKING TO MYSELF.
...PLUS I'M IN DESPERATE NEED OF BREAKFAST. RIGHT, NO WORRIES.
WELL, AT LEAST THE SNOW WILL MAKE EVERYTHING LOOK CLEAN.
NEXT: BLIZZARD!

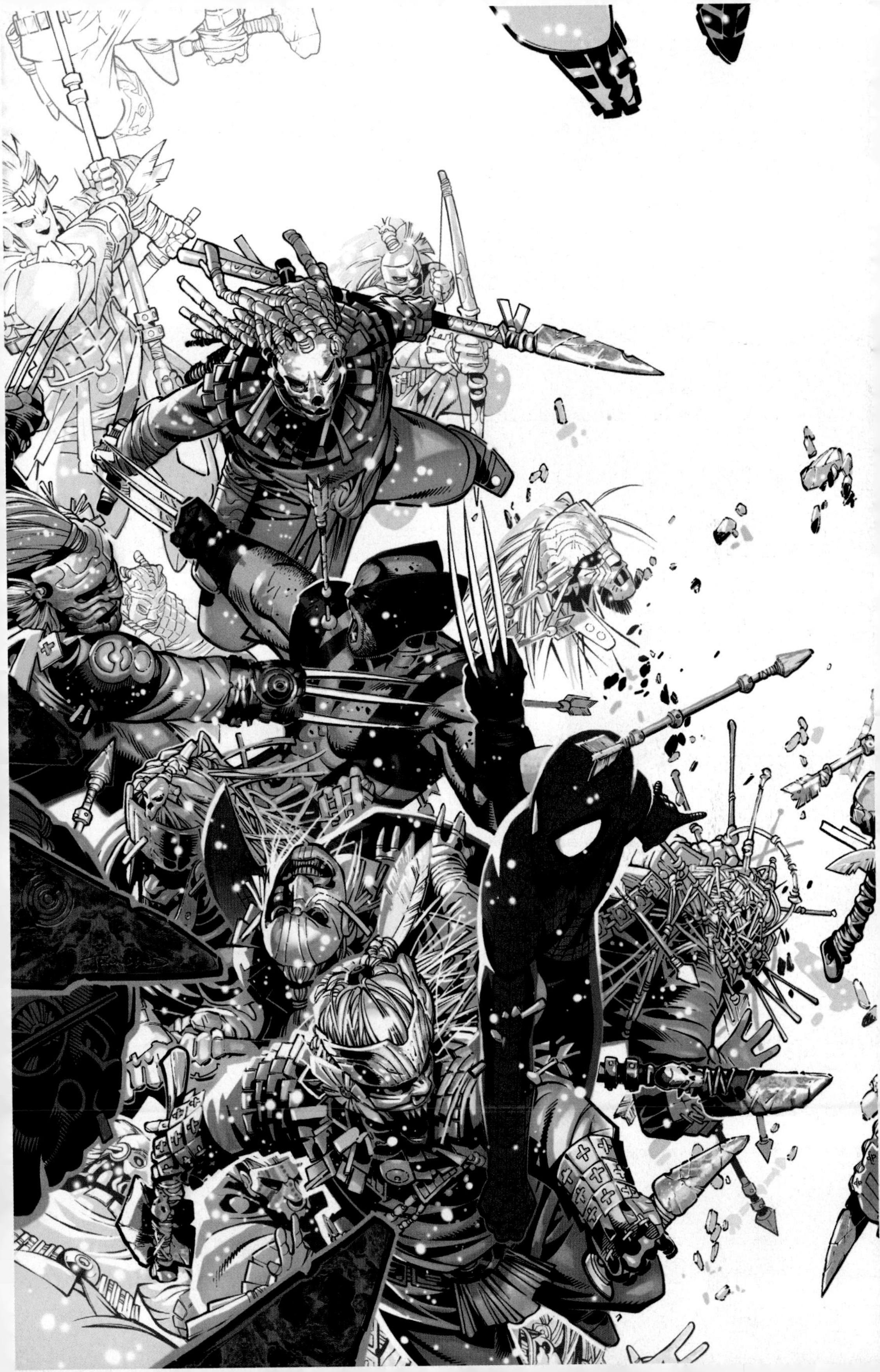

I SHOULD HAVE JUST LEFT...

THUNK! THUNK! THUNK!

THUNK!

BUT AUNT MAY DOESN'T BUY THE *FUN* CEREAL, AND A FREE BREAKFAST IS A FREE BREAKFAST.

WHIT

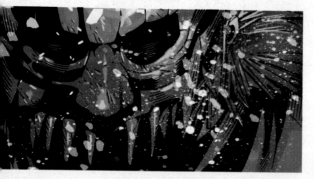

BUT, OBVIOUSLY, I SHOULD HAVE JUST LEFT.

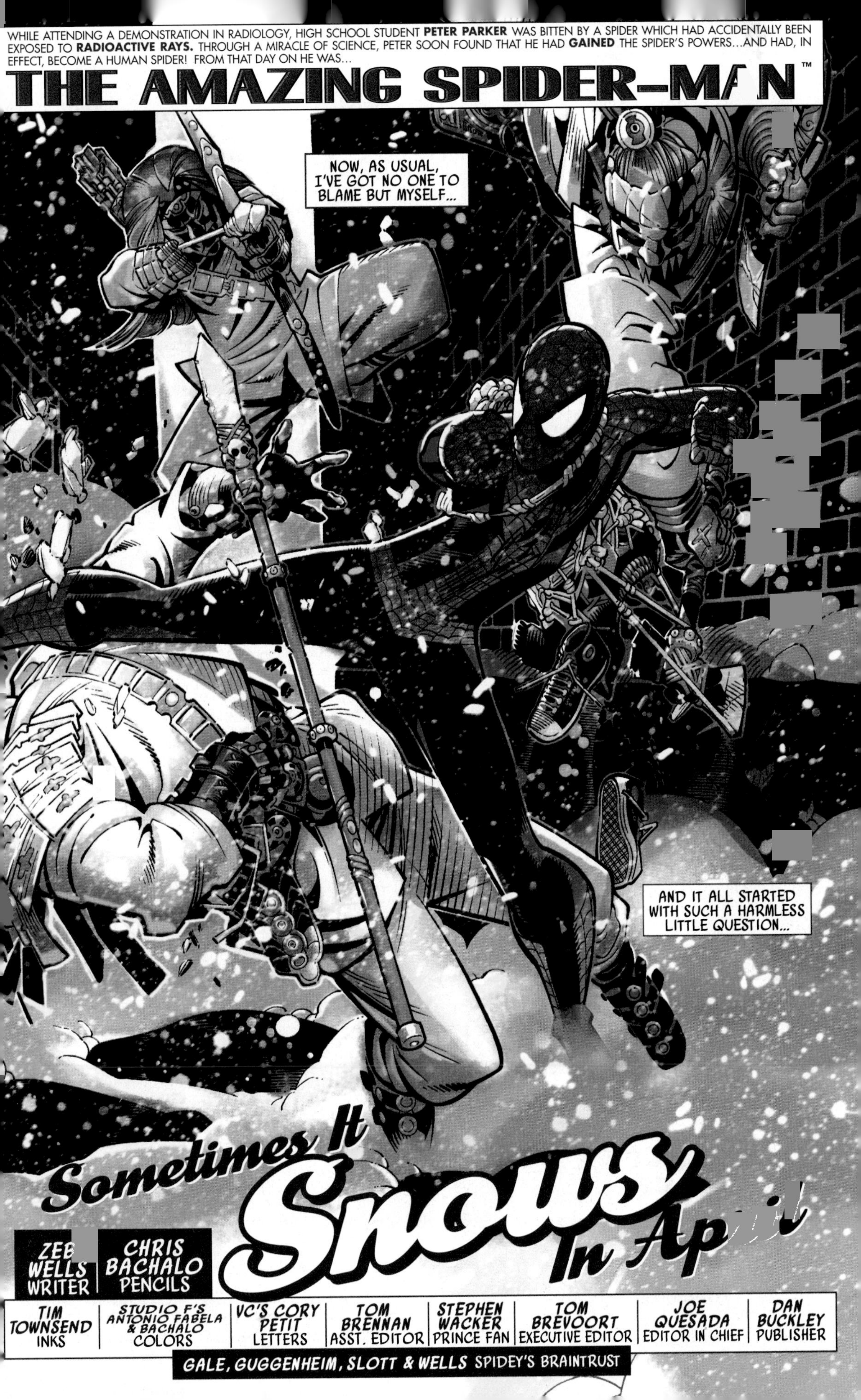
WHILE ATTENDING A DEMONSTRATION IN RADIOLOGY, HIGH SCHOOL STUDENT PETER PARKER WAS BITTEN BY A SPIDER WHICH HAD ACCIDENTALLY BEEN EXPOSED TO RADIOACTIVE RAYS. THROUGH A MIRACLE OF SCIENCE, PETER SOON FOUND THAT HE HAD GAINED THE SPIDER'S POWERS...AND HAD, IN EFFECT, BECOME A HUMAN SPIDER! FROM THAT DAY ON HE WAS...
THE AMAZING SPIDER-MAN™
NOW, AS USUAL, I'VE GOT NO ONE TO BLAME BUT MYSELF...
AND IT ALL STARTED WITH SUCH A HARMLESS LITTLE QUESTION...
Sometimes It Snows In Ap il
ZEB WELLS WRITER
CHRIS BACHALO PENCILS
TIM TOWNSEND INKS
STUDIO F'S ANTONIO FABELA & BACHALO COLORS
VC'S CORY PETIT LETTERS
TOM BRENNAN ASST. EDITOR
STEPHEN WACKER PRINCE FAN
TOM BREVOORT EXECUTIVE EDITOR
JOE QUESADA EDITOR IN CHIEF
DAN BUCKLEY PUBLISHER
GALE, GUGGENHEIM, SLOTT & WELLS SPIDEY'S BRAINTRUST

HEY, WOLVERINE... IS THIS YOUR *FRUIT LOOT?*

GLUB GLUB

DIDN'T THINK SO.

THINK ANYONE WOULD MISS A BOWL?

DON'T KNOW.

THINK ANYONE WOULD MISS THE PRIZE?

I AIN'T RATTIN' ON YA. IT LOOKS LIKE YOU'VE GOT BIGGER PROBLEMS THAN THAT.

FRUIT LOOT

WHAT DO YOU MEAN?

THERE SOMETHIN' YOU WANNA TELL YOUR *"TEAMMATE,"* BIG GUY?

THE OFFICIAL NEWSPAPER O

DB

SPIDE KILLER

HEY, LISTEN. YOU DON'T THINK--

I MEAN, I'D NEVER--

RELAX. I KNOW YOU'RE NOT A KILLER.

YOU DON'T HAVE IT IN YOU.

YOU SAY THAT LIKE IT'S A BAD THING.

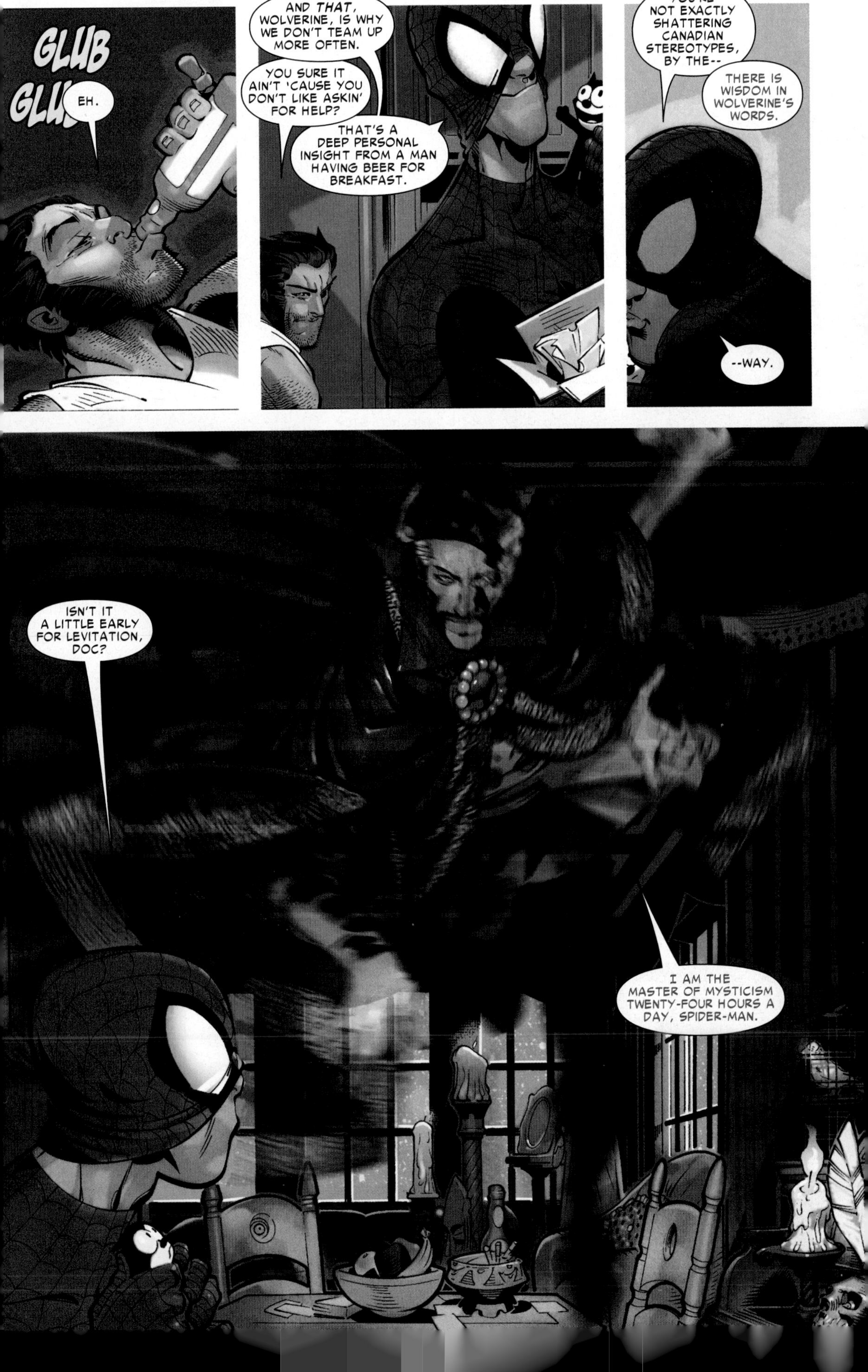
GLUB GLUB
EH.
AND THAT, WOLVERINE, IS WHY WE DON'T TEAM UP MORE OFTEN.
YOU SURE IT AIN'T 'CAUSE YOU DON'T LIKE ASKIN' FOR HELP?
THAT'S A DEEP PERSONAL INSIGHT FROM A MAN HAVING BEER FOR BREAKFAST.
YOU'RE NOT EXACTLY SHATTERING CANADIAN STEREOTYPES, BY THE--
THERE IS WISDOM IN WOLVERINE'S WORDS.
--WAY.
ISN'T IT A LITTLE EARLY FOR LEVITATION, DOC?
I AM THE MASTER OF MYSTICISM TWENTY-FOUR HOURS A DAY, SPIDER-MAN.

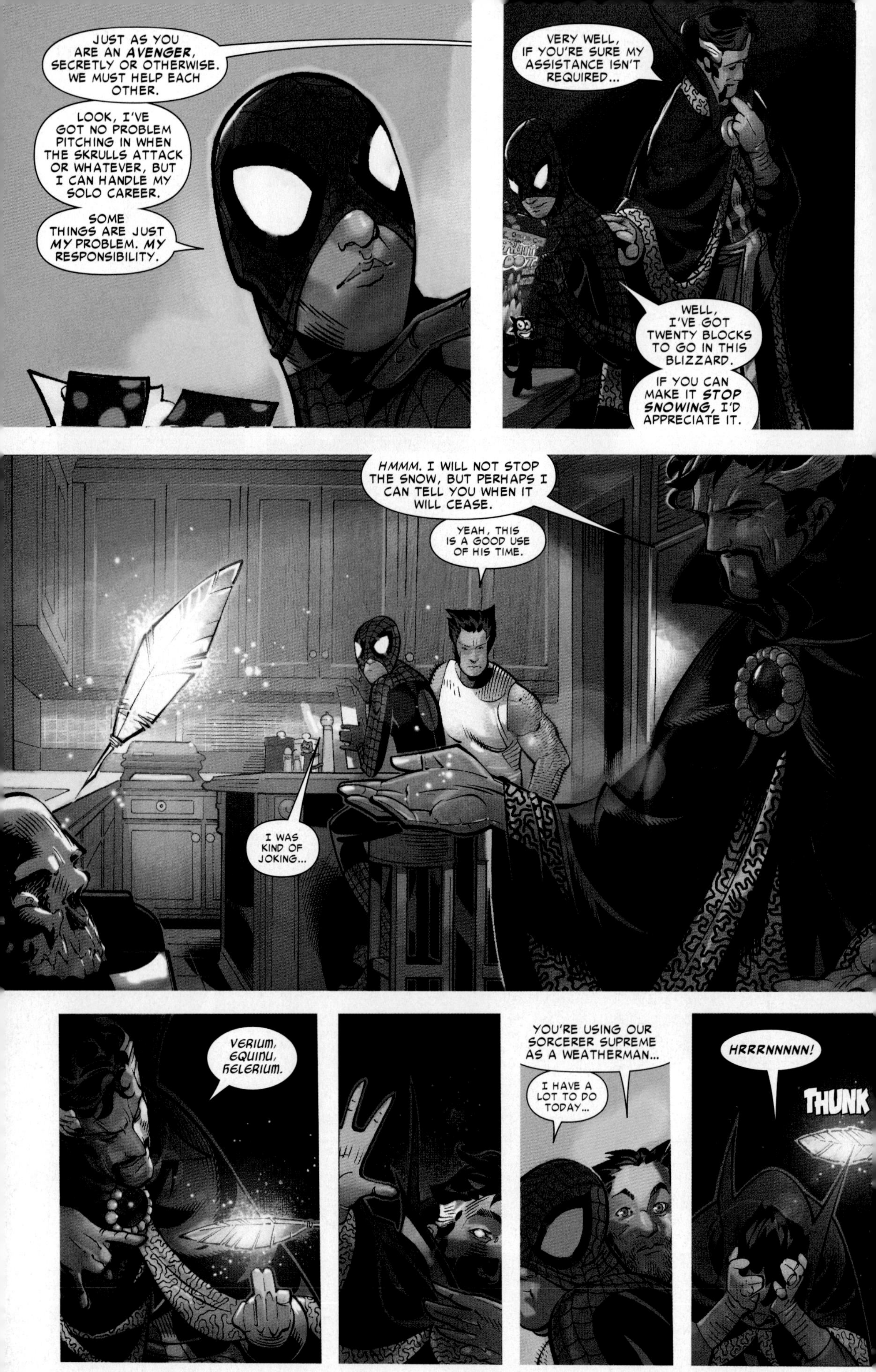
JUST AS YOU ARE AN AVENGER, SECRETLY OR OTHERWISE. WE MUST HELP EACH OTHER.
LOOK, I'VE GOT NO PROBLEM PITCHING IN WHEN THE SKRULLS ATTACK OR WHATEVER, BUT I CAN HANDLE MY SOLO CAREER.
SOME THINGS ARE JUST MY PROBLEM. MY RESPONSIBILITY.
VERY WELL, IF YOU'RE SURE MY ASSISTANCE ISN'T REQUIRED...
WELL, I'VE GOT TWENTY BLOCKS TO GO IN THIS BLIZZARD.
IF YOU CAN MAKE IT STOP SNOWING, I'D APPRECIATE IT.
HMMM. I WILL NOT STOP THE SNOW, BUT PERHAPS I CAN TELL YOU WHEN IT WILL CEASE.
YEAH, THIS IS A GOOD USE OF HIS TIME.
I WAS KIND OF JOKING...
VERIUM, EQUINU, FELERIUM.
YOU'RE USING OUR SORCERER SUPREME AS A WEATHERMAN...
I HAVE A LOT TO DO TODAY...
HRRRNNNNN!
THUNK

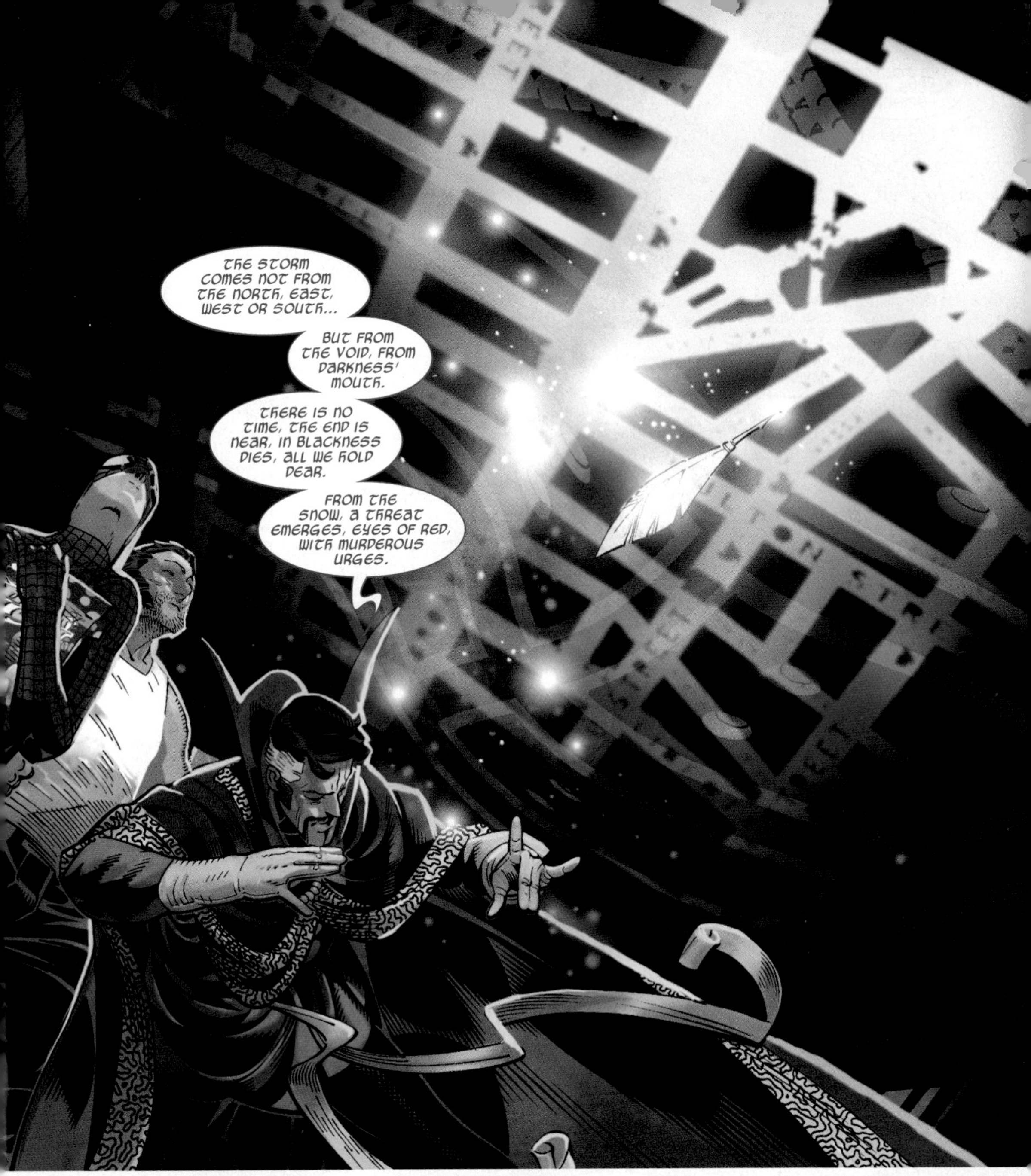
THE STORM COMES NOT FROM THE NORTH, EAST, WEST OR SOUTH...
BUT FROM THE VOID, FROM DARKNESS' MOUTH.
THERE IS NO TIME, THE END IS NEAR, IN BLACKNESS DIES, ALL WE HOLD DEAR.
FROM THE SNOW, A THREAT EMERGES, EYES OF RED, WITH MURDEROUS URGES.

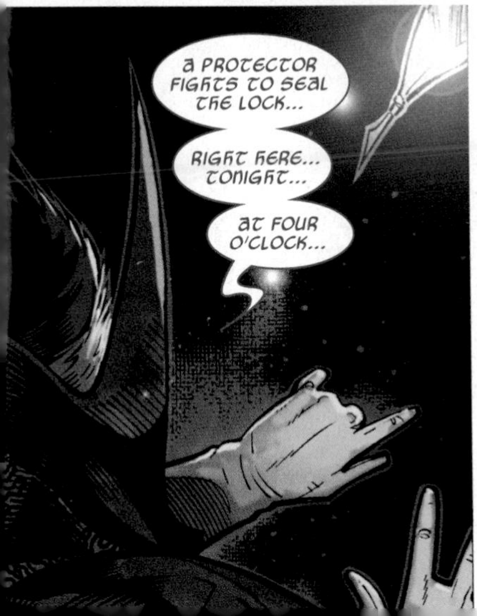
A PROTECTOR FIGHTS TO SEAL THE LOCK...
RIGHT HERE... TONIGHT...
AT FOUR O'CLOCK...

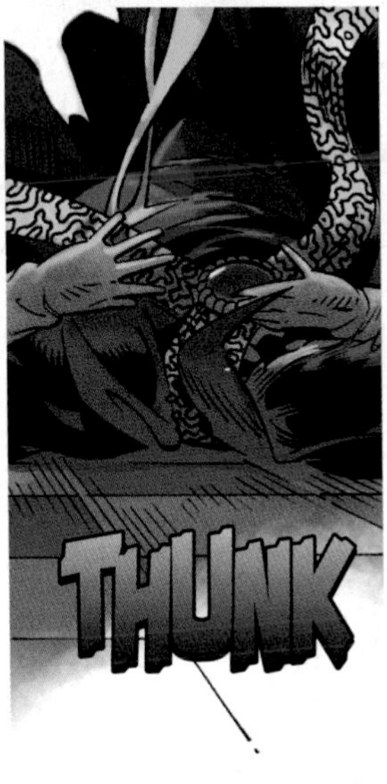
THUNK

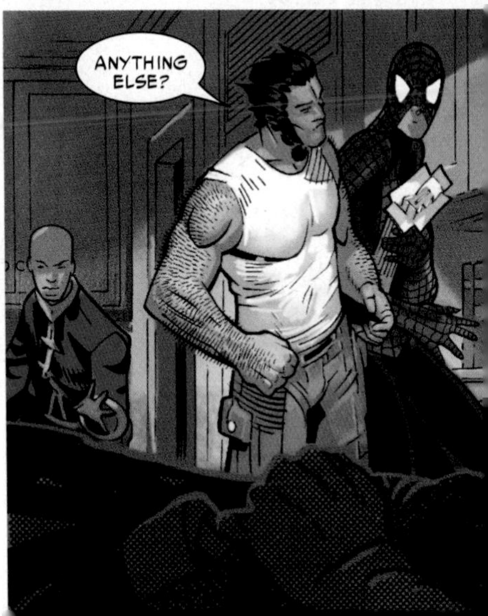
ANYTHING ELSE?

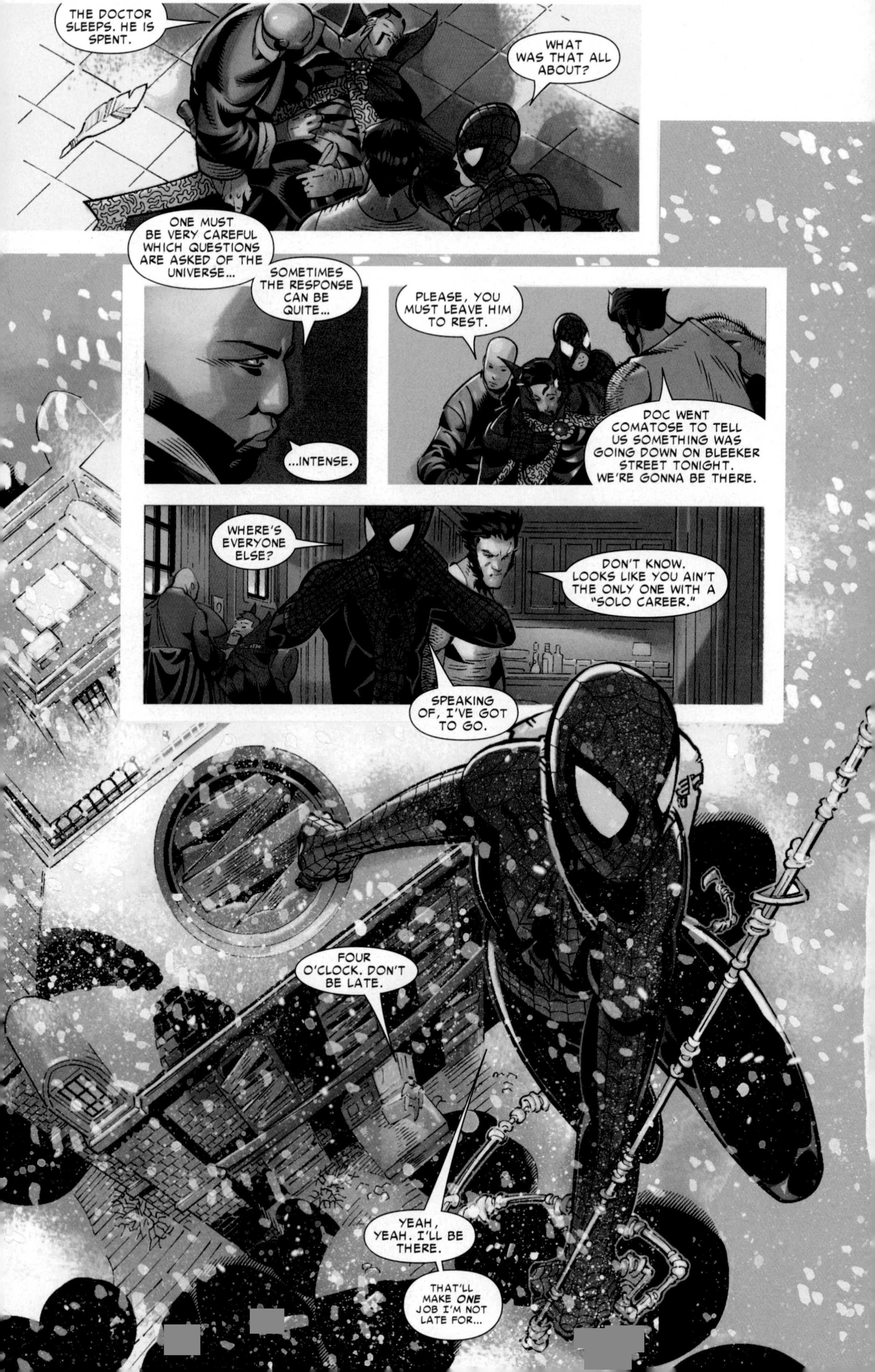
THE DOCTOR SLEEPS. HE IS SPENT.
WHAT WAS THAT ALL ABOUT?
ONE MUST BE VERY CAREFUL WHICH QUESTIONS ARE ASKED OF THE UNIVERSE...
SOMETIMES THE RESPONSE CAN BE QUITE...
...INTENSE.
PLEASE, YOU MUST LEAVE HIM TO REST.
DOC WENT COMATOSE TO TELL US SOMETHING WAS GOING DOWN ON BLEEKER STREET TONIGHT. WE'RE GONNA BE THERE.
WHERE'S EVERYONE ELSE?
DON'T KNOW. LOOKS LIKE YOU AIN'T THE ONLY ONE WITH A "SOLO CAREER."
SPEAKING OF, I'VE GOT TO GO.
FOUR O'CLOCK. DON'T BE LATE.
YEAH, YEAH. I'LL BE THERE.
THAT'LL MAKE *ONE* JOB I'M NOT LATE FOR...

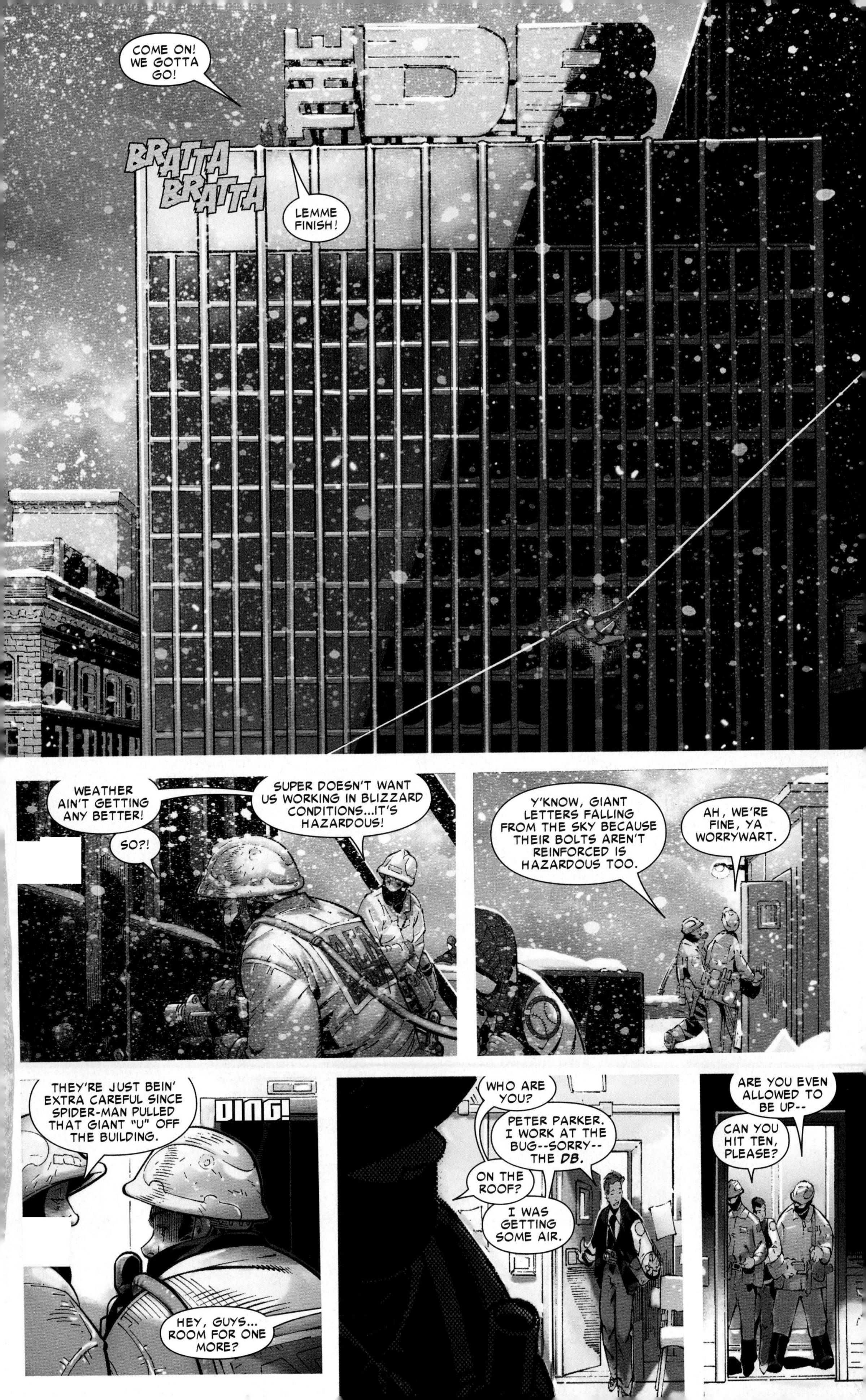
COME ON! WE GOTTA GO!
THE DB
BRATTA BRATTA
LEMME FINISH!
WEATHER AIN'T GETTING ANY BETTER!
SUPER DOESN'T WANT US WORKING IN BLIZZARD CONDITIONS...IT'S HAZARDOUS!
SO?!
Y'KNOW, GIANT LETTERS FALLING FROM THE SKY BECAUSE THEIR BOLTS AREN'T REINFORCED IS HAZARDOUS TOO.
AH, WE'RE FINE, YA WORRYWART.
THEY'RE JUST BEIN' EXTRA CAREFUL SINCE SPIDER-MAN PULLED THAT GIANT "U" OFF THE BUILDING.
DING!
HEY, GUYS... ROOM FOR ONE MORE?
WHO ARE YOU?
PETER PARKER. I WORK AT THE BUG--SORRY-- THE DB.
ON THE ROOF?
I WAS GETTING SOME AIR.
ARE YOU EVEN ALLOWED TO BE UP--
CAN YOU HIT TEN, PLEASE?

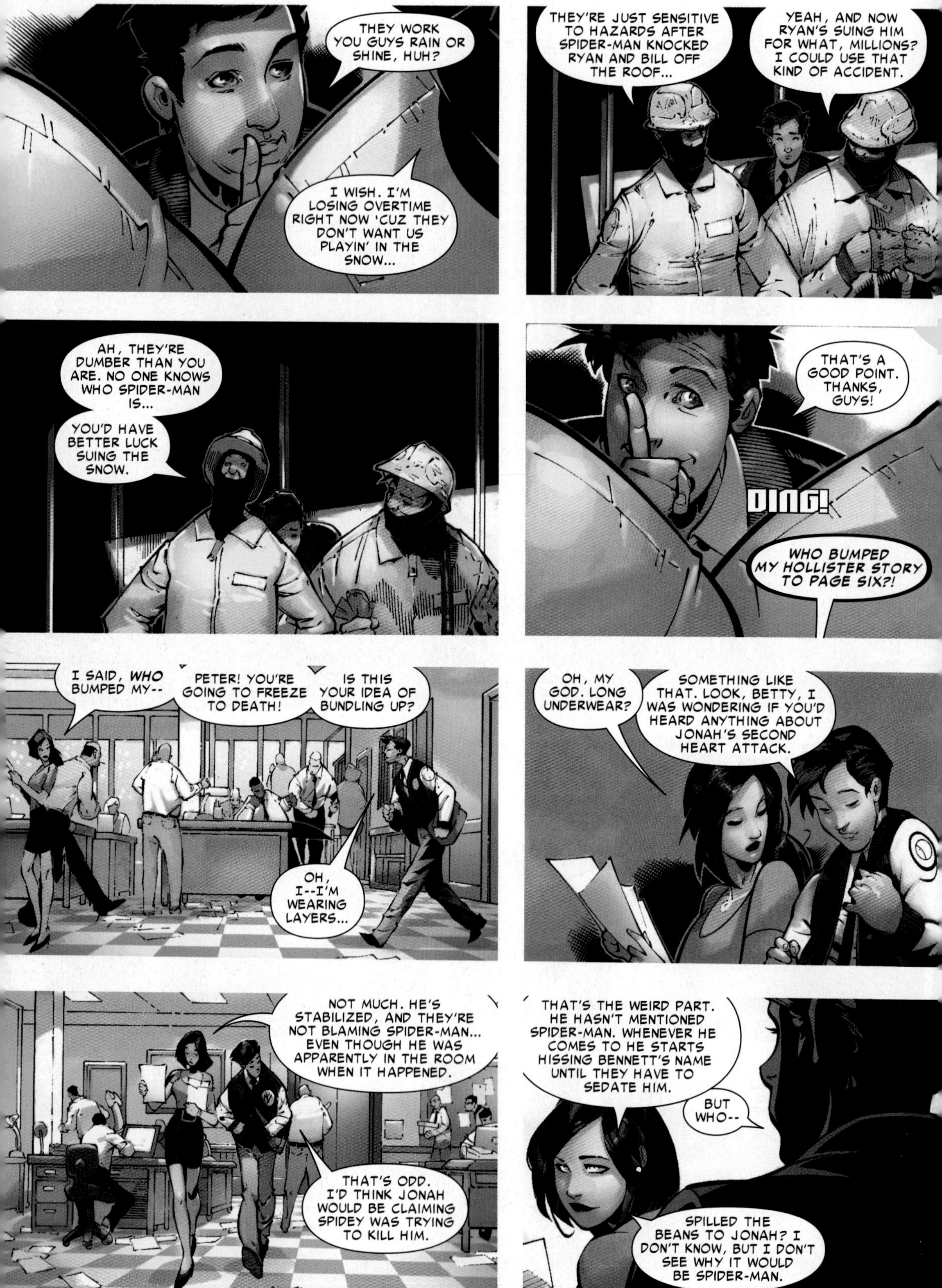
THEY WORK YOU GUYS RAIN OR SHINE, HUH?
I WISH. I'M LOSING OVERTIME RIGHT NOW 'CUZ THEY DON'T WANT US PLAYIN' IN THE SNOW...
THEY'RE JUST SENSITIVE TO HAZARDS AFTER SPIDER-MAN KNOCKED RYAN AND BILL OFF THE ROOF...
YEAH, AND NOW RYAN'S SUING HIM FOR WHAT, MILLIONS? I COULD USE THAT KIND OF ACCIDENT.
AH, THEY'RE DUMBER THAN YOU ARE. NO ONE KNOWS WHO SPIDER-MAN IS...
YOU'D HAVE BETTER LUCK SUING THE SNOW.
THAT'S A GOOD POINT. THANKS, GUYS!
DING!
WHO BUMPED MY HOLLISTER STORY TO PAGE SIX?!
I SAID, WHO BUMPED MY--
PETER! YOU'RE GOING TO FREEZE TO DEATH!
IS THIS YOUR IDEA OF BUNDLING UP?
OH, I--I'M WEARING LAYERS...
OH, MY GOD. LONG UNDERWEAR?
SOMETHING LIKE THAT. LOOK, BETTY, I WAS WONDERING IF YOU'D HEARD ANYTHING ABOUT JONAH'S SECOND HEART ATTACK.
NOT MUCH. HE'S STABILIZED, AND THEY'RE NOT BLAMING SPIDER-MAN... EVEN THOUGH HE WAS APPARENTLY IN THE ROOM WHEN IT HAPPENED.
THAT'S ODD. I'D THINK JONAH WOULD BE CLAIMING SPIDEY WAS TRYING TO KILL HIM.
THAT'S THE WEIRD PART. HE HASN'T MENTIONED SPIDER-MAN. WHENEVER HE COMES TO HE STARTS HISSING BENNETT'S NAME UNTIL THEY HAVE TO SEDATE HIM.
BUT WHO--
SPILLED THE BEANS TO JONAH? I DON'T KNOW, BUT I DON'T SEE WHY IT WOULD BE SPIDER-MAN.

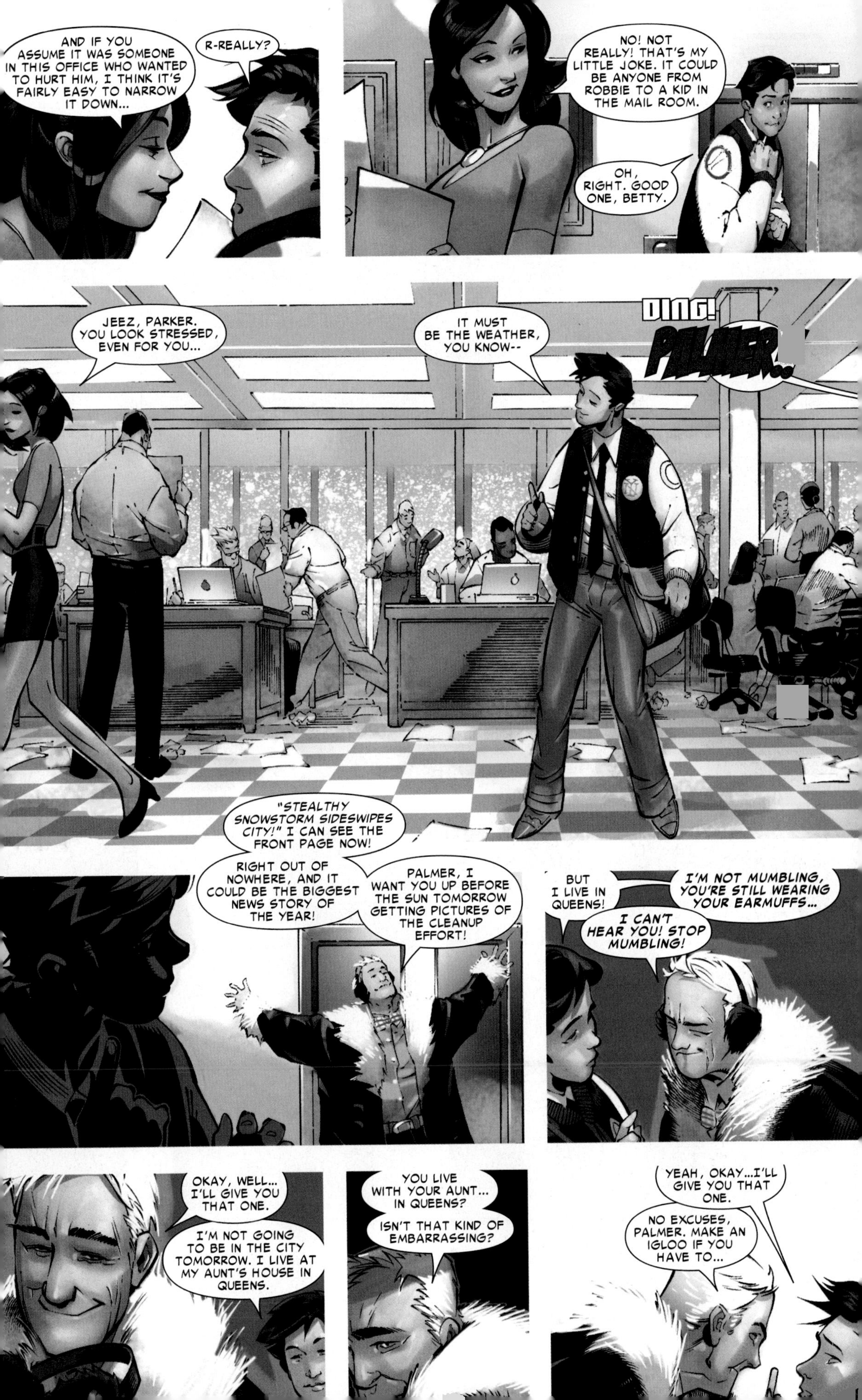
AND IF YOU ASSUME IT WAS SOMEONE IN THIS OFFICE WHO WANTED TO HURT HIM, I THINK IT'S FAIRLY EASY TO NARROW IT DOWN...
R-REALLY?
NO! NOT REALLY! THAT'S MY LITTLE JOKE. IT COULD BE ANYONE FROM ROBBIE TO A KID IN THE MAIL ROOM.
OH, RIGHT. GOOD ONE, BETTY.
JEEZ, PARKER. YOU LOOK STRESSED, EVEN FOR YOU...
IT MUST BE THE WEATHER, YOU KNOW--
DING!
PALMER...
"STEALTHY SNOWSTORM SIDESWIPES CITY!" I CAN SEE THE FRONT PAGE NOW!
RIGHT OUT OF NOWHERE, AND IT COULD BE THE BIGGEST NEWS STORY OF THE YEAR!
PALMER, I WANT YOU UP BEFORE THE SUN TOMORROW GETTING PICTURES OF THE CLEANUP EFFORT!
BUT I LIVE IN QUEENS!
I CAN'T HEAR YOU! STOP MUMBLING!
I'M NOT MUMBLING, YOU'RE STILL WEARING YOUR EARMUFFS...
OKAY, WELL... I'LL GIVE YOU THAT ONE.
I'M NOT GOING TO BE IN THE CITY TOMORROW. I LIVE AT MY AUNT'S HOUSE IN QUEENS.
YOU LIVE WITH YOUR AUNT... IN QUEENS?
ISN'T THAT KIND OF EMBARRASSING?
YEAH, OKAY...I'LL GIVE YOU THAT ONE.
NO EXCUSES, PALMER. MAKE AN IGLOO IF YOU HAVE TO...

"...JUST GET OUT THERE AND DO YOUR JOB!"

STUPID DEXTER BENNETT... EASY FOR YOU TO SAY...

COME ON, WOLVERINE! WHERE ARE YOU...?

I DON'T EVEN KNOW WHAT I'M LOOKING FOR.

JEEZ, MAYBE I SHOULDN'T HAVE WEBBED UP MY JACKET WITH THE REST OF MY CIVIES...

B-BUT I REMEMBER HOW RIDICULOUS A BLUE HOODY LOOKS OVER THIS COSTUME, I DOUBT A YANKEES JACKET WOULD BE MUCH BETTER--

WAIT A MINUTE.

HEY, BUDDY! YOU'RE NOT RUNNING FROM A THREAT WITH RED EYES AND "MURDEROUS URGES," ARE YOU?

⸗HUFF⸗

⸗HUFF⸗

⸗HUFF⸗

NO! PLEASE!

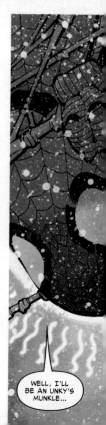

WELL, I'LL BE AN UNKY'S MUNKLE...

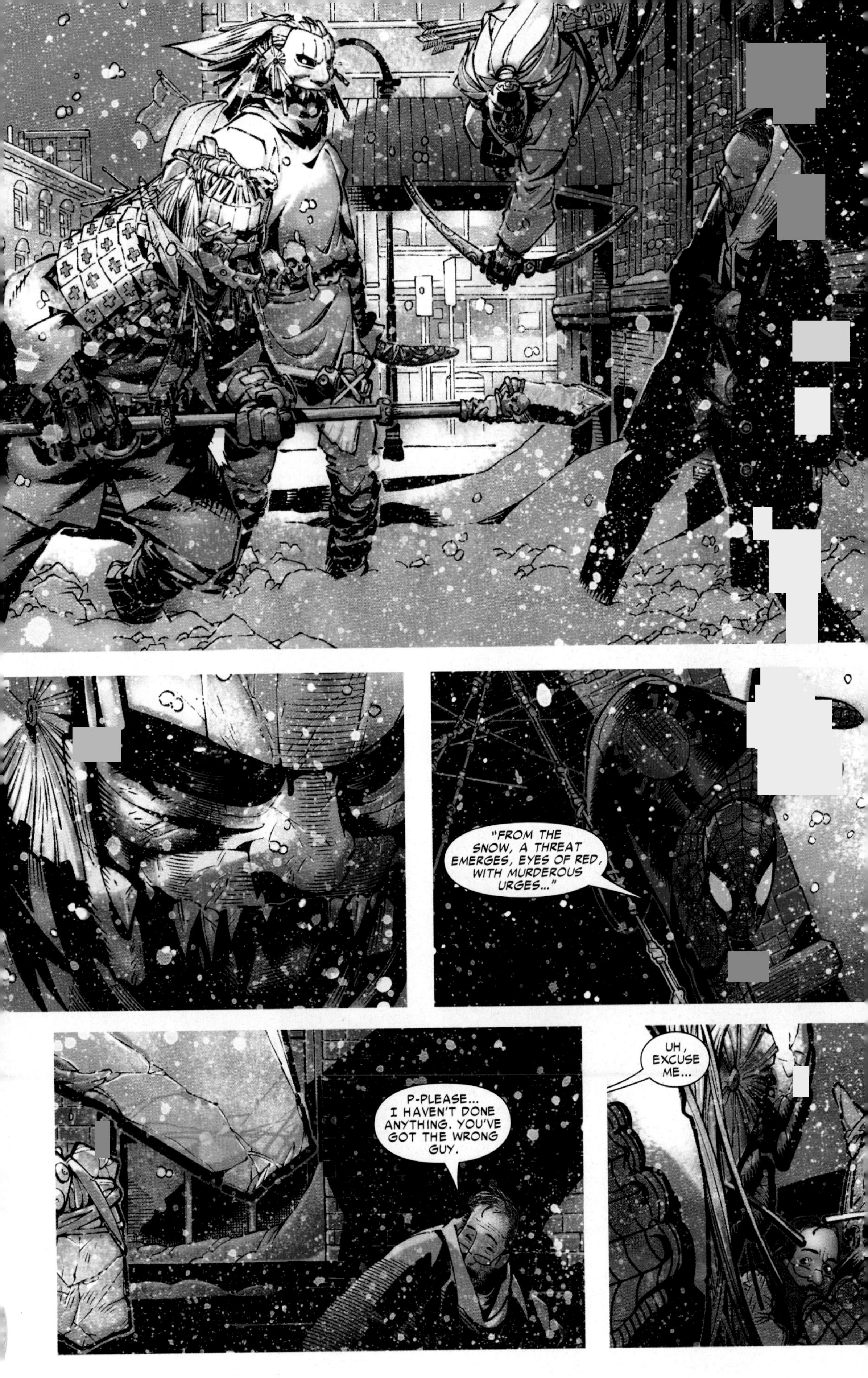
"FROM THE SNOW, A THREAT EMERGES, EYES OF RED, WITH MURDEROUS URGES..."
P-PLEASE... I HAVEN'T DONE ANYTHING. YOU'VE GOT THE WRONG GUY.
UH, EXCUSE ME...

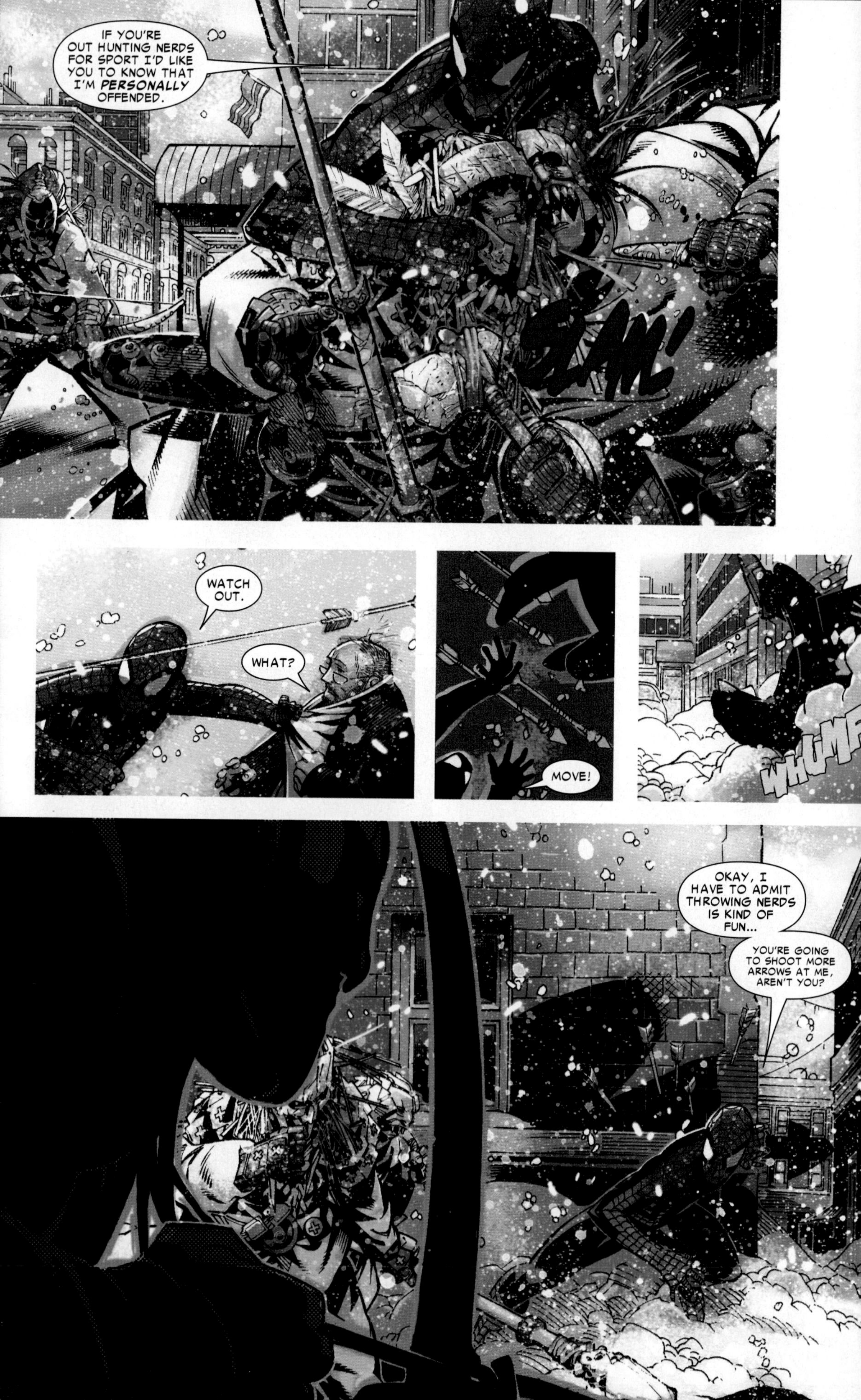
IF YOU'RE OUT HUNTING NERDS FOR SPORT I'D LIKE YOU TO KNOW THAT I'M *PERSONALLY* OFFENDED.
WATCH OUT.
WHAT?
MOVE!
OKAY, I HAVE TO ADMIT THROWING NERDS IS KIND OF FUN...
YOU'RE GOING TO SHOOT MORE ARROWS AT ME, AREN'T YOU?

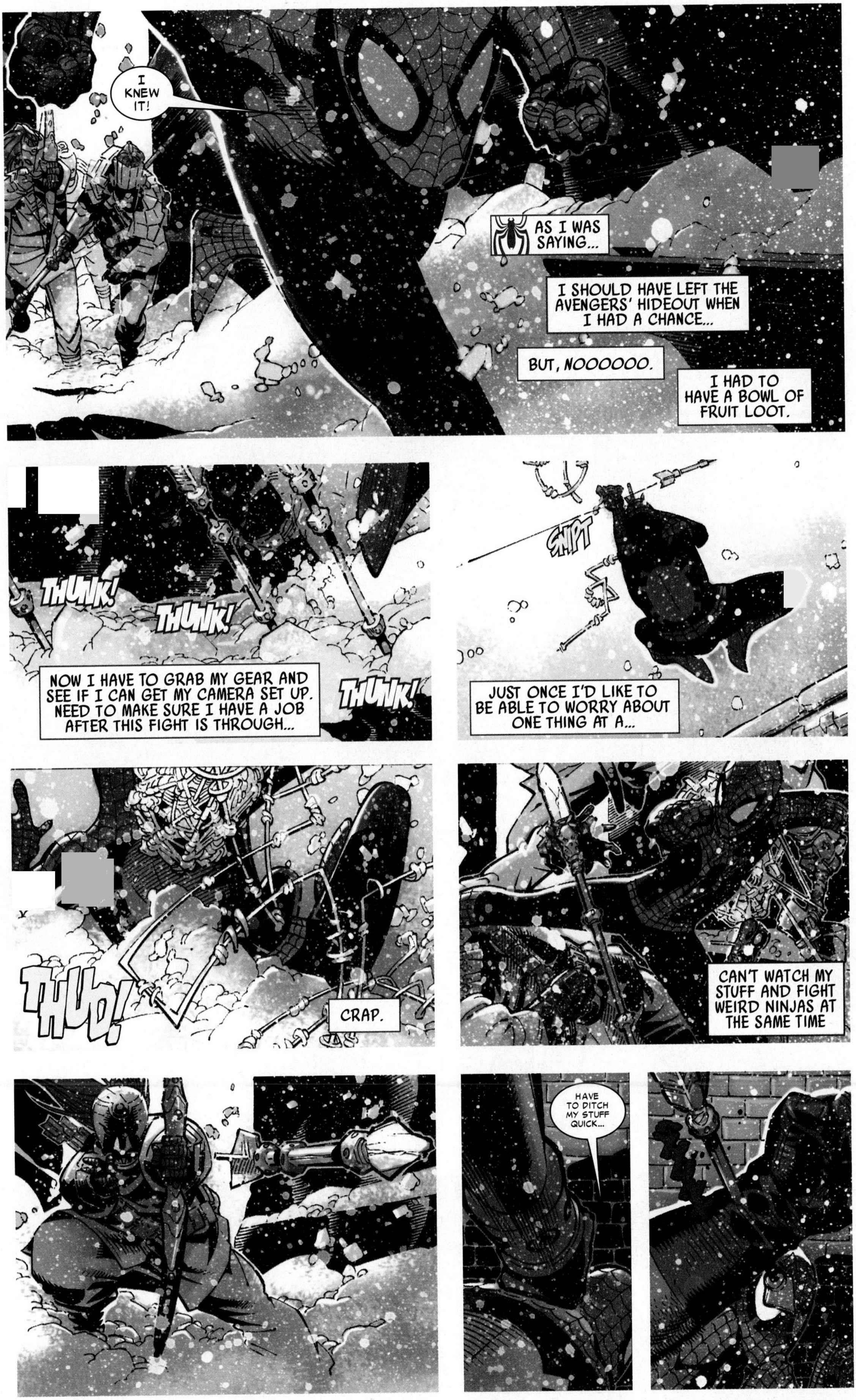
I KNEW IT!
AS I WAS SAYING...
I SHOULD HAVE LEFT THE AVENGERS' HIDEOUT WHEN I HAD A CHANCE...
BUT, NOOOOOO.
I HAD TO HAVE A BOWL OF FRUIT LOOT.
THUNK!
THUNK!
NOW I HAVE TO GRAB MY GEAR AND SEE IF I CAN GET MY CAMERA SET UP. NEED TO MAKE SURE I HAVE A JOB AFTER THIS FIGHT IS THROUGH...
THUNK!
SNIPT
JUST ONCE I'D LIKE TO BE ABLE TO WORRY ABOUT ONE THING AT A...
THUD!
CRAP.
CAN'T WATCH MY STUFF AND FIGHT WEIRD NINJAS AT THE SAME TIME
HAVE TO DITCH MY STUFF QUICK...

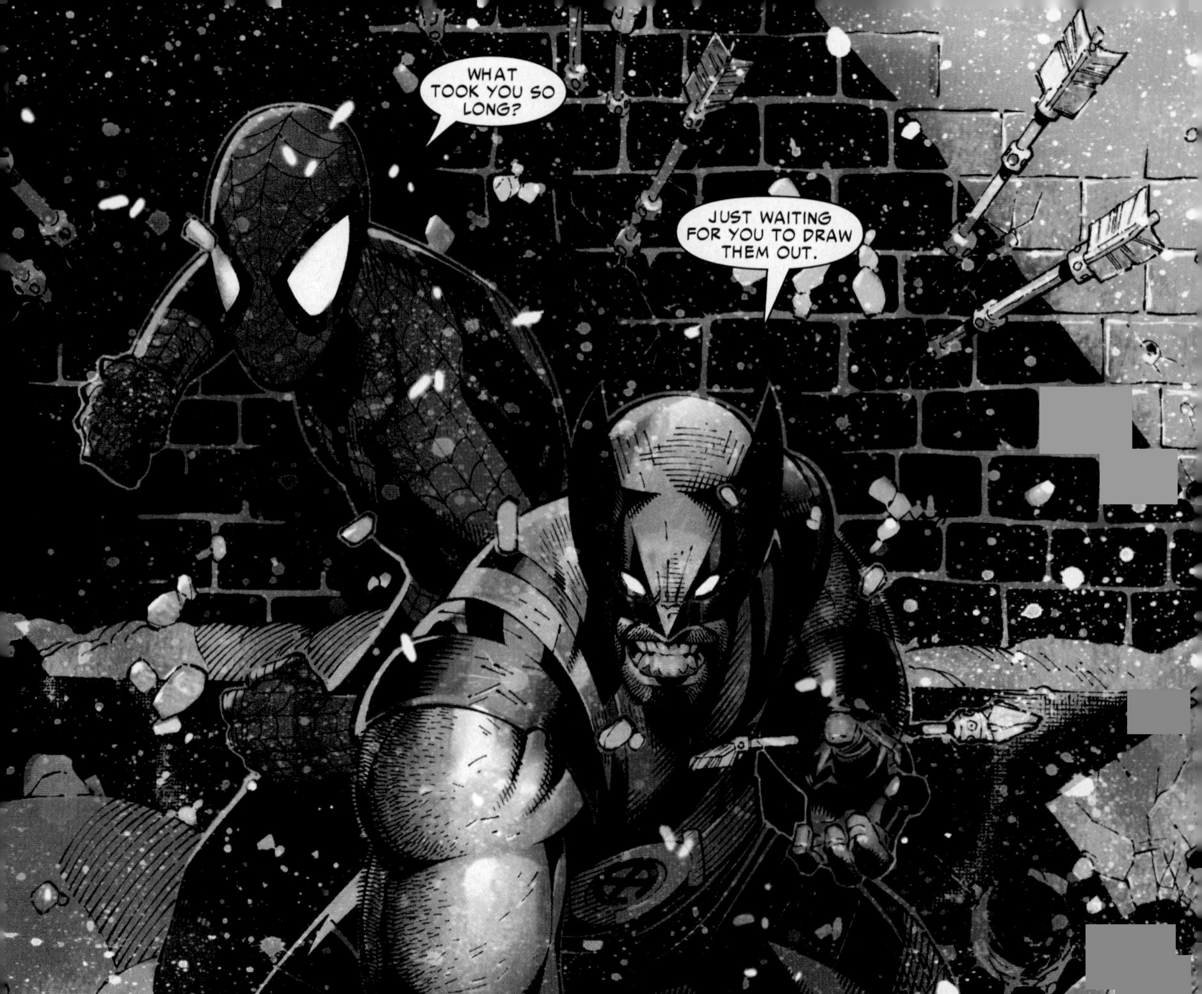
WHAT TOOK YOU SO LONG?
JUST WAITING FOR YOU TO DRAW THEM OUT.

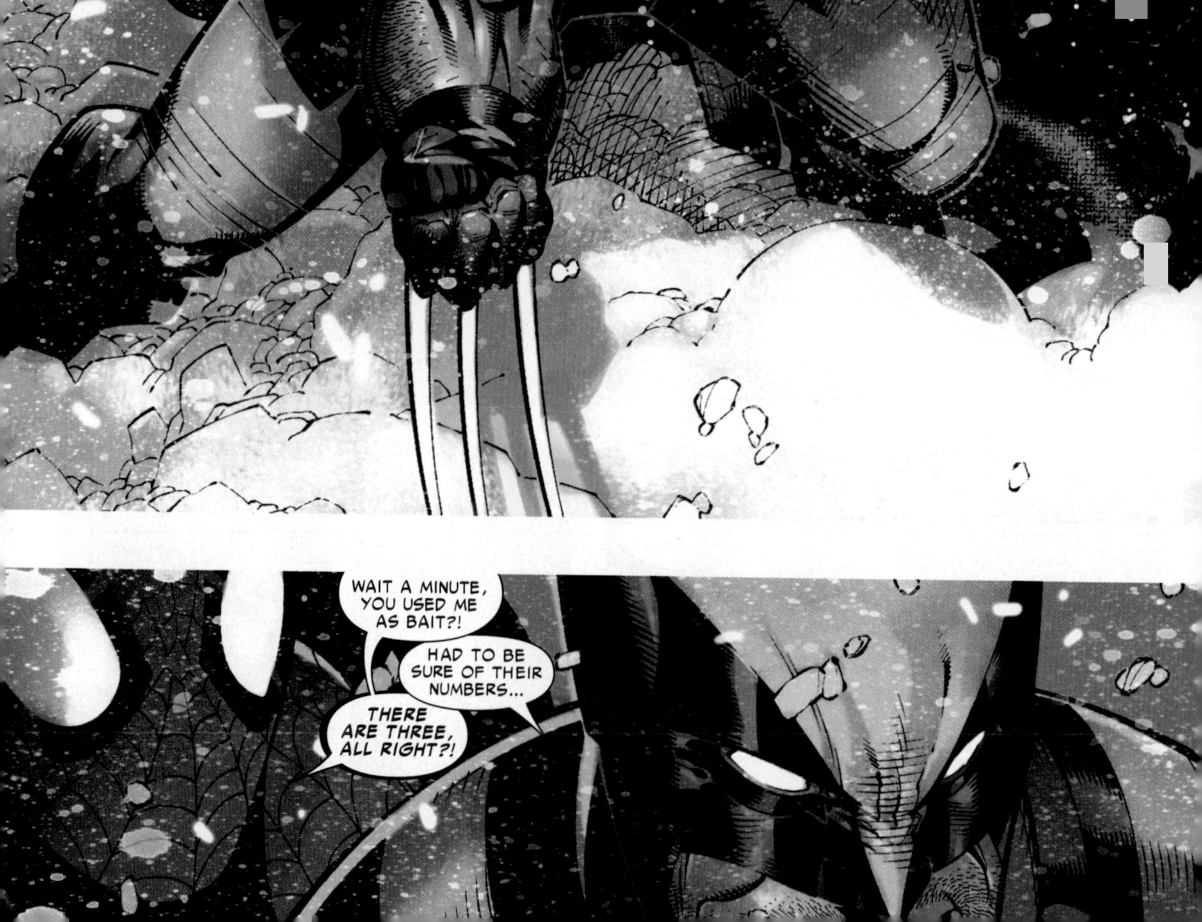
WAIT A MINUTE, YOU USED ME AS BAIT?!
HAD TO BE SURE OF THEIR NUMBERS...
THERE ARE THREE, ALL RIGHT?!

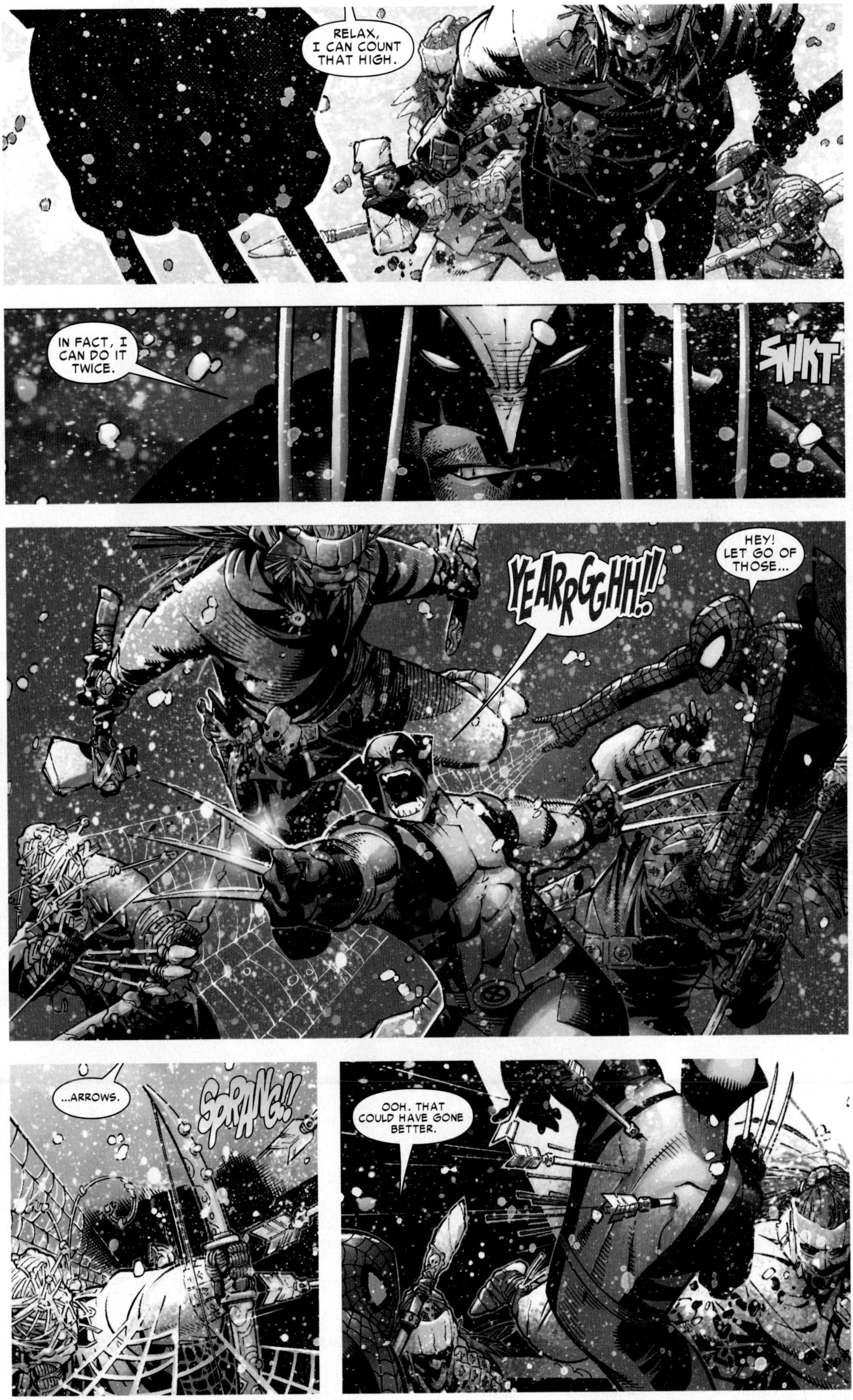
RELAX, I CAN COUNT THAT HIGH.
IN FACT, I CAN DO IT TWICE.
SNIKT
YEARRGGHH!!!
HEY! LET GO OF THOSE...
...ARROWS.
SPRANG!!
OOH. THAT COULD HAVE GONE BETTER.

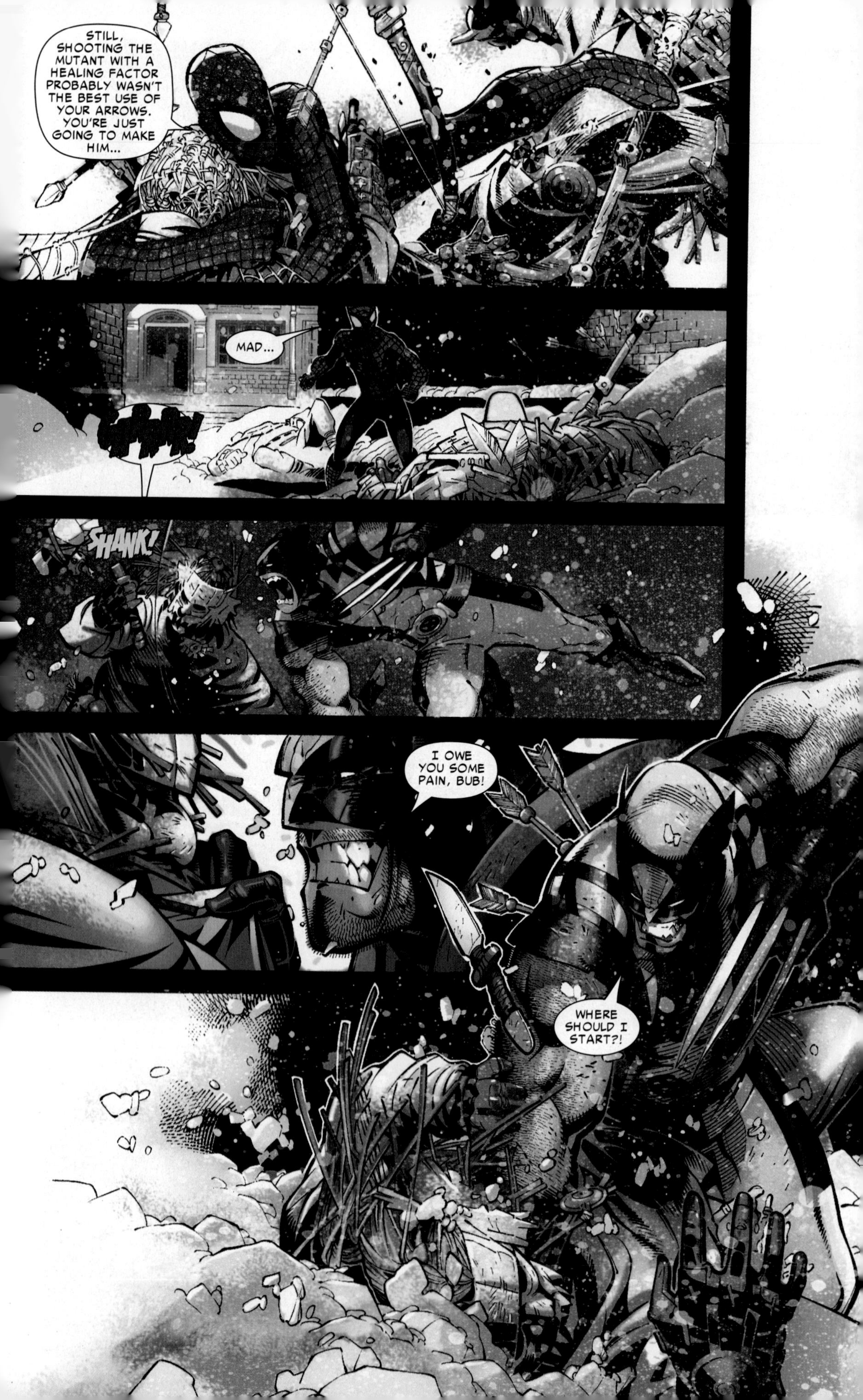
STILL, SHOOTING THE MUTANT WITH A HEALING FACTOR PROBABLY WASN'T THE BEST USE OF YOUR ARROWS. YOU'RE JUST GOING TO MAKE HIM...
MAD...
SHANK!
I OWE YOU SOME PAIN, BUB!
WHERE SHOULD I START?!

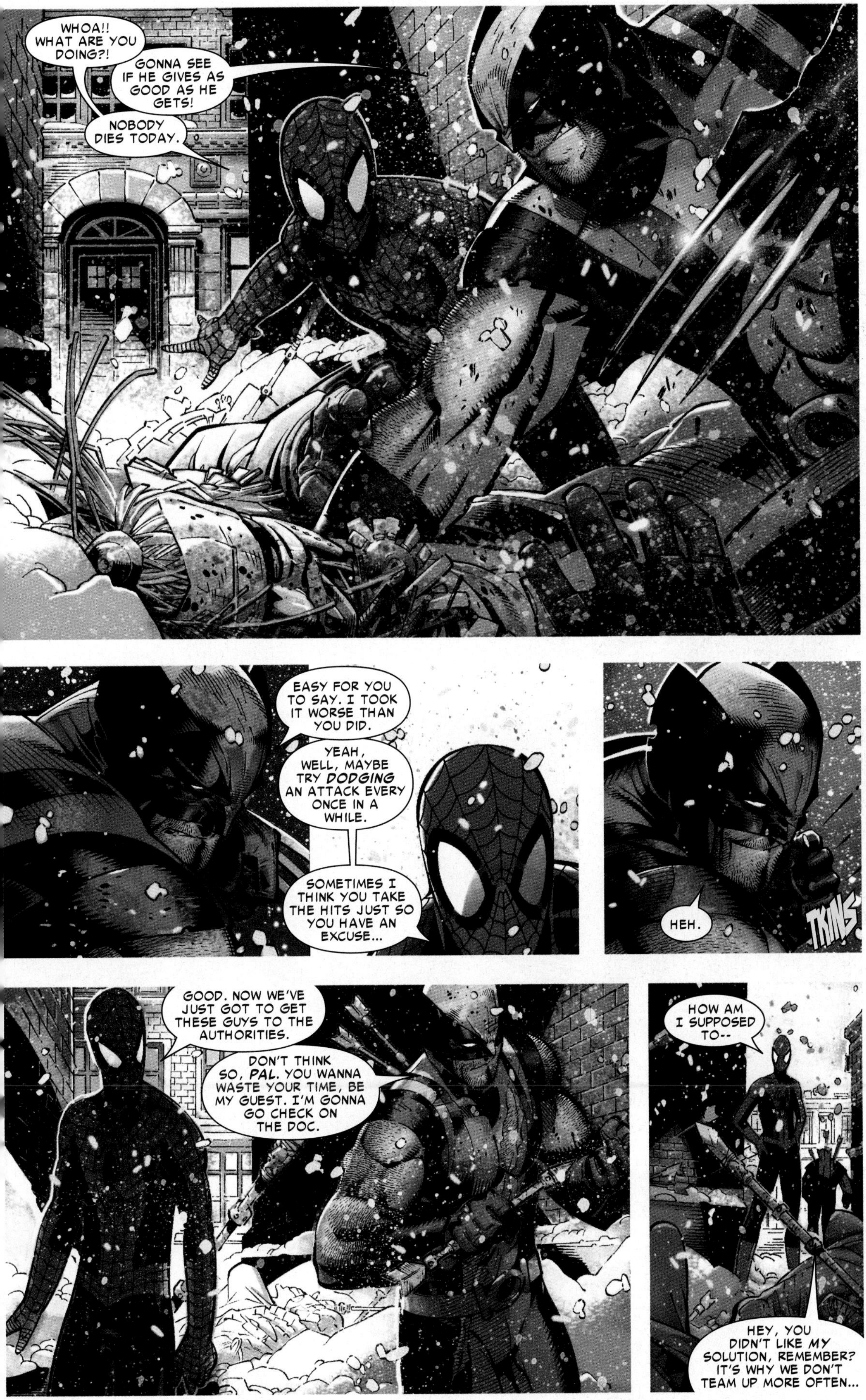
WHOA!! WHAT ARE YOU DOING?!
GONNA SEE IF HE GIVES AS GOOD AS HE GETS!
NOBODY DIES TODAY.
EASY FOR YOU TO SAY. I TOOK IT WORSE THAN YOU DID.
YEAH, WELL, MAYBE TRY DODGING AN ATTACK EVERY ONCE IN A WHILE.
SOMETIMES I THINK YOU TAKE THE HITS JUST SO YOU HAVE AN EXCUSE...
HEH.
TKING
GOOD. NOW WE'VE JUST GOT TO GET THESE GUYS TO THE AUTHORITIES.
DON'T THINK SO, PAL. YOU WANNA WASTE YOUR TIME, BE MY GUEST. I'M GONNA GO CHECK ON THE DOC.
HOW AM I SUPPOSED TO--
HEY, YOU DIDN'T LIKE MY SOLUTION, REMEMBER? IT'S WHY WE DON'T TEAM UP MORE OFTEN...

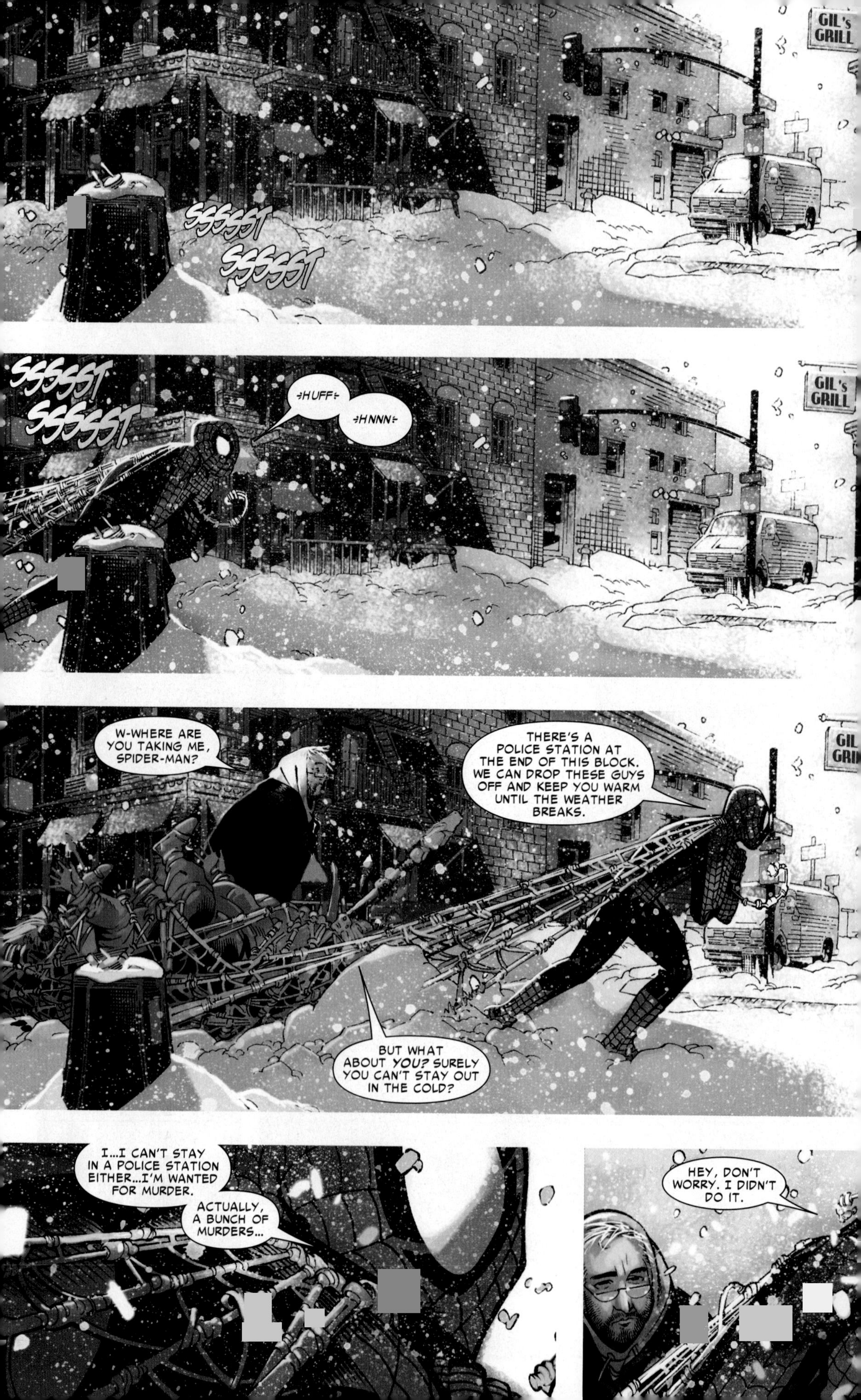
GIL's GRILL
SSSSST
SSSSST
SSSSST
SSSSST
HUFF
HNNN
W-WHERE ARE YOU TAKING ME, SPIDER-MAN?
THERE'S A POLICE STATION AT THE END OF THIS BLOCK. WE CAN DROP THESE GUYS OFF AND KEEP YOU WARM UNTIL THE WEATHER BREAKS.
BUT WHAT ABOUT *YOU?* SURELY YOU CAN'T STAY OUT IN THE COLD?
I...I CAN'T STAY IN A POLICE STATION EITHER...I'M WANTED FOR MURDER.
ACTUALLY, A BUNCH OF MURDERS...
HEY, DON'T WORRY. I DIDN'T DO IT.

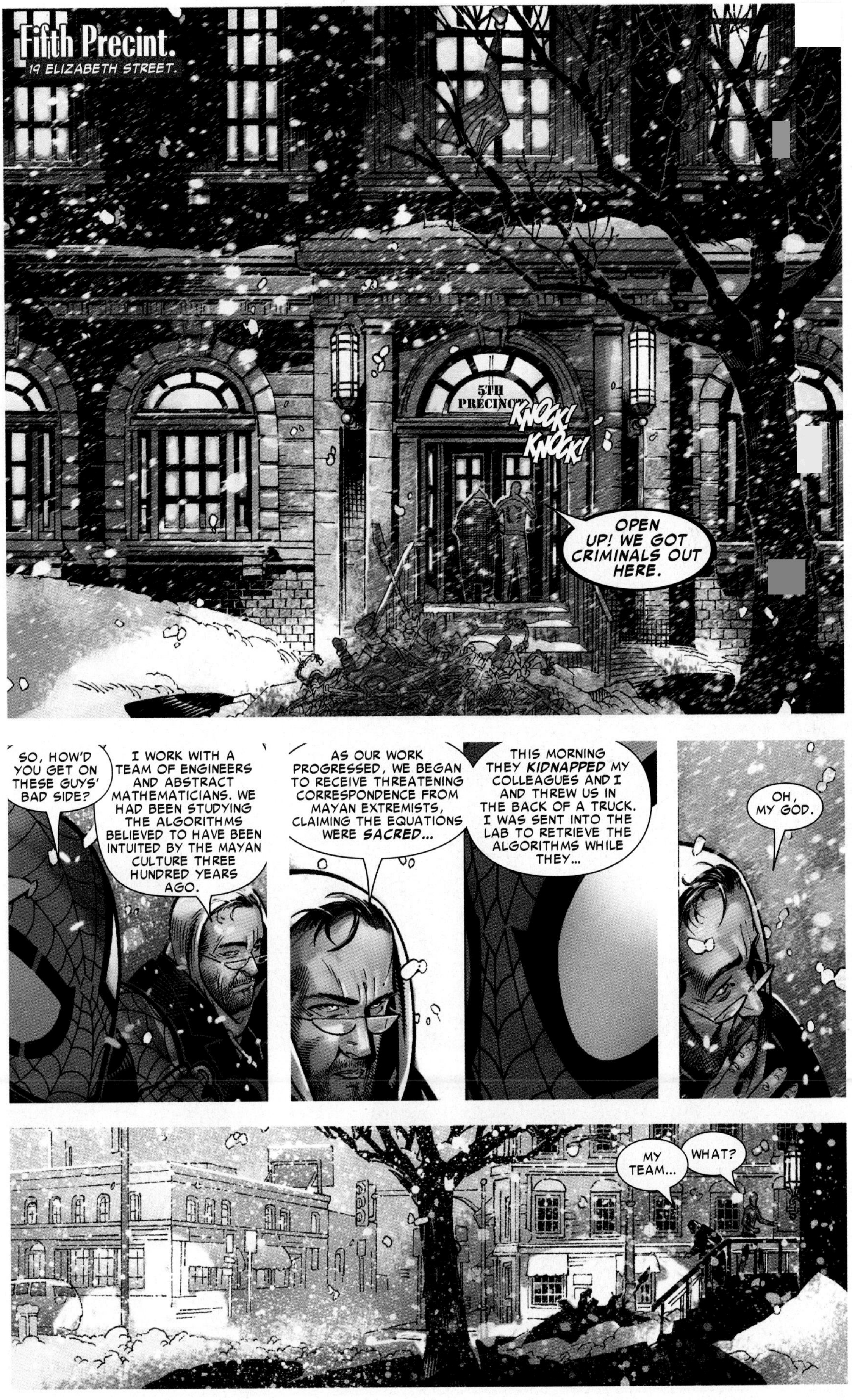
Fifth Precint.
19 ELIZABETH STREET.
5TH PRECINCT
KNOCK! KNOCK!
OPEN UP! WE GOT CRIMINALS OUT HERE.
SO, HOW'D YOU GET ON THESE GUYS' BAD SIDE?
I WORK WITH A TEAM OF ENGINEERS AND ABSTRACT MATHEMATICIANS. WE HAD BEEN STUDYING THE ALGORITHMS BELIEVED TO HAVE BEEN INTUITED BY THE MAYAN CULTURE THREE HUNDRED YEARS AGO.
AS OUR WORK PROGRESSED, WE BEGAN TO RECEIVE THREATENING CORRESPONDENCE FROM MAYAN EXTREMISTS, CLAIMING THE EQUATIONS WERE SACRED...
THIS MORNING THEY KIDNAPPED MY COLLEAGUES AND I AND THREW US IN THE BACK OF A TRUCK. I WAS SENT INTO THE LAB TO RETRIEVE THE ALGORITHMS WHILE THEY...
OH, MY GOD.
MY TEAM...
WHAT?

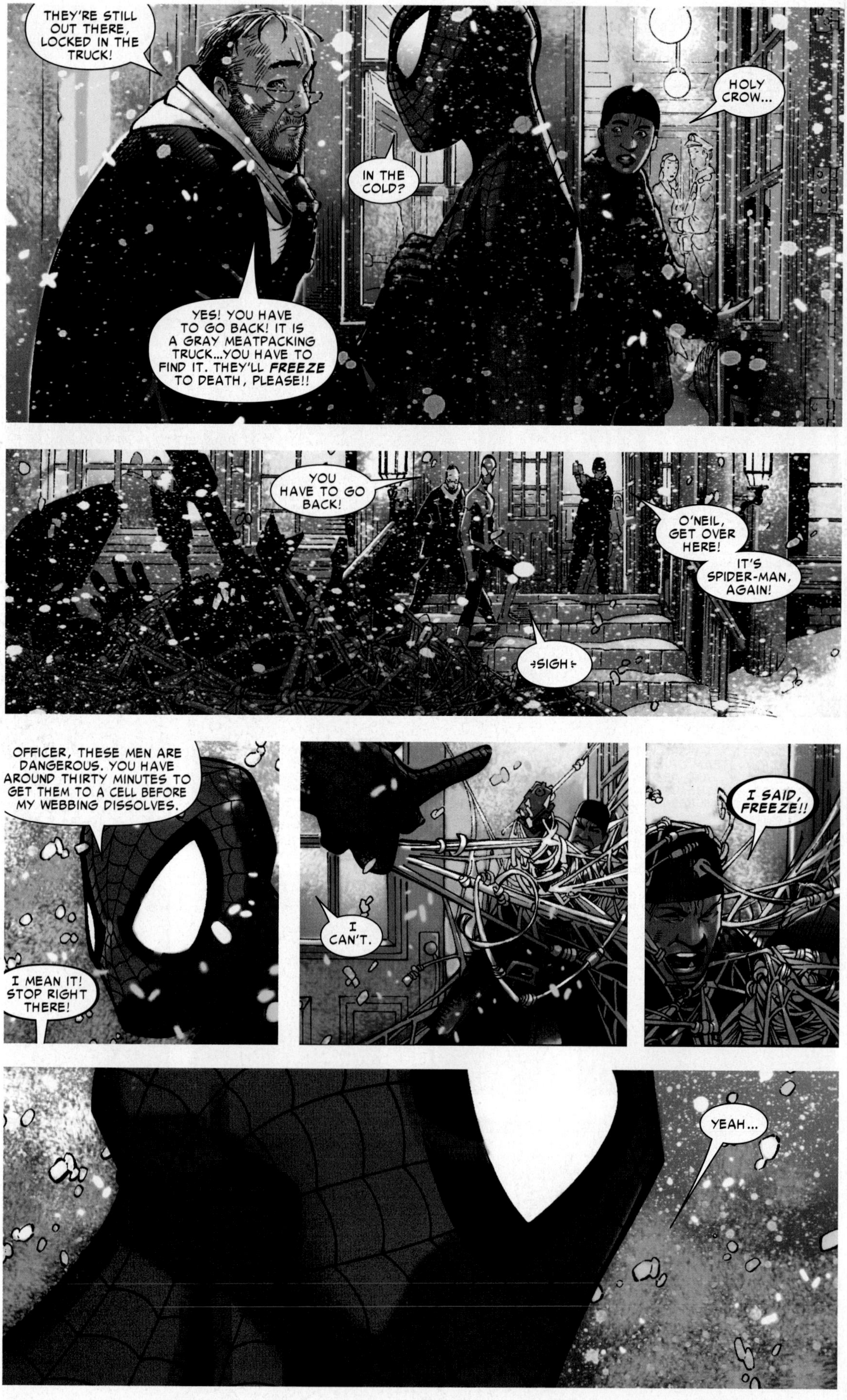
THEY'RE STILL OUT THERE, LOCKED IN THE TRUCK!
IN THE COLD?
HOLY CROW...
YES! YOU HAVE TO GO BACK! IT IS A GRAY MEATPACKING TRUCK...YOU HAVE TO FIND IT. THEY'LL *FREEZE* TO DEATH, PLEASE!!
YOU HAVE TO GO BACK!
O'NEIL, GET OVER HERE!
IT'S SPIDER-MAN, AGAIN!
SIGH
OFFICER, THESE MEN ARE DANGEROUS. YOU HAVE AROUND THIRTY MINUTES TO GET THEM TO A CELL BEFORE MY WEBBING DISSOLVES.
I MEAN IT! STOP RIGHT THERE!
I CAN'T.
I SAID, FREEZE!!
YEAH...

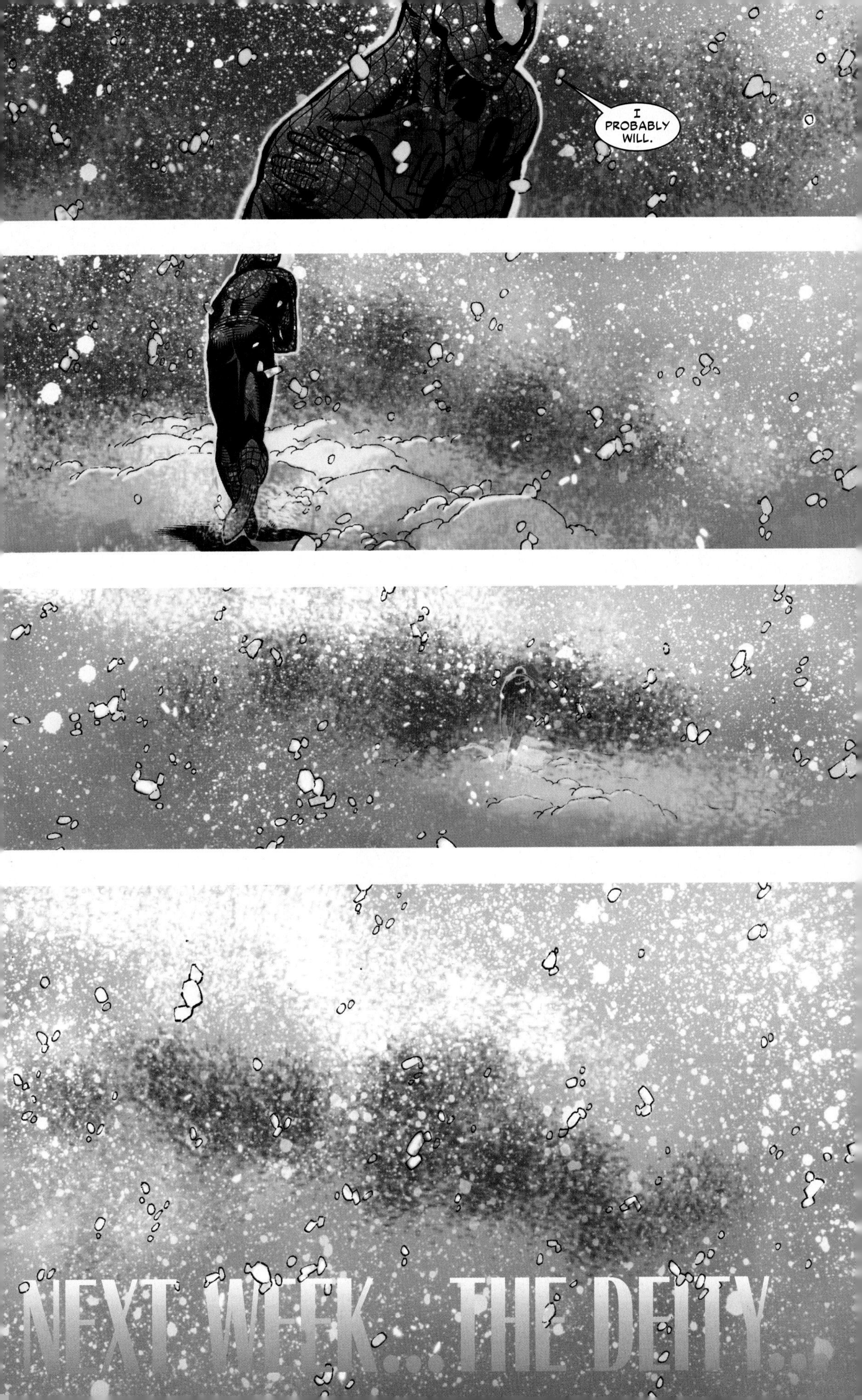
I PROBABLY WILL.
NEXT WEEK... THE DEITY...

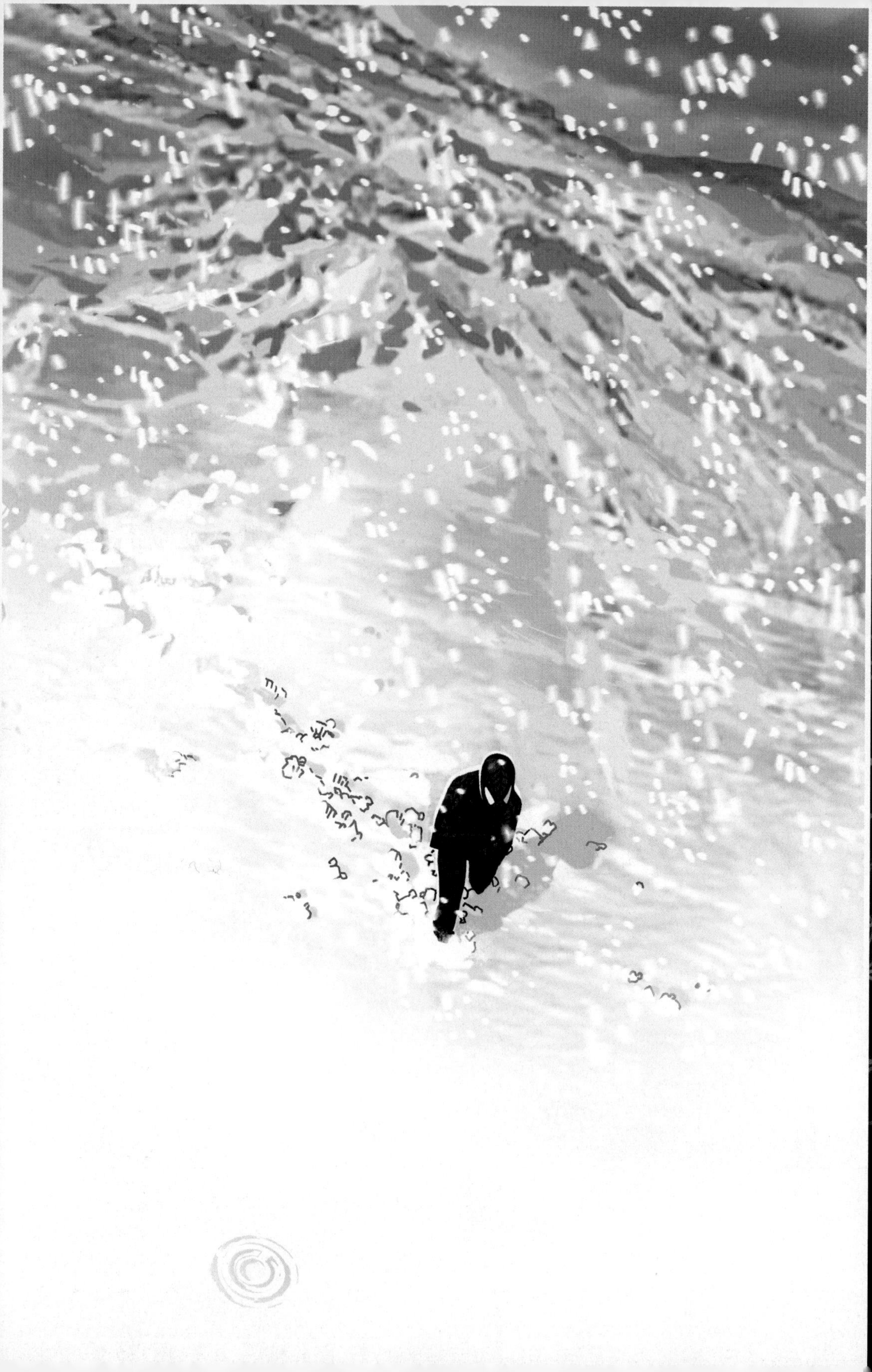

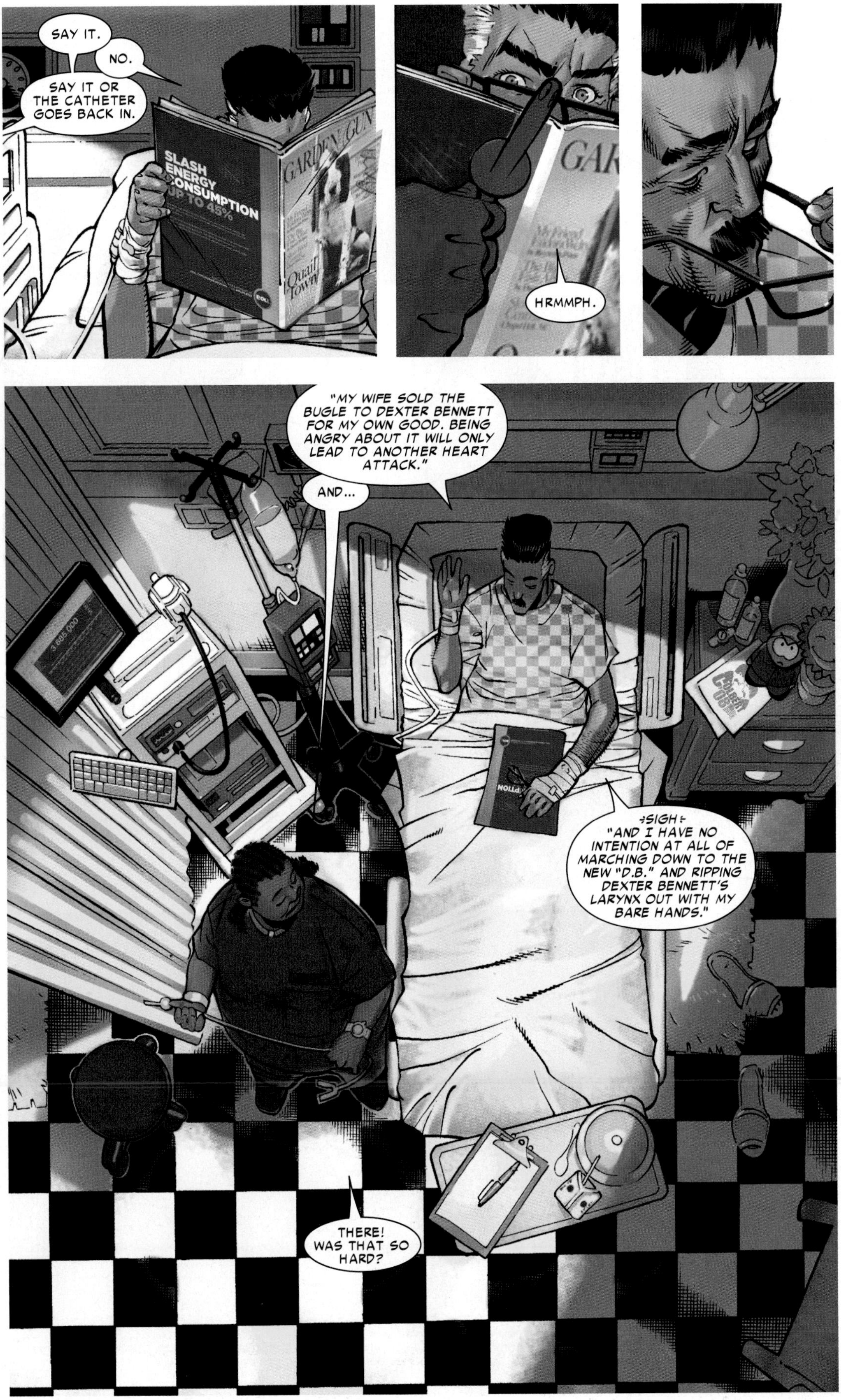
SAY IT.
NO.
SAY IT OR THE CATHETER GOES BACK IN.
SLASH ENERGY CONSUMPTION UP TO 45%
GARDEN & GUN
HRMMPH.
"MY WIFE SOLD THE BUGLE TO DEXTER BENNETT FOR MY OWN GOOD. BEING ANGRY ABOUT IT WILL ONLY LEAD TO ANOTHER HEART ATTACK."
AND...
⸗SIGH⸗ "AND I HAVE NO INTENTION AT ALL OF MARCHING DOWN TO THE NEW "D.B." AND RIPPING DEXTER BENNETT'S LARYNX OUT WITH MY BARE HANDS."
THERE! WAS THAT SO HARD?

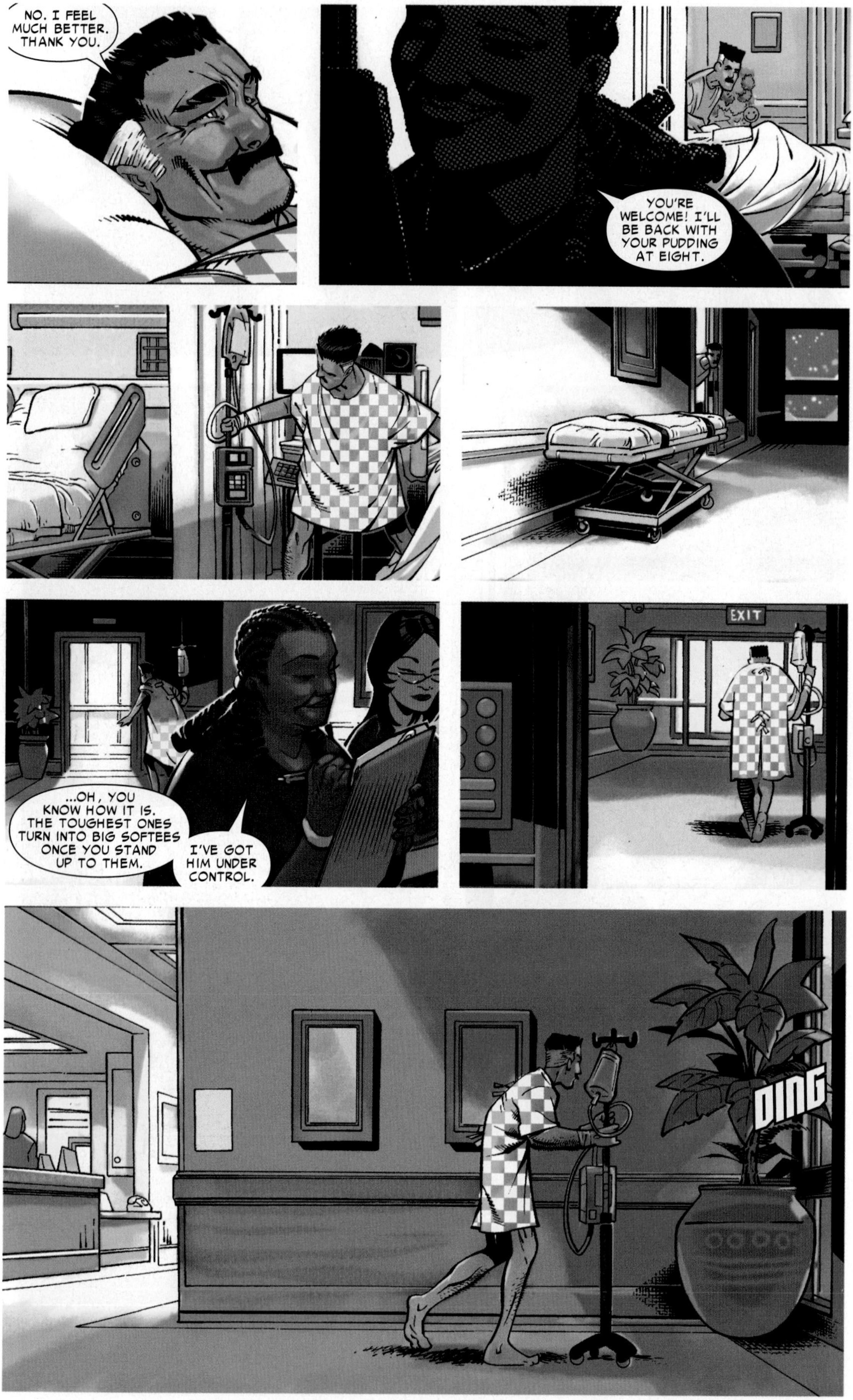
NO. I FEEL MUCH BETTER. THANK YOU.
YOU'RE WELCOME! I'LL BE BACK WITH YOUR PUDDING AT EIGHT.
EXIT
...OH, YOU KNOW HOW IT IS. THE TOUGHEST ONES TURN INTO BIG SOFTEES ONCE YOU STAND UP TO THEM.
I'VE GOT HIM UNDER CONTROL.
DING

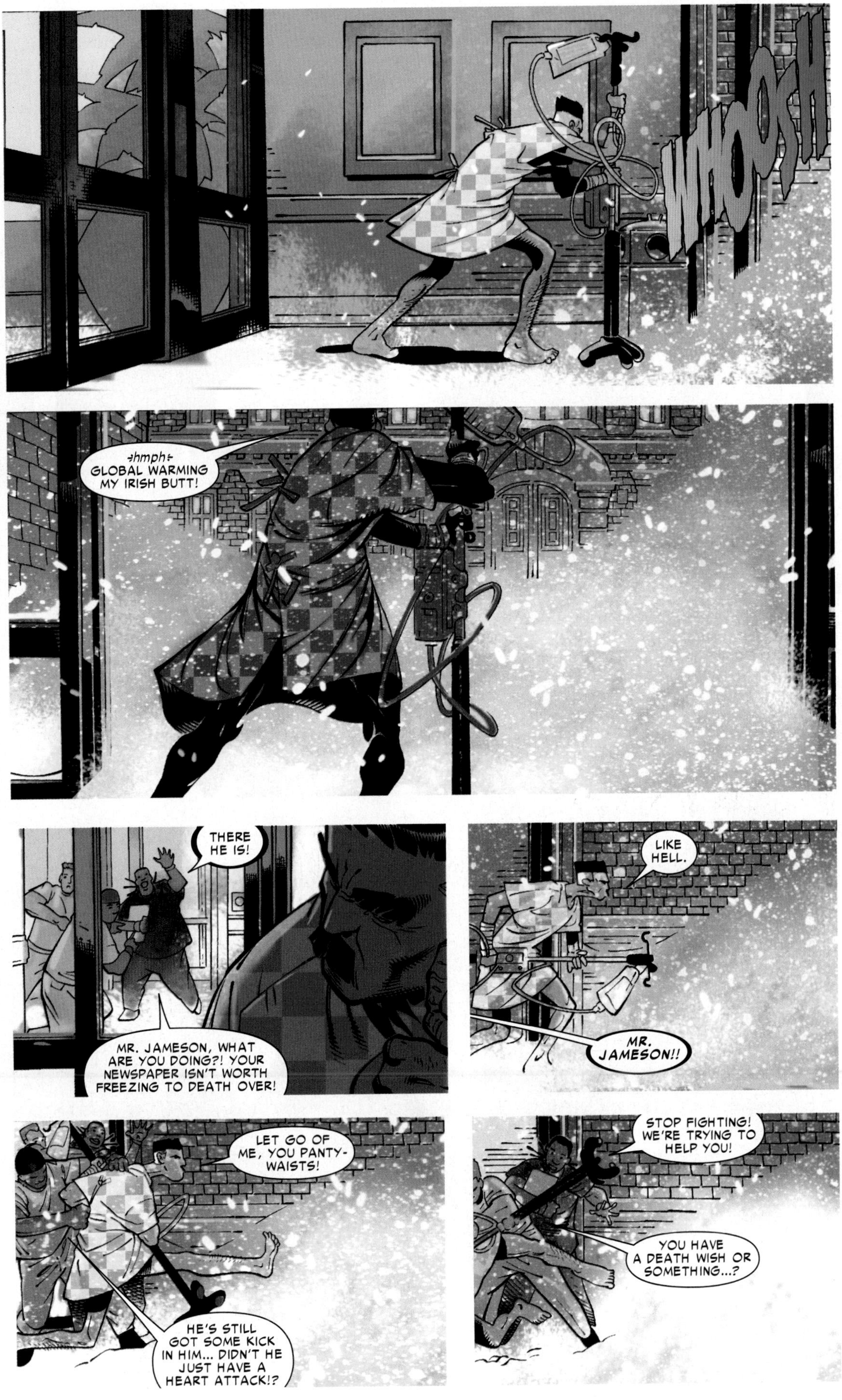
WHOOSH
-hmph-
GLOBAL WARMING MY IRISH BUTT!
THERE HE IS!
MR. JAMESON, WHAT ARE YOU DOING?! YOUR NEWSPAPER ISN'T WORTH FREEZING TO DEATH OVER!
LIKE HELL.
MR. JAMESON!!
LET GO OF ME, YOU PANTY-WAISTS!
HE'S STILL GOT SOME KICK IN HIM... DIDN'T HE JUST HAVE A HEART ATTACK!?
STOP FIGHTING! WE'RE TRYING TO HELP YOU!
YOU HAVE A DEATH WISH OR SOMETHING...?

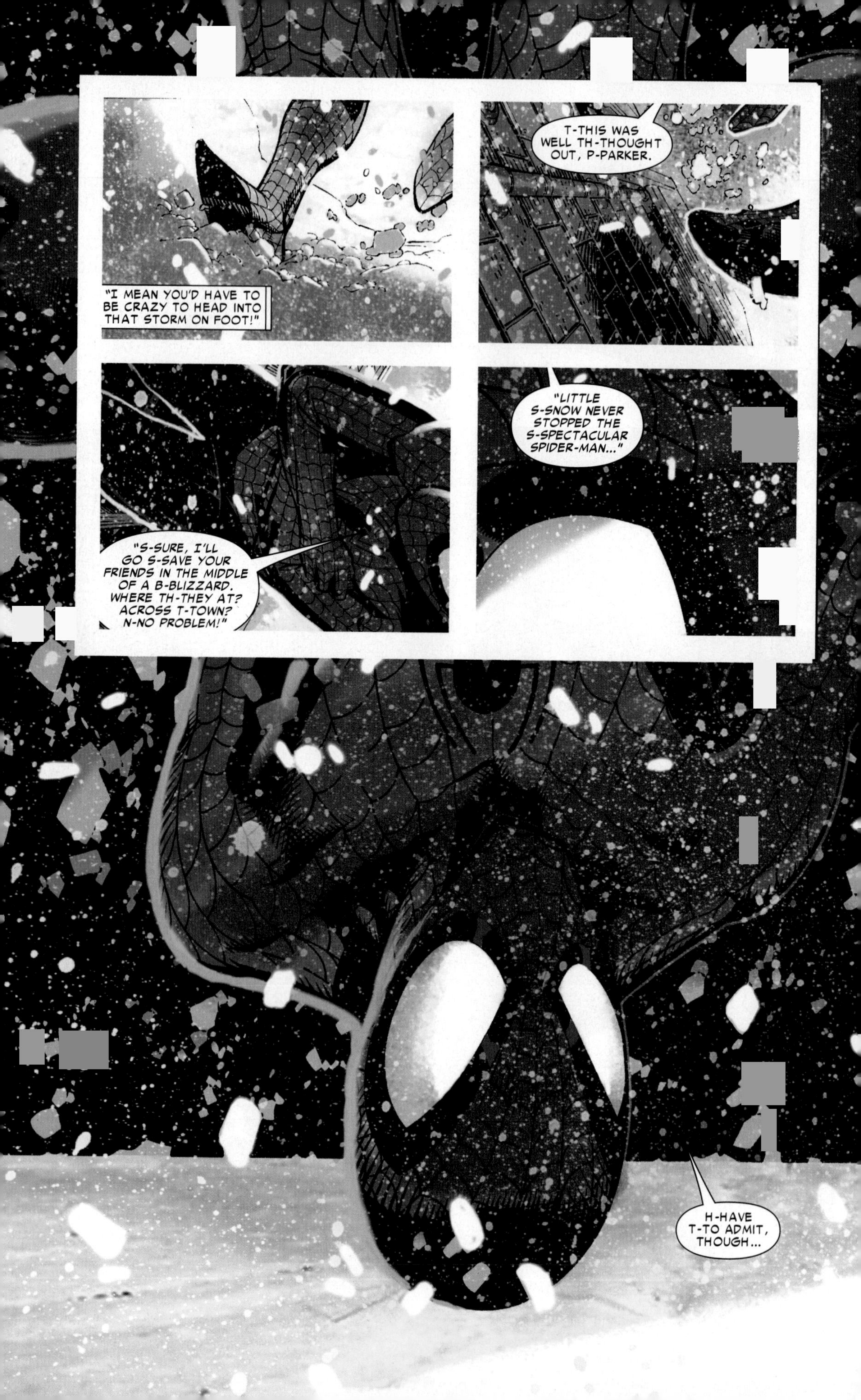
"I MEAN YOU'D HAVE TO BE CRAZY TO HEAD INTO THAT STORM ON FOOT!"
T-THIS WAS WELL TH-THOUGHT OUT, P-PARKER.
"S-SURE, I'LL GO S-SAVE YOUR FRIENDS IN THE MIDDLE OF A B-BLIZZARD. WHERE TH-THEY AT? ACROSS T-TOWN? N-NO PROBLEM!"
"LITTLE S-SNOW NEVER STOPPED THE S-SPECTACULAR SPIDER-MAN..."
H-HAVE T-TO ADMIT, THOUGH...

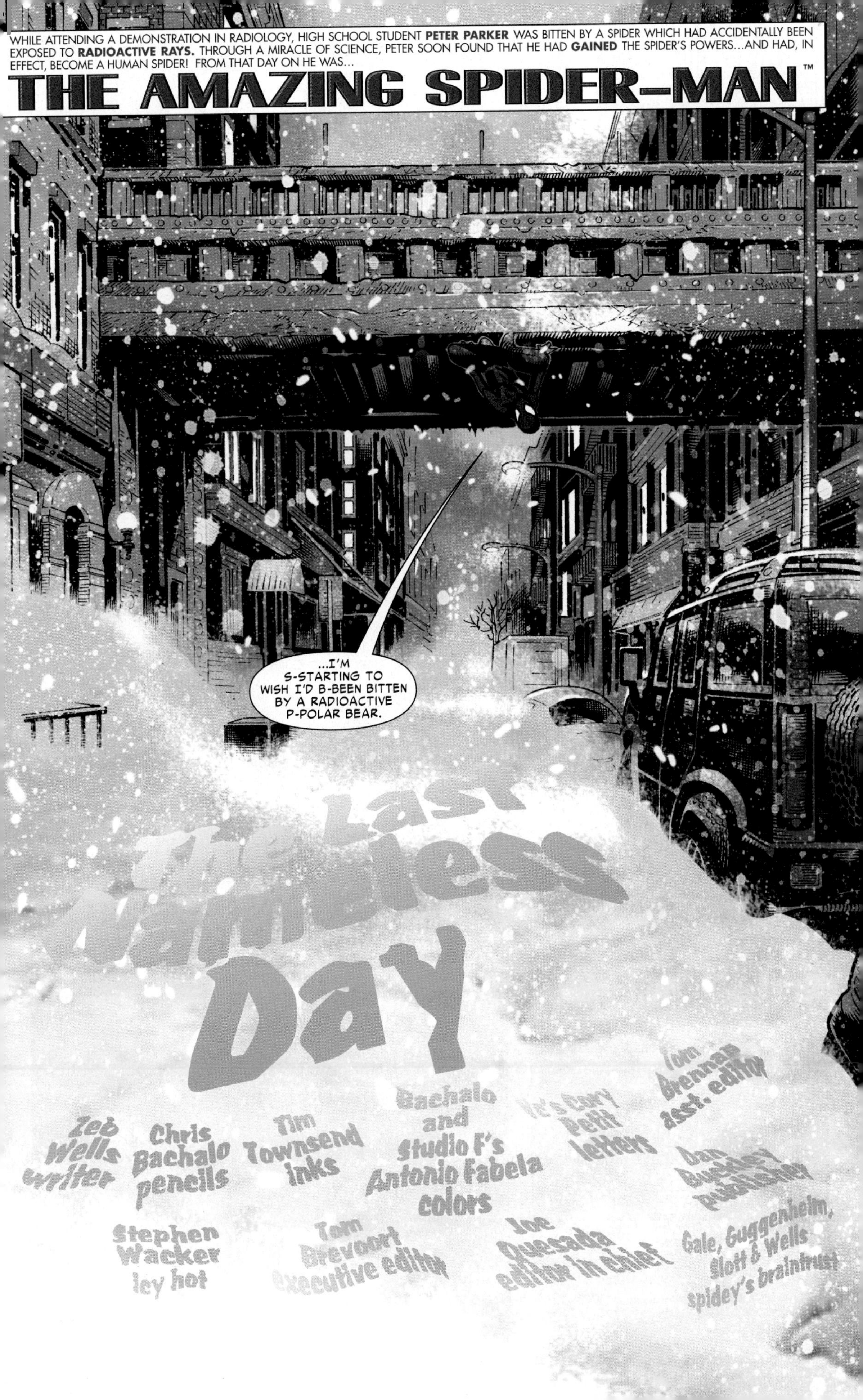
WHILE ATTENDING A DEMONSTRATION IN RADIOLOGY, HIGH SCHOOL STUDENT PETER PARKER WAS BITTEN BY A SPIDER WHICH HAD ACCIDENTALLY BEEN EXPOSED TO RADIOACTIVE RAYS. THROUGH A MIRACLE OF SCIENCE, PETER SOON FOUND THAT HE HAD GAINED THE SPIDER'S POWERS...AND HAD, IN EFFECT, BECOME A HUMAN SPIDER! FROM THAT DAY ON HE WAS...
THE AMAZING SPIDER-MAN™
...I'M S-STARTING TO WISH I'D B-BEEN BITTEN BY A RADIOACTIVE P-POLAR BEAR.
The Last Nameless Day
Zeb Wells writer
Chris Bachalo pencils
Tim Townsend inks
Bachalo and Studio F's Antonio Fabela colors
VC's Cory Petit letters
Tom Brennan asst. editor
Dan Buckley publisher
Stephen Wacker icy hot
Tom Brevoort executive editor
Joe Quesada editor in chief
Gale, Guggenheim, Slott & Wells spidey's braintrust

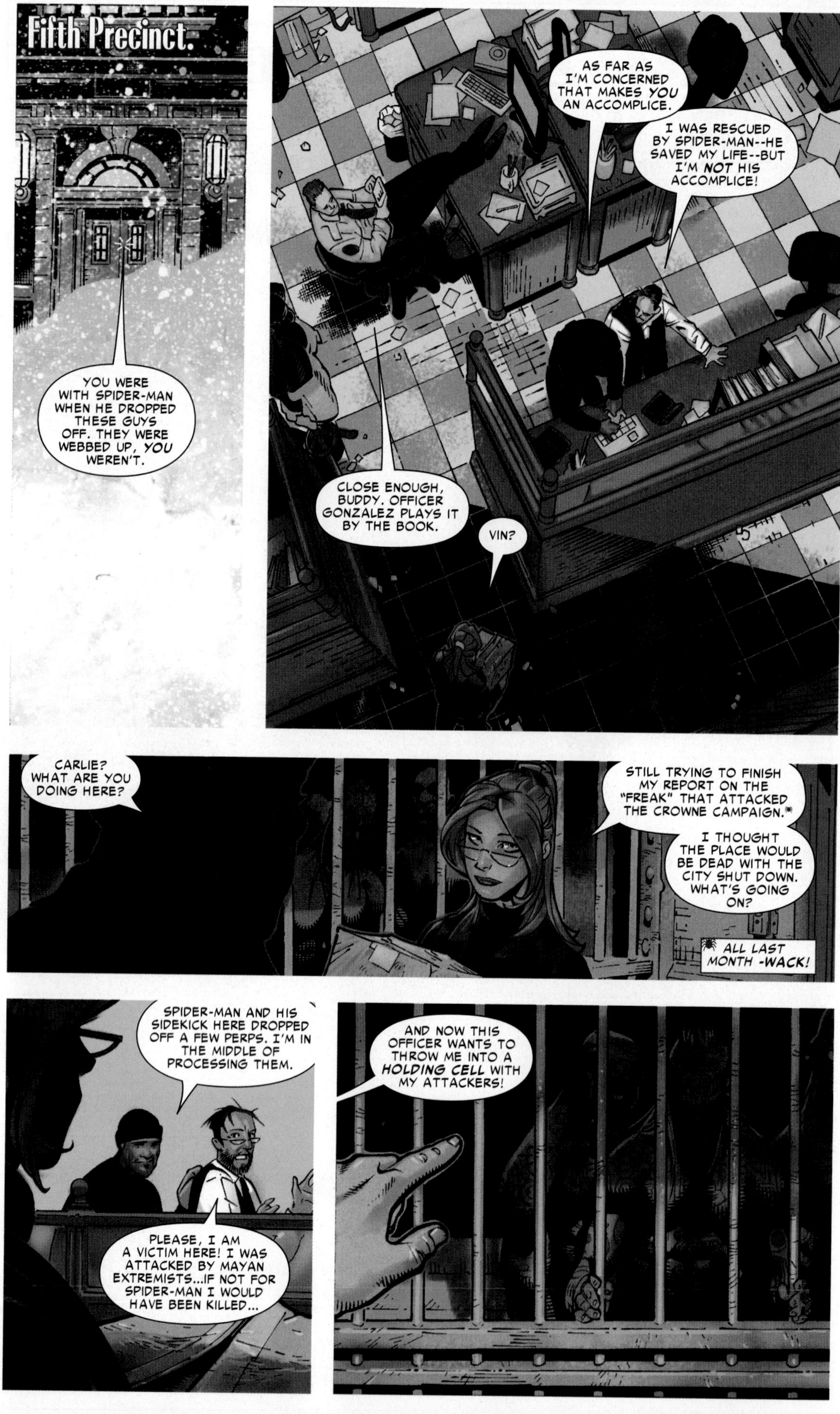
Fifth Precinct.
YOU WERE WITH SPIDER-MAN WHEN HE DROPPED THESE GUYS OFF. THEY WERE WEBBED UP, YOU WEREN'T.
AS FAR AS I'M CONCERNED THAT MAKES YOU AN ACCOMPLICE.
I WAS RESCUED BY SPIDER-MAN--HE SAVED MY LIFE--BUT I'M NOT HIS ACCOMPLICE!
CLOSE ENOUGH, BUDDY. OFFICER GONZALEZ PLAYS IT BY THE BOOK.
VIN?
CARLIE? WHAT ARE YOU DOING HERE?
STILL TRYING TO FINISH MY REPORT ON THE "FREAK" THAT ATTACKED THE CROWNE CAMPAIGN.*
I THOUGHT THE PLACE WOULD BE DEAD WITH THE CITY SHUT DOWN. WHAT'S GOING ON?
*ALL LAST MONTH -WACK!
SPIDER-MAN AND HIS SIDEKICK HERE DROPPED OFF A FEW PERPS. I'M IN THE MIDDLE OF PROCESSING THEM.
PLEASE, I AM A VICTIM HERE! I WAS ATTACKED BY MAYAN EXTREMISTS...IF NOT FOR SPIDER-MAN I WOULD HAVE BEEN KILLED...
AND NOW THIS OFFICER WANTS TO THROW ME INTO A HOLDING CELL WITH MY ATTACKERS!

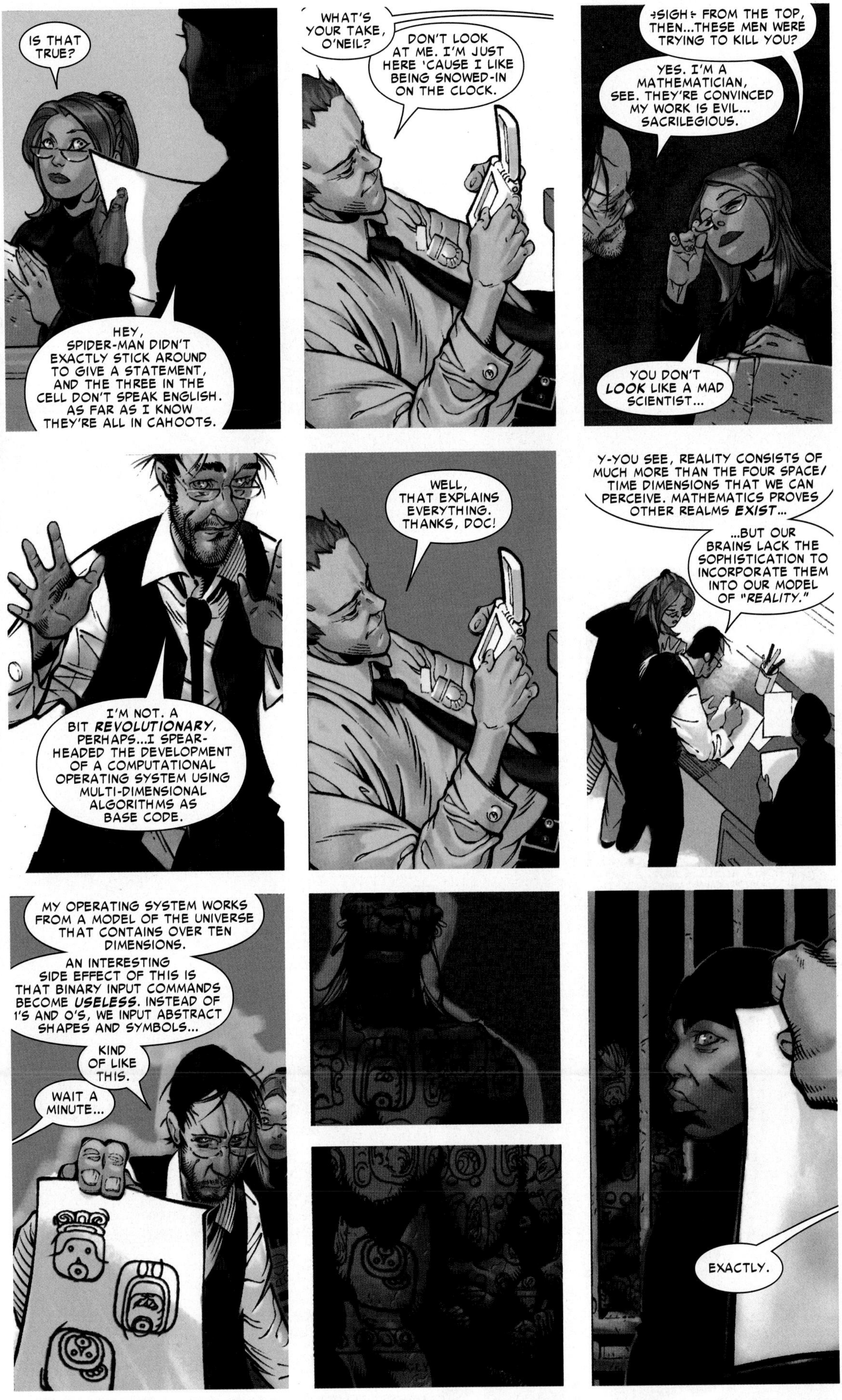
IS THAT TRUE?
HEY, SPIDER-MAN DIDN'T EXACTLY STICK AROUND TO GIVE A STATEMENT, AND THE THREE IN THE CELL DON'T SPEAK ENGLISH. AS FAR AS I KNOW THEY'RE ALL IN CAHOOTS.
WHAT'S YOUR TAKE, O'NEIL?
DON'T LOOK AT ME. I'M JUST HERE 'CAUSE I LIKE BEING SNOWED-IN ON THE CLOCK.
÷SIGH÷ FROM THE TOP, THEN...THESE MEN WERE TRYING TO KILL YOU?
YES. I'M A MATHEMATICIAN, SEE. THEY'RE CONVINCED MY WORK IS EVIL... SACRILEGIOUS.
YOU DON'T LOOK LIKE A MAD SCIENTIST...
I'M NOT. A BIT REVOLUTIONARY, PERHAPS...I SPEARHEADED THE DEVELOPMENT OF A COMPUTATIONAL OPERATING SYSTEM USING MULTI-DIMENSIONAL ALGORITHMS AS BASE CODE.
WELL, THAT EXPLAINS EVERYTHING. THANKS, DOC!
Y-YOU SEE, REALITY CONSISTS OF MUCH MORE THAN THE FOUR SPACE/TIME DIMENSIONS THAT WE CAN PERCEIVE. MATHEMATICS PROVES OTHER REALMS EXIST...
...BUT OUR BRAINS LACK THE SOPHISTICATION TO INCORPORATE THEM INTO OUR MODEL OF "REALITY."
MY OPERATING SYSTEM WORKS FROM A MODEL OF THE UNIVERSE THAT CONTAINS OVER TEN DIMENSIONS.
AN INTERESTING SIDE EFFECT OF THIS IS THAT BINARY INPUT COMMANDS BECOME USELESS. INSTEAD OF 1'S AND 0'S, WE INPUT ABSTRACT SHAPES AND SYMBOLS...
KIND OF LIKE THIS.
WAIT A MINUTE...
EXACTLY.

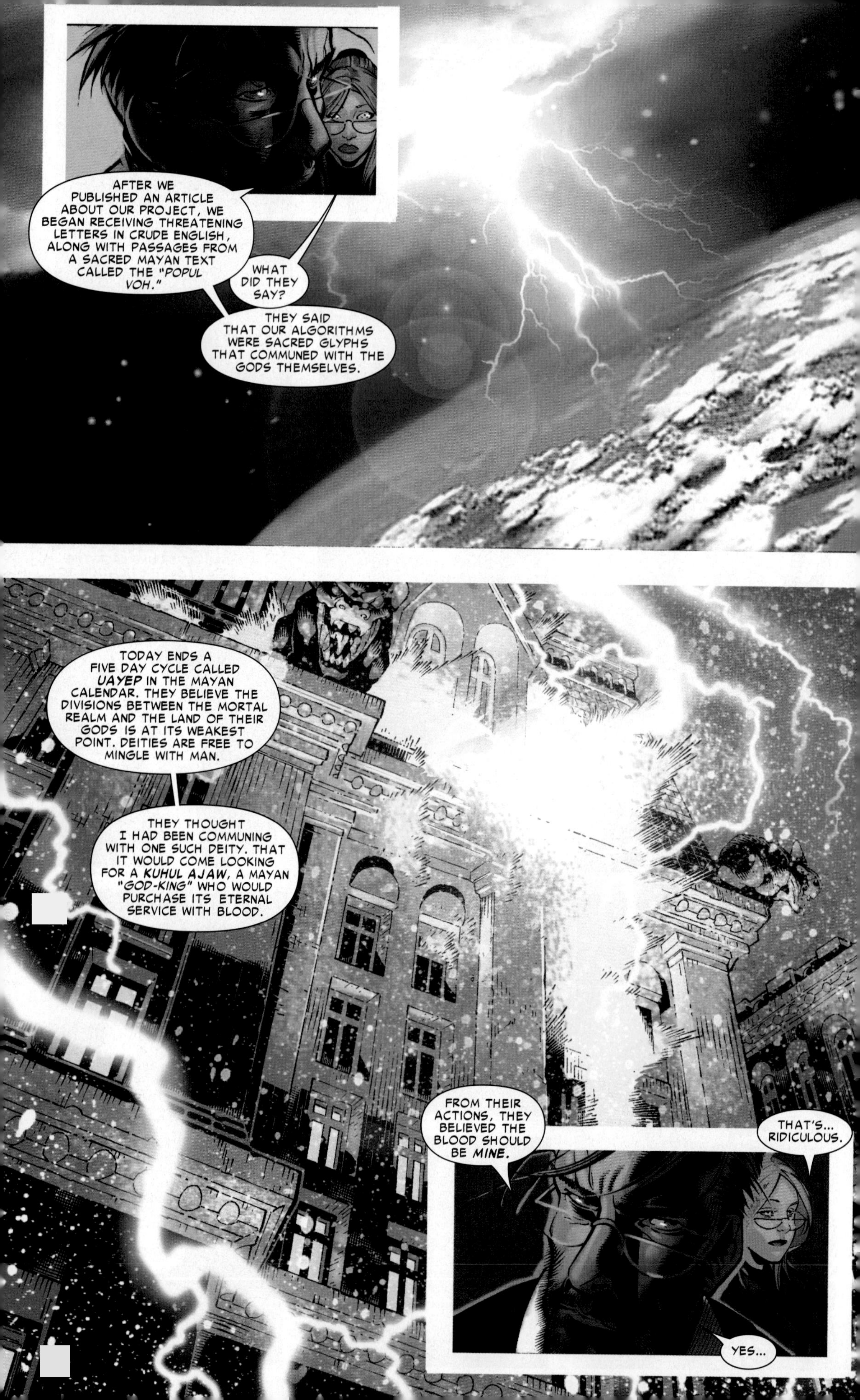
AFTER WE PUBLISHED AN ARTICLE ABOUT OUR PROJECT, WE BEGAN RECEIVING THREATENING LETTERS IN CRUDE ENGLISH, ALONG WITH PASSAGES FROM A SACRED MAYAN TEXT CALLED THE "POPUL VOH."
WHAT DID THEY SAY?
THEY SAID THAT OUR ALGORITHMS WERE SACRED GLYPHS THAT COMMUNED WITH THE GODS THEMSELVES.
TODAY ENDS A FIVE DAY CYCLE CALLED UAYEP IN THE MAYAN CALENDAR. THEY BELIEVE THE DIVISIONS BETWEEN THE MORTAL REALM AND THE LAND OF THEIR GODS IS AT ITS WEAKEST POINT. DEITIES ARE FREE TO MINGLE WITH MAN.
THEY THOUGHT I HAD BEEN COMMUNING WITH ONE SUCH DEITY. THAT IT WOULD COME LOOKING FOR A KUHUL AJAW, A MAYAN "GOD-KING" WHO WOULD PURCHASE ITS ETERNAL SERVICE WITH BLOOD.
FROM THEIR ACTIONS, THEY BELIEVED THE BLOOD SHOULD BE MINE.
THAT'S... RIDICULOUS.
YES...

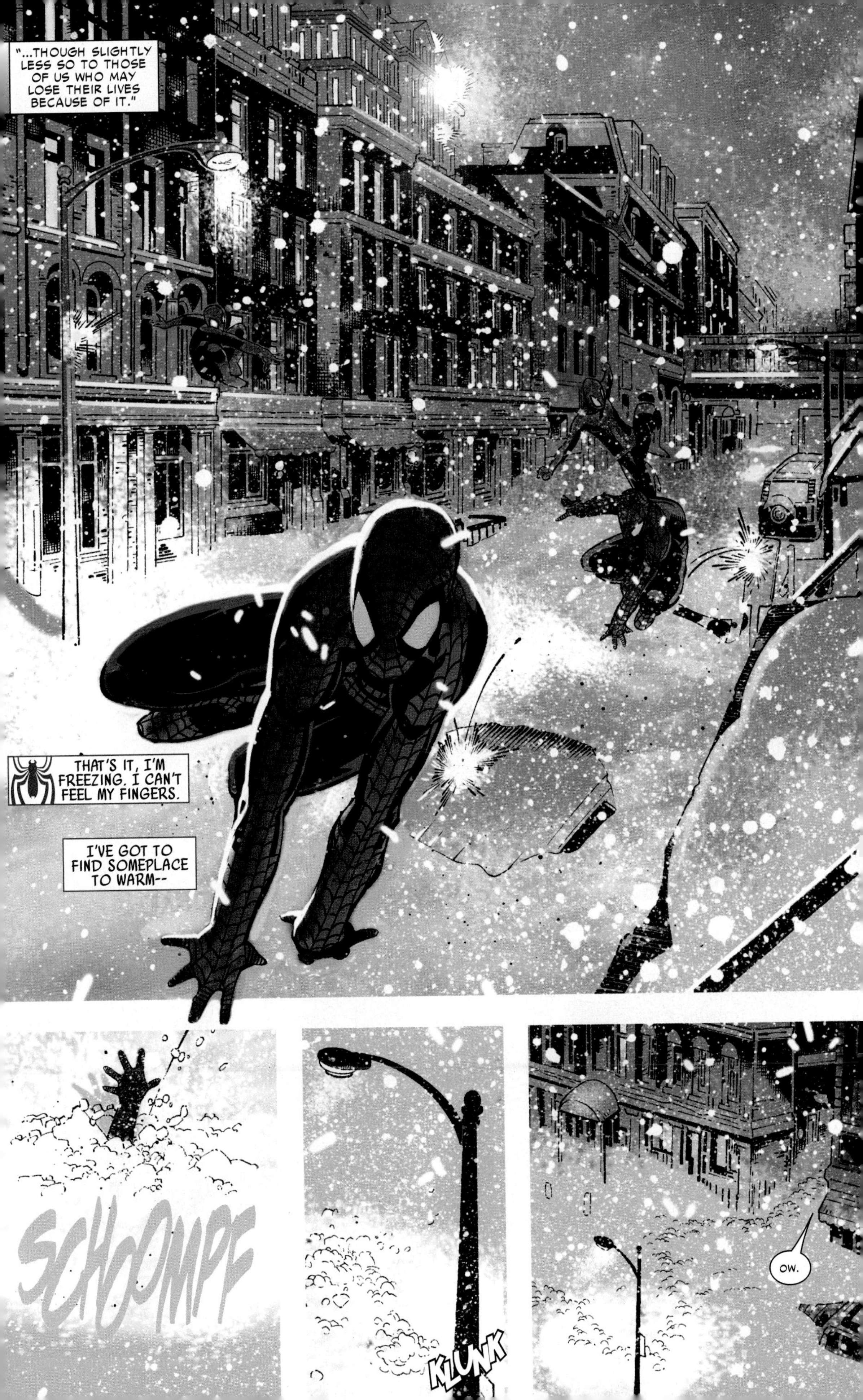
"...THOUGH SLIGHTLY LESS SO TO THOSE OF US WHO MAY LOSE THEIR LIVES BECAUSE OF IT."
THAT'S IT, I'M FREEZING. I CAN'T FEEL MY FINGERS.
I'VE GOT TO FIND SOMEPLACE TO WARM--
SCHOOMPF
KLUNK
OW.

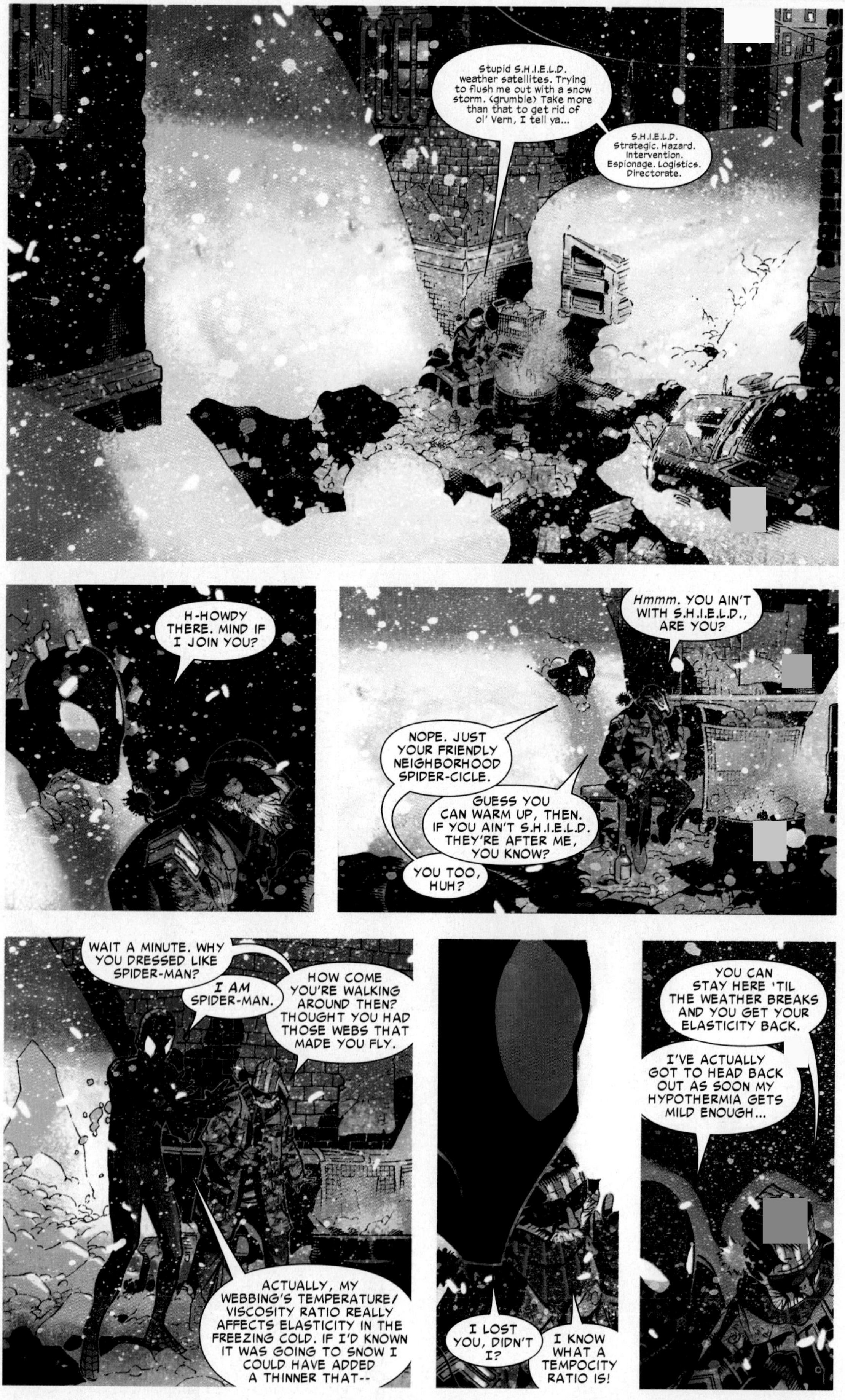

Stupid S.H.I.E.L.D. weather satellites. Trying to flush me out with a snow storm. (grumble) Take more than that to get rid of ol' Vern, I tell ya...
S.H.I.E.L.D. Strategic. Hazard. Intervention. Espionage. Logistics. Directorate.
H-HOWDY THERE. MIND IF I JOIN YOU?
Hmmm. YOU AIN'T WITH S.H.I.E.L.D., ARE YOU?
NOPE. JUST YOUR FRIENDLY NEIGHBORHOOD SPIDER-CICLE.
GUESS YOU CAN WARM UP, THEN. IF YOU AIN'T S.H.I.E.L.D. THEY'RE AFTER ME, YOU KNOW?
YOU TOO, HUH?
WAIT A MINUTE. WHY YOU DRESSED LIKE SPIDER-MAN?
I AM SPIDER-MAN.
HOW COME YOU'RE WALKING AROUND THEN? THOUGHT YOU HAD THOSE WEBS THAT MADE YOU FLY.
ACTUALLY, MY WEBBING'S TEMPERATURE/ VISCOSITY RATIO REALLY AFFECTS ELASTICITY IN THE FREEZING COLD. IF I'D KNOWN IT WAS GOING TO SNOW I COULD HAVE ADDED A THINNER THAT--
I LOST YOU, DIDN'T I?
I KNOW WHAT A TEMPOCITY RATIO IS!
YOU CAN STAY HERE 'TIL THE WEATHER BREAKS AND YOU GET YOUR ELASTICITY BACK.
I'VE ACTUALLY GOT TO HEAD BACK OUT AS SOON MY HYPOTHERMIA GETS MILD ENOUGH...

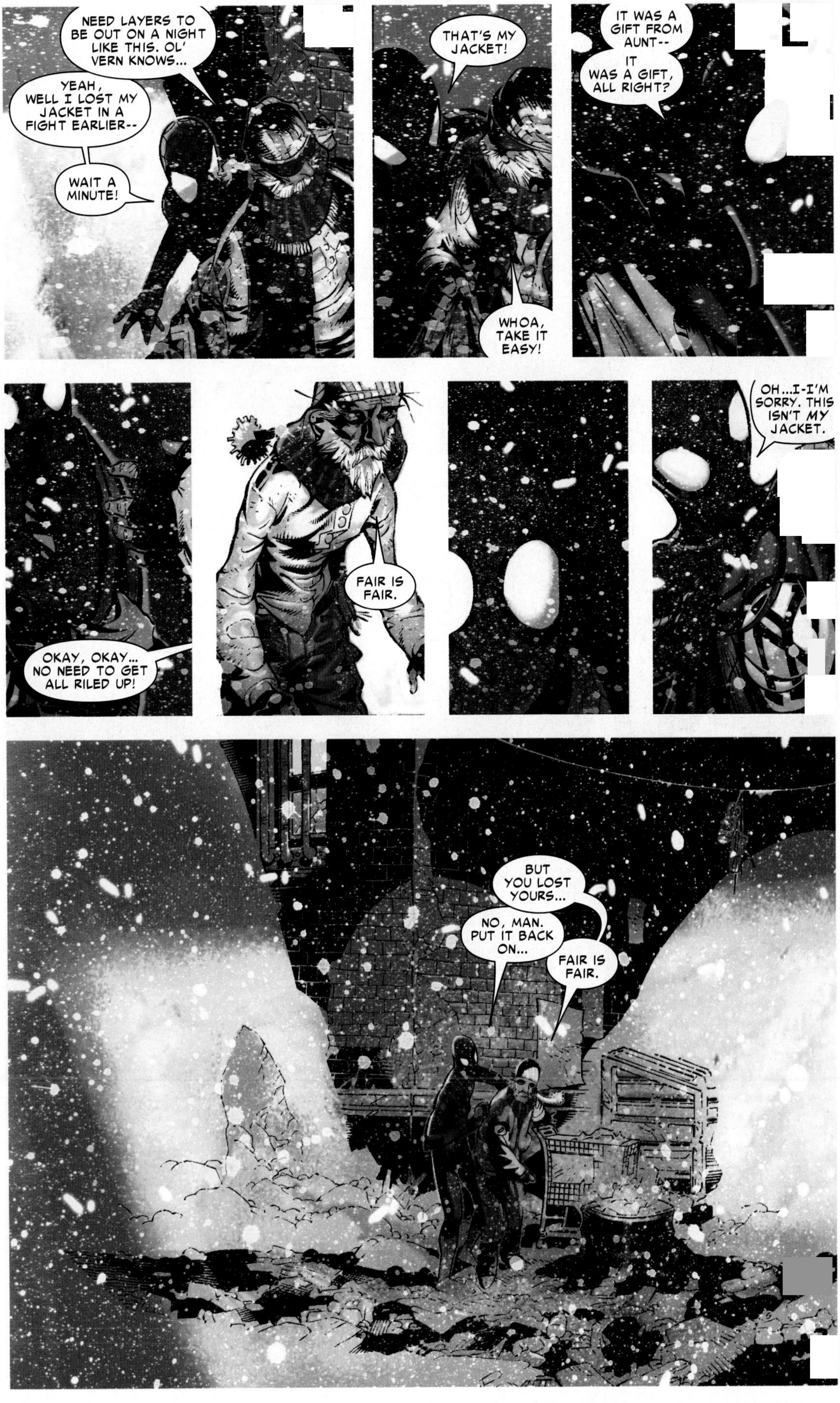
NEED LAYERS TO BE OUT ON A NIGHT LIKE THIS. OL' VERN KNOWS...
YEAH, WELL I LOST MY JACKET IN A FIGHT EARLIER--
WAIT A MINUTE!
THAT'S MY JACKET!
WHOA, TAKE IT EASY!
IT WAS A GIFT FROM AUNT--
IT WAS A GIFT, ALL RIGHT?
OKAY, OKAY... NO NEED TO GET ALL RILED UP!
FAIR IS FAIR.
OH...I-I'M SORRY. THIS ISN'T MY JACKET.
BUT YOU LOST YOURS...
NO, MAN. PUT IT BACK ON...
FAIR IS FAIR.

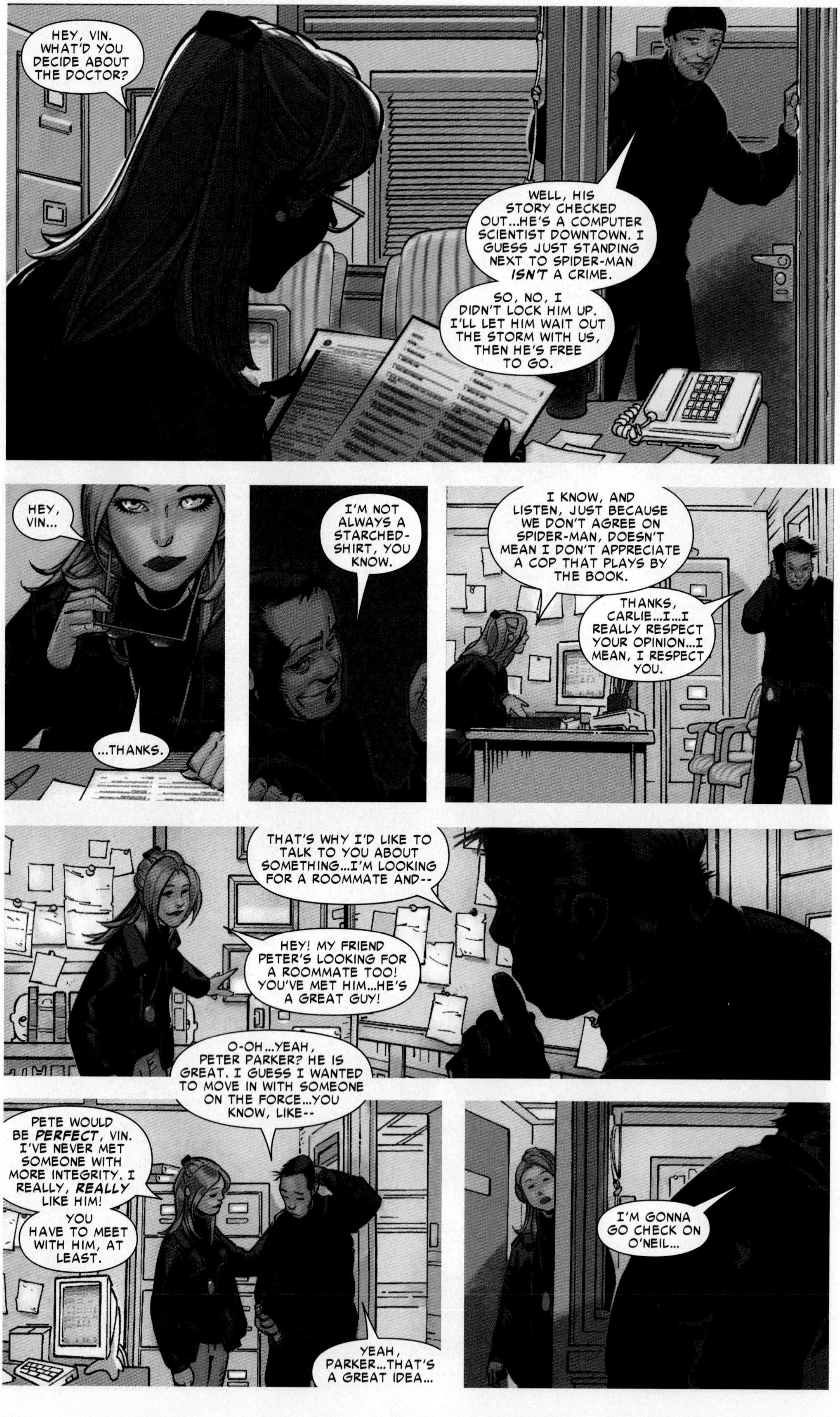
HEY, VIN. WHAT'D YOU DECIDE ABOUT THE DOCTOR?
WELL, HIS STORY CHECKED OUT...HE'S A COMPUTER SCIENTIST DOWNTOWN. I GUESS JUST STANDING NEXT TO SPIDER-MAN *ISN'T* A CRIME.
SO, NO, I DIDN'T LOCK HIM UP. I'LL LET HIM WAIT OUT THE STORM WITH US, THEN HE'S FREE TO GO.
HEY, VIN...
...THANKS.
I'M NOT ALWAYS A STARCHED-SHIRT, YOU KNOW.
I KNOW, AND LISTEN, JUST BECAUSE WE DON'T AGREE ON SPIDER-MAN, DOESN'T MEAN I DON'T APPRECIATE A COP THAT PLAYS BY THE BOOK.
THANKS, CARLIE...I...I REALLY RESPECT YOUR OPINION...I MEAN, I RESPECT YOU.
THAT'S WHY I'D LIKE TO TALK TO YOU ABOUT SOMETHING...I'M LOOKING FOR A ROOMMATE AND--
HEY! MY FRIEND PETER'S LOOKING FOR A ROOMMATE TOO! YOU'VE MET HIM...HE'S A GREAT GUY!
O-OH...YEAH, PETER PARKER? HE IS GREAT. I GUESS I WANTED TO MOVE IN WITH SOMEONE ON THE FORCE...YOU KNOW, LIKE--
PETE WOULD BE *PERFECT*, VIN. I'VE NEVER MET SOMEONE WITH MORE INTEGRITY. I REALLY, *REALLY* LIKE HIM!
YOU HAVE TO MEET WITH HIM, AT LEAST.
YEAH, PARKER...THAT'S A GREAT IDEA...
I'M GONNA GO CHECK ON O'NEIL...

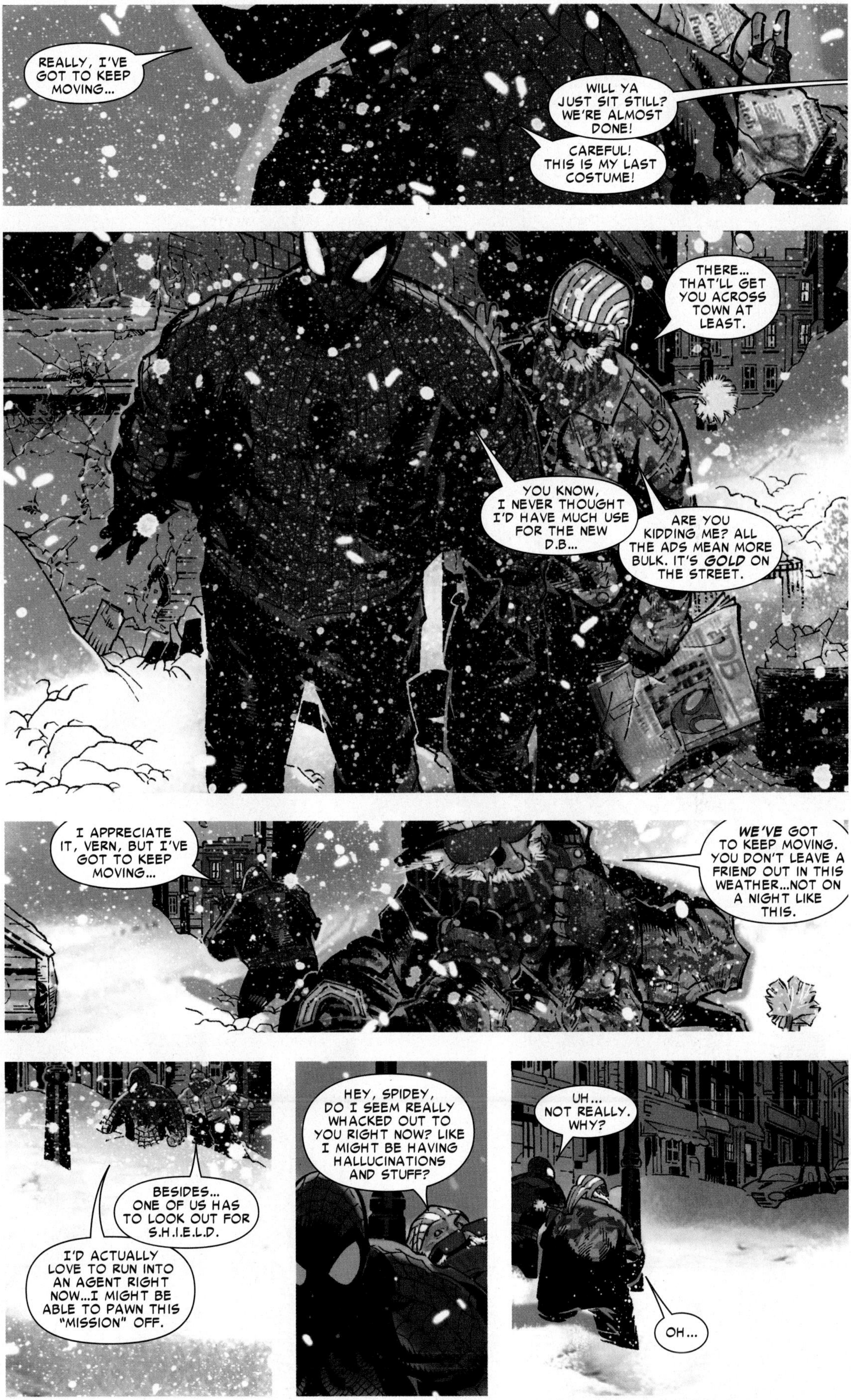
REALLY, I'VE GOT TO KEEP MOVING...
WILL YA JUST SIT STILL? WE'RE ALMOST DONE!
CAREFUL! THIS IS MY LAST COSTUME!
THERE... THAT'LL GET YOU ACROSS TOWN AT LEAST.
YOU KNOW, I NEVER THOUGHT I'D HAVE MUCH USE FOR THE NEW D.B...
ARE YOU KIDDING ME? ALL THE ADS MEAN MORE BULK. IT'S GOLD ON THE STREET.
I APPRECIATE IT, VERN, BUT I'VE GOT TO KEEP MOVING...
WE'VE GOT TO KEEP MOVING. YOU DON'T LEAVE A FRIEND OUT IN THIS WEATHER...NOT ON A NIGHT LIKE THIS.
BESIDES... ONE OF US HAS TO LOOK OUT FOR S.H.I.E.L.D.
I'D ACTUALLY LOVE TO RUN INTO AN AGENT RIGHT NOW...I MIGHT BE ABLE TO PAWN THIS "MISSION" OFF.
HEY, SPIDEY, DO I SEEM REALLY WHACKED OUT TO YOU RIGHT NOW? LIKE I MIGHT BE HAVING HALLUCINATIONS AND STUFF?
UH... NOT REALLY. WHY?
OH...

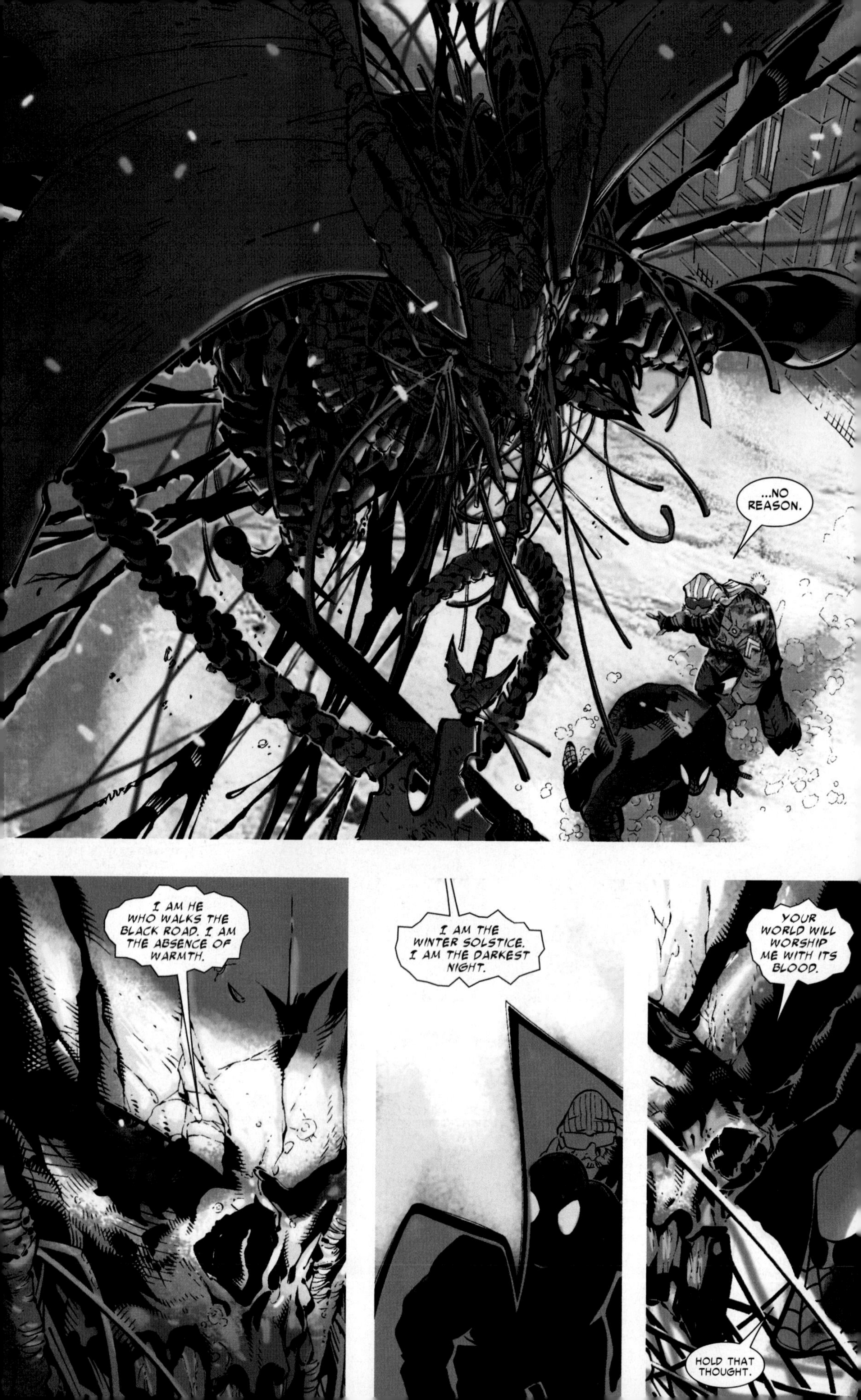
...NO REASON.
I AM HE WHO WALKS THE BLACK ROAD. I AM THE ABSENCE OF WARMTH.
I AM THE WINTER SOLSTICE. I AM THE DARKEST NIGHT.
YOUR WORLD WILL WORSHIP ME WITH ITS BLOOD.
HOLD THAT THOUGHT.

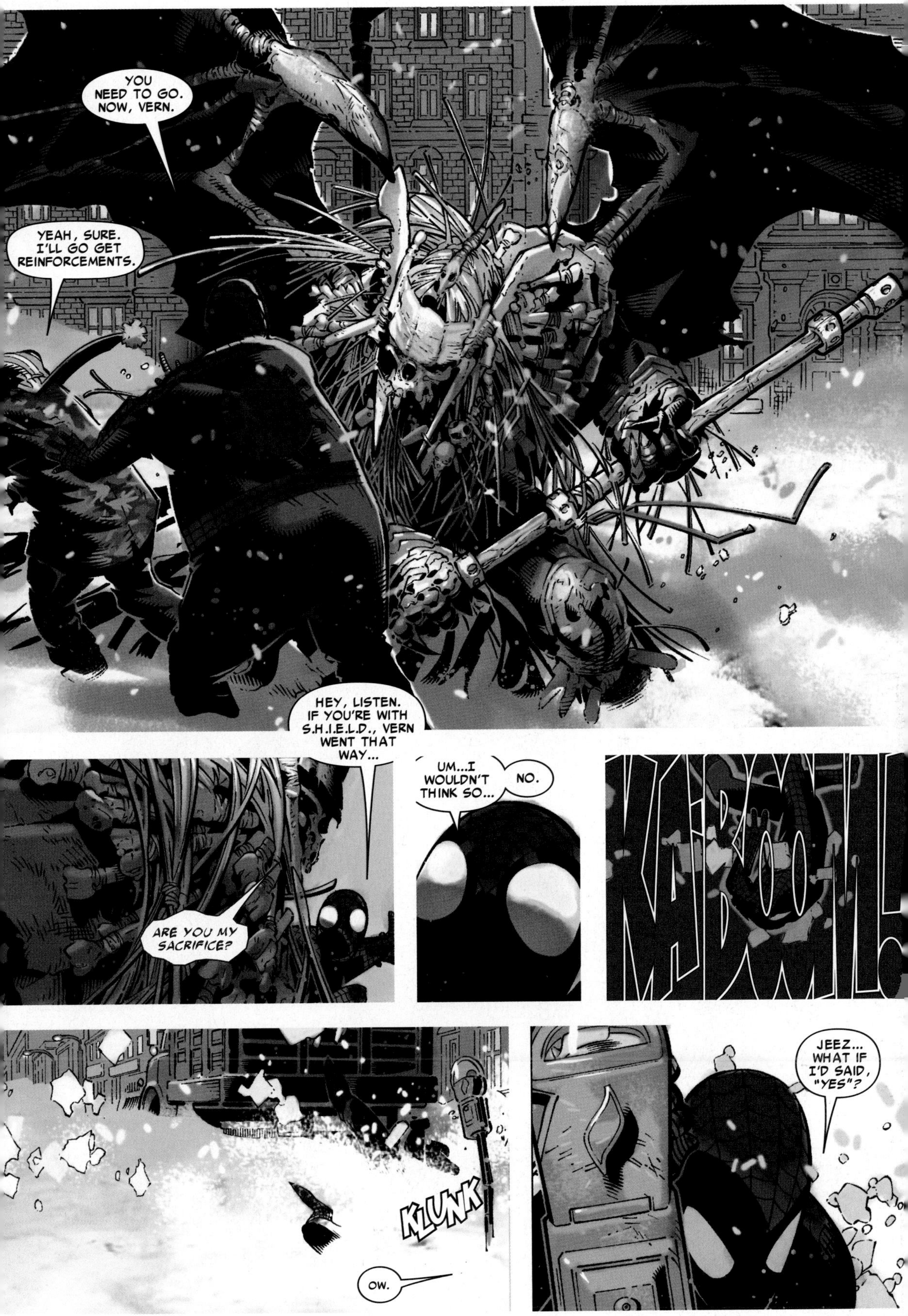
YOU NEED TO GO. NOW, VERN.
YEAH, SURE. I'LL GO GET REINFORCEMENTS.
HEY, LISTEN. IF YOU'RE WITH S.H.I.E.L.D., VERN WENT THAT WAY...
ARE YOU MY SACRIFICE?
UM...I WOULDN'T THINK SO...
NO.
KA-BOOM!
KLUNK
OW.
JEEZ... WHAT IF I'D SAID, "YES"?

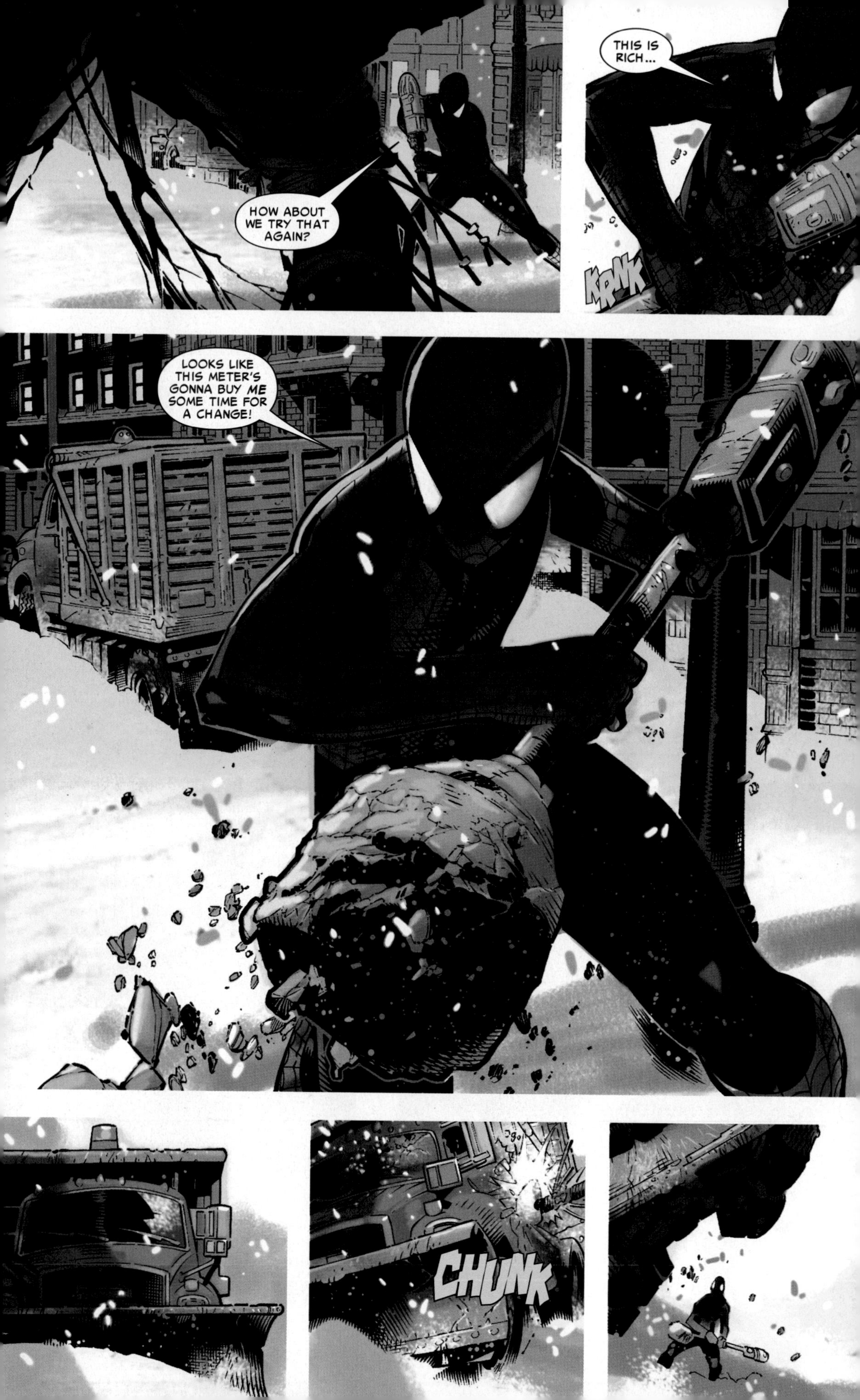
HOW ABOUT WE TRY THAT AGAIN?
THIS IS RICH...
KRNK
LOOKS LIKE THIS METER'S GONNA BUY *ME* SOME TIME FOR A CHANGE!
CHUNK

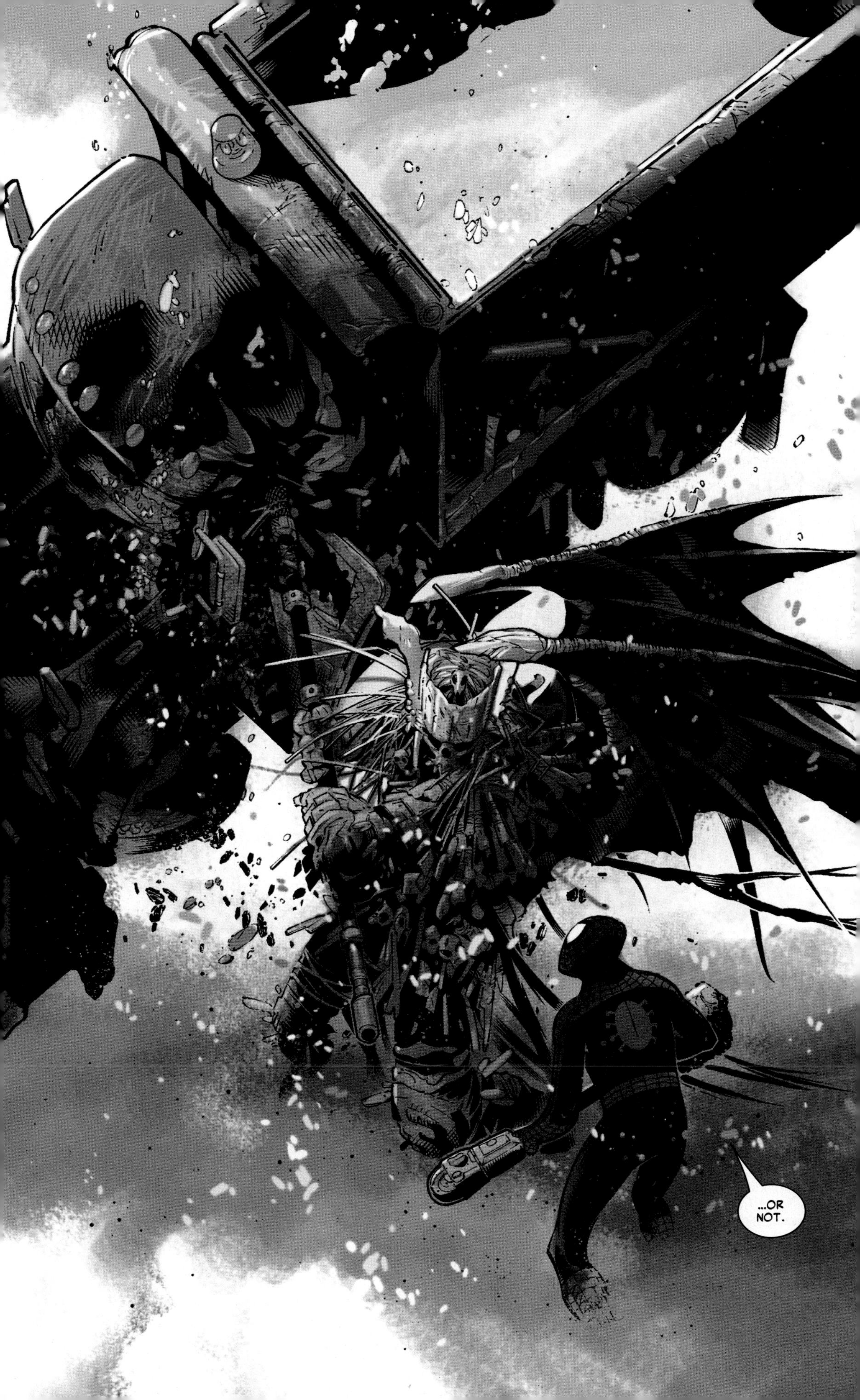
...OR NOT.

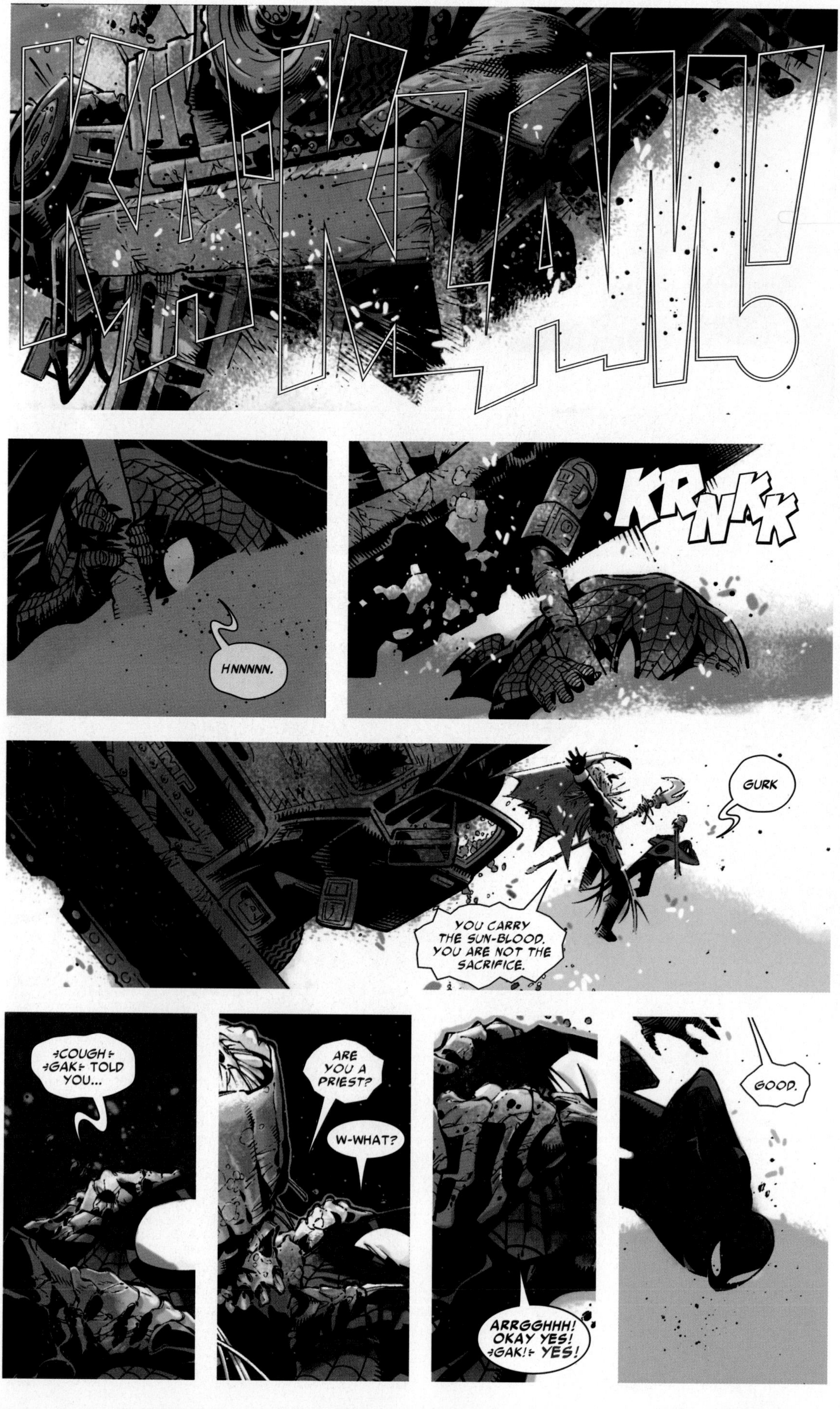
KA-KLAM!
HNNNNN.
KRNKK
GURK
YOU CARRY THE SUN-BLOOD. YOU ARE NOT THE SACRIFICE.
COUGH *GAK* TOLD YOU...
ARE YOU A PRIEST?
W-WHAT?
ARRGGHHH! OKAY YES! *GAK!* YES!
GOOD.

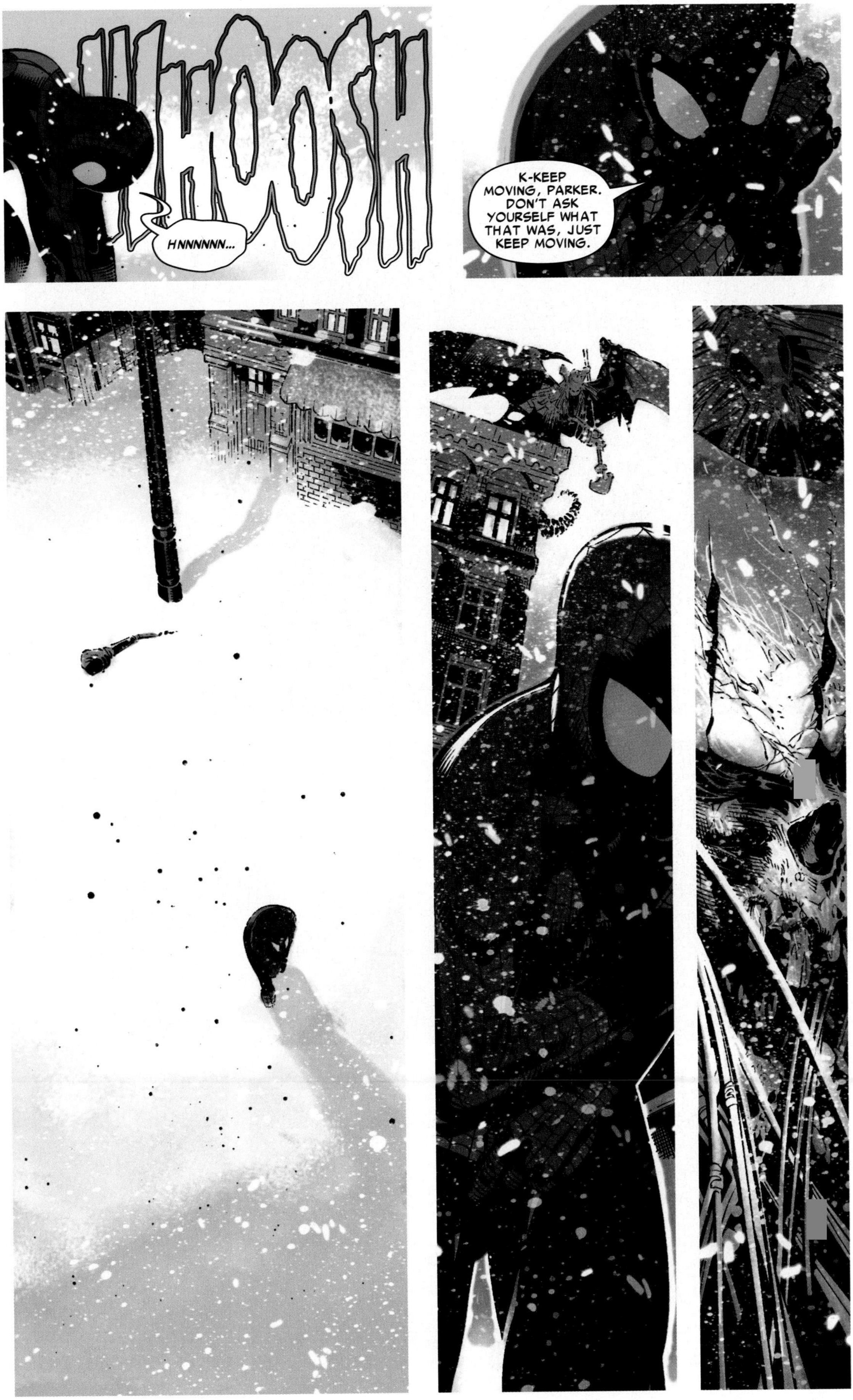
WHOOSH
HNNNNNN...
K-KEEP MOVING, PARKER. DON'T ASK YOURSELF WHAT THAT WAS, JUST KEEP MOVING.

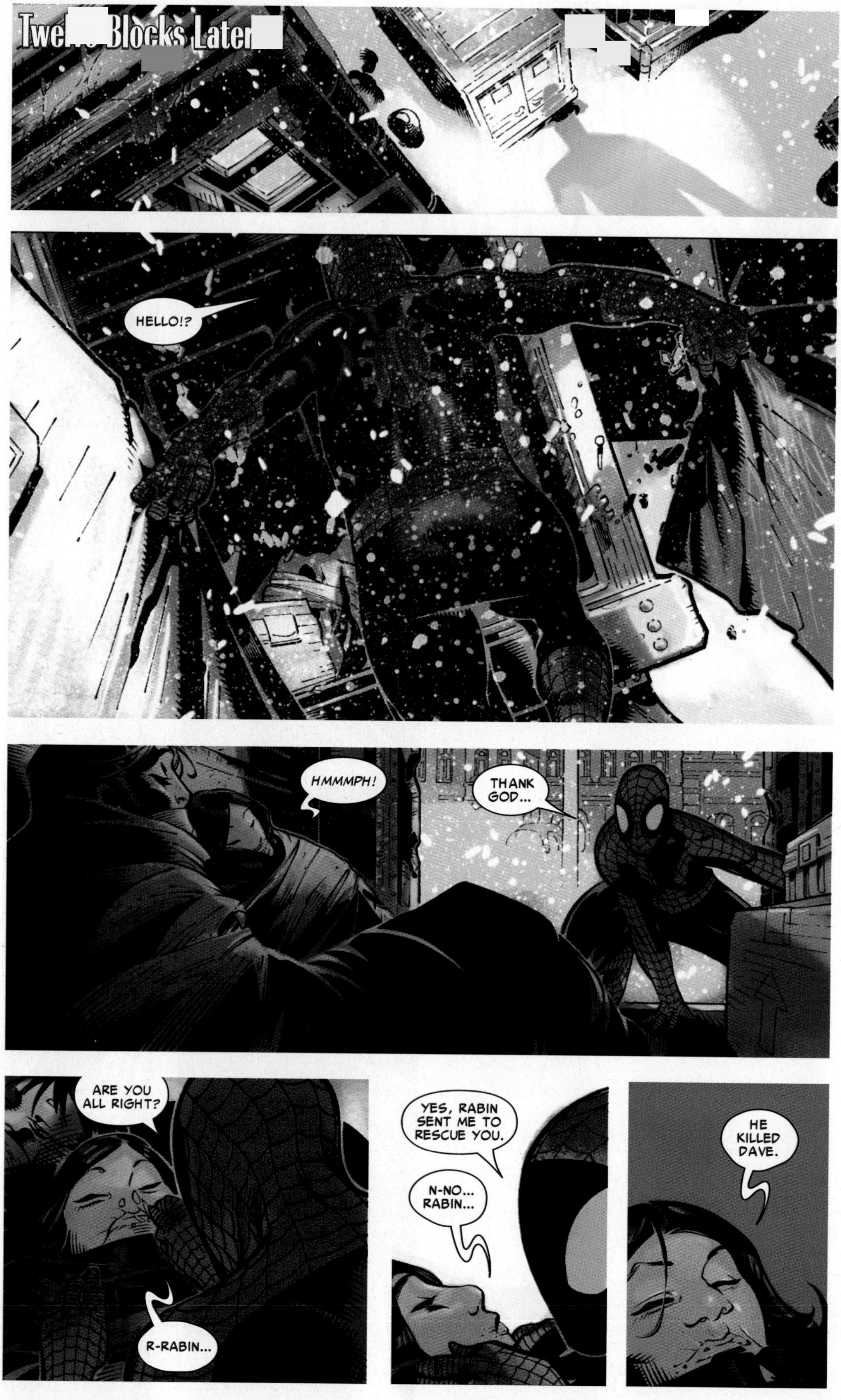
Blocks Later
HELLO!?
HMMMPH!
THANK GOD...
ARE YOU ALL RIGHT?
R-RABIN...
YES, RABIN SENT ME TO RESCUE YOU.
N-NO... RABIN...
HE KILLED DAVE.

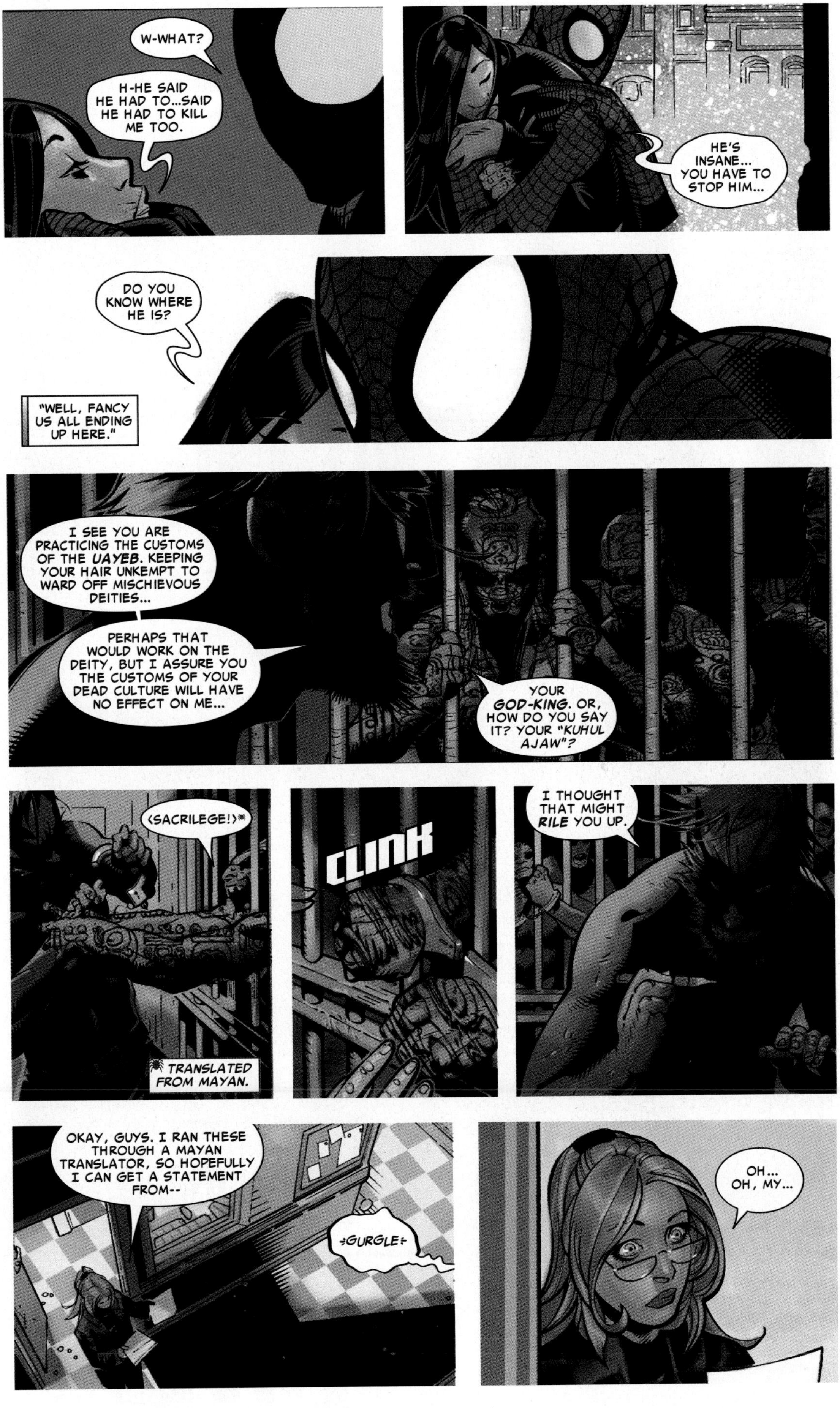
W-WHAT?
H-HE SAID HE HAD TO...SAID HE HAD TO KILL ME TOO.
HE'S INSANE... YOU HAVE TO STOP HIM...
DO YOU KNOW WHERE HE IS?
"WELL, FANCY US ALL ENDING UP HERE."
I SEE YOU ARE PRACTICING THE CUSTOMS OF THE *UAYEB*. KEEPING YOUR HAIR UNKEMPT TO WARD OFF MISCHIEVOUS DEITIES...
PERHAPS THAT WOULD WORK ON THE DEITY, BUT I ASSURE YOU THE CUSTOMS OF YOUR DEAD CULTURE WILL HAVE NO EFFECT ON ME...
YOUR ***GOD-KING***. OR, HOW DO YOU SAY IT? YOUR "*KUHUL AJAW*"?
‹SACRILEGE!›
TRANSLATED FROM MAYAN.
CLINK
I THOUGHT THAT MIGHT ***RILE*** YOU UP.
OKAY, GUYS. I RAN THESE THROUGH A MAYAN TRANSLATOR, SO HOPEFULLY I CAN GET A STATEMENT FROM--
GURGLE
OH... OH, MY...

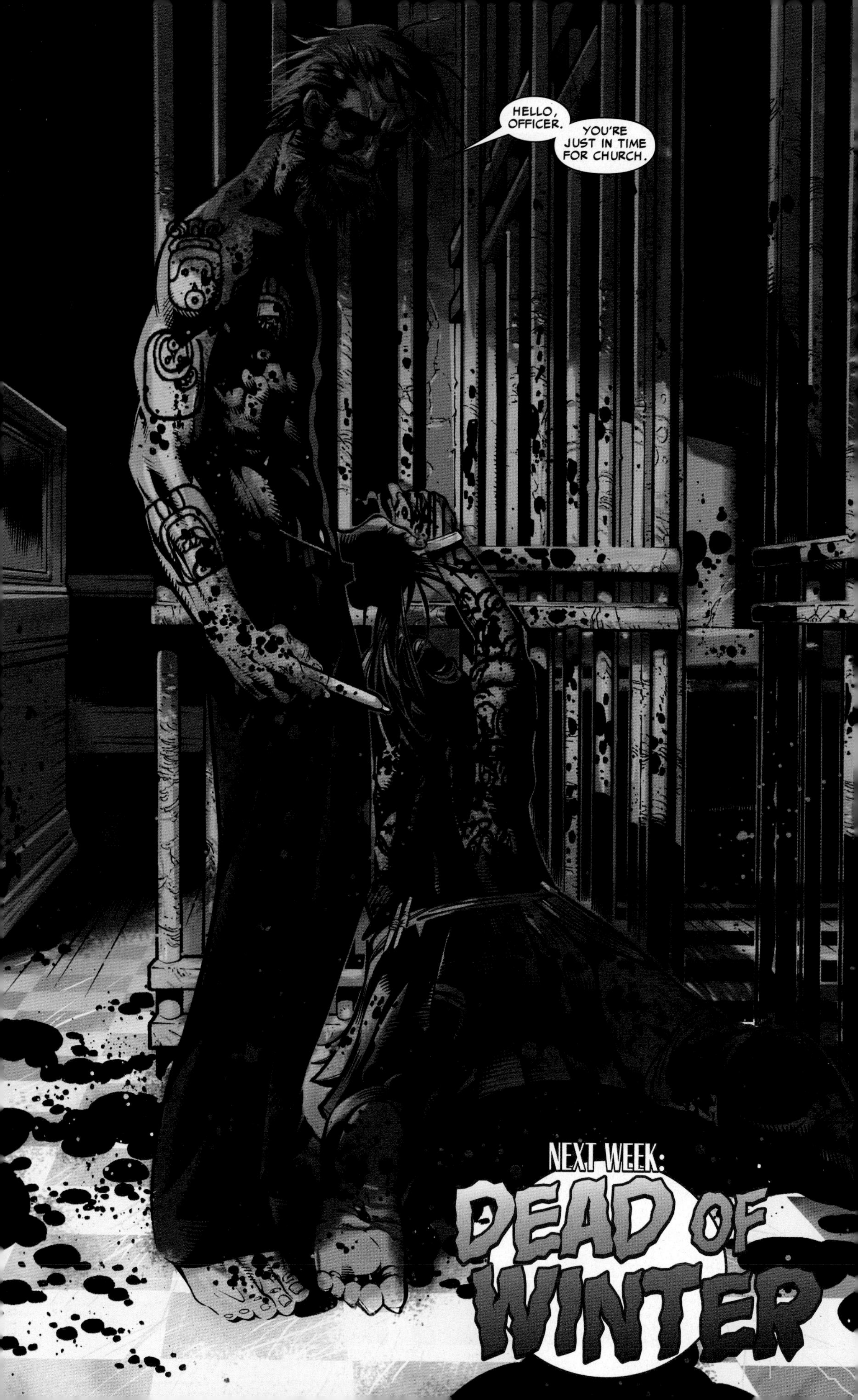
HELLO, OFFICER.
YOU'RE JUST IN TIME FOR CHURCH.
NEXT WEEK:
DEAD OF WINTER

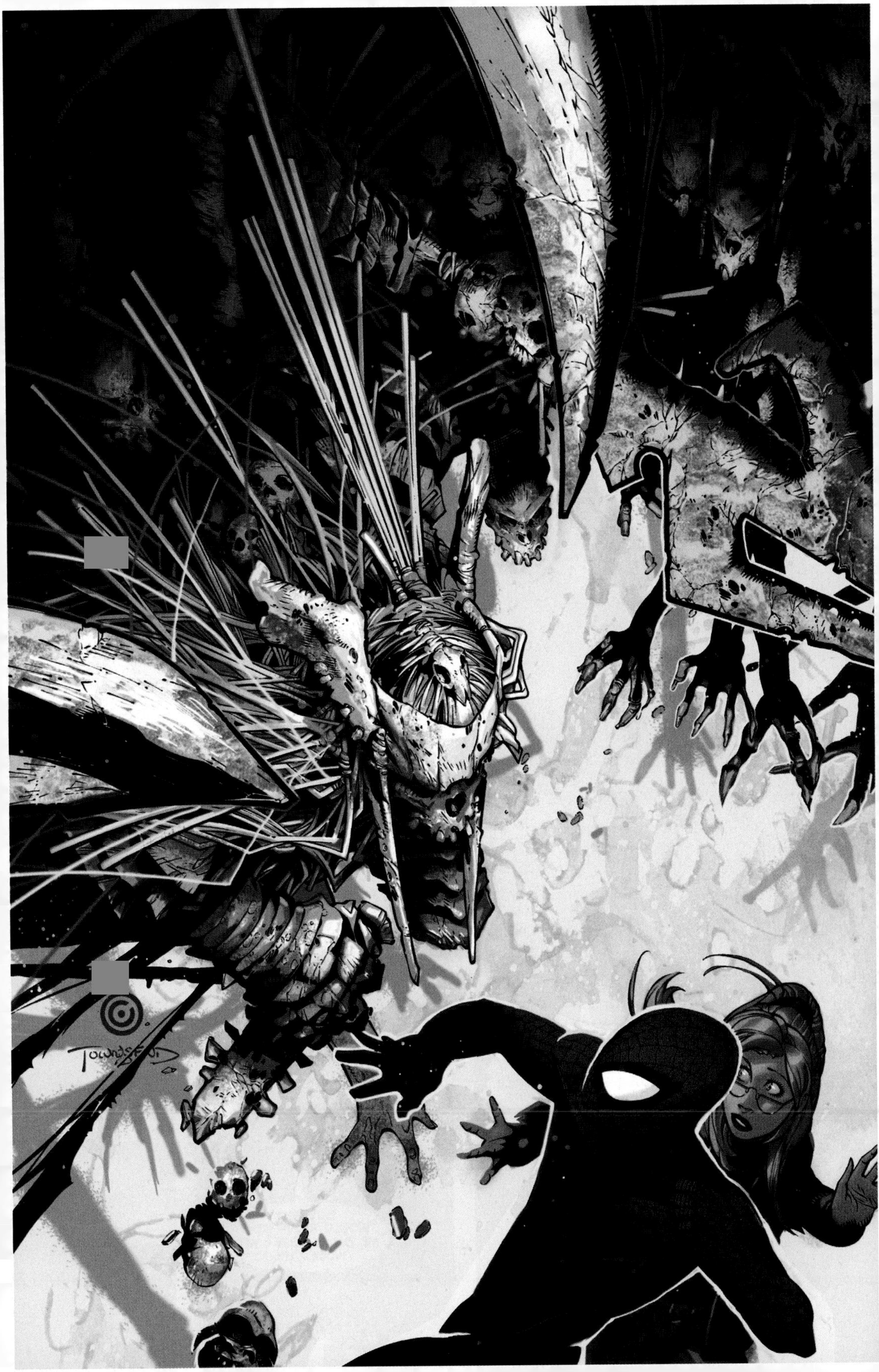

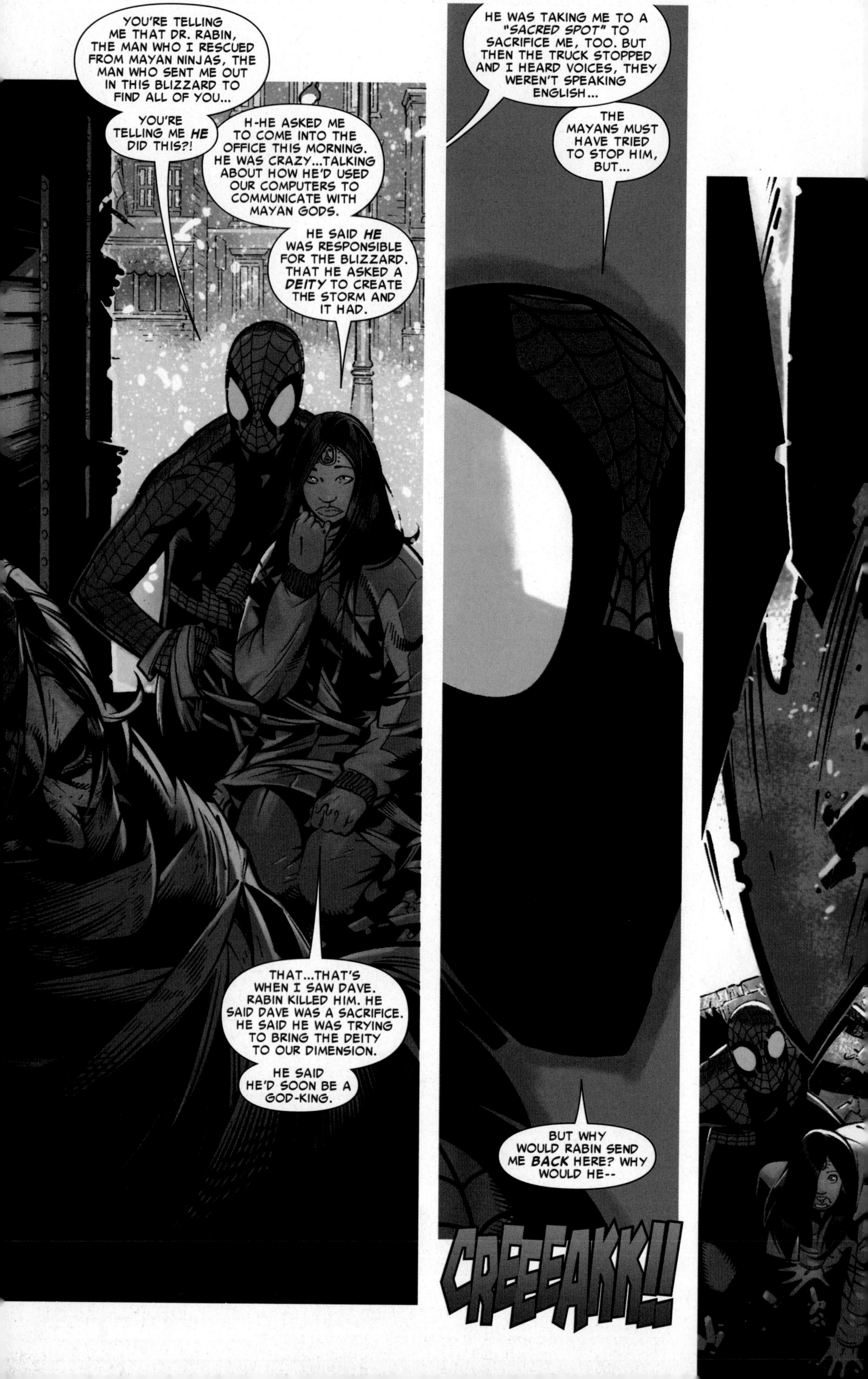
YOU'RE TELLING ME THAT DR. RABIN, THE MAN WHO I RESCUED FROM MAYAN NINJAS, THE MAN WHO SENT ME OUT IN THIS BLIZZARD TO FIND ALL OF YOU...
YOU'RE TELLING ME HE DID THIS?!
H-HE ASKED ME TO COME INTO THE OFFICE THIS MORNING. HE WAS CRAZY...TALKING ABOUT HOW HE'D USED OUR COMPUTERS TO COMMUNICATE WITH MAYAN GODS.
HE SAID HE WAS RESPONSIBLE FOR THE BLIZZARD. THAT HE ASKED A DEITY TO CREATE THE STORM AND IT HAD.
THAT...THAT'S WHEN I SAW DAVE. RABIN KILLED HIM. HE SAID DAVE WAS A SACRIFICE. HE SAID HE WAS TRYING TO BRING THE DEITY TO OUR DIMENSION.
HE SAID HE'D SOON BE A GOD-KING.
HE WAS TAKING ME TO A "SACRED SPOT" TO SACRIFICE ME, TOO. BUT THEN THE TRUCK STOPPED AND I HEARD VOICES, THEY WEREN'T SPEAKING ENGLISH...
THE MAYANS MUST HAVE TRIED TO STOP HIM, BUT...
BUT WHY WOULD RABIN SEND ME BACK HERE? WHY WOULD HE--
CREEEAKK!!

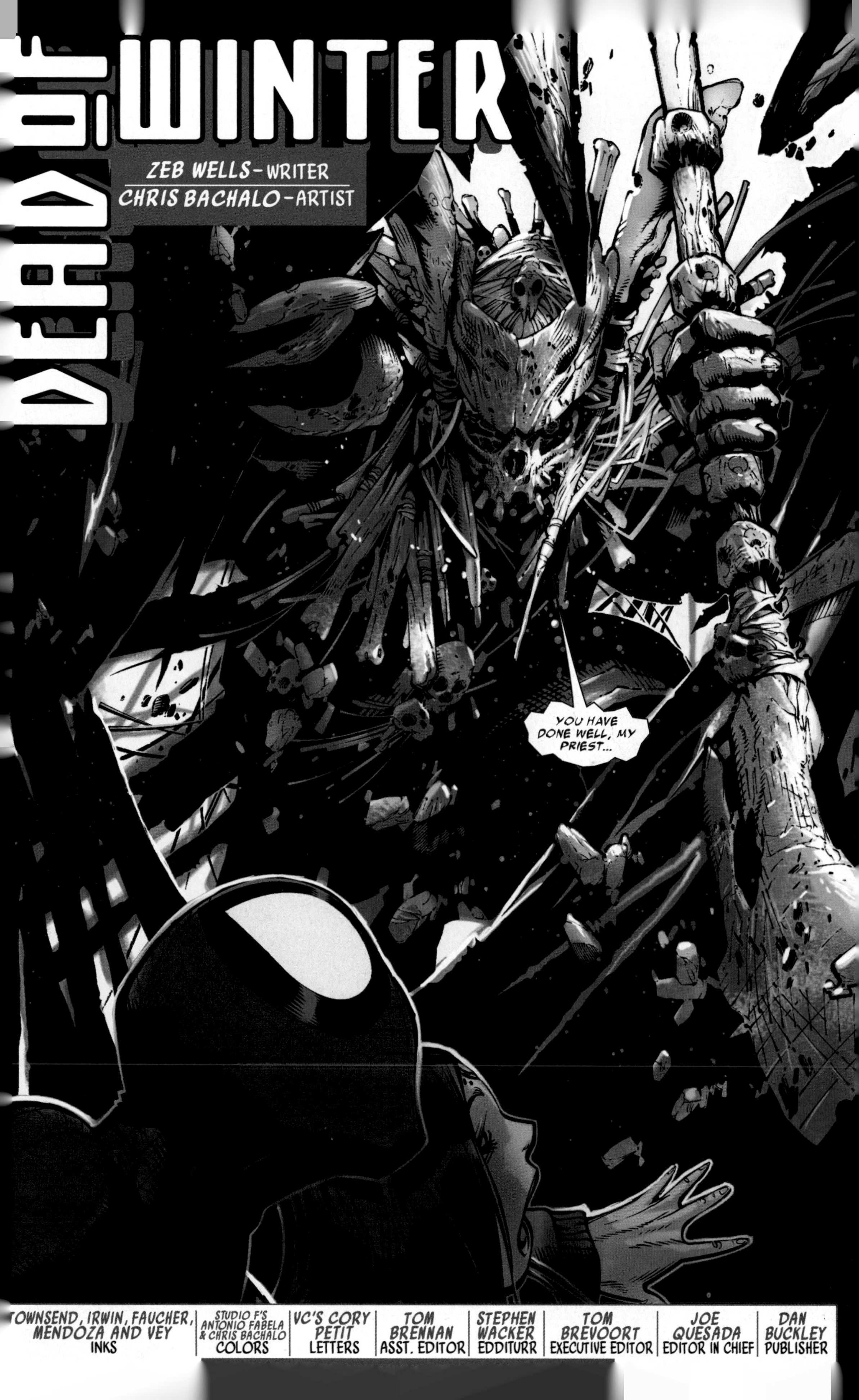
DEAD OF WINTER
ZEB WELLS-WRITER
CHRIS BACHALO-ARTIST
YOU HAVE DONE WELL, MY PRIEST...
TOWNSEND, IRWIN, FAUCHER, MENDOZA AND VEY INKS
STUDIO F'S ANTONIO FABELA & CHRIS BACHALO COLORS
VC'S CORY PETIT LETTERS
TOM BRENNAN ASST. EDITOR
STEPHEN WACKER EDDITURR
TOM BREVOORT EXECUTIVE EDITOR
JOE QUESADA EDITOR IN CHIEF
DAN BUCKLEY PUBLISHER

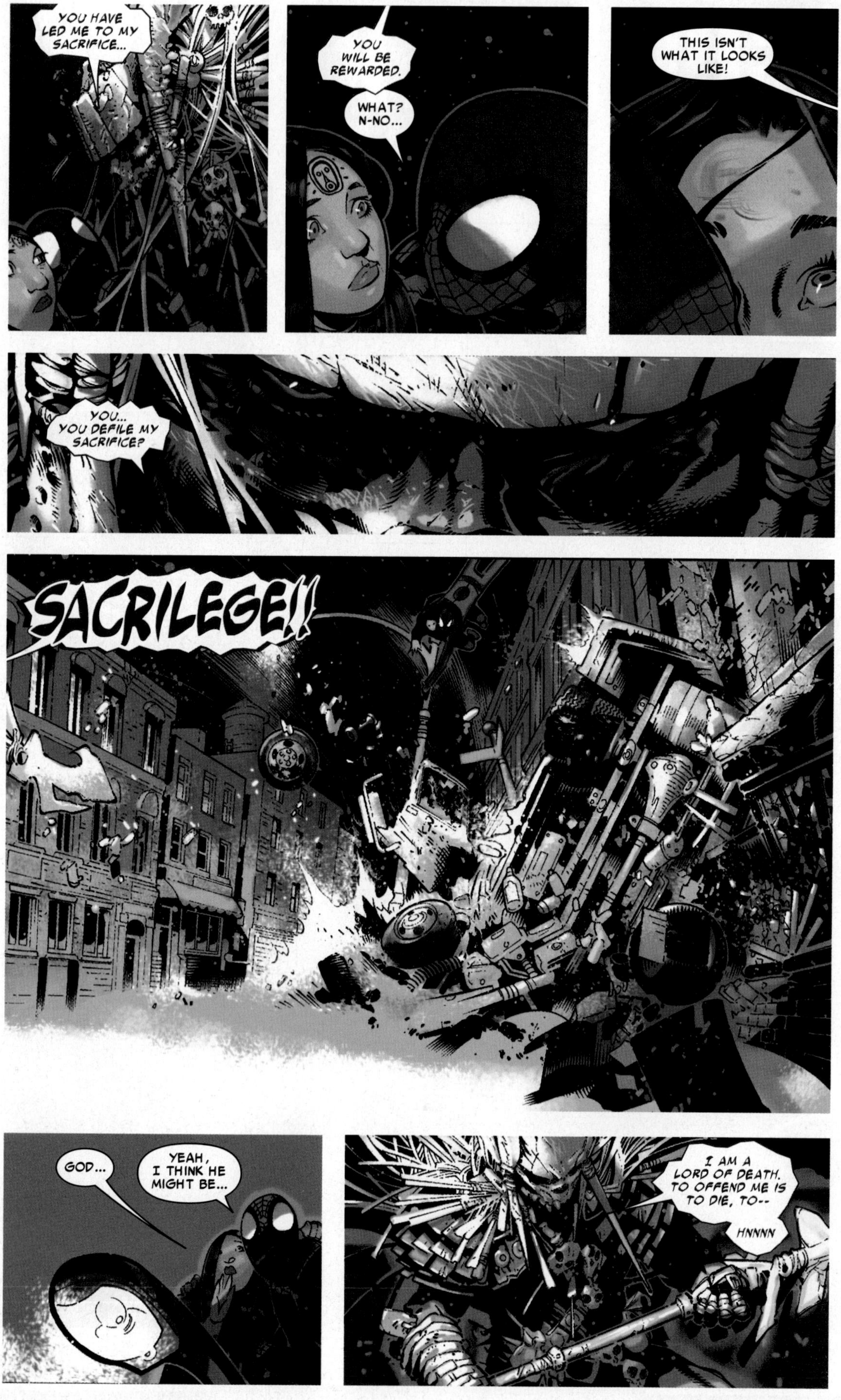
YOU HAVE LED ME TO MY SACRIFICE...
YOU WILL BE REWARDED.
WHAT? N-NO...
THIS ISN'T WHAT IT LOOKS LIKE!
YOU... YOU DEFILE MY SACRIFICE?
SACRILEGE!!
GOD...
YEAH, I THINK HE MIGHT BE...
I AM A LORD OF DEATH. TO OFFEND ME IS TO DIE, TO--
HNNNN

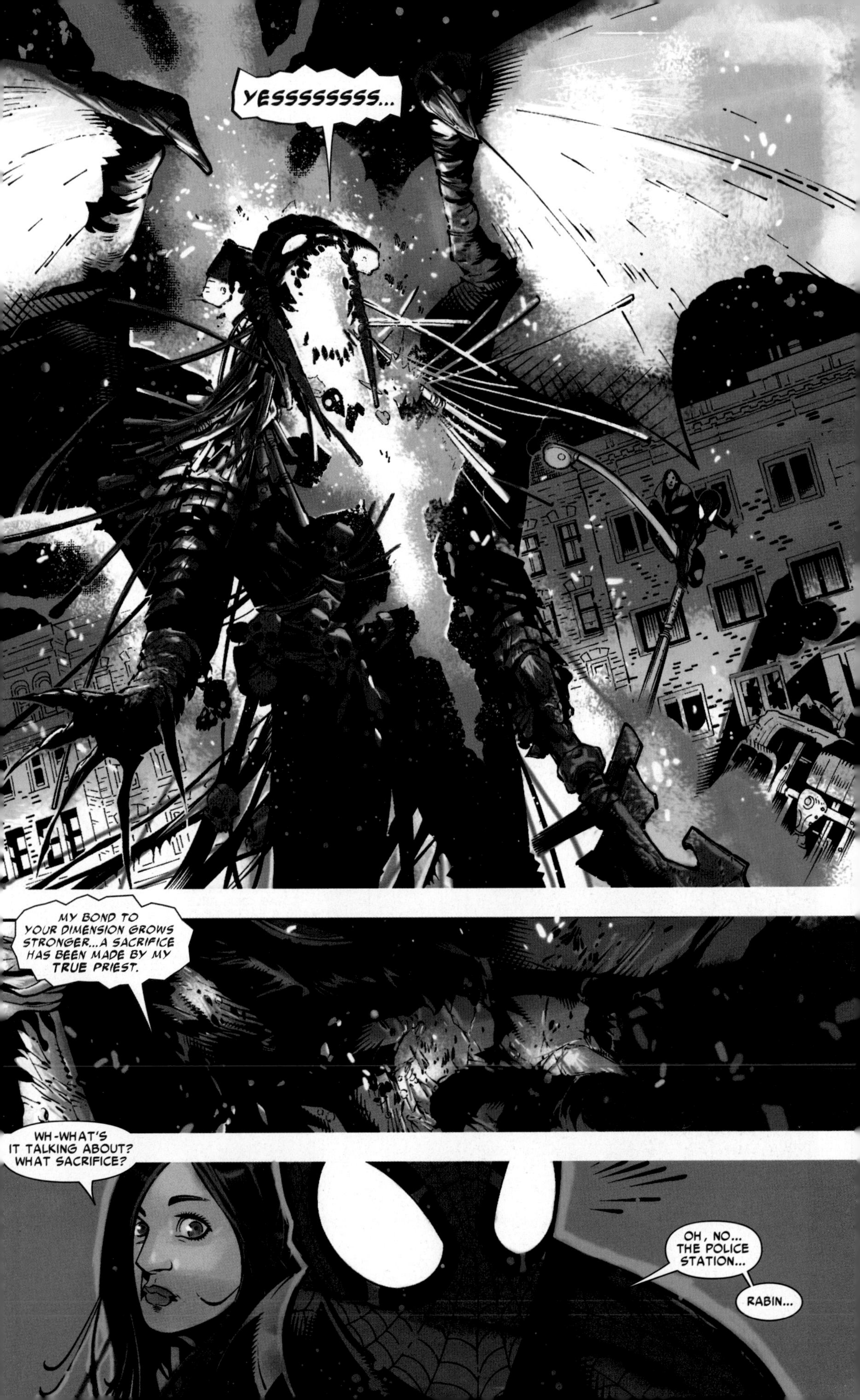
YESSSSSSSS...
MY BOND TO YOUR DIMENSION GROWS STRONGER...A SACRIFICE HAS BEEN MADE BY MY TRUE PRIEST.
WH-WHAT'S IT TALKING ABOUT? WHAT SACRIFICE?
OH, NO... THE POLICE STATION...
RABIN...

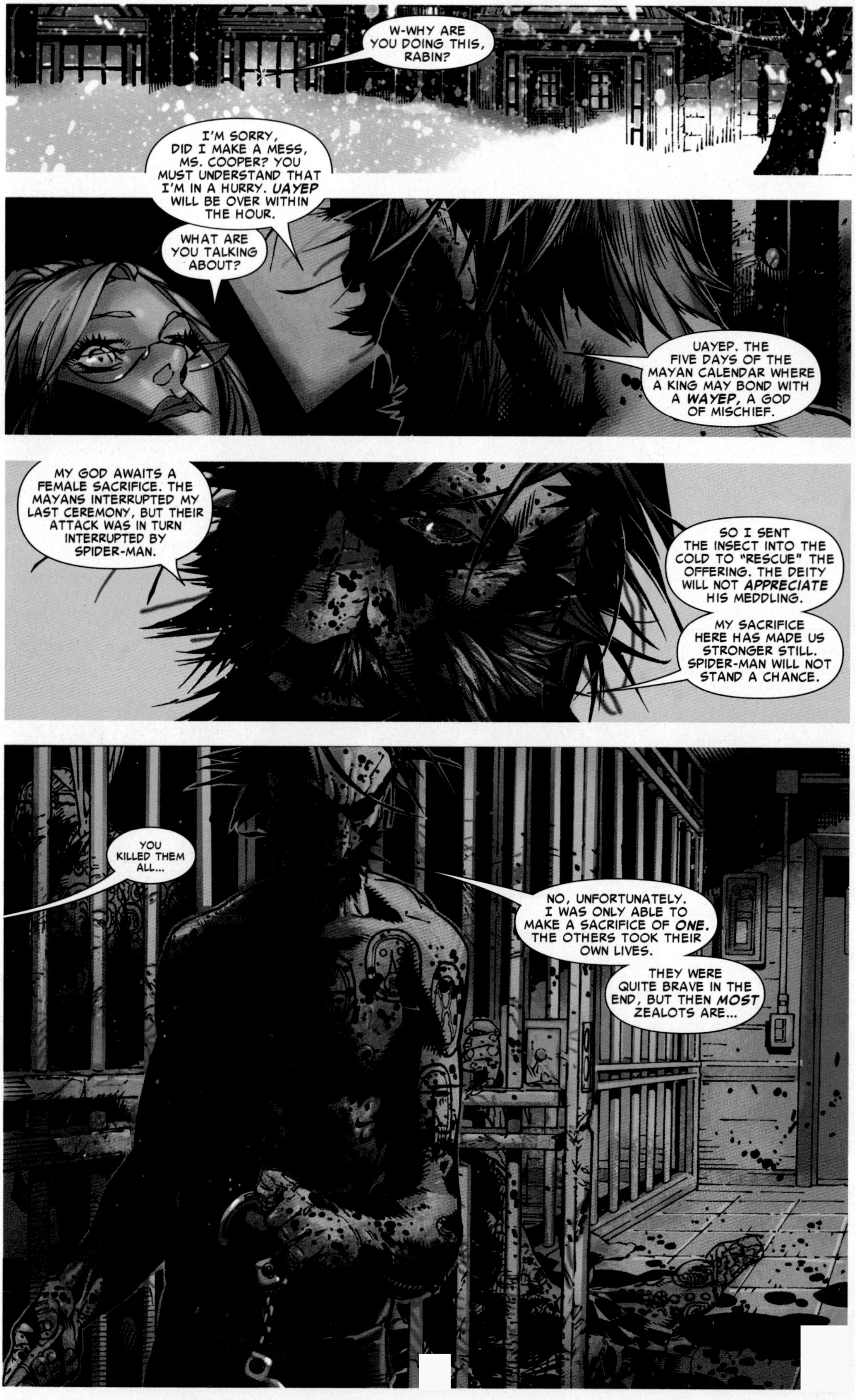
W-WHY ARE YOU DOING THIS, RABIN?
I'M SORRY, DID I MAKE A MESS, MS. COOPER? YOU MUST UNDERSTAND THAT I'M IN A HURRY. UAYEP WILL BE OVER WITHIN THE HOUR.
WHAT ARE YOU TALKING ABOUT?
UAYEP. THE FIVE DAYS OF THE MAYAN CALENDAR WHERE A KING MAY BOND WITH A WAYEP, A GOD OF MISCHIEF.
MY GOD AWAITS A FEMALE SACRIFICE. THE MAYANS INTERRUPTED MY LAST CEREMONY, BUT THEIR ATTACK WAS IN TURN INTERRUPTED BY SPIDER-MAN.
SO I SENT THE INSECT INTO THE COLD TO "RESCUE" THE OFFERING. THE DEITY WILL NOT APPRECIATE HIS MEDDLING.
MY SACRIFICE HERE HAS MADE US STRONGER STILL. SPIDER-MAN WILL NOT STAND A CHANCE.
YOU KILLED THEM ALL...
NO, UNFORTUNATELY. I WAS ONLY ABLE TO MAKE A SACRIFICE OF ONE. THE OTHERS TOOK THEIR OWN LIVES.
THEY WERE QUITE BRAVE IN THE END, BUT THEN MOST ZEALOTS ARE...

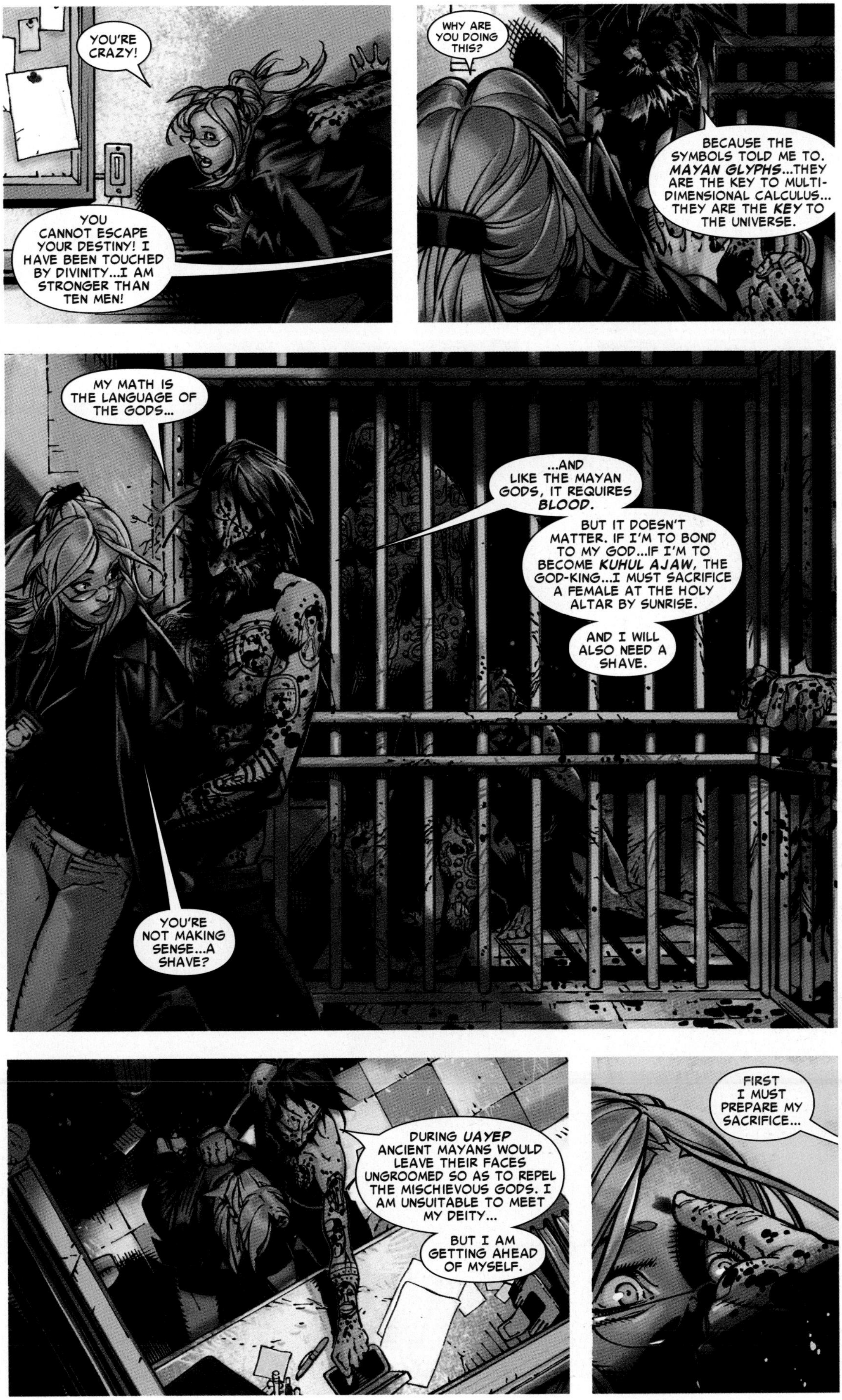
YOU'RE CRAZY!
YOU CANNOT ESCAPE YOUR DESTINY! I HAVE BEEN TOUCHED BY DIVINITY...I AM STRONGER THAN TEN MEN!
WHY ARE YOU DOING THIS?
BECAUSE THE SYMBOLS TOLD ME TO. MAYAN GLYPHS...THEY ARE THE KEY TO MULTI-DIMENSIONAL CALCULUS... THEY ARE THE KEY TO THE UNIVERSE.
MY MATH IS THE LANGUAGE OF THE GODS...
...AND LIKE THE MAYAN GODS, IT REQUIRES BLOOD.
BUT IT DOESN'T MATTER. IF I'M TO BOND TO MY GOD...IF I'M TO BECOME KUHUL AJAW, THE GOD-KING...I MUST SACRIFICE A FEMALE AT THE HOLY ALTAR BY SUNRISE.
AND I WILL ALSO NEED A SHAVE.
YOU'RE NOT MAKING SENSE...A SHAVE?
DURING UAYEP ANCIENT MAYANS WOULD LEAVE THEIR FACES UNGROOMED SO AS TO REPEL THE MISCHIEVOUS GODS. I AM UNSUITABLE TO MEET MY DEITY...
BUT I AM GETTING AHEAD OF MYSELF.
FIRST I MUST PREPARE MY SACRIFICE...

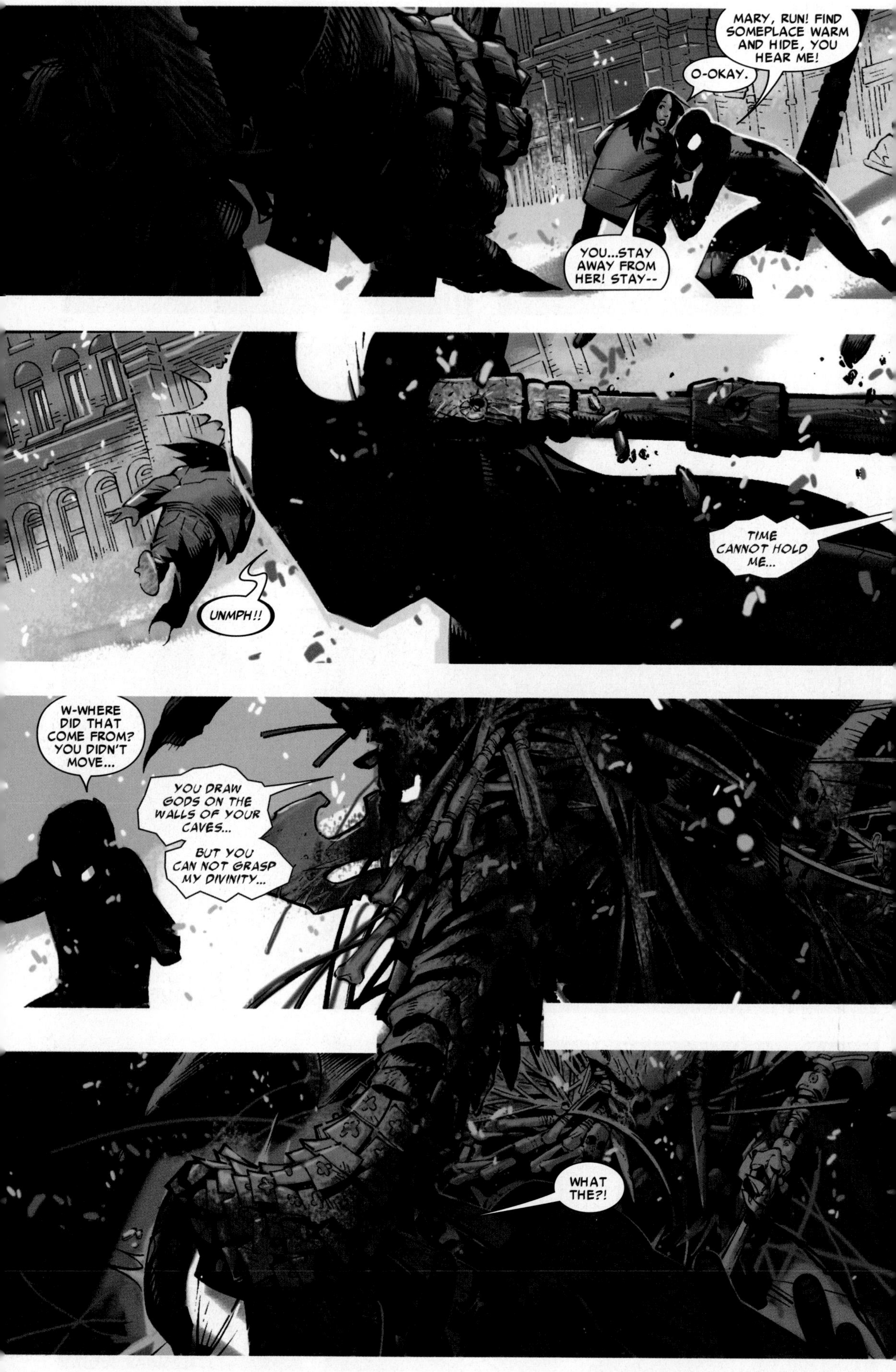
MARY, RUN! FIND SOMEPLACE WARM AND HIDE, YOU HEAR ME!
O-OKAY.
YOU...STAY AWAY FROM HER! STAY--
TIME CANNOT HOLD ME...
UNMPH!!
W-WHERE DID THAT COME FROM? YOU DIDN'T MOVE...
YOU DRAW GODS ON THE WALLS OF YOUR CAVES...
BUT YOU CAN NOT GRASP MY DIVINITY...
WHAT THE?!

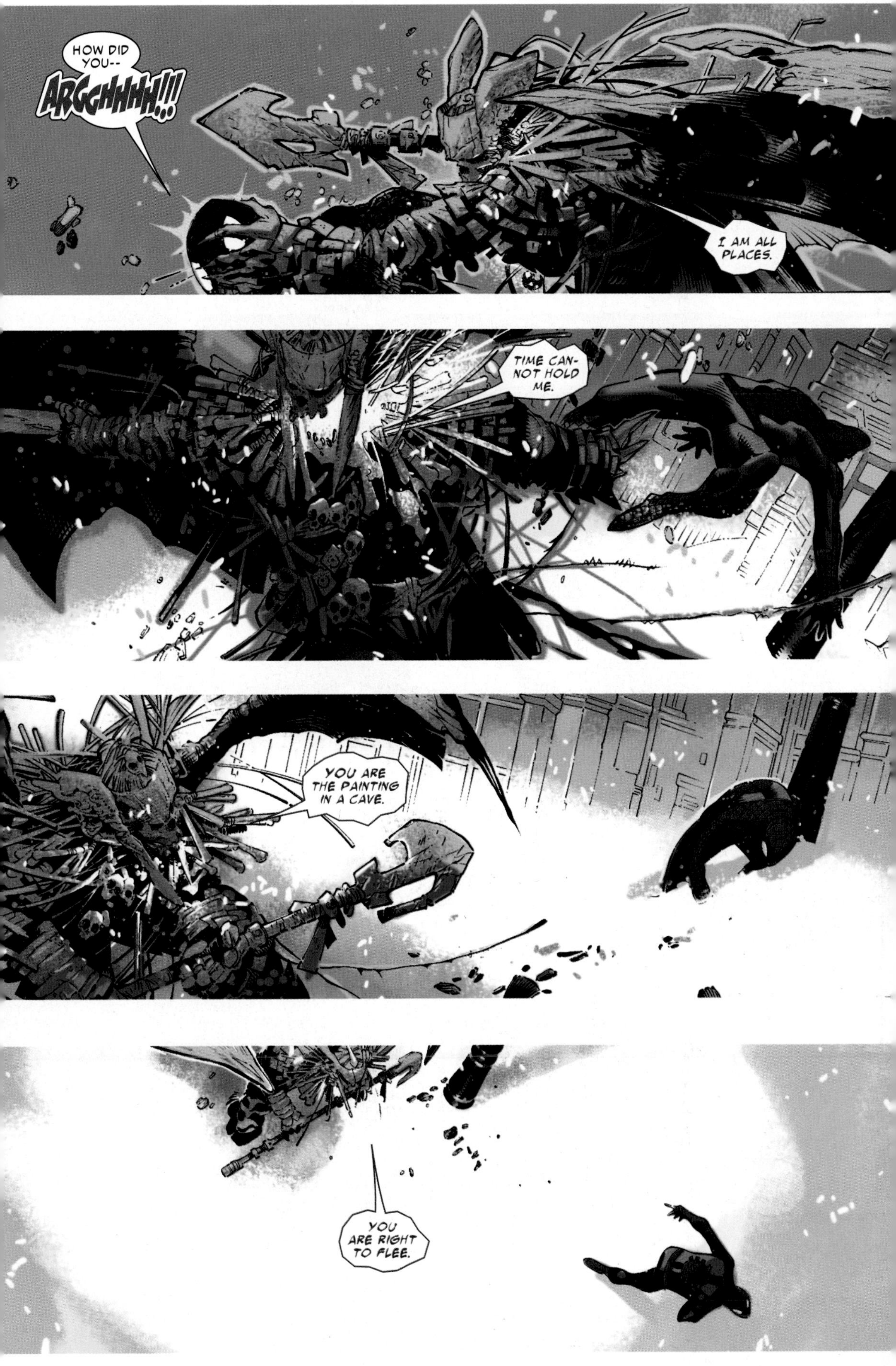
HOW DID YOU--
ARGGHHHH!!!
I AM ALL PLACES.
TIME CAN-NOT HOLD ME.
YOU ARE THE PAINTING IN A CAVE.
YOU ARE RIGHT TO FLEE.

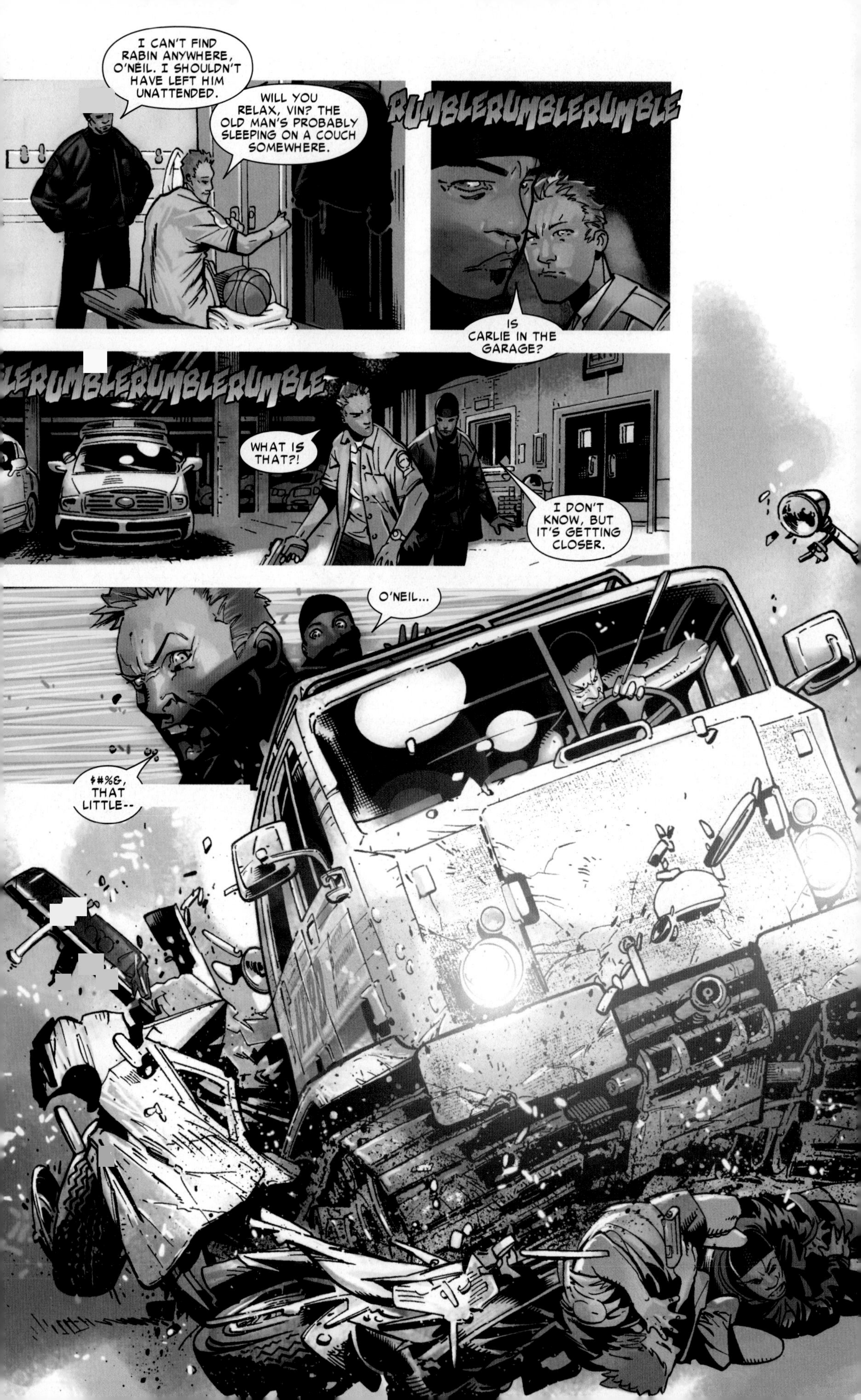

I CAN'T FIND RABIN ANYWHERE, O'NEIL. I SHOULDN'T HAVE LEFT HIM UNATTENDED.
WILL YOU RELAX, VIN? THE OLD MAN'S PROBABLY SLEEPING ON A COUCH SOMEWHERE.
RUMBLERUMBLERUMBLE
IS CARLIE IN THE GARAGE?
LERUMBLERUMBLERUMBLE
WHAT IS THAT?!
I DON'T KNOW, BUT IT'S GETTING CLOSER.
O'NEIL...
$#%&, THAT LITTLE--

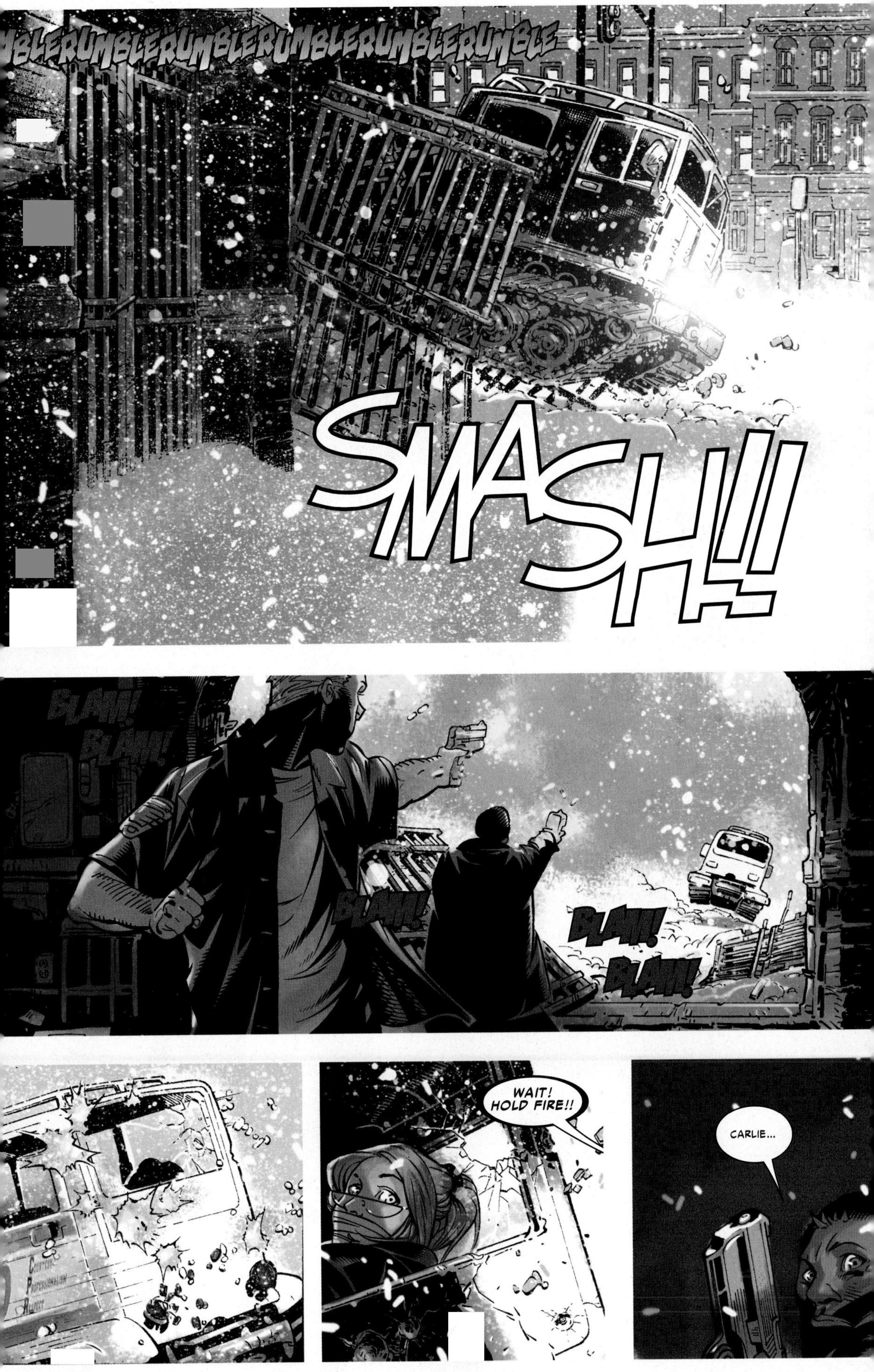
MBLERUMBLERUMBLERUMBLERUMBLERUMBLE
SMASH!!!
BLAM!
BLAM!
BLAM!
BLAM!
BLAM!
WAIT! HOLD FIRE!!
CARLIE...

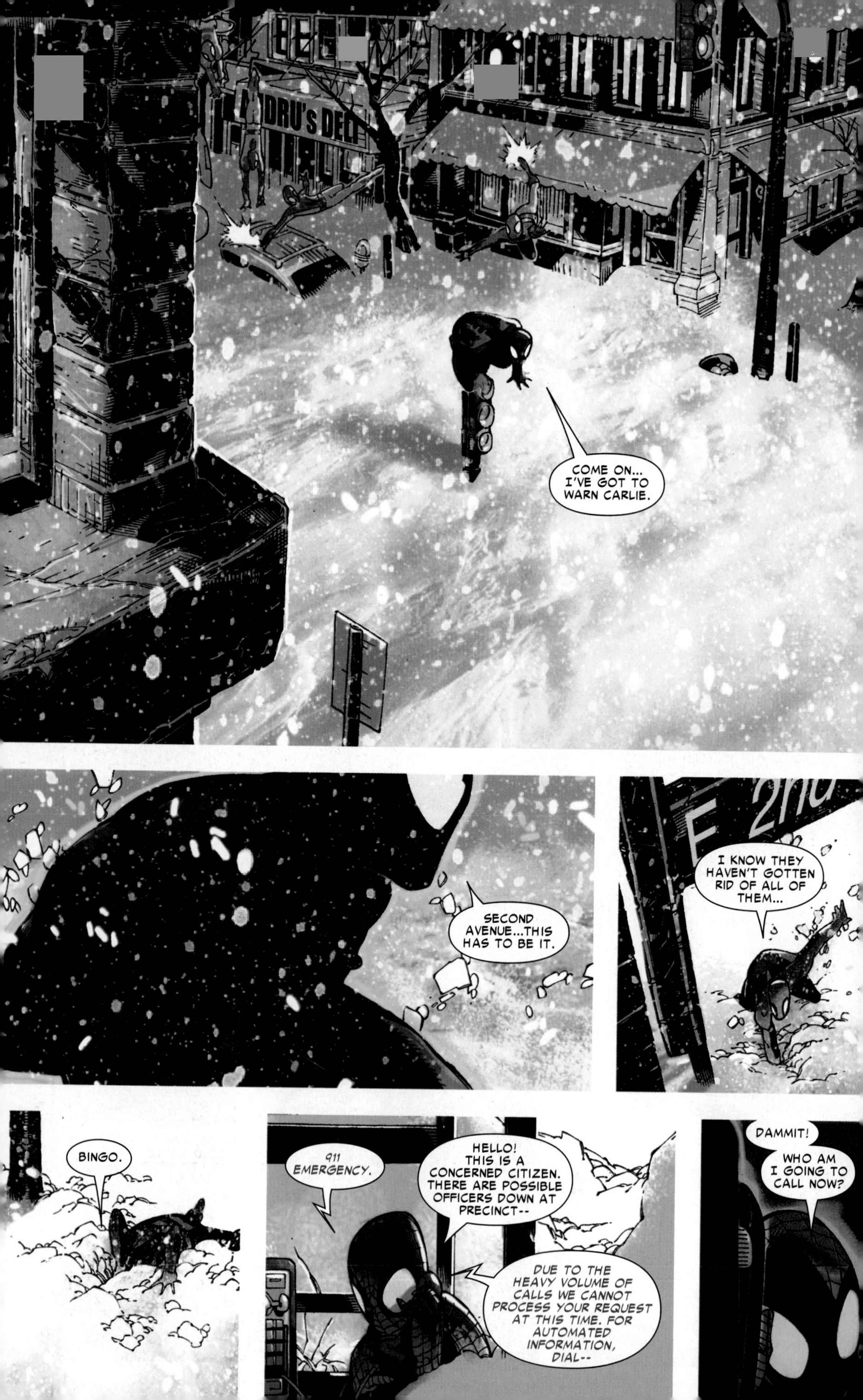
COME ON... I'VE GOT TO WARN CARLIE.
SECOND AVENUE...THIS HAS TO BE IT.
I KNOW THEY HAVEN'T GOTTEN RID OF ALL OF THEM...
BINGO.
911 EMERGENCY.
HELLO! THIS IS A CONCERNED CITIZEN. THERE ARE POSSIBLE OFFICERS DOWN AT PRECINCT--
DUE TO THE HEAVY VOLUME OF CALLS WE CANNOT PROCESS YOUR REQUEST AT THIS TIME. FOR AUTOMATED INFORMATION, DIAL--
DAMMIT!
WHO AM I GOING TO CALL NOW?

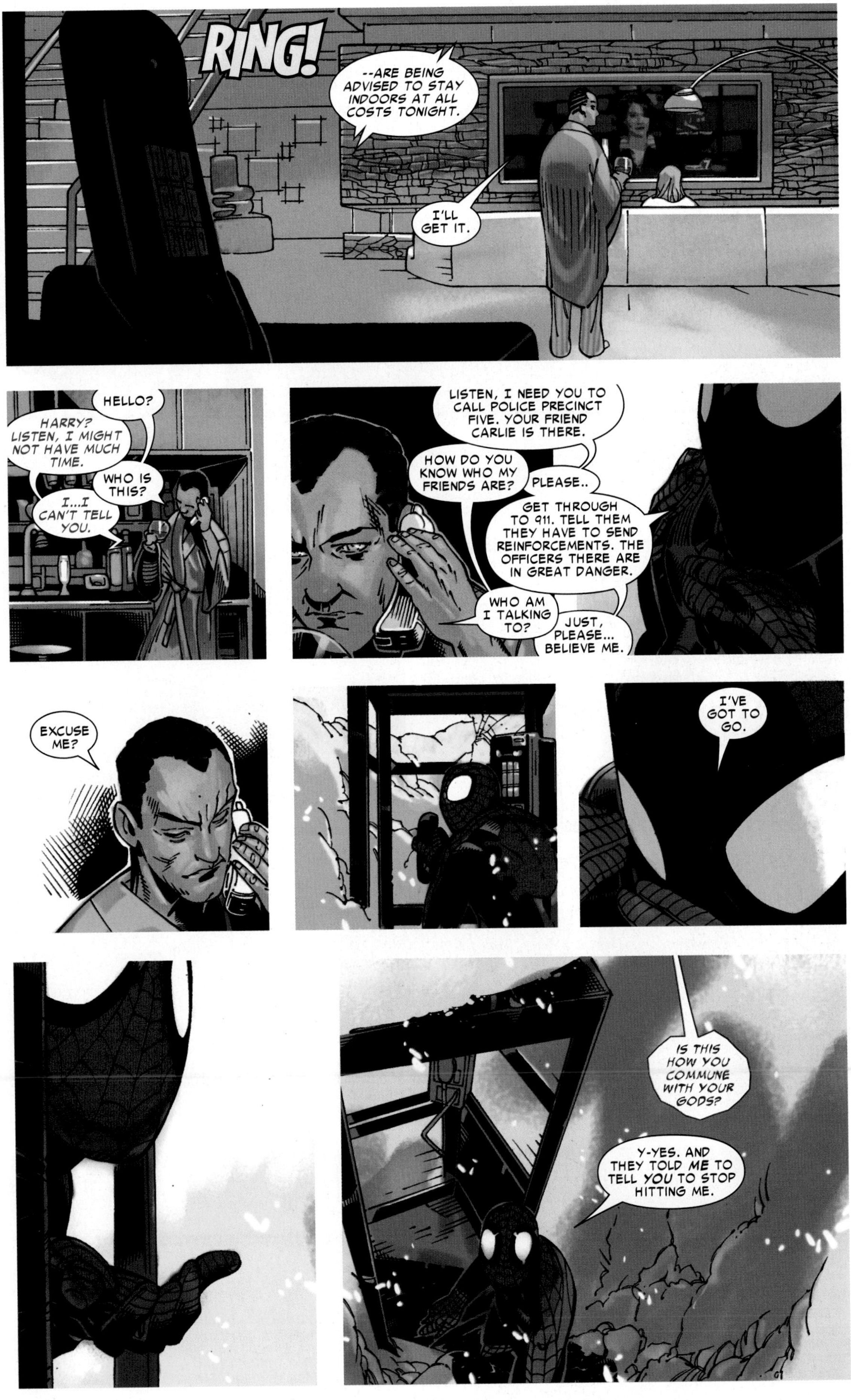
RING!
--ARE BEING ADVISED TO STAY INDOORS AT ALL COSTS TONIGHT.
I'LL GET IT.
HELLO?
HARRY? LISTEN, I MIGHT NOT HAVE MUCH TIME.
WHO IS THIS?
I...I CAN'T TELL YOU.
LISTEN, I NEED YOU TO CALL POLICE PRECINCT FIVE. YOUR FRIEND CARLIE IS THERE.
HOW DO YOU KNOW WHO MY FRIENDS ARE?
PLEASE..
GET THROUGH TO 911. TELL THEM THEY HAVE TO SEND REINFORCEMENTS. THE OFFICERS THERE ARE IN GREAT DANGER.
WHO AM I TALKING TO?
JUST, PLEASE... BELIEVE ME.
EXCUSE ME?
I'VE GOT TO GO.
IS THIS HOW YOU COMMUNE WITH YOUR GODS?
Y-YES. AND THEY TOLD ME TO TELL YOU TO STOP HITTING ME.

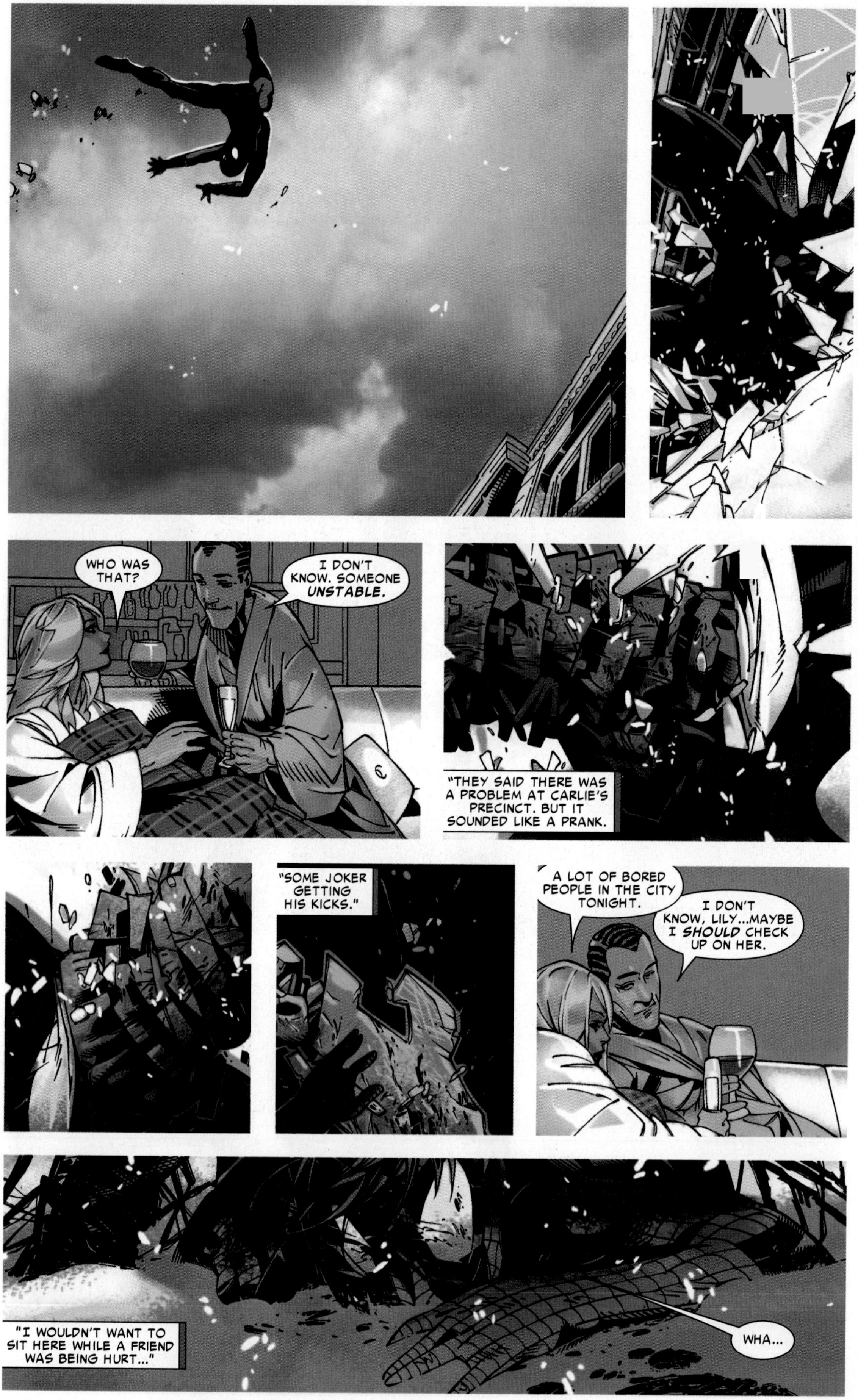
WHO WAS THAT?
I DON'T KNOW. SOMEONE *UNSTABLE.*
"THEY SAID THERE WAS A PROBLEM AT CARLIE'S PRECINCT. BUT IT SOUNDED LIKE A PRANK.
"SOME JOKER GETTING HIS KICKS."
A LOT OF BORED PEOPLE IN THE CITY TONIGHT.
I DON'T KNOW, LILY...MAYBE I *SHOULD* CHECK UP ON HER.
"I WOULDN'T WANT TO SIT HERE WHILE A FRIEND WAS BEING HURT..."
WHA...

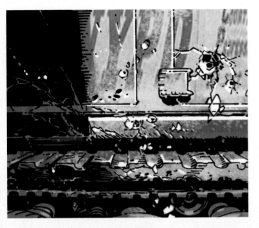

C-CARLIE... THANK GOD. I HOPE YOU BROUGHT EVERYBODY...

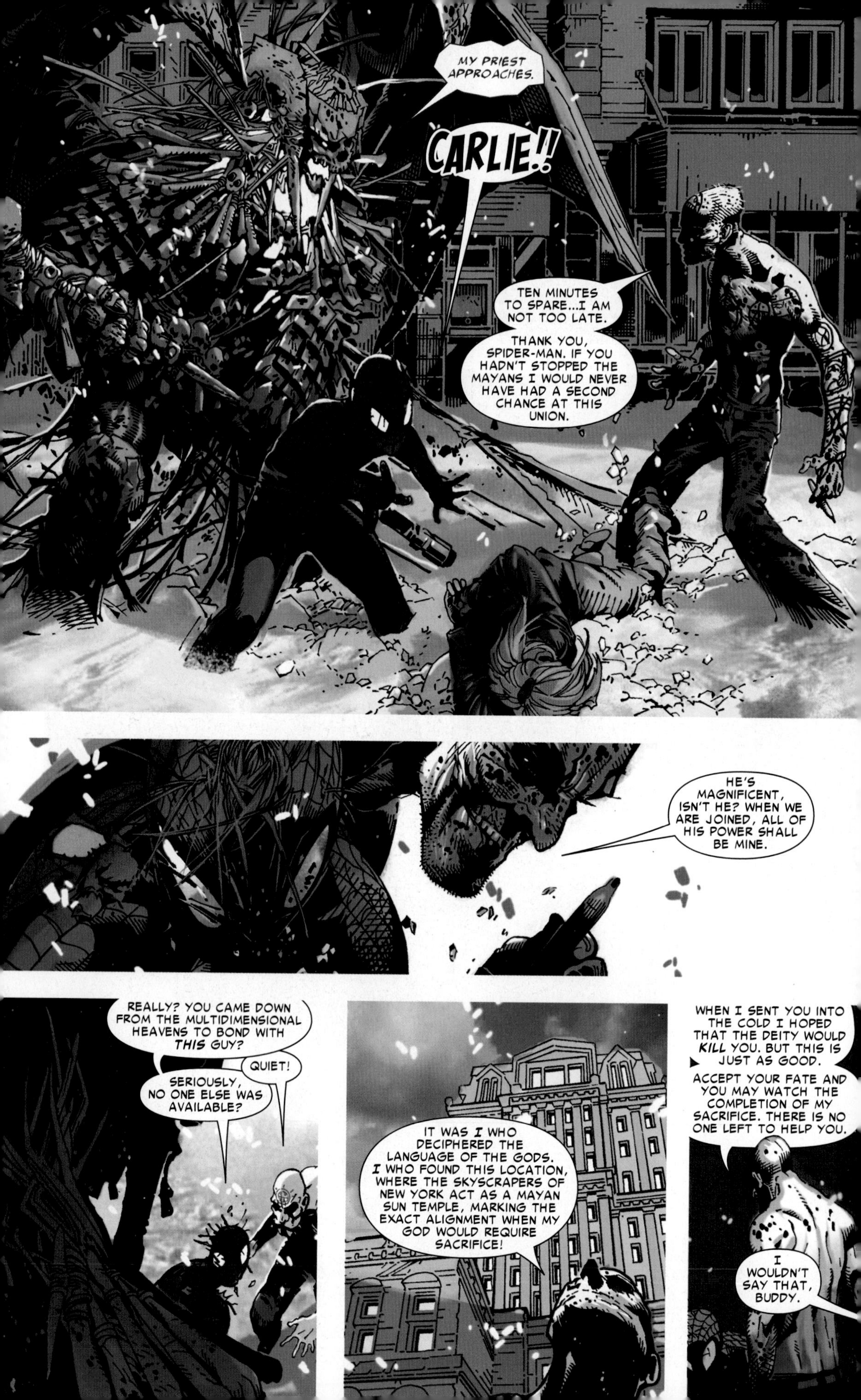
MY PRIEST APPROACHES.
CARLIE!!
TEN MINUTES TO SPARE...I AM NOT TOO LATE.
THANK YOU, SPIDER-MAN. IF YOU HADN'T STOPPED THE MAYANS I WOULD NEVER HAVE HAD A SECOND CHANCE AT THIS UNION.
HE'S MAGNIFICENT, ISN'T HE? WHEN WE ARE JOINED, ALL OF HIS POWER SHALL BE MINE.
REALLY? YOU CAME DOWN FROM THE MULTIDIMENSIONAL HEAVENS TO BOND WITH THIS GUY?
QUIET!
SERIOUSLY, NO ONE ELSE WAS AVAILABLE?
IT WAS I WHO DECIPHERED THE LANGUAGE OF THE GODS. I WHO FOUND THIS LOCATION, WHERE THE SKYSCRAPERS OF NEW YORK ACT AS A MAYAN SUN TEMPLE, MARKING THE EXACT ALIGNMENT WHEN MY GOD WOULD REQUIRE SACRIFICE!
WHEN I SENT YOU INTO THE COLD I HOPED THAT THE DEITY WOULD KILL YOU. BUT THIS IS JUST AS GOOD.
ACCEPT YOUR FATE AND YOU MAY WATCH THE COMPLETION OF MY SACRIFICE. THERE IS NO ONE LEFT TO HELP YOU.
I WOULDN'T SAY THAT, BUDDY.

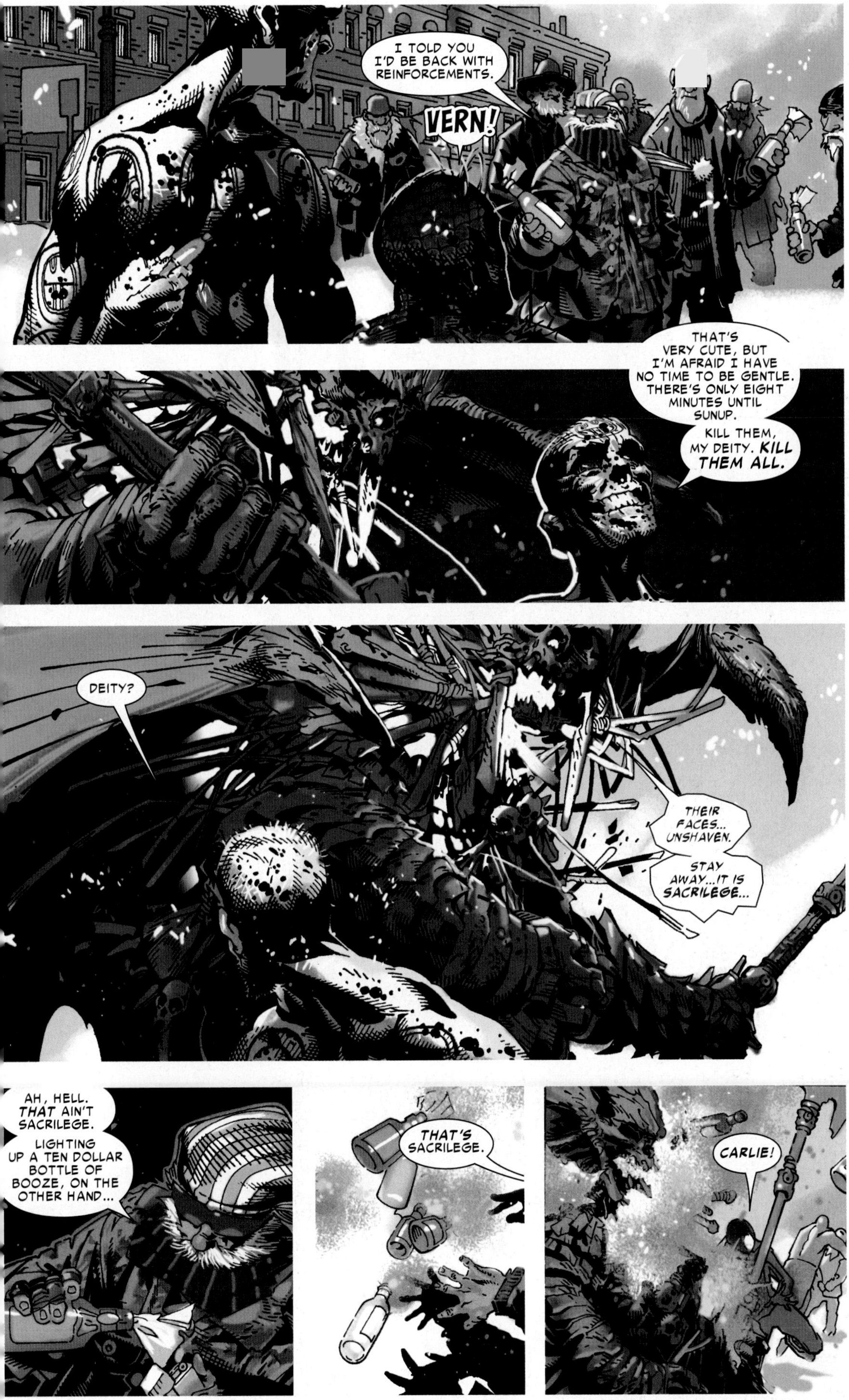

I TOLD YOU I'D BE BACK WITH REINFORCEMENTS.
VERN!
THAT'S VERY CUTE, BUT I'M AFRAID I HAVE NO TIME TO BE GENTLE. THERE'S ONLY EIGHT MINUTES UNTIL SUNUP.
KILL THEM, MY DEITY. KILL THEM ALL.
DEITY?
THEIR FACES... UNSHAVEN.
STAY AWAY...IT IS SACRILEGE...
AH, HELL. THAT AIN'T SACRILEGE.
LIGHTING UP A TEN DOLLAR BOTTLE OF BOOZE, ON THE OTHER HAND...
THAT'S SACRILEGE.
CARLIE!

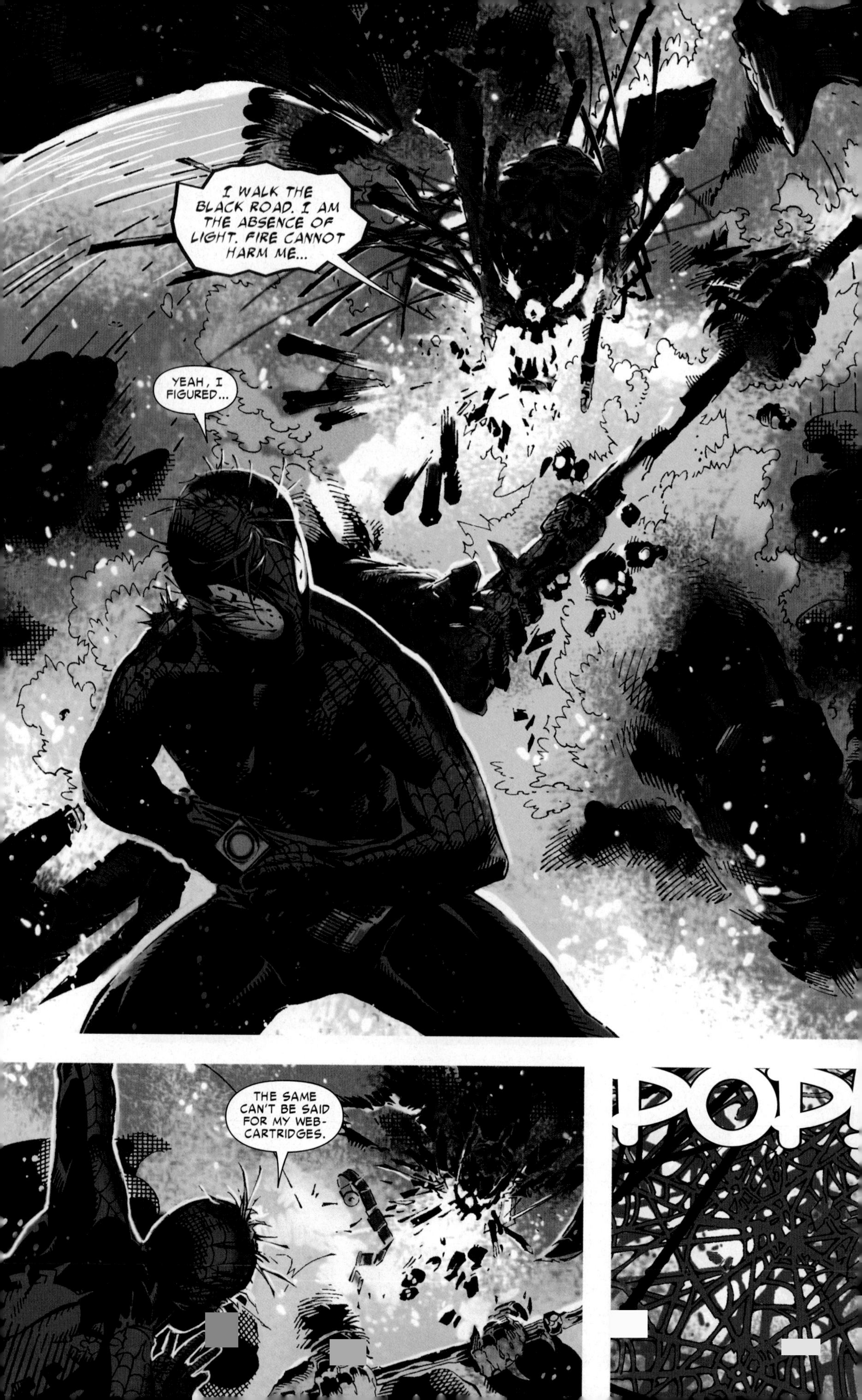
I WALK THE BLACK ROAD. I AM THE ABSENCE OF LIGHT. FIRE CANNOT HARM ME...
YEAH, I FIGURED...
THE SAME CAN'T BE SAID FOR MY WEB-CARTRIDGES.
POP

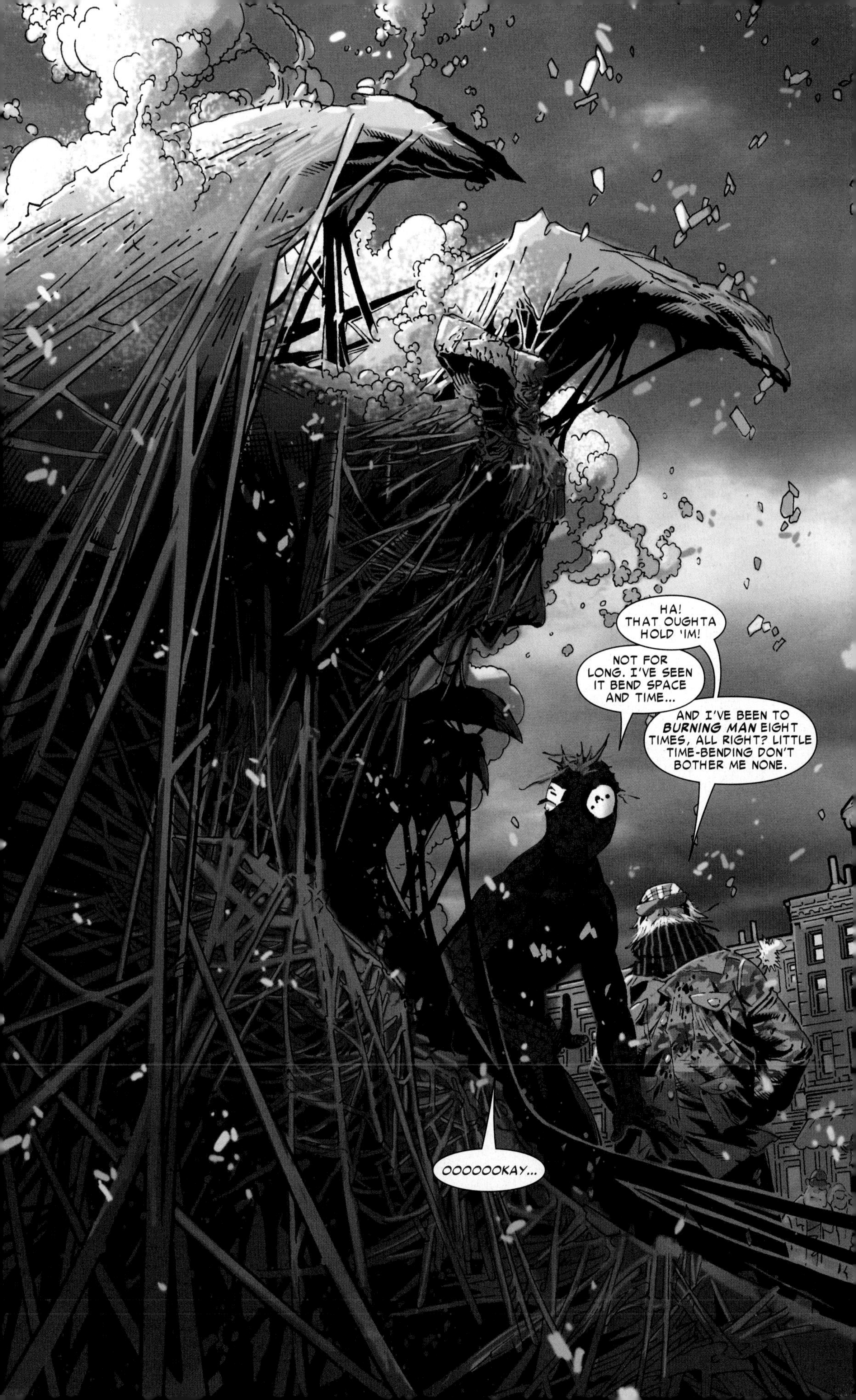
HA! THAT OUGHTA HOLD 'IM!
NOT FOR LONG. I'VE SEEN IT BEND SPACE AND TIME...
AND I'VE BEEN TO *BURNING MAN* EIGHT TIMES, ALL RIGHT? LITTLE TIME-BENDING DON'T BOTHER ME NONE.
OOOOOOKAY...

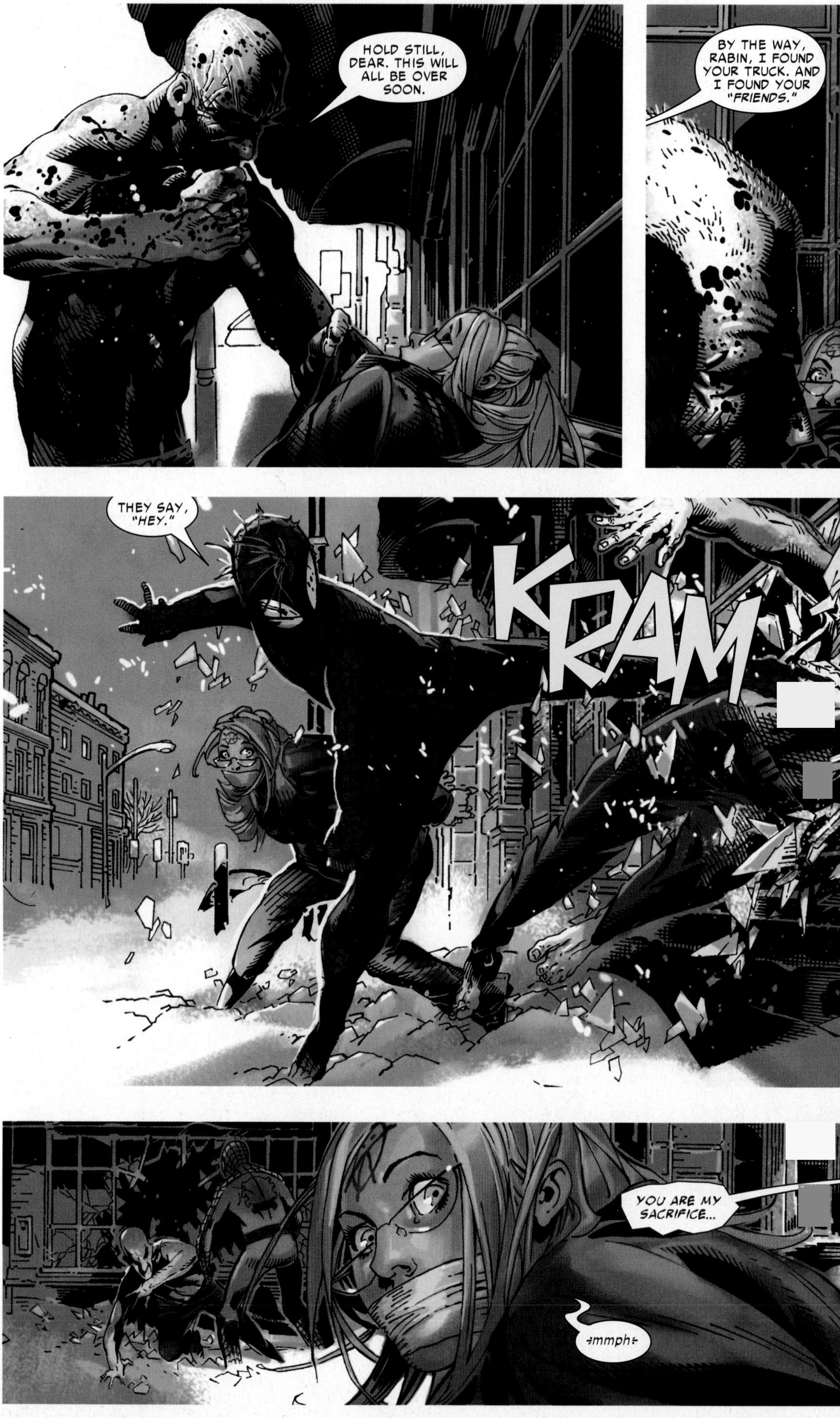
HOLD STILL, DEAR. THIS WILL ALL BE OVER SOON.
BY THE WAY, RABIN, I FOUND YOUR TRUCK. AND I FOUND YOUR "FRIENDS."
THEY SAY, "HEY."
KRAM
YOU ARE MY SACRIFICE...
-mmph-

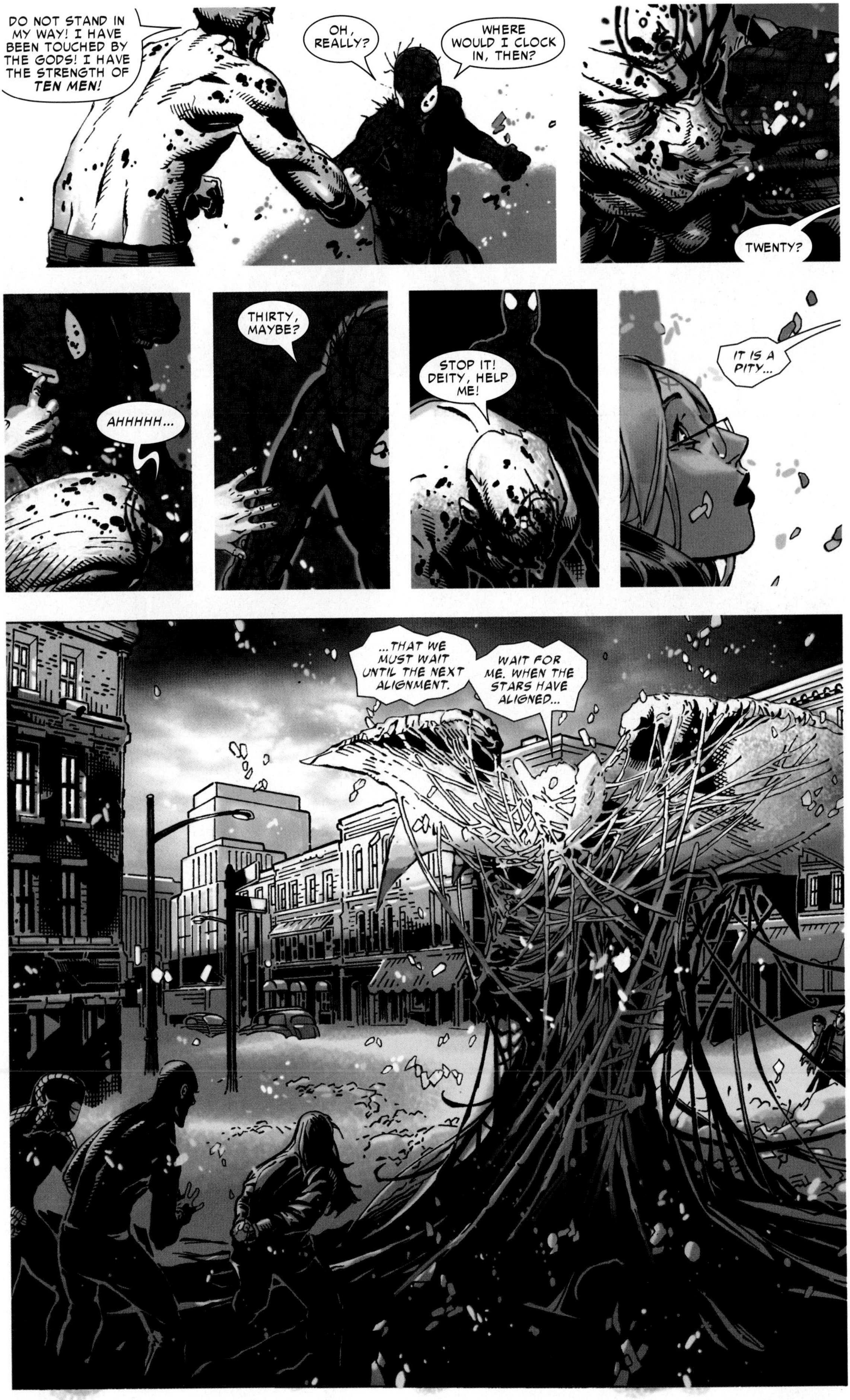
DO NOT STAND IN MY WAY! I HAVE BEEN TOUCHED BY THE GODS! I HAVE THE STRENGTH OF *TEN MEN!*
OH, REALLY?
WHERE WOULD I CLOCK IN, THEN?
TWENTY?
AHHHHH...
THIRTY, MAYBE?
STOP IT! DEITY, HELP ME!
IT IS A PITY...
...THAT WE MUST WAIT UNTIL THE NEXT ALIGNMENT.
WAIT FOR ME. WHEN THE STARS HAVE ALIGNED...

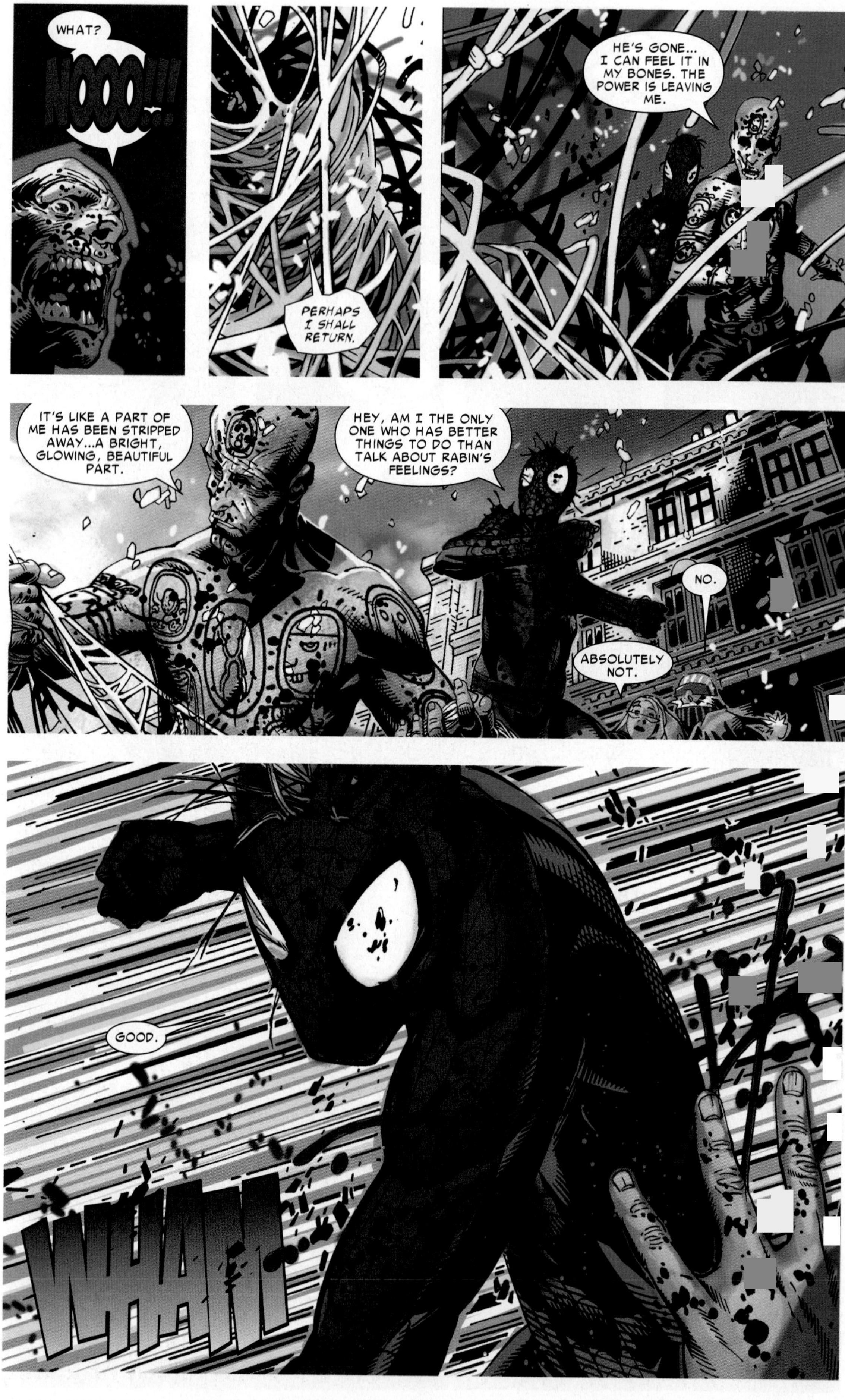
WHAT?
NOOO..!!!
PERHAPS I SHALL RETURN.
HE'S GONE... I CAN FEEL IT IN MY BONES. THE POWER IS LEAVING ME.
IT'S LIKE A PART OF ME HAS BEEN STRIPPED AWAY...A BRIGHT, GLOWING, BEAUTIFUL PART.
HEY, AM I THE ONLY ONE WHO HAS BETTER THINGS TO DO THAN TALK ABOUT RABIN'S FEELINGS?
NO.
ABSOLUTELY NOT.
GOOD.
WHAM

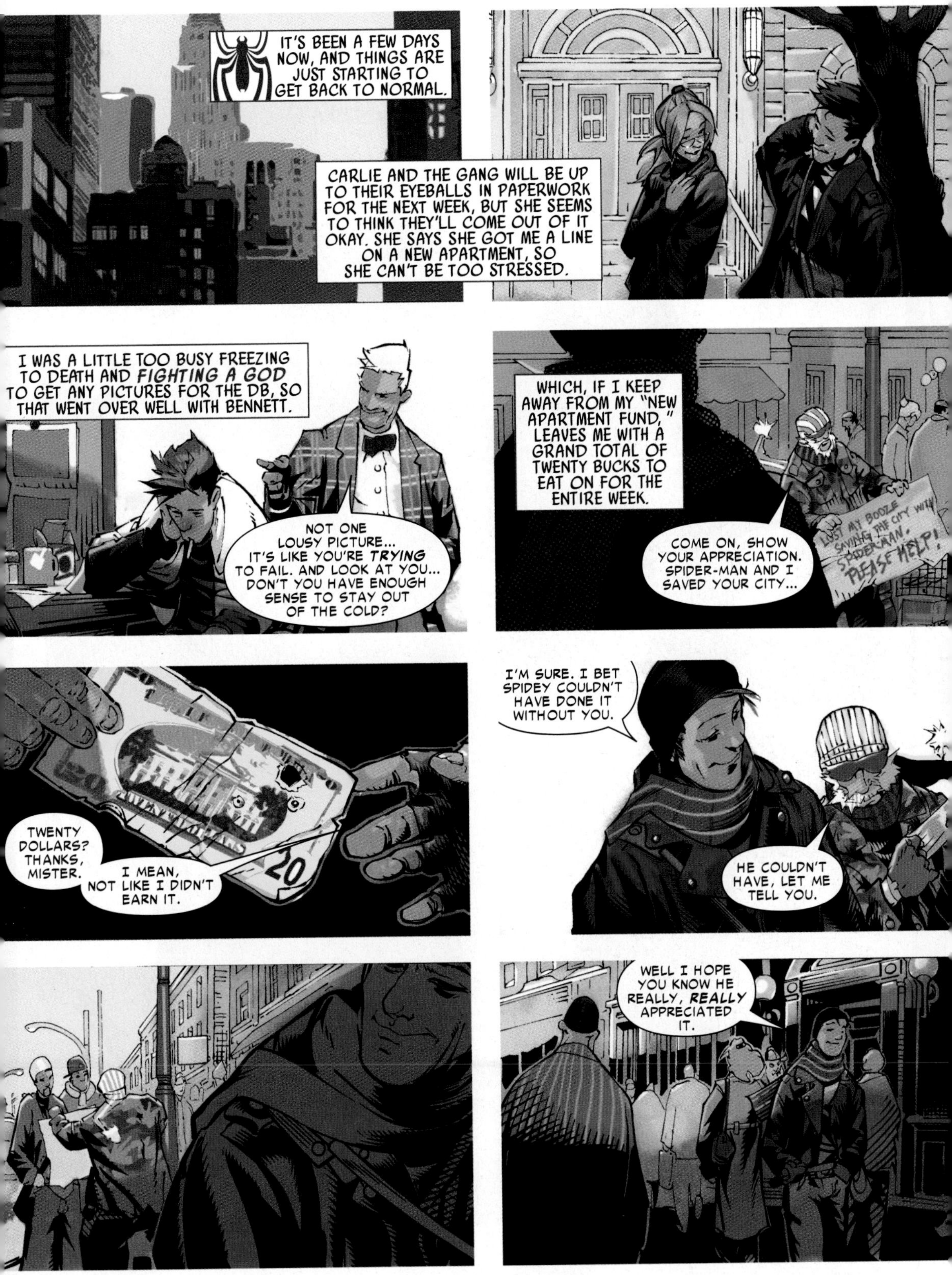
IT'S BEEN A FEW DAYS NOW, AND THINGS ARE JUST STARTING TO GET BACK TO NORMAL.
CARLIE AND THE GANG WILL BE UP TO THEIR EYEBALLS IN PAPERWORK FOR THE NEXT WEEK, BUT SHE SEEMS TO THINK THEY'LL COME OUT OF IT OKAY. SHE SAYS SHE GOT ME A LINE ON A NEW APARTMENT, SO SHE CAN'T BE TOO STRESSED.
I WAS A LITTLE TOO BUSY FREEZING TO DEATH AND FIGHTING A GOD TO GET ANY PICTURES FOR THE DB, SO THAT WENT OVER WELL WITH BENNETT.
NOT ONE LOUSY PICTURE... IT'S LIKE YOU'RE TRYING TO FAIL. AND LOOK AT YOU... DON'T YOU HAVE ENOUGH SENSE TO STAY OUT OF THE COLD?
WHICH, IF I KEEP AWAY FROM MY "NEW APARTMENT FUND," LEAVES ME WITH A GRAND TOTAL OF TWENTY BUCKS TO EAT ON FOR THE ENTIRE WEEK.
LOST MY BOOZE SAVING THE CITY WITH SPIDER-MAN. PLEASE HELP!
COME ON, SHOW YOUR APPRECIATION. SPIDER-MAN AND I SAVED YOUR CITY...
TWENTY DOLLARS? THANKS, MISTER.
I MEAN, NOT LIKE I DIDN'T EARN IT.
I'M SURE. I BET SPIDEY COULDN'T HAVE DONE IT WITHOUT YOU.
HE COULDN'T HAVE, LET ME TELL YOU.
WELL I HOPE YOU KNOW HE REALLY, REALLY APPRECIATED IT.

NEXT: FREAK'S BACK (AND HE'S BRINGING BARRY KITSON WITH HIM!)

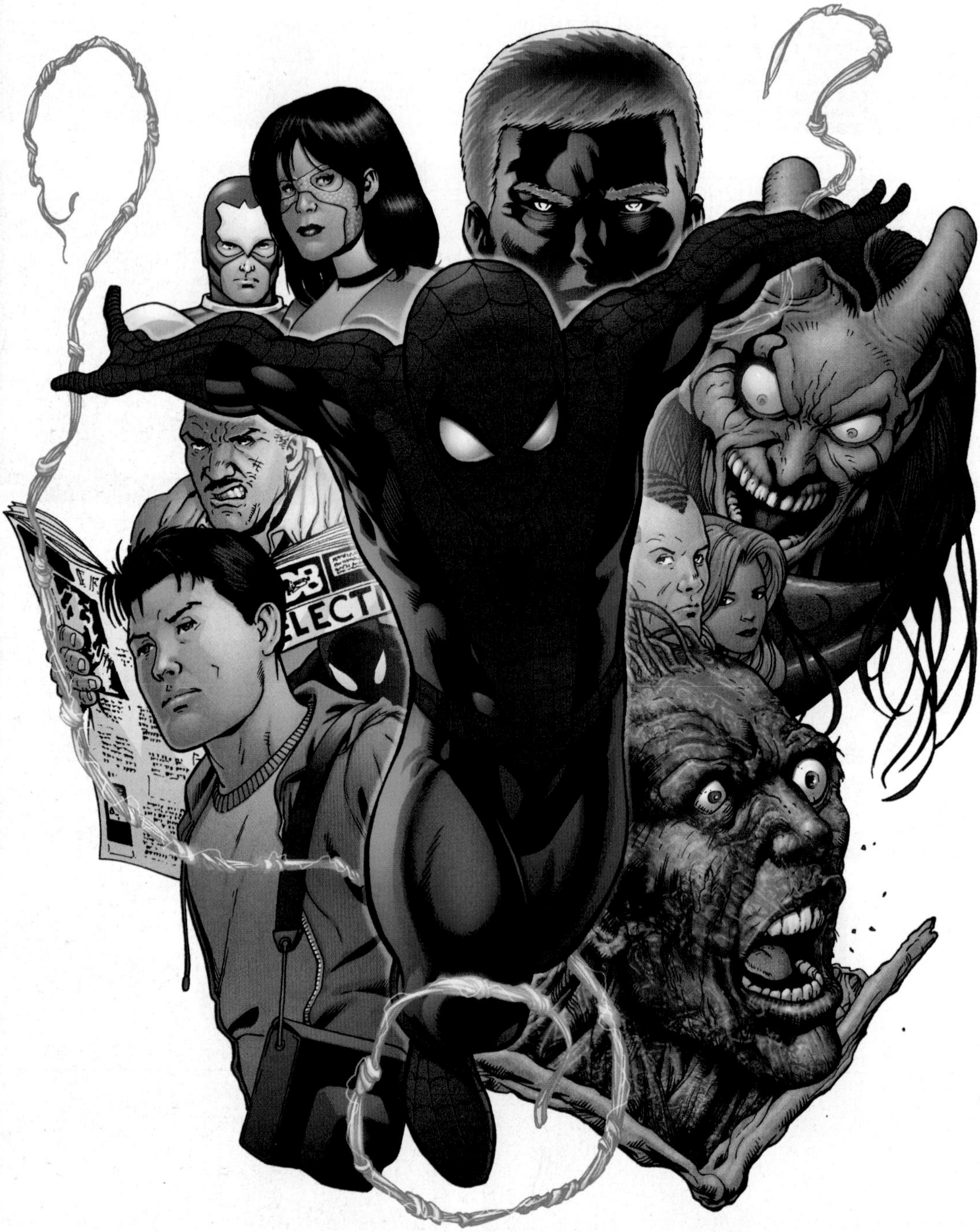

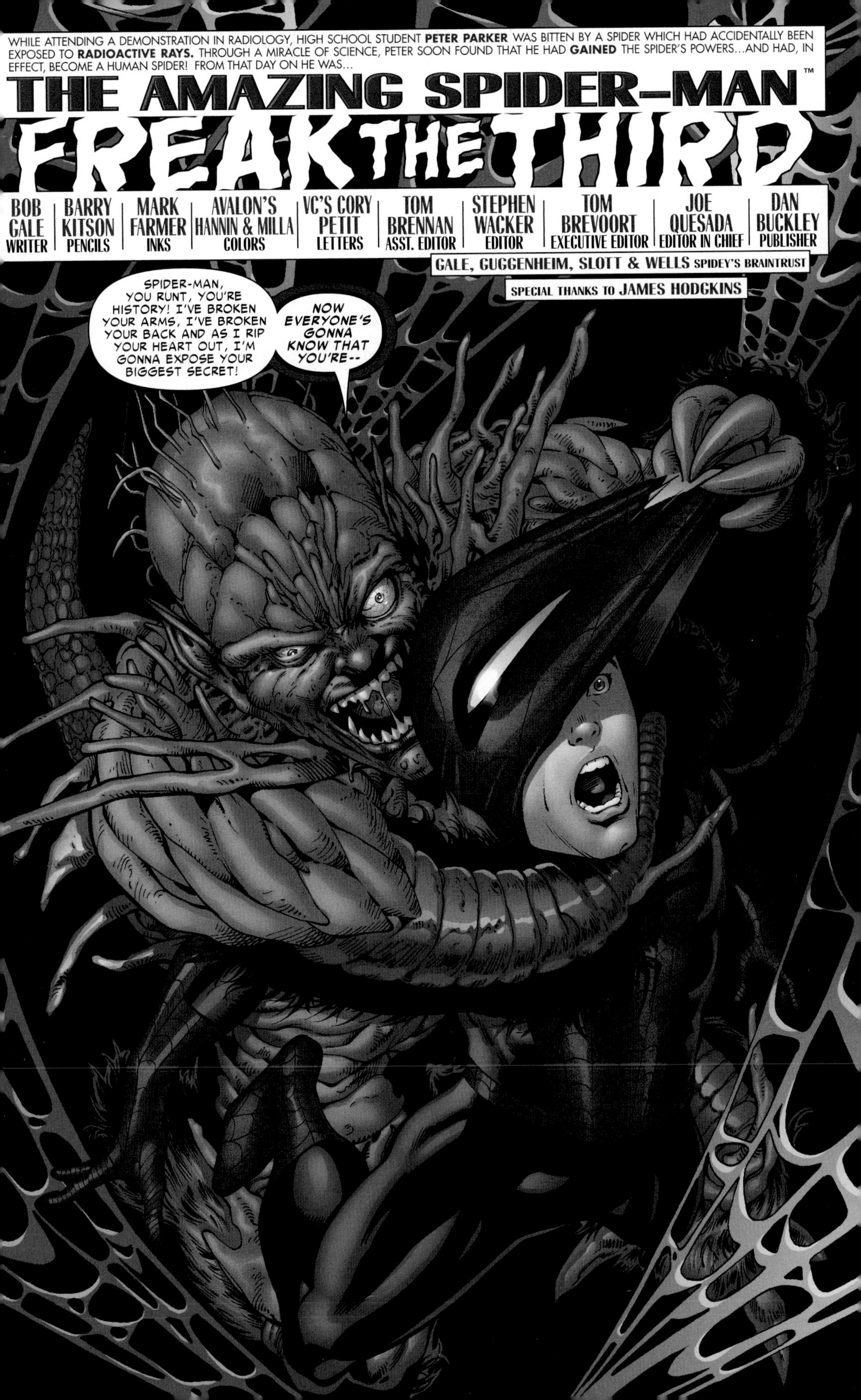
WHILE ATTENDING A DEMONSTRATION IN RADIOLOGY, HIGH SCHOOL STUDENT PETER PARKER WAS BITTEN BY A SPIDER WHICH HAD ACCIDENTALLY BEEN EXPOSED TO RADIOACTIVE RAYS. THROUGH A MIRACLE OF SCIENCE, PETER SOON FOUND THAT HE HAD GAINED THE SPIDER'S POWERS...AND HAD, IN EFFECT, BECOME A HUMAN SPIDER! FROM THAT DAY ON HE WAS...
THE AMAZING SPIDER-MAN™
FREAK THE THIRD
BOB GALE WRITER
BARRY KITSON PENCILS
MARK FARMER INKS
AVALON'S HANNIN & MILLA COLORS
VC'S CORY PETIT LETTERS
TOM BRENNAN ASST. EDITOR
STEPHEN WACKER EDITOR
TOM BREVOORT EXECUTIVE EDITOR
JOE QUESADA EDITOR IN CHIEF
DAN BUCKLEY PUBLISHER
GALE, GUGGENHEIM, SLOTT & WELLS SPIDEY'S BRAINTRUST
SPECIAL THANKS TO JAMES HODGKINS
SPIDER-MAN, YOU RUNT, YOU'RE HISTORY! I'VE BROKEN YOUR ARMS, I'VE BROKEN YOUR BACK AND AS I RIP YOUR HEART OUT, I'M GONNA EXPOSE YOUR BIGGEST SECRET!
NOW EVERYONE'S GONNA KNOW THAT YOU'RE--

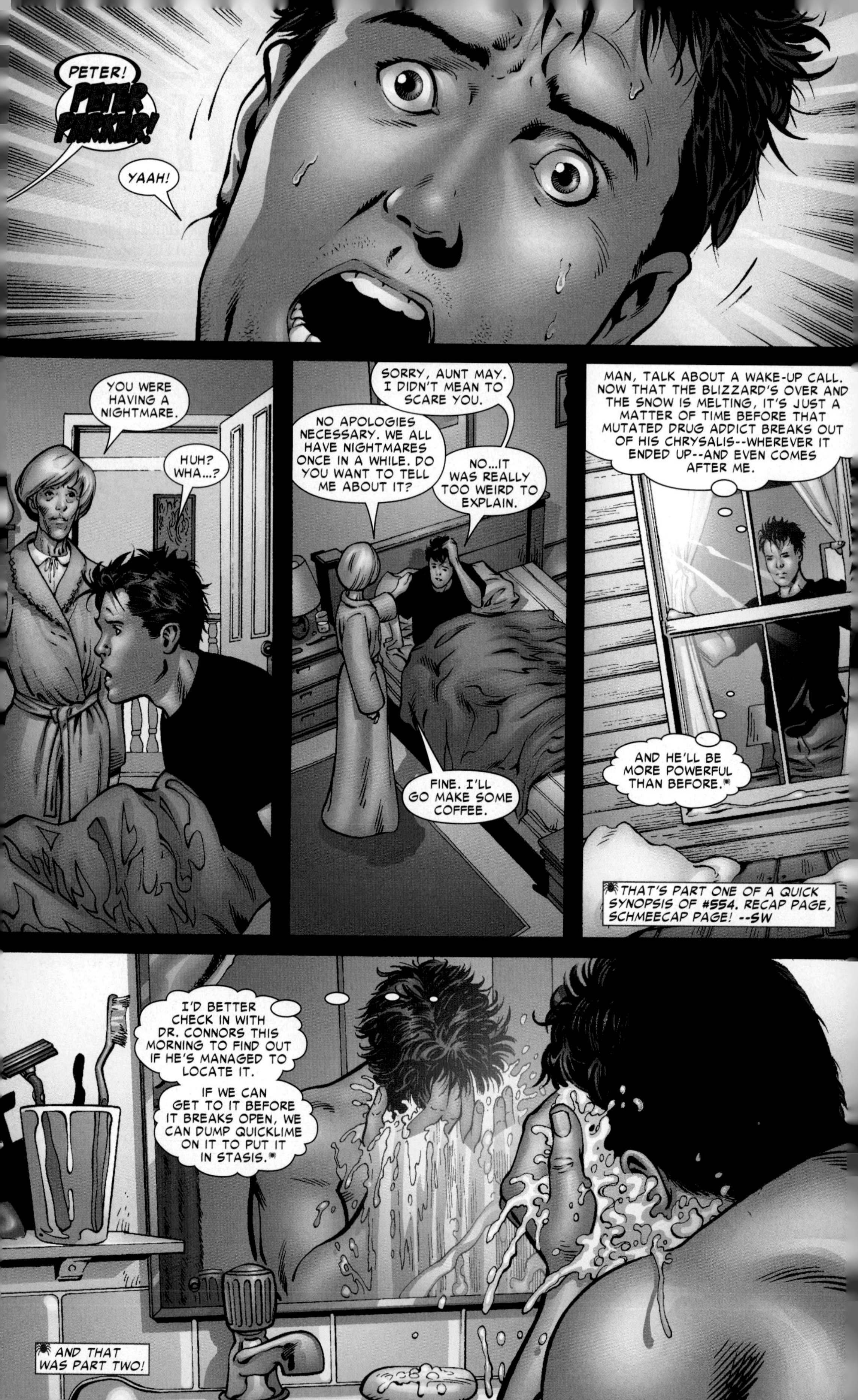
PETER!
PETER PARKER!
YAAH!
YOU WERE HAVING A NIGHTMARE.
HUH? WHA...?
SORRY, AUNT MAY. I DIDN'T MEAN TO SCARE YOU.
NO APOLOGIES NECESSARY. WE ALL HAVE NIGHTMARES ONCE IN A WHILE. DO YOU WANT TO TELL ME ABOUT IT?
NO...IT WAS REALLY TOO WEIRD TO EXPLAIN.
FINE. I'LL GO MAKE SOME COFFEE.
MAN, TALK ABOUT A WAKE-UP CALL. NOW THAT THE BLIZZARD'S OVER AND THE SNOW IS MELTING, IT'S JUST A MATTER OF TIME BEFORE THAT MUTATED DRUG ADDICT BREAKS OUT OF HIS CHRYSALIS--WHEREVER IT ENDED UP--AND EVEN COMES AFTER ME.
AND HE'LL BE MORE POWERFUL THAN BEFORE.*
*THAT'S PART ONE OF A QUICK SYNOPSIS OF #554. RECAP PAGE, SCHMEECAP PAGE! --SW
I'D BETTER CHECK IN WITH DR. CONNORS THIS MORNING TO FIND OUT IF HE'S MANAGED TO LOCATE IT.
IF WE CAN GET TO IT BEFORE IT BREAKS OPEN, WE CAN DUMP QUICKLIME ON IT TO PUT IT IN STASIS.*
*AND THAT WAS PART TWO!

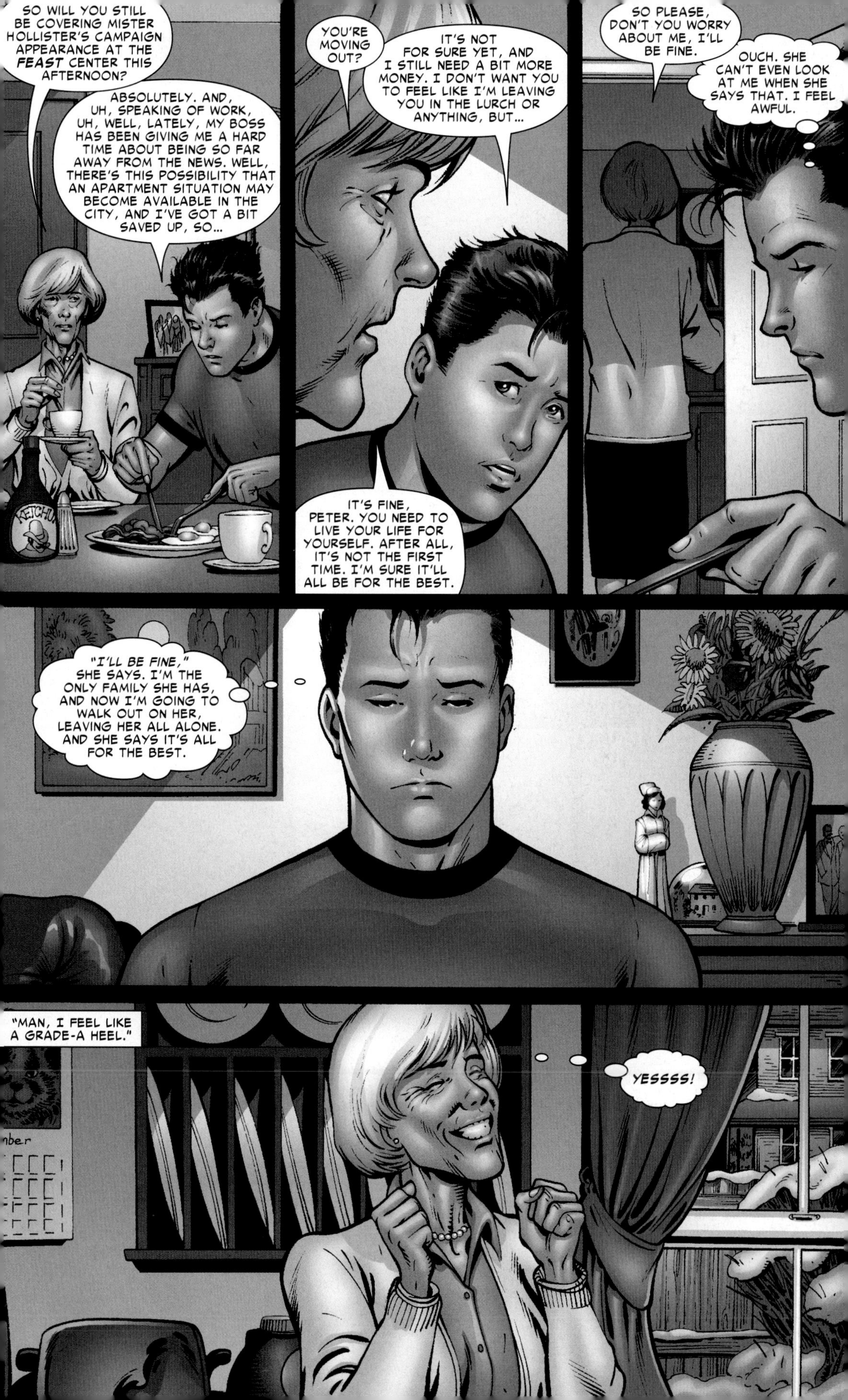
SO WILL YOU STILL BE COVERING MISTER HOLLISTER'S CAMPAIGN APPEARANCE AT THE *FEAST* CENTER THIS AFTERNOON?
ABSOLUTELY. AND, UH, SPEAKING OF WORK, UH, WELL, LATELY, MY BOSS HAS BEEN GIVING ME A HARD TIME ABOUT BEING SO FAR AWAY FROM THE NEWS. WELL, THERE'S THIS POSSIBILITY THAT AN APARTMENT SITUATION MAY BECOME AVAILABLE IN THE CITY, AND I'VE GOT A BIT SAVED UP, SO...
KETCHUP
YOU'RE MOVING OUT?
IT'S NOT FOR SURE YET, AND I STILL NEED A BIT MORE MONEY. I DON'T WANT YOU TO FEEL LIKE I'M LEAVING YOU IN THE LURCH OR ANYTHING, BUT...
IT'S FINE, PETER. YOU NEED TO LIVE YOUR LIFE FOR YOURSELF. AFTER ALL, IT'S NOT THE FIRST TIME. I'M SURE IT'LL ALL BE FOR THE BEST.
SO PLEASE, DON'T YOU WORRY ABOUT ME, I'LL BE FINE.
OUCH. SHE CAN'T EVEN LOOK AT ME WHEN SHE SAYS THAT. I FEEL AWFUL.
"I'LL BE FINE," SHE SAYS. I'M THE ONLY FAMILY SHE HAS, AND NOW I'M GOING TO WALK OUT ON HER, LEAVING HER ALL ALONE. AND SHE SAYS IT'S ALL FOR THE BEST.
"MAN, I FEEL LIKE A GRADE-A HEEL."
YESSSS!

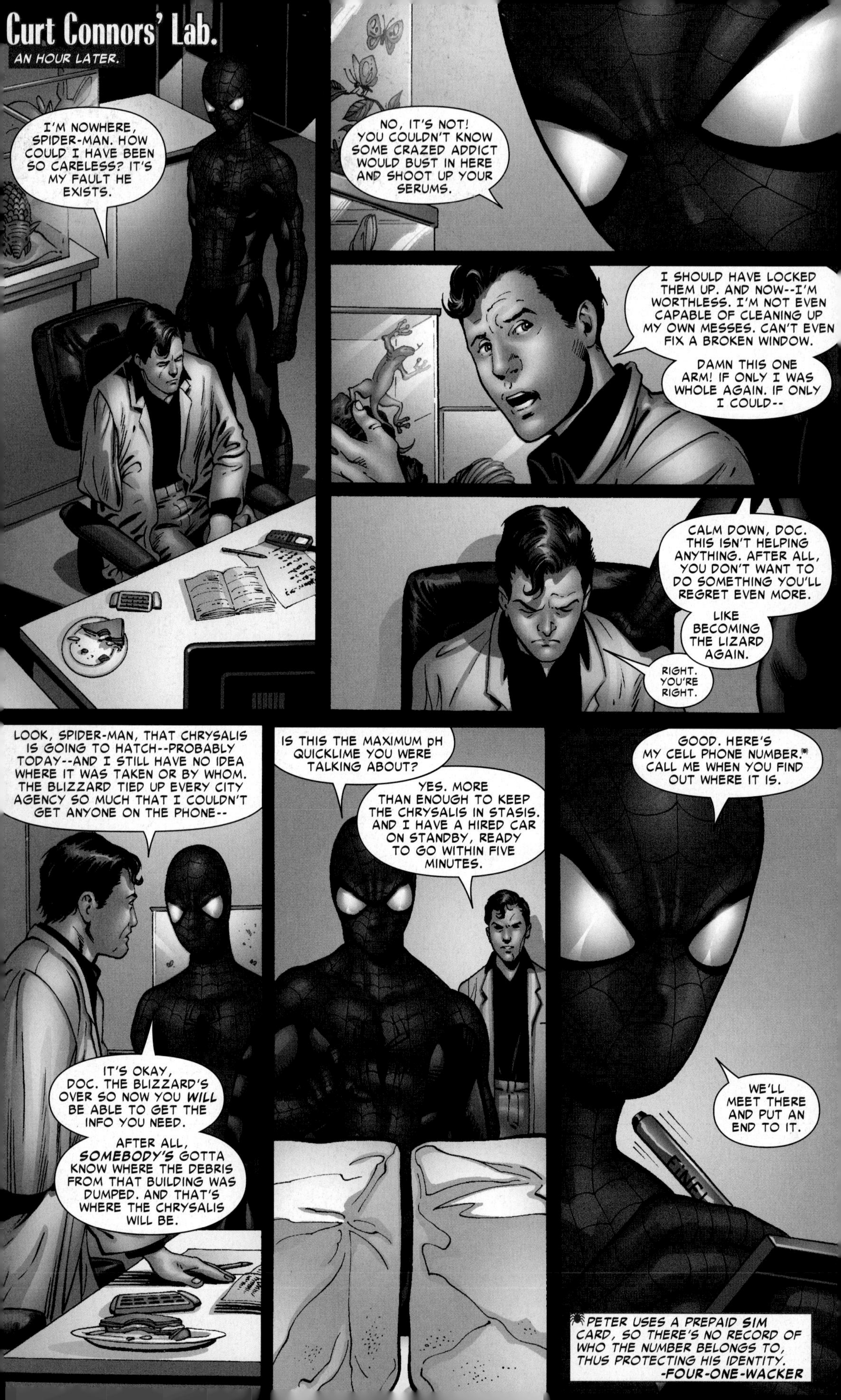
Curt Connors' Lab.
AN HOUR LATER.
I'M NOWHERE, SPIDER-MAN. HOW COULD I HAVE BEEN SO CARELESS? IT'S MY FAULT HE EXISTS.
NO, IT'S NOT! YOU COULDN'T KNOW SOME CRAZED ADDICT WOULD BUST IN HERE AND SHOOT UP YOUR SERUMS.
I SHOULD HAVE LOCKED THEM UP. AND NOW--I'M WORTHLESS. I'M NOT EVEN CAPABLE OF CLEANING UP MY OWN MESSES. CAN'T EVEN FIX A BROKEN WINDOW.
DAMN THIS ONE ARM! IF ONLY I WAS WHOLE AGAIN. IF ONLY I COULD--
CALM DOWN, DOC. THIS ISN'T HELPING ANYTHING. AFTER ALL, YOU DON'T WANT TO DO SOMETHING YOU'LL REGRET EVEN MORE.
LIKE BECOMING THE LIZARD AGAIN.
RIGHT. YOU'RE RIGHT.
LOOK, SPIDER-MAN, THAT CHRYSALIS IS GOING TO HATCH--PROBABLY TODAY--AND I STILL HAVE NO IDEA WHERE IT WAS TAKEN OR BY WHOM. THE BLIZZARD TIED UP EVERY CITY AGENCY SO MUCH THAT I COULDN'T GET ANYONE ON THE PHONE--
IT'S OKAY, DOC. THE BLIZZARD'S OVER SO NOW YOU *WILL* BE ABLE TO GET THE INFO YOU NEED.
AFTER ALL, ***SOMEBODY'S*** GOTTA KNOW WHERE THE DEBRIS FROM THAT BUILDING WAS DUMPED. AND THAT'S WHERE THE CHRYSALIS WILL BE.
IS THIS THE MAXIMUM pH QUICKLIME YOU WERE TALKING ABOUT?
YES. MORE THAN ENOUGH TO KEEP THE CHRYSALIS IN STASIS. AND I HAVE A HIRED CAR ON STANDBY, READY TO GO WITHIN FIVE MINUTES.
GOOD. HERE'S MY CELL PHONE NUMBER.*
CALL ME WHEN YOU FIND OUT WHERE IT IS.
WE'LL MEET THERE AND PUT AN END TO IT.
*PETER USES A PREPAID *SIM* CARD, SO THERE'S NO RECORD OF WHO THE NUMBER BELONGS TO, THUS PROTECTING HIS IDENTITY. -FOUR-ONE-WACKER

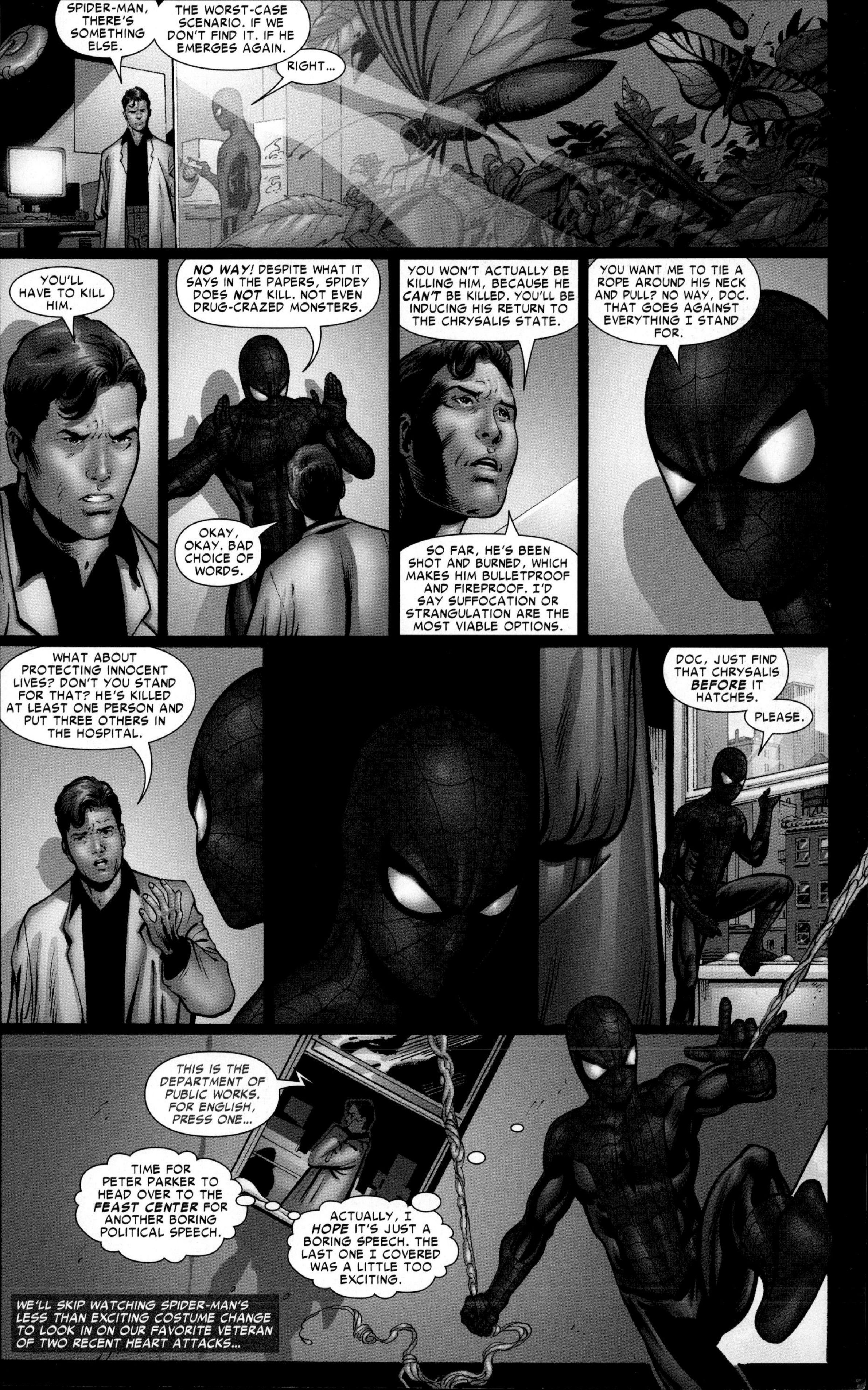
SPIDER-MAN, THERE'S SOMETHING ELSE.
THE WORST-CASE SCENARIO. IF WE DON'T FIND IT. IF HE EMERGES AGAIN.
RIGHT...
YOU'LL HAVE TO KILL HIM.
NO WAY! DESPITE WHAT IT SAYS IN THE PAPERS, SPIDEY DOES NOT KILL. NOT EVEN DRUG-CRAZED MONSTERS.
OKAY, OKAY. BAD CHOICE OF WORDS.
YOU WON'T ACTUALLY BE KILLING HIM, BECAUSE HE CAN'T BE KILLED. YOU'LL BE INDUCING HIS RETURN TO THE CHRYSALIS STATE.
SO FAR, HE'S BEEN SHOT AND BURNED, WHICH MAKES HIM BULLETPROOF AND FIREPROOF. I'D SAY SUFFOCATION OR STRANGULATION ARE THE MOST VIABLE OPTIONS.
YOU WANT ME TO TIE A ROPE AROUND HIS NECK AND PULL? NO WAY, DOC. THAT GOES AGAINST EVERYTHING I STAND FOR.
WHAT ABOUT PROTECTING INNOCENT LIVES? DON'T YOU STAND FOR THAT? HE'S KILLED AT LEAST ONE PERSON AND PUT THREE OTHERS IN THE HOSPITAL.
DOC, JUST FIND THAT CHRYSALIS BEFORE IT HATCHES.
PLEASE.
THIS IS THE DEPARTMENT OF PUBLIC WORKS. FOR ENGLISH, PRESS ONE...
TIME FOR PETER PARKER TO HEAD OVER TO THE FEAST CENTER FOR ANOTHER BORING POLITICAL SPEECH.
ACTUALLY, I HOPE IT'S JUST A BORING SPEECH. THE LAST ONE I COVERED WAS A LITTLE TOO EXCITING.
WE'LL SKIP WATCHING SPIDER-MAN'S LESS THAN EXCITING COSTUME CHANGE TO LOOK IN ON OUR FAVORITE VETERAN OF TWO RECENT HEART ATTACKS...

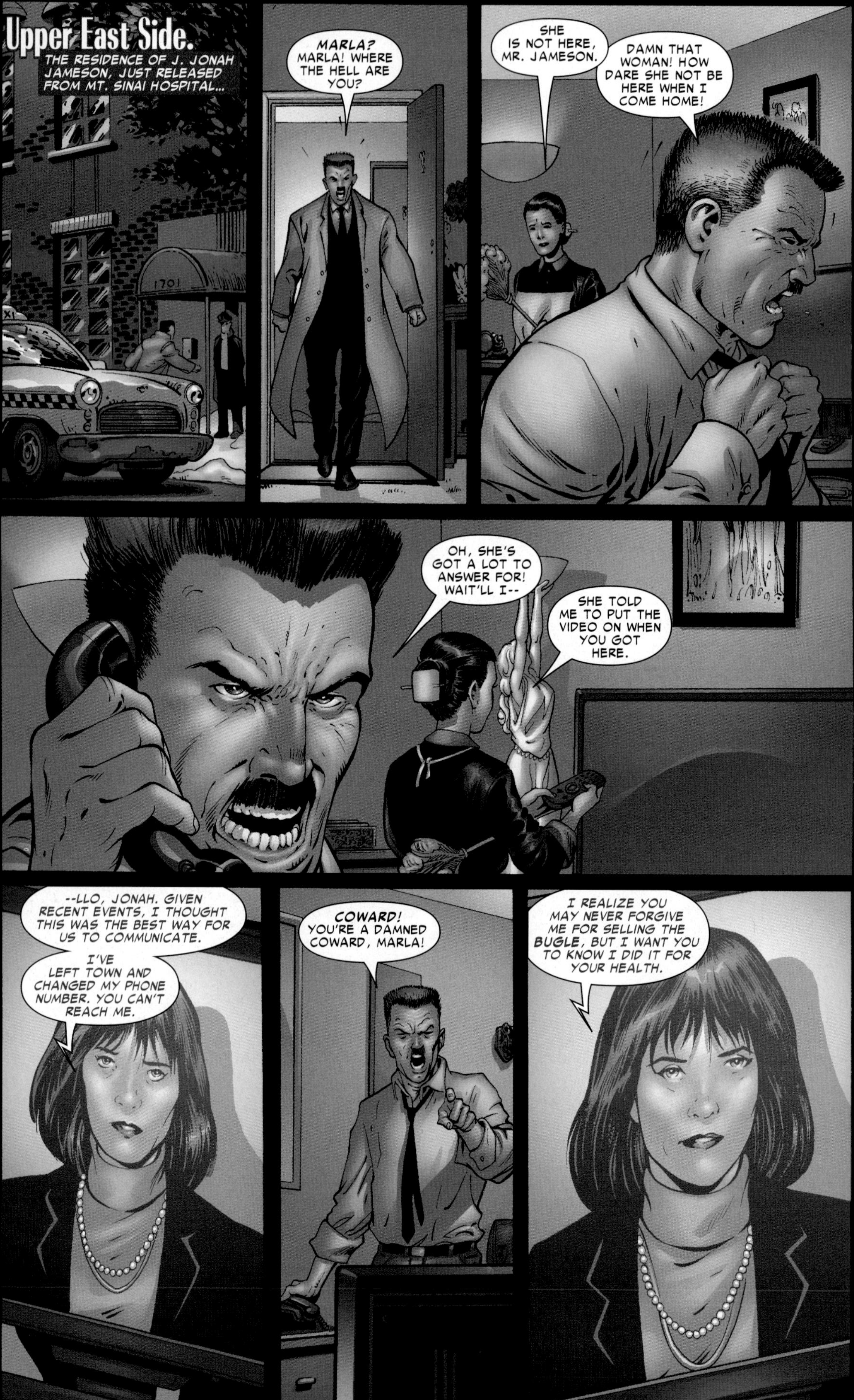

Upper East Side.
THE RESIDENCE OF J. JONAH JAMESON, JUST RELEASED FROM MT. SINAI HOSPITAL...
MARLA? MARLA! WHERE THE HELL ARE YOU?
SHE IS NOT HERE, MR. JAMESON.
DAMN THAT WOMAN! HOW DARE SHE NOT BE HERE WHEN I COME HOME!
OH, SHE'S GOT A LOT TO ANSWER FOR! WAIT'LL I--
SHE TOLD ME TO PUT THE VIDEO ON WHEN YOU GOT HERE.
--LLO, JONAH. GIVEN RECENT EVENTS, I THOUGHT THIS WAS THE BEST WAY FOR US TO COMMUNICATE.
I'VE LEFT TOWN AND CHANGED MY PHONE NUMBER. YOU CAN'T REACH ME.
COWARD! YOU'RE A DAMNED COWARD, MARLA!
I REALIZE YOU MAY NEVER FORGIVE ME FOR SELLING THE BUGLE, BUT I WANT YOU TO KNOW I DID IT FOR YOUR HEALTH.

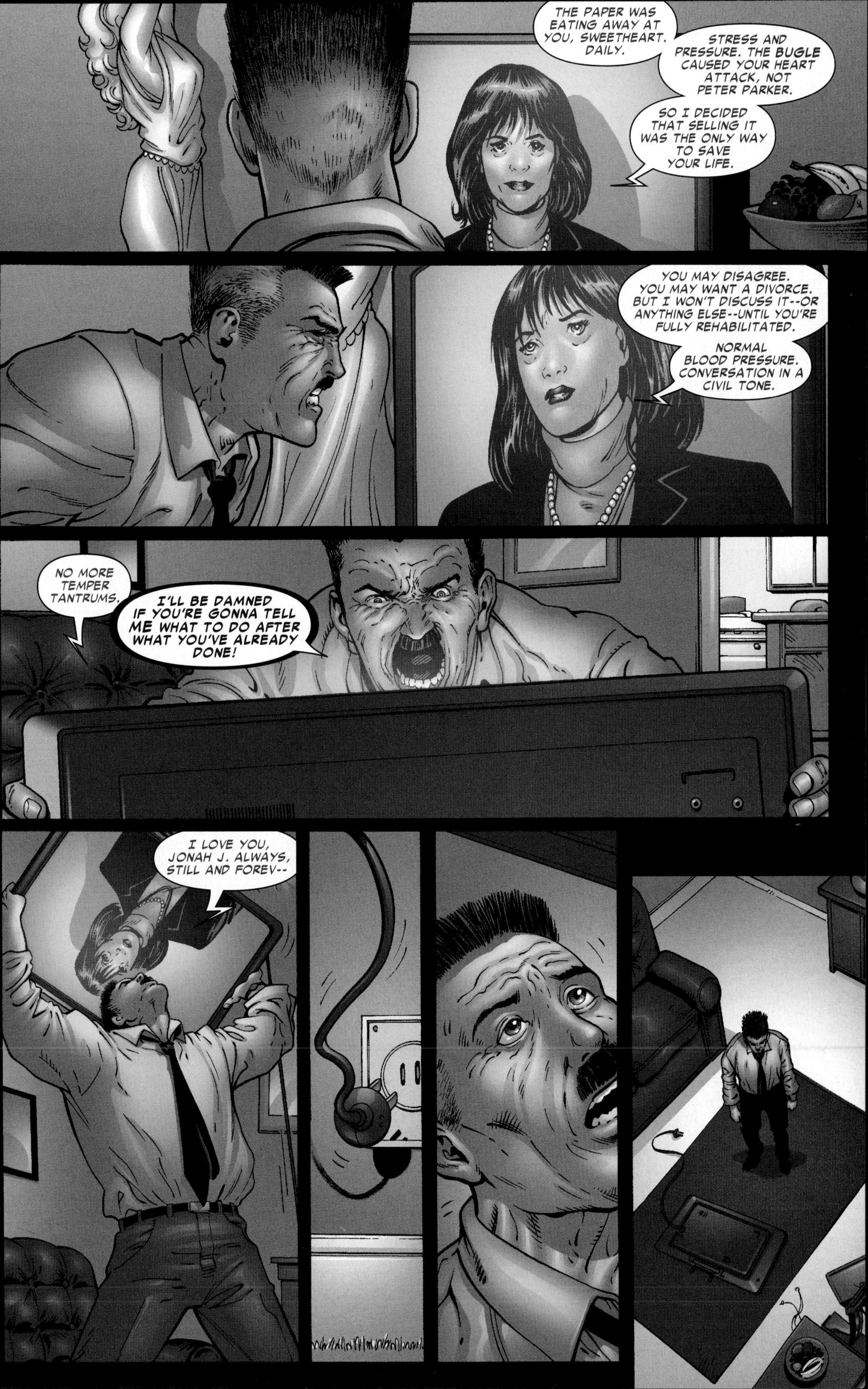
THE PAPER WAS EATING AWAY AT YOU, SWEETHEART. DAILY.
STRESS AND PRESSURE. THE BUGLE CAUSED YOUR HEART ATTACK, NOT PETER PARKER.
SO I DECIDED THAT SELLING IT WAS THE ONLY WAY TO SAVE YOUR LIFE.
YOU MAY DISAGREE. YOU MAY WANT A DIVORCE. BUT I WON'T DISCUSS IT--OR ANYTHING ELSE--UNTIL YOU'RE FULLY REHABILITATED.
NORMAL BLOOD PRESSURE. CONVERSATION IN A CIVIL TONE.
NO MORE TEMPER TANTRUMS.
I'LL BE DAMNED IF YOU'RE GONNA TELL ME WHAT TO DO AFTER WHAT YOU'VE ALREADY DONE!
I LOVE YOU, JONAH J. ALWAYS, STILL AND FOREV--

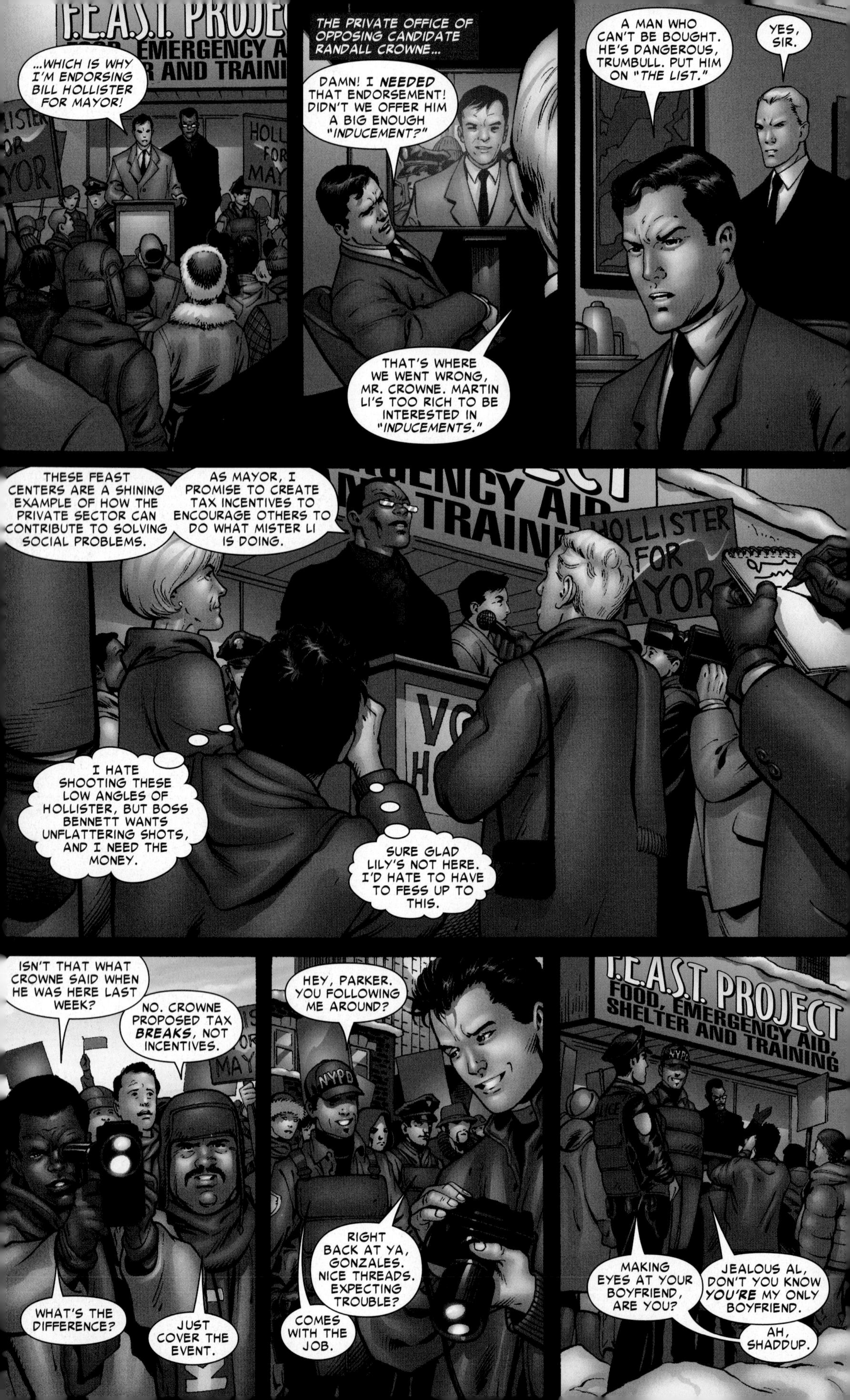
F.E.A.S.T. PROJECT
FOOD, EMERGENCY AID, SHELTER AND TRAINING
...WHICH IS WHY I'M ENDORSING BILL HOLLISTER FOR MAYOR!
HOLLISTER FOR MAYOR
THE PRIVATE OFFICE OF OPPOSING CANDIDATE RANDALL CROWNE...
DAMN! I NEEDED THAT ENDORSEMENT! DIDN'T WE OFFER HIM A BIG ENOUGH "INDUCEMENT?"
THAT'S WHERE WE WENT WRONG, MR. CROWNE. MARTIN LI'S TOO RICH TO BE INTERESTED IN "INDUCEMENTS."
A MAN WHO CAN'T BE BOUGHT. HE'S DANGEROUS, TRUMBULL. PUT HIM ON "THE LIST."
YES, SIR.
THESE FEAST CENTERS ARE A SHINING EXAMPLE OF HOW THE PRIVATE SECTOR CAN CONTRIBUTE TO SOLVING SOCIAL PROBLEMS.
AS MAYOR, I PROMISE TO CREATE TAX INCENTIVES TO ENCOURAGE OTHERS TO DO WHAT MISTER LI IS DOING.
HOLLISTER FOR MAYOR
I HATE SHOOTING THESE LOW ANGLES OF HOLLISTER, BUT BOSS BENNETT WANTS UNFLATTERING SHOTS, AND I NEED THE MONEY.
SURE GLAD LILY'S NOT HERE. I'D HATE TO HAVE TO FESS UP TO THIS.
ISN'T THAT WHAT CROWNE SAID WHEN HE WAS HERE LAST WEEK?
NO. CROWNE PROPOSED TAX BREAKS, NOT INCENTIVES.
WHAT'S THE DIFFERENCE?
JUST COVER THE EVENT.
HEY, PARKER. YOU FOLLOWING ME AROUND?
NYPD
RIGHT BACK AT YA, GONZALES. NICE THREADS. EXPECTING TROUBLE?
COMES WITH THE JOB.
F.E.A.S.T. PROJECT
FOOD, EMERGENCY AID, SHELTER AND TRAINING
MAKING EYES AT YOUR BOYFRIEND, ARE YOU?
JEALOUS AL, DON'T YOU KNOW YOU'RE MY ONLY BOYFRIEND.
AH, SHADDUP.

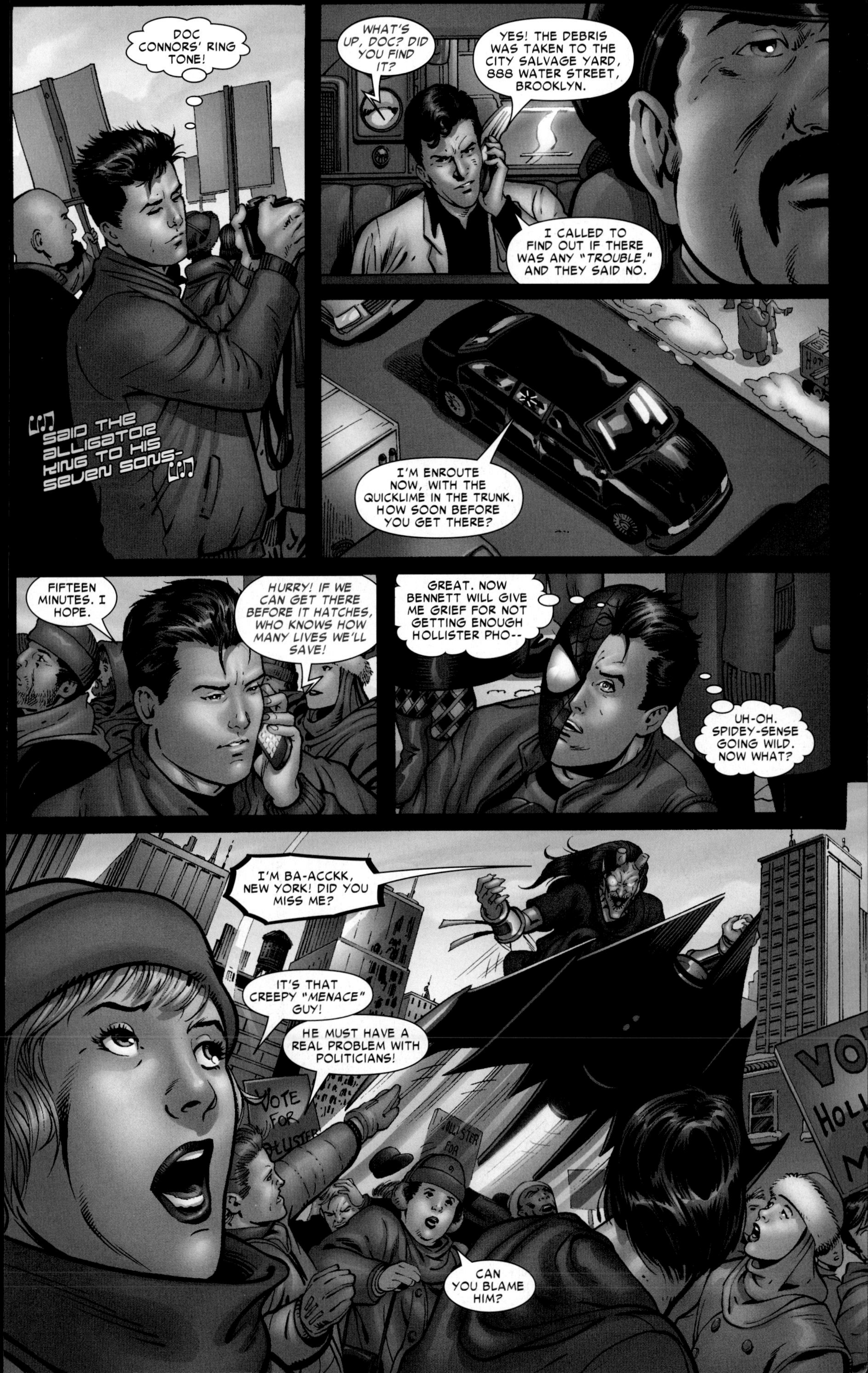
DOC CONNORS' RING TONE!
♫ SAID THE ALLIGATOR KING TO HIS SEVEN SONS- ♫
WHAT'S UP, DOC? DID YOU FIND IT?
YES! THE DEBRIS WAS TAKEN TO THE CITY SALVAGE YARD, 888 WATER STREET, BROOKLYN.
I CALLED TO FIND OUT IF THERE WAS ANY "TROUBLE," AND THEY SAID NO.
I'M ENROUTE NOW, WITH THE QUICKLIME IN THE TRUNK. HOW SOON BEFORE YOU GET THERE?
FIFTEEN MINUTES. I HOPE.
HURRY! IF WE CAN GET THERE BEFORE IT HATCHES, WHO KNOWS HOW MANY LIVES WE'LL SAVE!
GREAT. NOW BENNETT WILL GIVE ME GRIEF FOR NOT GETTING ENOUGH HOLLISTER PHO--
UH-OH. SPIDEY-SENSE GOING WILD. NOW WHAT?
I'M BA-ACCKK, NEW YORK! DID YOU MISS ME?
IT'S THAT CREEPY "MENACE" GUY!
HE MUST HAVE A REAL PROBLEM WITH POLITICIANS!
CAN YOU BLAME HIM?

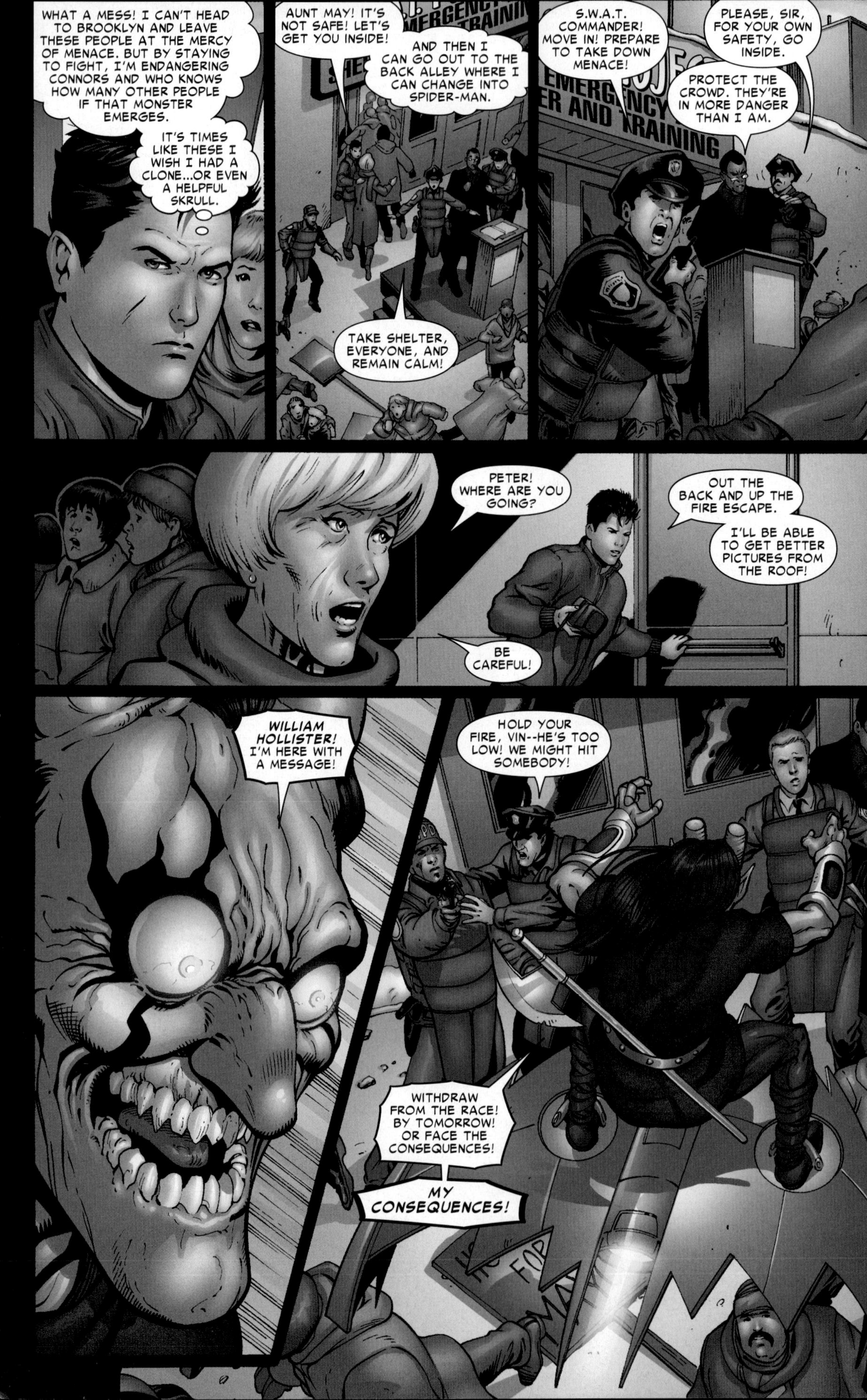
WHAT A MESS! I CAN'T HEAD TO BROOKLYN AND LEAVE THESE PEOPLE AT THE MERCY OF MENACE. BUT BY STAYING TO FIGHT, I'M ENDANGERING CONNORS AND WHO KNOWS HOW MANY OTHER PEOPLE IF THAT MONSTER EMERGES.
IT'S TIMES LIKE THESE I WISH I HAD A CLONE...OR EVEN A HELPFUL SKRULL.
AUNT MAY! IT'S NOT SAFE! LET'S GET YOU INSIDE!
AND THEN I CAN GO OUT TO THE BACK ALLEY WHERE I CAN CHANGE INTO SPIDER-MAN.
TAKE SHELTER, EVERYONE, AND REMAIN CALM!
S.W.A.T. COMMANDER! MOVE IN! PREPARE TO TAKE DOWN MENACE!
PLEASE, SIR, FOR YOUR OWN SAFETY, GO INSIDE.
PROTECT THE CROWD. THEY'RE IN MORE DANGER THAN I AM.
EMERGENCY
ER AND TRAINING
PETER! WHERE ARE YOU GOING?
OUT THE BACK AND UP THE FIRE ESCAPE.
I'LL BE ABLE TO GET BETTER PICTURES FROM THE ROOF!
BE CAREFUL!
WILLIAM HOLLISTER! I'M HERE WITH A MESSAGE!
HOLD YOUR FIRE, VIN--HE'S TOO LOW! WE MIGHT HIT SOMEBODY!
WITHDRAW FROM THE RACE! BY TOMORROW! OR FACE THE CONSEQUENCES!
MY CONSEQUENCES!

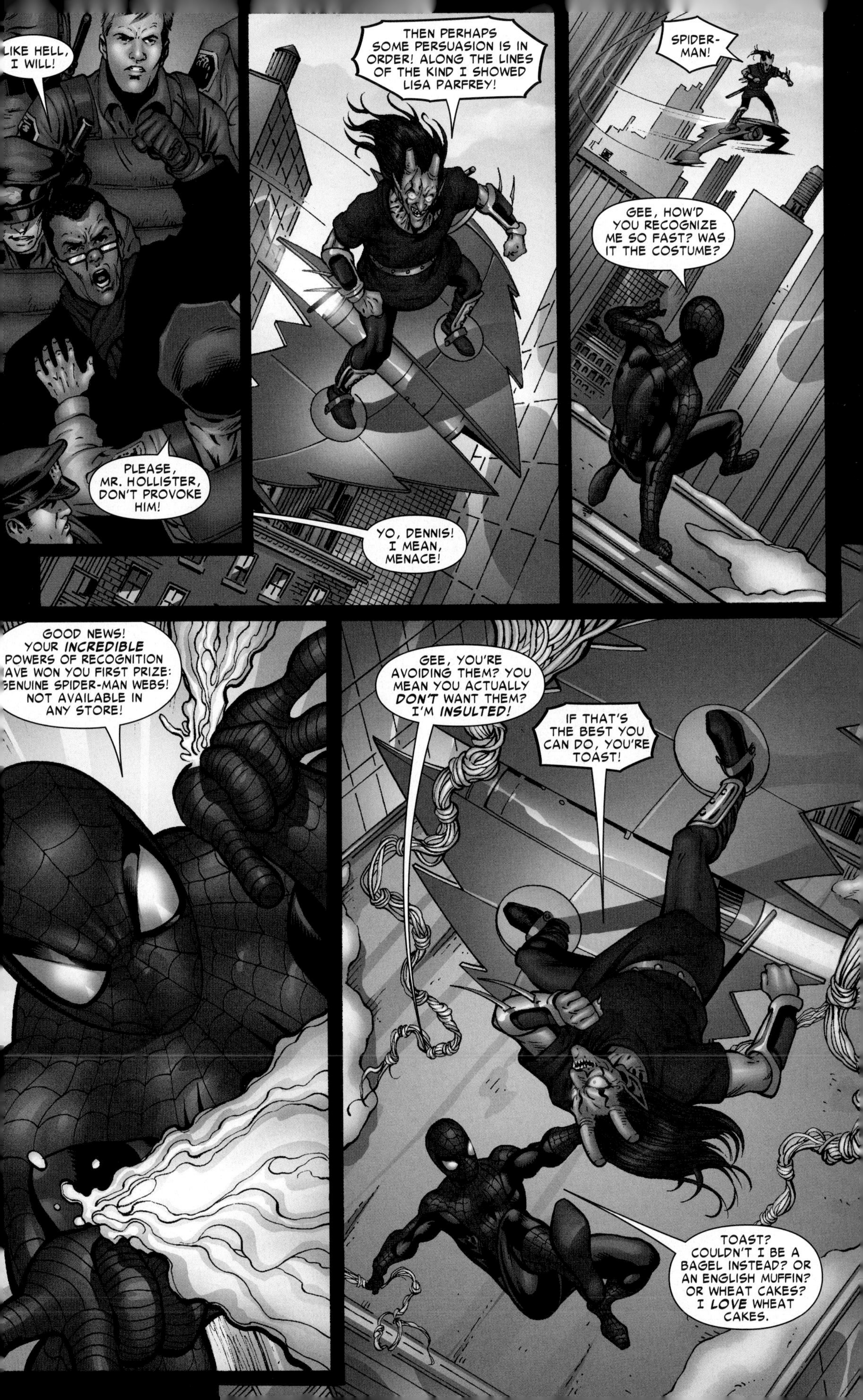
LIKE HELL, I WILL!
THEN PERHAPS SOME PERSUASION IS IN ORDER! ALONG THE LINES OF THE KIND I SHOWED LISA PARFREY!
PLEASE, MR. HOLLISTER, DON'T PROVOKE HIM!
YO, DENNIS! I MEAN, MENACE!
SPIDER-MAN!
GEE, HOW'D YOU RECOGNIZE ME SO FAST? WAS IT THE COSTUME?
GOOD NEWS! YOUR INCREDIBLE POWERS OF RECOGNITION AVE WON YOU FIRST PRIZE: GENUINE SPIDER-MAN WEBS! NOT AVAILABLE IN ANY STORE!
GEE, YOU'RE AVOIDING THEM? YOU MEAN YOU ACTUALLY DON'T WANT THEM? I'M INSULTED!
IF THAT'S THE BEST YOU CAN DO, YOU'RE TOAST!
TOAST? COULDN'T I BE A BAGEL INSTEAD? OR AN ENGLISH MUFFIN? OR WHEAT CAKES? I LOVE WHEAT CAKES.

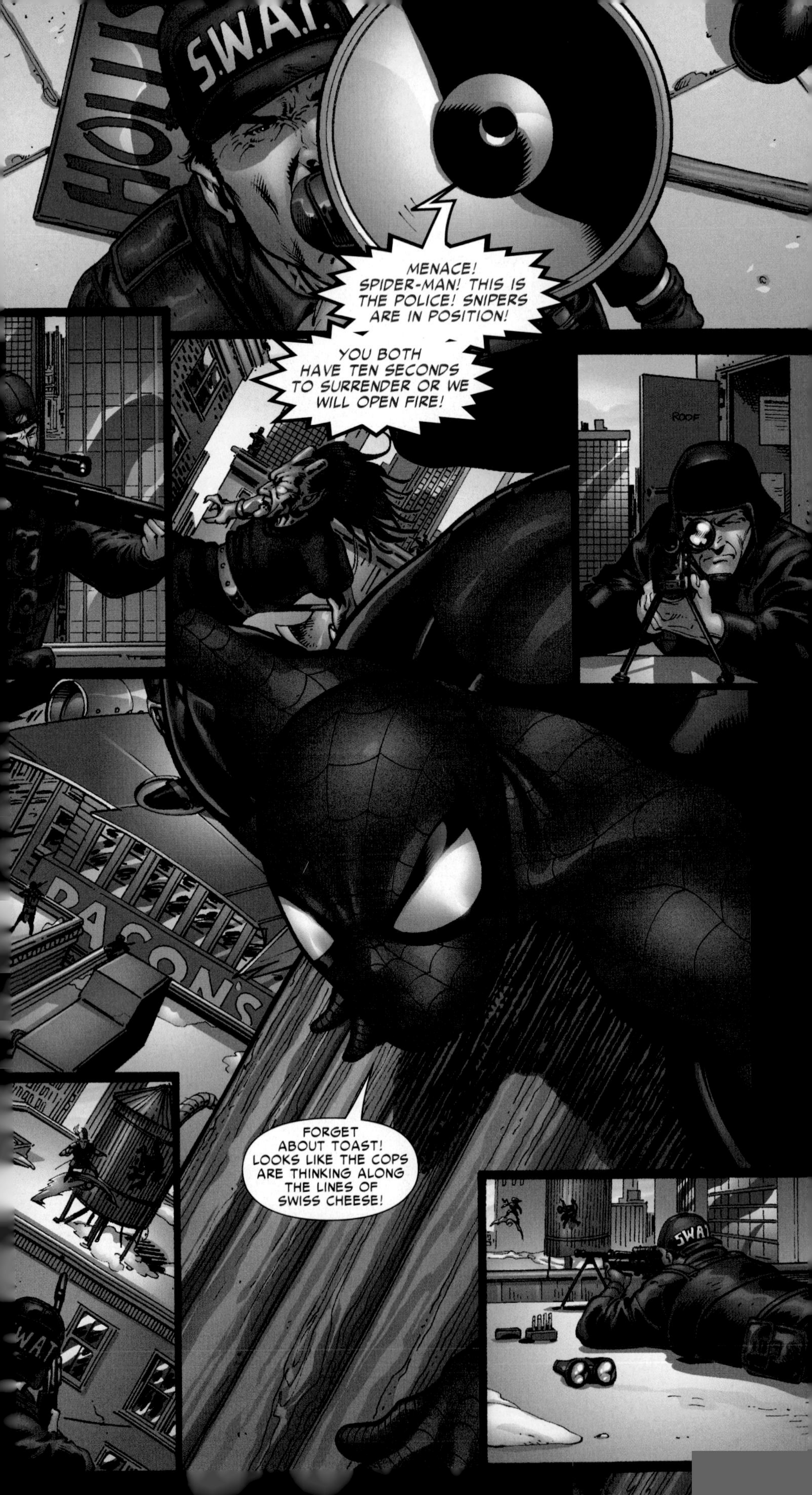
S.W.A.T.
MENACE! SPIDER-MAN! THIS IS THE POLICE! SNIPERS ARE IN POSITION!
YOU BOTH HAVE TEN SECONDS TO SURRENDER OR WE WILL OPEN FIRE!
ROOF
BACON'S
FORGET ABOUT TOAST! LOOKS LIKE THE COPS ARE THINKING ALONG THE LINES OF SWISS CHEESE!
SWAT
SWAT

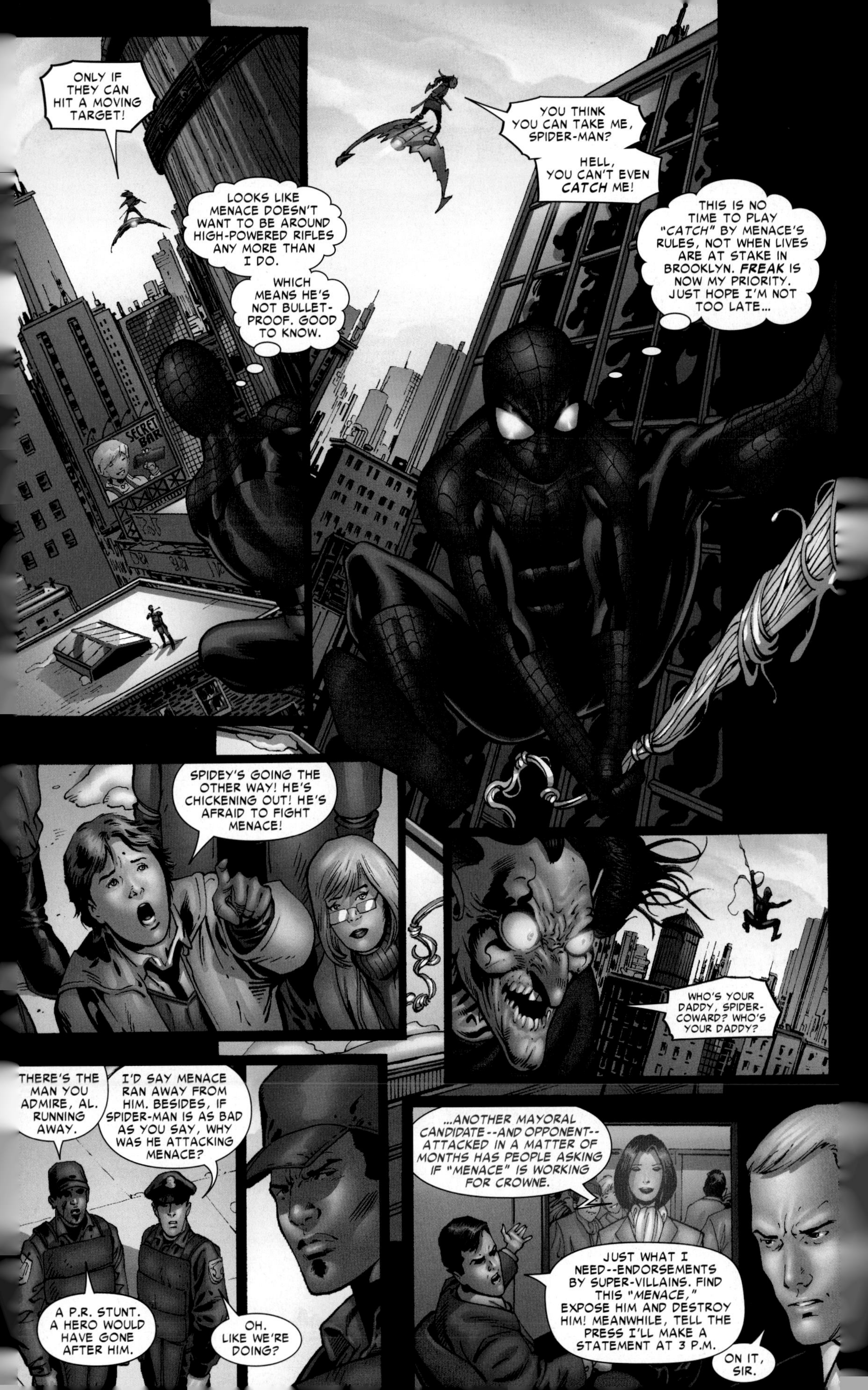

ONLY IF THEY CAN HIT A MOVING TARGET!
YOU THINK YOU CAN TAKE ME, SPIDER-MAN?
HELL, YOU CAN'T EVEN CATCH ME!
LOOKS LIKE MENACE DOESN'T WANT TO BE AROUND HIGH-POWERED RIFLES ANY MORE THAN I DO.
WHICH MEANS HE'S NOT BULLET-PROOF. GOOD TO KNOW.
THIS IS NO TIME TO PLAY "CATCH" BY MENACE'S RULES, NOT WHEN LIVES ARE AT STAKE IN BROOKLYN. FREAK IS NOW MY PRIORITY. JUST HOPE I'M NOT TOO LATE...
SECRET BAR
SPIDEY'S GOING THE OTHER WAY! HE'S CHICKENING OUT! HE'S AFRAID TO FIGHT MENACE!
WHO'S YOUR DADDY, SPIDER-COWARD? WHO'S YOUR DADDY?
THERE'S THE MAN YOU ADMIRE, AL. RUNNING AWAY.
I'D SAY MENACE RAN AWAY FROM HIM. BESIDES, IF SPIDER-MAN IS AS BAD AS YOU SAY, WHY WAS HE ATTACKING MENACE?
A P.R. STUNT. A HERO WOULD HAVE GONE AFTER HIM.
OH. LIKE WE'RE DOING?
...ANOTHER MAYORAL CANDIDATE--AND OPPONENT--ATTACKED IN A MATTER OF MONTHS HAS PEOPLE ASKING IF "MENACE" IS WORKING FOR CROWNE.
JUST WHAT I NEED--ENDORSEMENTS BY SUPER-VILLAINS. FIND THIS "MENACE," EXPOSE HIM AND DESTROY HIM! MEANWHILE, TELL THE PRESS I'LL MAKE A STATEMENT AT 3 P.M.
ON IT, SIR.

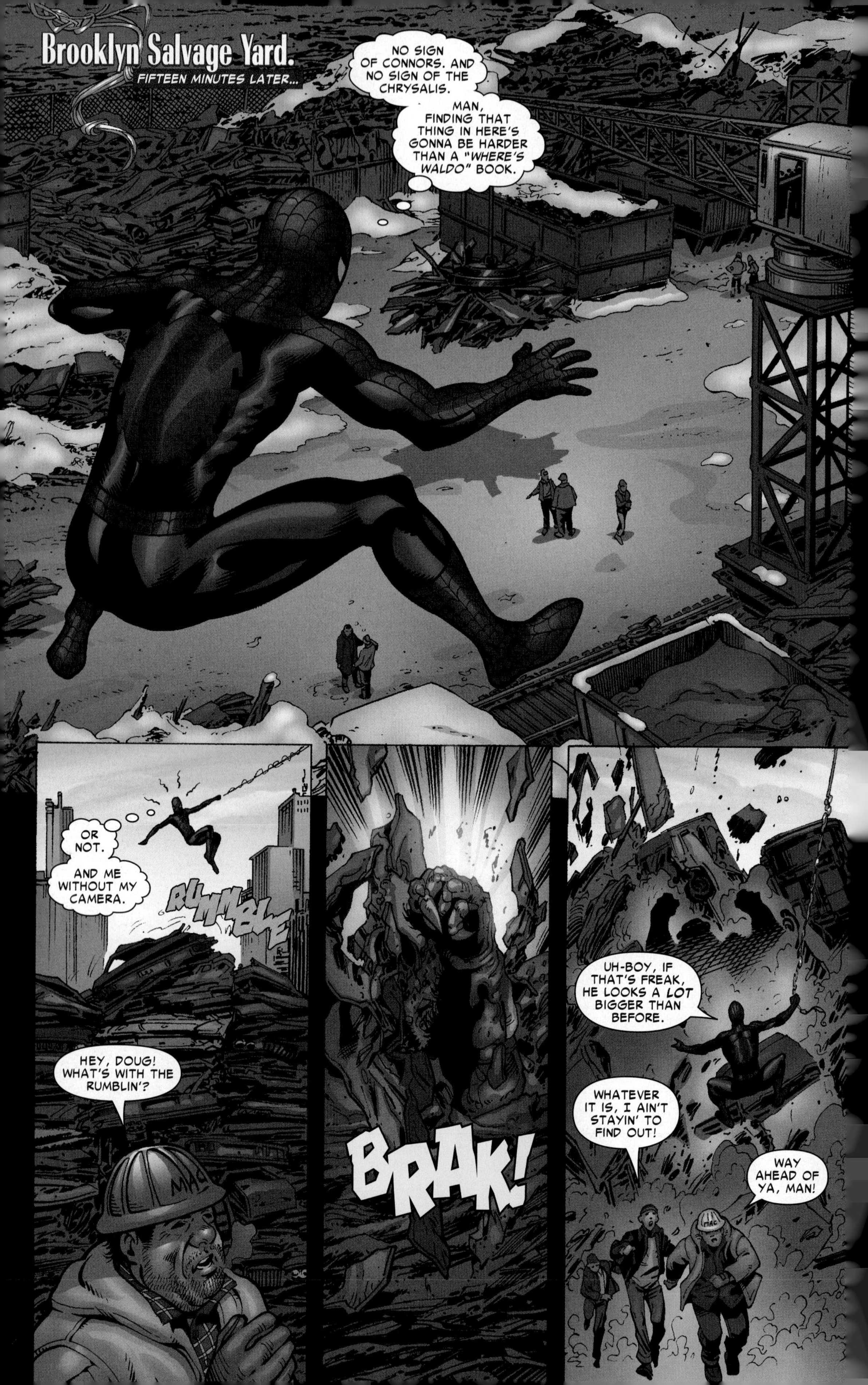

Brooklyn Salvage Yard.
FIFTEEN MINUTES LATER...
NO SIGN OF CONNORS. AND NO SIGN OF THE CHRYSALIS.
MAN, FINDING THAT THING IN HERE'S GONNA BE HARDER THAN A "WHERE'S WALDO" BOOK.
OR NOT.
AND ME WITHOUT MY CAMERA.
RUMMBLE
HEY, DOUG! WHAT'S WITH THE RUMBLIN'?
BRAK!
UH-BOY, IF THAT'S FREAK, HE LOOKS A LOT BIGGER THAN BEFORE.
WHATEVER IT IS, I AIN'T STAYIN' TO FIND OUT!
WAY AHEAD OF YA, MAN!

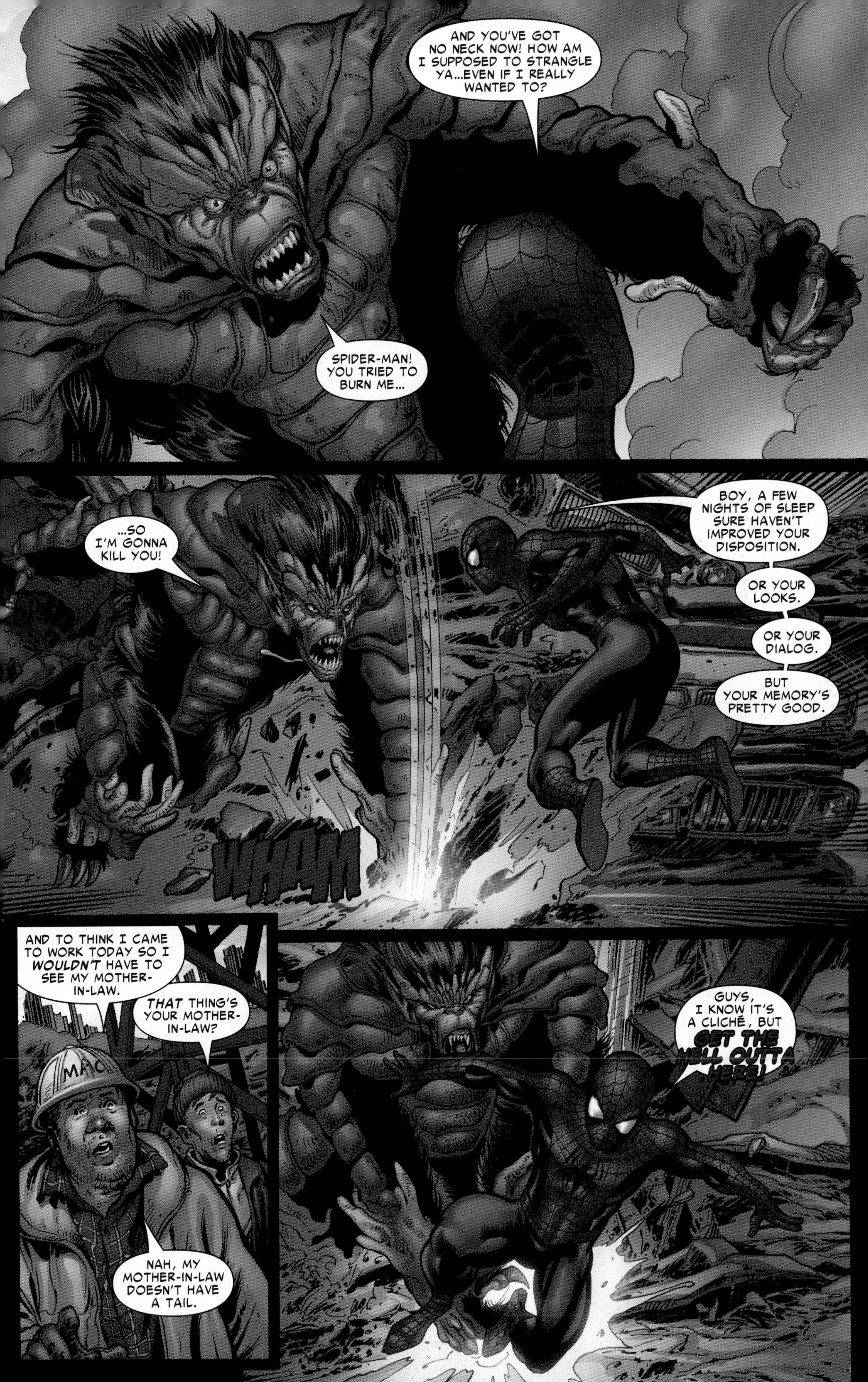
SPIDER-MAN! YOU TRIED TO BURN ME...
AND YOU'VE GOT NO NECK NOW! HOW AM I SUPPOSED TO STRANGLE YA...EVEN IF I REALLY WANTED TO?
...SO I'M GONNA KILL YOU!
BOY, A FEW NIGHTS OF SLEEP SURE HAVEN'T IMPROVED YOUR DISPOSITION.
OR YOUR LOOKS.
OR YOUR DIALOG.
BUT YOUR MEMORY'S PRETTY GOOD.
WHAM
AND TO THINK I CAME TO WORK TODAY SO I *WOULDN'T* HAVE TO SEE MY MOTHER-IN-LAW.
THAT THING'S YOUR MOTHER-IN-LAW?
NAH, MY MOTHER-IN-LAW DOESN'T HAVE A TAIL.
MAC
GUYS, I KNOW IT'S A CLICHÉ, BUT **GET THE HELL OUTTA HERE!**

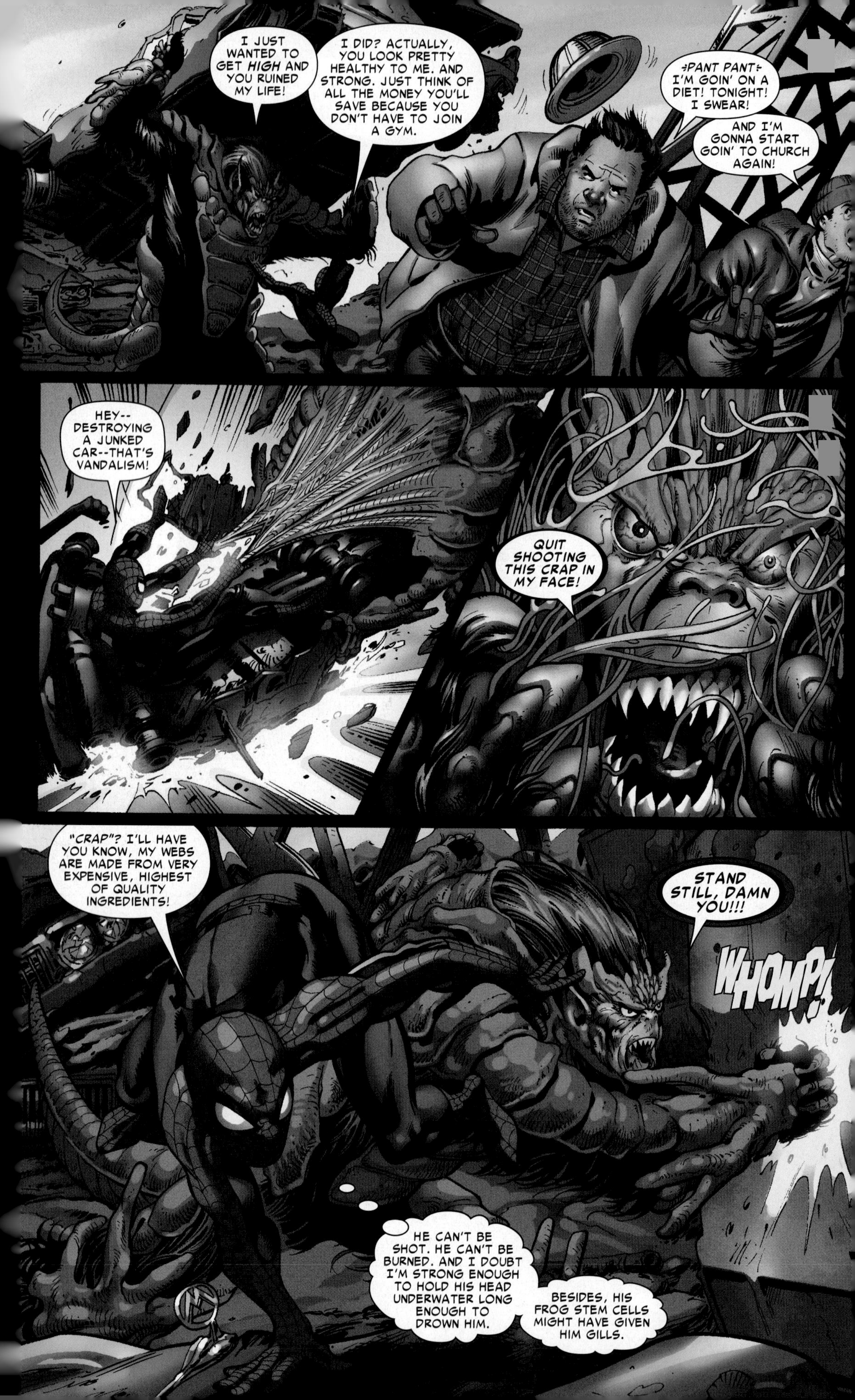
I JUST WANTED TO GET HIGH AND YOU RUINED MY LIFE!
I DID? ACTUALLY, YOU LOOK PRETTY HEALTHY TO ME. AND STRONG. JUST THINK OF ALL THE MONEY YOU'LL SAVE BECAUSE YOU DON'T HAVE TO JOIN A GYM.
PANT PANT I'M GOIN' ON A DIET! TONIGHT! I SWEAR!
AND I'M GONNA START GOIN' TO CHURCH AGAIN!
HEY--DESTROYING A JUNKED CAR--THAT'S VANDALISM!
QUIT SHOOTING THIS CRAP IN MY FACE!
"CRAP"? I'LL HAVE YOU KNOW, MY WEBS ARE MADE FROM VERY EXPENSIVE, HIGHEST OF QUALITY INGREDIENTS!
STAND STILL, DAMN YOU!!!
WHOMP!
HE CAN'T BE SHOT. HE CAN'T BE BURNED. AND I DOUBT I'M STRONG ENOUGH TO HOLD HIS HEAD UNDERWATER LONG ENOUGH TO DROWN HIM.
BESIDES, HIS FROG STEM CELLS MIGHT HAVE GIVEN HIM GILLS.

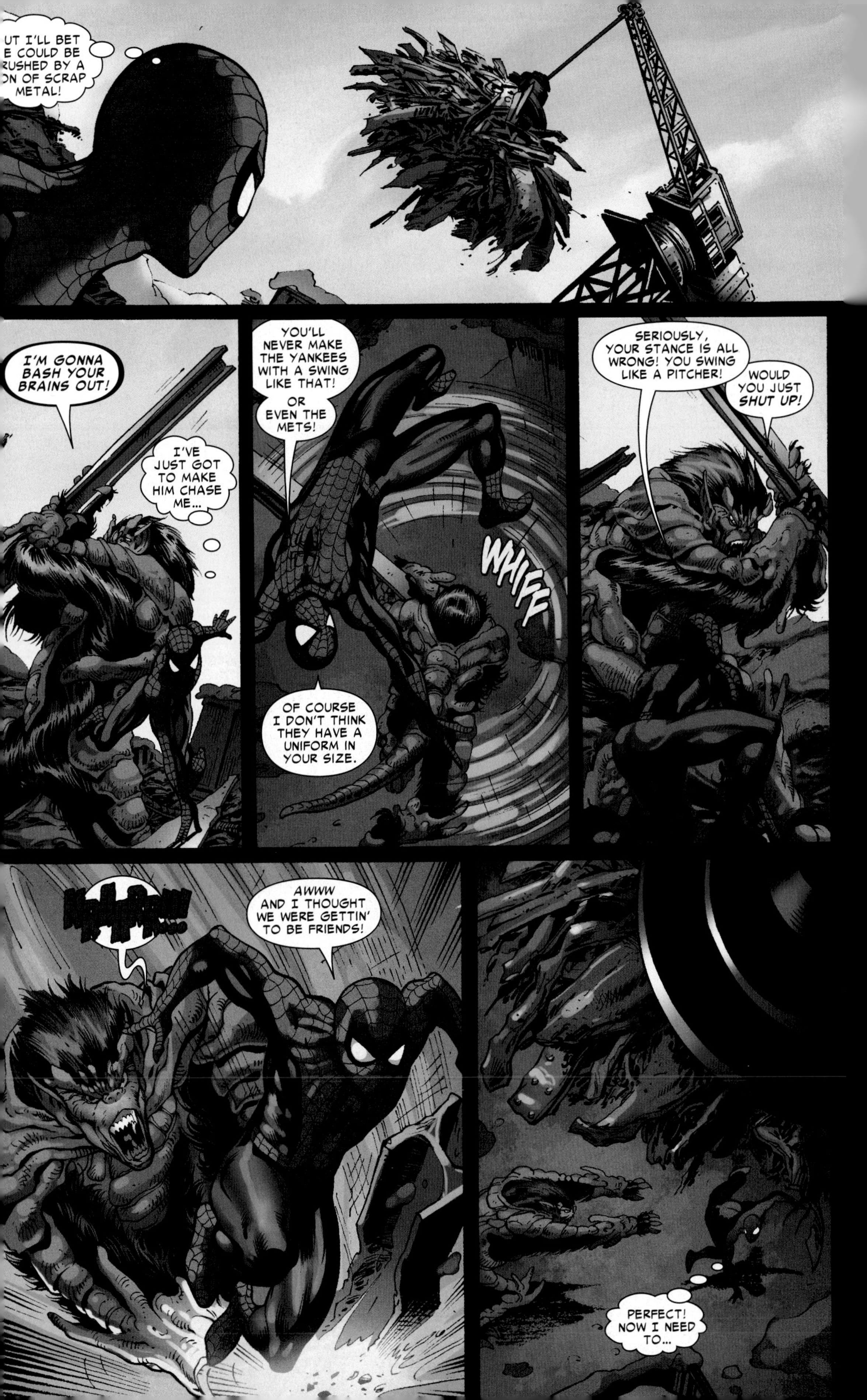
UT I'LL BET E COULD BE RUSHED BY A ON OF SCRAP METAL!
I'M GONNA BASH YOUR BRAINS OUT!
I'VE JUST GOT TO MAKE HIM CHASE ME...
YOU'LL NEVER MAKE THE YANKEES WITH A SWING LIKE THAT!
OR EVEN THE METS!
WHIFF
OF COURSE I DON'T THINK THEY HAVE A UNIFORM IN YOUR SIZE.
SERIOUSLY, YOUR STANCE IS ALL WRONG! YOU SWING LIKE A PITCHER!
WOULD YOU JUST SHUT UP!
AWWW AND I THOUGHT WE WERE GETTIN' TO BE FRIENDS!
PERFECT! NOW I NEED TO...

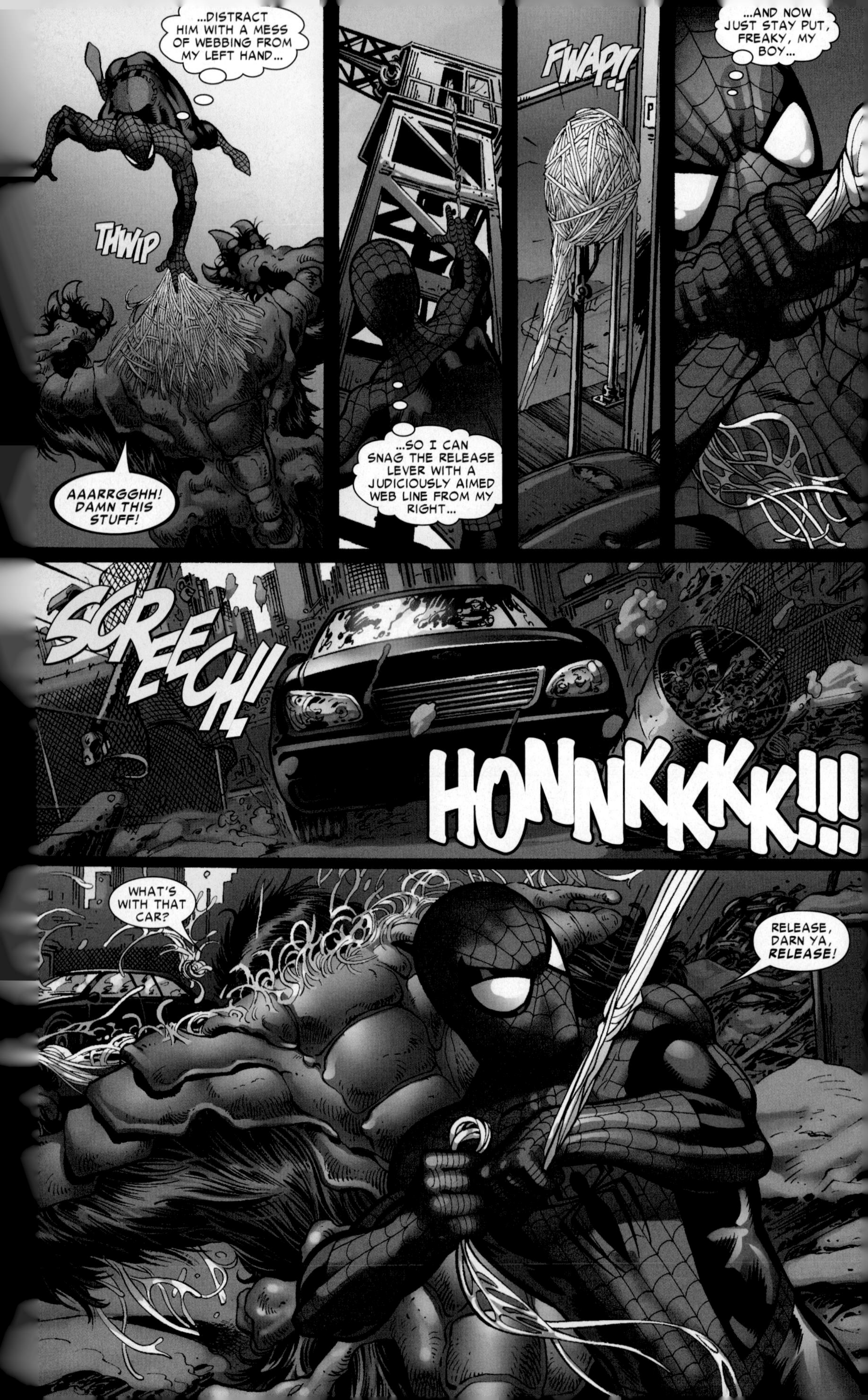
...DISTRACT HIM WITH A MESS OF WEBBING FROM MY LEFT HAND...
THWIP
AAARRGGHH! DAMN THIS STUFF!
...SO I CAN SNAG THE RELEASE LEVER WITH A JUDICIOUSLY AIMED WEB LINE FROM MY RIGHT...
FWAP!!
...AND NOW JUST STAY PUT, FREAKY, MY BOY...
SCREECH!
HONNKKKK!!!
WHAT'S WITH THAT CAR?
RELEASE, DARN YA, RELEASE!

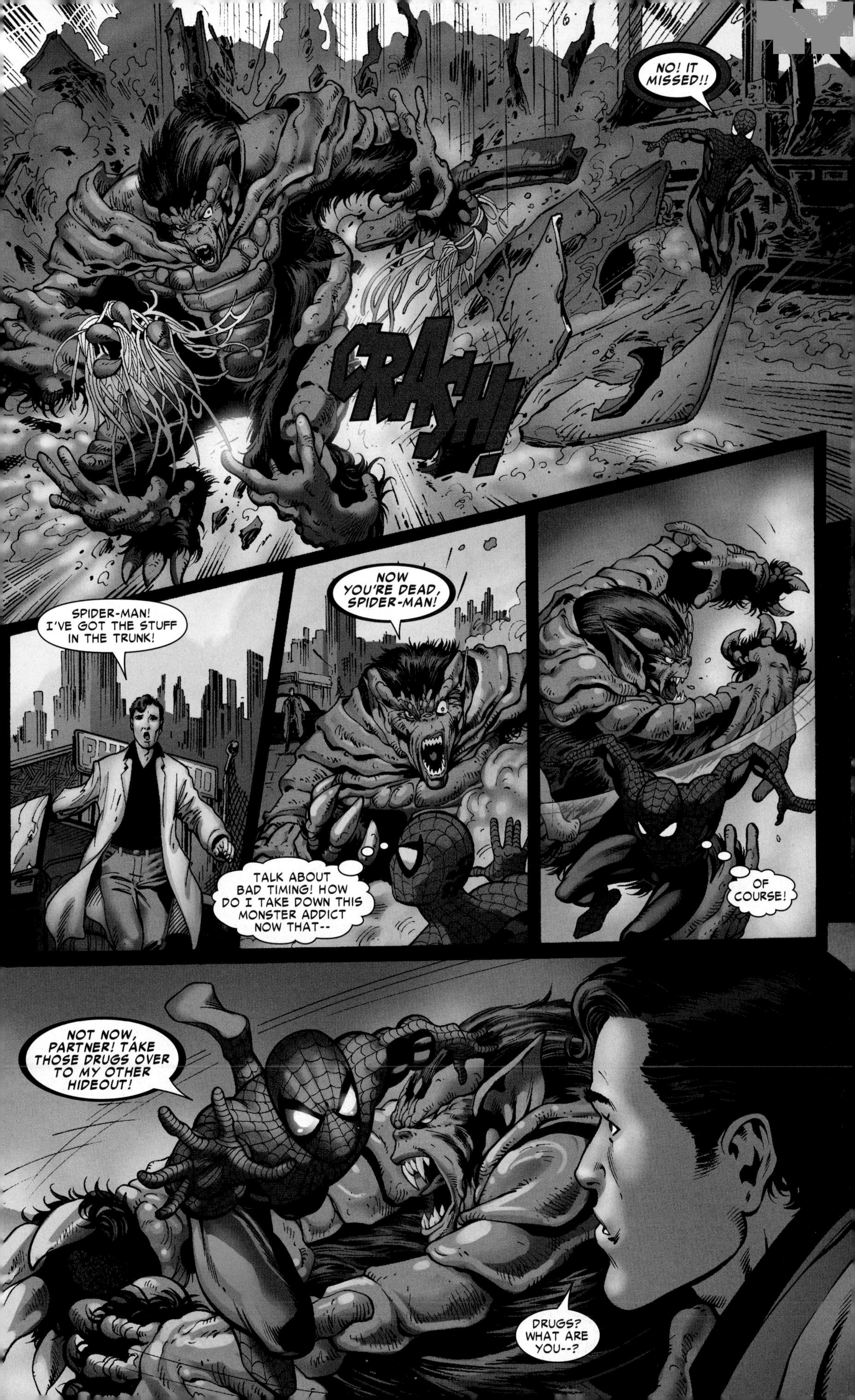
NO! IT MISSED!!
CRASH!
SPIDER-MAN! I'VE GOT THE STUFF IN THE TRUNK!
NOW YOU'RE DEAD, SPIDER-MAN!
TALK ABOUT BAD TIMING! HOW DO I TAKE DOWN THIS MONSTER ADDICT NOW THAT--
OF COURSE!
NOT NOW, PARTNER! TAKE THOSE DRUGS OVER TO MY OTHER HIDEOUT!
DRUGS? WHAT ARE YOU--?

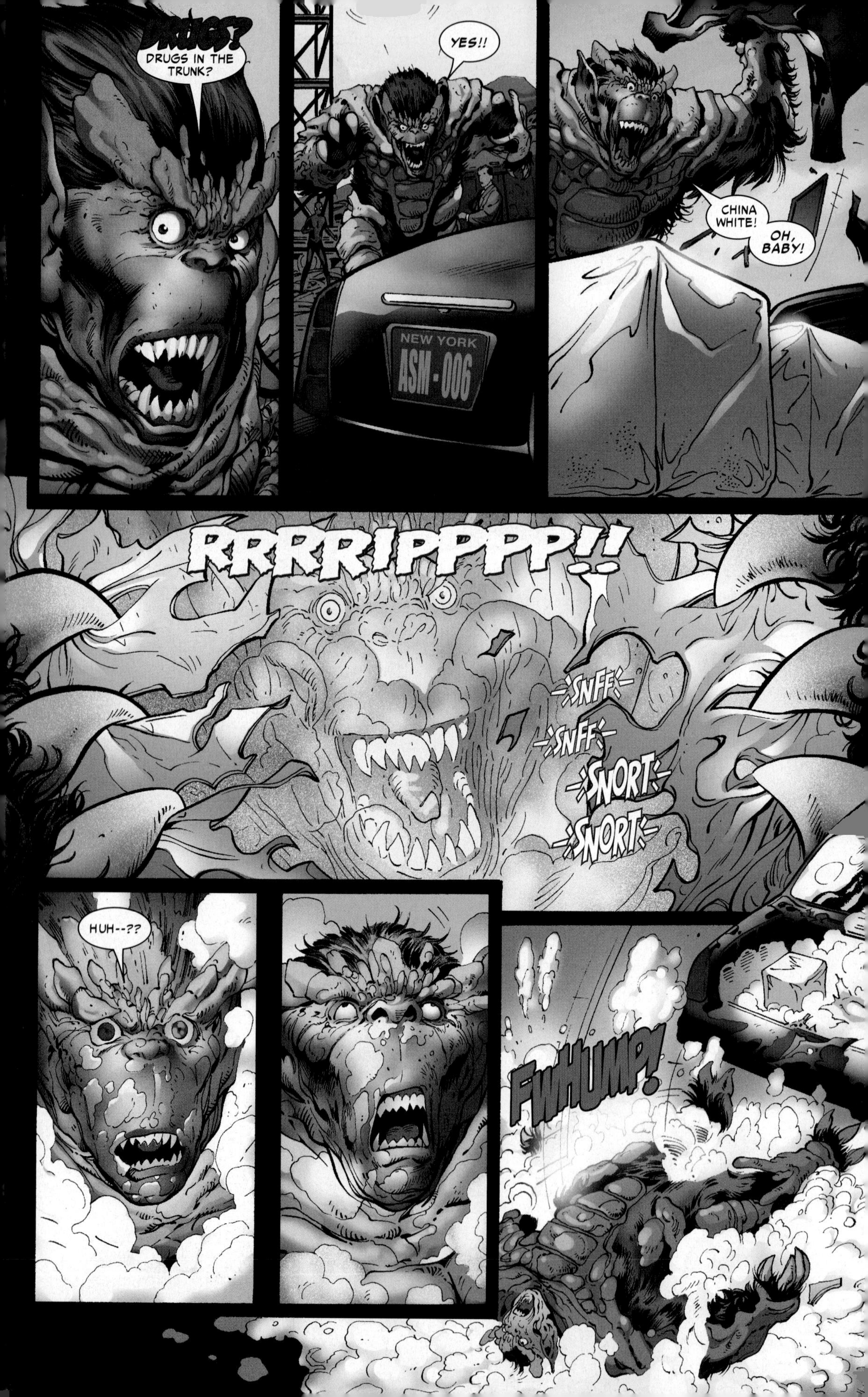
DRUGS?
DRUGS IN THE TRUNK?
YES!!
NEW YORK
ASM - 006
CHINA WHITE!
OH, BABY!
RRRRIPPPPP!!
SNFF
SNFF
SNORT
SNORT
HUH--??
FWHUMP!

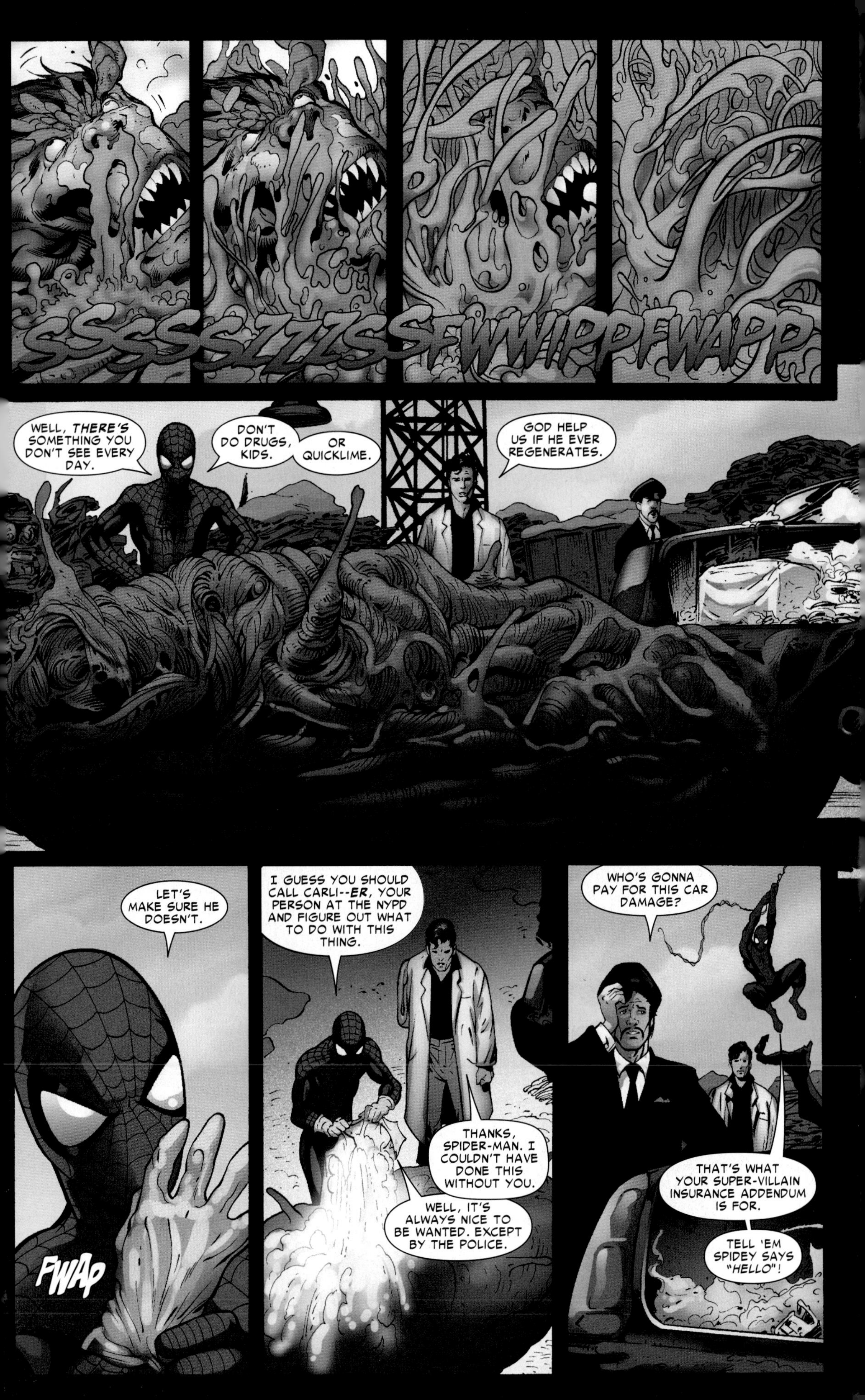
SSSSSIZZZSSFWWIPPFWAPP
WELL, *THERE'S* SOMETHING YOU DON'T SEE EVERY DAY.
DON'T DO DRUGS, KIDS.
OR QUICKLIME.
GOD HELP US IF HE EVER REGENERATES.
LET'S MAKE SURE HE DOESN'T.
FWAP
I GUESS YOU SHOULD CALL CARLI--*ER*, YOUR PERSON AT THE NYPD AND FIGURE OUT WHAT TO DO WITH THIS THING.
THANKS, SPIDER-MAN. I COULDN'T HAVE DONE THIS WITHOUT YOU.
WELL, IT'S ALWAYS NICE TO BE WANTED. EXCEPT BY THE POLICE.
WHO'S GONNA PAY FOR THIS CAR DAMAGE?
THAT'S WHAT YOUR SUPER-VILLAIN INSURANCE ADDENDUM IS FOR.
TELL 'EM SPIDEY SAYS "*HELLO*"!

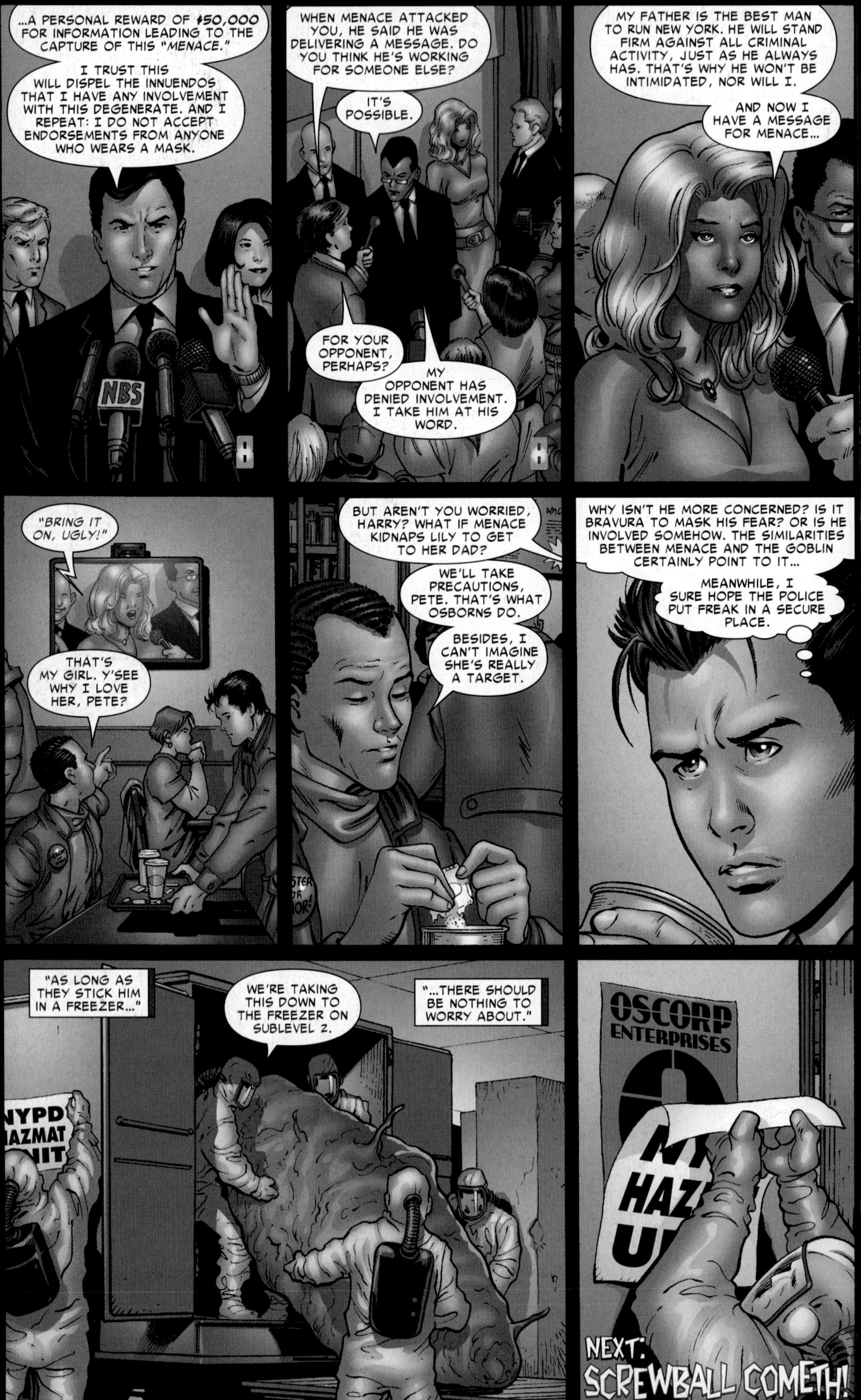
...A PERSONAL REWARD OF $50,000 FOR INFORMATION LEADING TO THE CAPTURE OF THIS "MENACE."
I TRUST THIS WILL DISPEL THE INNUENDOS THAT I HAVE ANY INVOLVEMENT WITH THIS DEGENERATE. AND I REPEAT: I DO NOT ACCEPT ENDORSEMENTS FROM ANYONE WHO WEARS A MASK.
NBS
WHEN MENACE ATTACKED YOU, HE SAID HE WAS DELIVERING A MESSAGE. DO YOU THINK HE'S WORKING FOR SOMEONE ELSE?
IT'S POSSIBLE.
FOR YOUR OPPONENT, PERHAPS?
MY OPPONENT HAS DENIED INVOLVEMENT. I TAKE HIM AT HIS WORD.
MY FATHER IS THE BEST MAN TO RUN NEW YORK. HE WILL STAND FIRM AGAINST ALL CRIMINAL ACTIVITY, JUST AS HE ALWAYS HAS. THAT'S WHY HE WON'T BE INTIMIDATED, NOR WILL I.
AND NOW I HAVE A MESSAGE FOR MENACE...
"BRING IT ON, UGLY!"
THAT'S MY GIRL. Y'SEE WHY I LOVE HER, PETE?
BUT AREN'T YOU WORRIED, HARRY? WHAT IF MENACE KIDNAPS LILY TO GET TO HER DAD?
WE'LL TAKE PRECAUTIONS, PETE. THAT'S WHAT OSBORNS DO.
BESIDES, I CAN'T IMAGINE SHE'S REALLY A TARGET.
WHY ISN'T HE MORE CONCERNED? IS IT BRAVURA TO MASK HIS FEAR? OR IS HE INVOLVED SOMEHOW. THE SIMILARITIES BETWEEN MENACE AND THE GOBLIN CERTAINLY POINT TO IT...
MEANWHILE, I SURE HOPE THE POLICE PUT FREAK IN A SECURE PLACE.
"AS LONG AS THEY STICK HIM IN A FREEZER..."
WE'RE TAKING THIS DOWN TO THE FREEZER ON SUBLEVEL 2.
"...THERE SHOULD BE NOTHING TO WORRY ABOUT."
NYPD HAZMAT UNIT
OSCORP ENTERPRISES
NEXT: SCREWBALL COMETH!

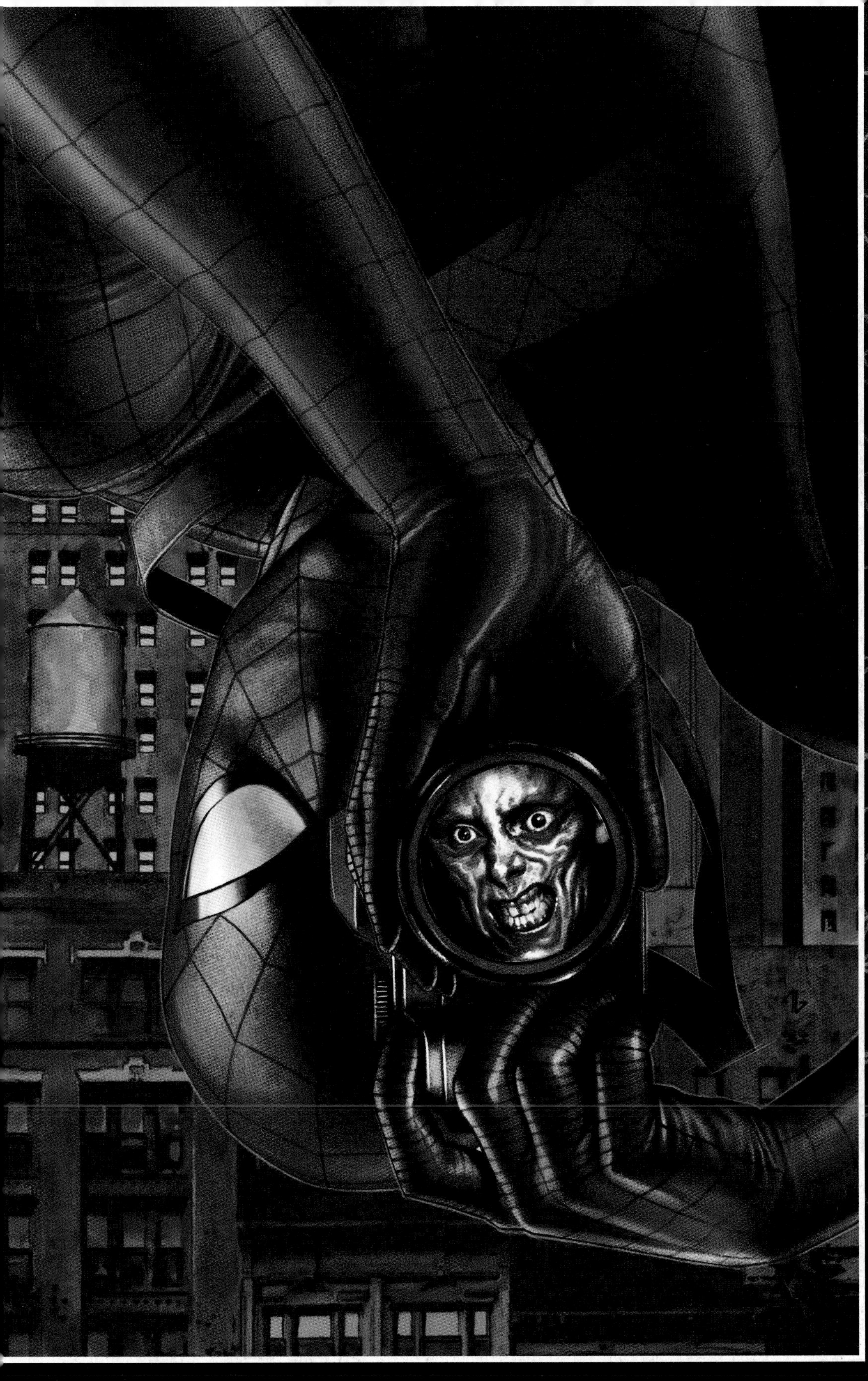

AMAZING SPIDER-MAN #552 VARIANT BY ADI GRANOV

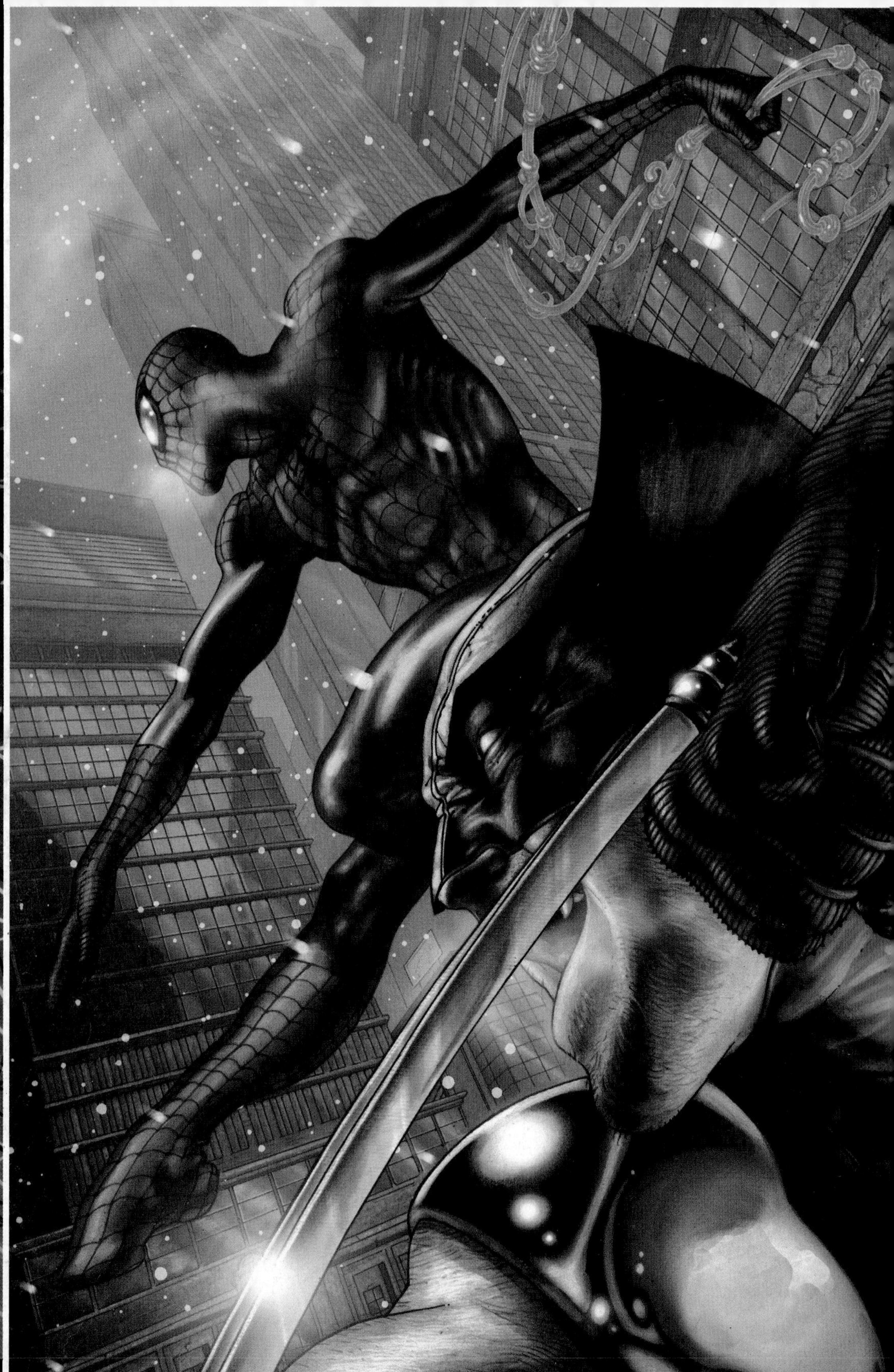

BIANCHI